ADOBE PHOTOSHOP 2023 COMPLETE GUIDE FOR BEGINNERS

ANISHE MORRISA

Copyright © 2023 Anishe Morrisa
All rights reserved.

COPYRIGHT

Adobe Photoshop 2023 Complete Guide for Beginners

First Edition

Copyright @ 2023 Anishe Morrisa

All rights reserved.

No part of this book may be reproduced, stored in a retrieval system, or transmitted in any form or by any means, without the prior written permission of the publisher, except in the case of brief quotations embedded in critical articles or reviews.

Every effort has been made in the preparation of this book to ensure the accuracy of the information presented. However, the information contained in this book is sold without warranty, either express or implied. Neither the author, nor Anishe Morrisa or its dealers and distributors, will be held liable for any damage caused or alleged to have been caused directly or indirectly by this book.

Anishe Morrisa has endeavored to provide trademark information about all the companies and products mentioned in this book by the appropriate use of capitals. However, Anishe Morrisa cannot guarantee the accuracy of this information.

ADOBE PHOTOSHOP 2023 COMPLETE GUIDE FOR BEGINNERS

INTRODUCTION

Welcome to **"Adobe Photoshop 2023 Complete Guide for Beginners**," a comprehensive journey through the intricate, yet highly rewarding world of Adobe Photoshop. This guide is designed to be your go-to resource for navigating the ever-evolving landscape of this incredibly powerful software. Whether you are a novice looking to dip your toes into the ocean of digital art and image manipulation or someone with a basic understanding of software looking to sharpen your skills, this book is tailored to help you achieve proficiency.

What to Expect

In today's world, Photoshop is not just a tool; it's a skill—one that is highly valued across various industries like design, photography, marketing, and beyond. As you flip through the pages of this guide, you'll uncover detailed, step-by-step instructions, peppered with illustrative examples and expert tips, designed to make your Photoshop journey both enjoyable and enlightening.

Starting with the basics, Chapter 1 lays down the foundation. From installation to understanding the user interface, you'll get a hands-on introduction to essential elements like tools, panels, and settings. Progressing through the chapters, you'll learn about everything from basic photo corrections, layering techniques, and working with selections, to advanced compositing, typographic design, and even video editing. By the time you reach the final chapter, you'll not only be familiar with Photoshop's extensive set of features but also capable of utilizing them in a way that enhances your work.

Special Features

What's New? Since this book focuses on the 2023 edition, you can expect an up-to-date guide on the latest tools and features. The book will delve into new additions like the "Live Gaussian Blur," a new slider for the 'replace-sky' feature, and much more.

Compatibility and Requirements: Chapter 1 will walk you through system requirements and compatibility checks to ensure your machine can handle the software without hitches.

Real-world Applications: Every chapter in this guide is framed in the context of real-world applications. Whether it's retouching a photo, designing a logo, or editing a video, you'll understand not just the 'how' but also the 'why' behind each tool and feature.

Advanced Techniques: For those seeking to go beyond the basics, this book includes advanced techniques, such as working with Camera Raw, mastering the art of masking and channels, and even dabbling in neural filters and 3D tools.

Frequently Asked Questions: Got questions? The FAQ section towards the end of the book will likely have the answers.

Extra Tips and Exercises: To help you practice and reinforce what you learn, the book is studded with practical exercises, and tips.

Your Journey Starts Here

Photoshop is more than just software; it's a canvas for creativity, a tool for visionaries, and a platform for innovation. As you navigate through the chapters of this guide, not only will you gain a robust understanding of Adobe Photoshop 2023, but you'll also unlock the potential to create and innovate like never before.

Ready to get started? Turn the page and embark on an adventure that promises to be both challenging and gratifying, as you master the art and science of Adobe Photoshop 2023.

Let's begin.

CONTENTS

COPYRIGHT iii
INTRODUCTION v
   What to Expect v
   Special Features v
   Your Journey Starts Here vi
CONTENTS vii

ABOUT ADOBE PHOTOSHOP 2023 1
   What's new in this edition? 2
      Create password-protected shareable links for your documents 2
      Snap Window support for Photoshop title bar available in the public app ... 2
      Faster and improved selections using the Object Selection tool 2
      Photo touch-up with smarter automatic features 2
      Cropping 3
      Brush updates 3
      Cloud-aided magic select tool 3
      Neural filters to restore old photos 3
      Materials based on substance 4
      The new material functions include: 4
      WebP image format support 4
   A new slider for the replace-sky feature 5
      Text recognition 5
      Content-based filler enables "AI" aid you to fill content gaps 5
   New blur option: Live Gaussian Blur 6
      Live Shapes 6
      Object Selection 6

Improved Performance 6

Prerequisites 6

Requirements for Adobe Photoshop 2023 8

Windows 8

macOS 10

Our Take on the Official Photoshop System Requirements 11

Installing Photoshop, Adobe Bridge, and Adobe Camera Raw 12

Installing Photoshop 12

Installing Adobe Bridge 12

Installing Adobe Camera Raw 14

Installing fonts 14

Windows 16

MacOS 16

Starting Adobe Photoshop 17

Starting Adobe Photoshop online 18

Restoring default preferences 19

Additional resources 21

Launching New Plugins 22

CHAPTER 1: GETTING STARTED 23

Starting to work in Adobe Photoshop 23

Understanding the Photoshop Interface 23

Creating a New Document 23

Using Layers 23

Adding Text To your Artwork 23

Utilizing the Selection Tools 24

Editing Images 24

Working with Masks 24

Using Filters	24
Exporting Your Artwork	24
Starting Photoshop	25
Using the Home screen	26
Accessing the Home Screen	26
Navigating the Home Screen	26
Opening a document	27
Launching Adobe Photoshop	27
Accessing the Open Dialog Box	28
Selecting a Document	28
Selecting Options	28
Opening the Document	28
Opening Multiple Documents	29
Opening Recent Documents	29
Using the tools	29
Selecting and using a tool from the Tools panel	31
Using the Zoom tool, for instance.	31
Sampling a color	33
Working with tools and tool properties	34
Setting the unit of measure	35
Undoing actions in Photoshop	36
More on Using the History Panel	37
Revert to a previous image state	39
Delete one or more image states	39
Create or replace a document with an image state	39
Set history options	40
Automatically Create First Snapshot	40
Automatically Create New Snapshot When Saving	40

Allow Non-Linear History 40
Show New Snapshot Dialog by Default 40
Make Layer Visibility Changes Undoable 41
Set Edit History Log options 41
More about panels and panel locations 42
Expanding and collapsing panels 42
Notes on Tools Panel and Option Bar 43

CHAPTER 2: BASIC PHOTO CORRECTIONS 45

Strategy for retouching 45
Using Filters for retouching 46
Resolution and image size 48
Opening a file with Adobe Bridge 53
Straightening and cropping the image in Photoshop 53
Adjusting the color and tone 55
Adjustment Layers 55
Color Balance 56
Selective Color 56
Color Lookup 56
The Spot Healing Brush tool 62
Getting Started 62
Using the Spot Healing Brush Tool 62
Tips for Effective Use 63
Advanced Techniques 64
Applying a content-aware patch 65
Repairing areas with the Clone Stamp tool 66
A few useful pointers while employing the Clone Stamp tool 68
Sharpening the image 68

CHAPTER 3: LAYER BASICS 73

About layers 73
- How do Layers Work? 73
- How to Use Photoshop Layers 73
- Using the Layers panel 74
- Understanding the Layers Panel 74
- Selecting Layers 76
- Moving Layers 76
- Layer Properties 76
- Grouping Layers 76

About the background layer 78
- Convert a background layer into a regular layer 79
- Rearranging layers 79

Applying gradient to a layer 81
- Tips for Applying Gradients in Photoshop 82

Duplicating a layer and adjusting the blending mode 82
Resizing and rotating layers 86
Using a filter to create artwork 88
Adding Text 89
Applying a layer style 90
Using the Gradients panel 93
Adding an adjustment layer 94
Using an effect more than once in a layer style 97
- Updating layer effects 97

Masking Objects in a Layer 99
Harmonizer Filter 99
Match Color Command 104
- Match color between two photos 104

Match color of two layers in the same picture 107

Save and apply adjustments in the Match Color command 109

Landscape Mixer Filter 109

Where to Find the Landscape Mixer 109

Creating a border from a selection 110

Layer Comps 113

Exercise 114

Change and edit a layer comp 116

Clear layer comp warnings 117

Delete a layer comp 117

Export layer comps 117

Flattening and storing files 118

Zooming and scrolling using the Navigator panel 119

Exploring design alternatives using Adobe Stock 121

CHAPTER 4: WORKING WITH SELECTIONS 123

About Selection and Selection Tools 123

1. Marquee tools 123

2. Lasso tools 124

3. Magic Wand tool 124

4. Quick Selection tool 125

5. Select and Mask 125

6. Object Selection Tool 125

Tips for Selection in Photoshop 126

Using cloud documents 126

Using the Marquee Tools 129

Rectangular Marquee tool 130

Elliptical Marquee tool 131

- Single Row Marquee tool ... 132
- Single Column Marquee tool ... 134
- Using the Magic Wand tool ... 135
- Using the Quick Selection tool ... 138
- Moving a specified area ... 139
  - Using the Object Selection tool ... 140
- Manipulating Selections ... 141
- Repositioning a selection marquee while creating it ... 141
- Moving selected pixels using a keyboard shortcut ... 143
- Moving a selection using the arrow keys ... 143
- Selecting with the lasso tools ... 145
  - The Lasso tool ... 145
  - The Polygonal Lasso tool ... 146
  - The Magnetic Lasso tool ... 147
  - Rotating a selection ... 148
- Selecting from a center point ... 150
  - Resizing and copying a selection ... 151
  - Moving and duplicating a selection concurrently ... 152
  - Copying selections ... 153
- Cropping a picture ... 153
  - How to Use the Crop Tool ... 154
  - How to utilize the Crop Presets ... 154
  - Using the Content-Aware Crop ... 155
  - Using the Perspective Crop ... 155
  - Useful advice for the Perspective Crop tool ... 156

CHAPTER 5: QUICK FIXES 157

Getting started 157

Improving a picture 158

Adjusting Color 158

    Adjusting Brightness and Contrast 158

Using Curves 159

    Using Levels 159

    Sharpening the Image 159

    Correcting the eye 159

    Tips for fixing red eye 161

Brightening an Image 161

    Method 1: Adjusting Brightness/Contrast 161

    Method 2: Using Levels 162

    Method 3: Using Curves 162

    Method 4: Using the Dodge Tool 164

Adjusting face features using Liquify 164

Control Other Options 169

Brush Tool Options 170

Face-Aware Liquify 171

    Using the tool 171

Blurring around a Subject 173

    Method 1: Using the Blur Gallery 173

    Method 2: Using the Gaussian Blur Filter 177

    Method 3: Using the Lens Blur Filter 179

Creating panoramic 180

Getting the best results with Photomerge 183

    Filling Empty Areas When Cropping in Adobe Photoshop 184

Correcting image distortion 185

Lens Correction Filter 186
Transform Tool 186
    Warp Tool 187
    Liquify Tool 187
Adaptive Wide-Angle Filter 187
    Extending depth of field 187
Removing objects with Content-Aware Fill 189
Adjusting perspective in a photograph 193
    Perspective Crop Tool 193
    Transform Tool 194
Transformations with the Content-Aware Move tool 195
Tips for utilizing the Content-Aware Move tool 197

CHAPTER 6: MASKS AND CHANNELS 201

Working with masks and channels 201
About Masks and Channels 201
Masks in Photoshop 201
    Channels in Photoshop 202
    Differences between Masks and Channels 202
Applications of Masks and Channels 203
Alpha channels, fast masks, clipping masks, layer masks, vector masks-what's the difference? 204
Using Select and Mask and Select Subject 205
    Select and Mask 205
Tips for Using Select and Mask and Select Subject 210
Getting better and faster outcomes with Select and Mask 211
Creating a quick mask 212
    Tips for utilizing Quick Mask mode 215

Manipulating a picture with Puppet Warp 216
    How to use Puppet Warp 216

Tips for using Puppet Warp 217

Using an alpha channel to create a shadow 218

Creating a pattern for the background 220
    Tips for generating a pattern for the background 221

Refining a mask 221

CHAPTER 7: TYPOGRAPHIC DESIGN 225

About type 225

Getting started 225
    Creating Text Layers 225
    Editing Text Layers 225
    Working with Text Styles 226
    Warping Text 226
    Creating a clipping mask from type 226

Adding guidelines to position type 227

Adding point type 228

Paragraph and character styles 231

Creating type on a Path 232

Creating a Type in a Circle 233

Warping point type 234

Designing paragraphs of type 237

Using guides for positioning 238

Adding paragraph type from a sticky note 238

CHAPTER 8: VECTOR DRAWING TECHNIQUES 241

About bitmap pictures and vector graphics 241

What is a pixel I hear you ask? 241

Rule of Thumb for picking a resolution 243

    Use High Resolution for Print 243

    Use Low Resolution for Web or Screen Graphics 243

Photoshop Raster Tools 244

    Pixel-based File Formats 244

    Vector images 244

Bitmap and Vector Side by Side 244

Photoshop Vector Tools 246

    Is Type in Photoshop Raster or Vector based? 246

About paths and the Pen tool 247

Getting started 248

    Understanding anchor points, handles, and line segments 248

Drawing a shape with the Pen tool 249

Creating curves and adjusting curves in shapes 251

Drawing paths with the pen tool 251

Straight line paths 252

    Drawing a straight line is easy; you could use the line tool or the pen tool 252

    Curved Paths 252

U-SHAPED CURVES 253

SIMPLE S CURVES 254

COMPLEX S CURVES 255

M CURVES 257

CLOSED PATHS 258

EXTRA TIP 260

Advanced approaches for producing complicated forms and patterns 260

Drawing trail traced from a Photo 261

Converting a path to a selection and a layer mask....................................262

Creating a logo with text and a custom shape..263

Guidelines for Designing a Great Logo 266

CHAPTER 9: ADVANCED COMPOSITING 269

Arranging layers 269

    1. Layer Order 269

    2. Layer Grouping 269

    3. Layer Blending Modes 269

    4. Layer Opacity...269

    5. Layer Masks 270

    6. Smart Objects 270

Using Smart Filters 270

Painting a layer 271

Adding a background 272

Using the History panel to undo modifications 273

Open the History Panel 273

Navigate the History States..274

    Undoing Edits 274

    Redoing Edits 275

Setting a Snapshot 275

    Clearing History States 275

History States 275

    Setting the number of History States. 275

    Layer Visibility...277

Improving a low-resolution picture 281

CHAPTER 10: PAINTING WITH THE MIXER BRUSH 285

    About the Mixer Brush 285

        How does the Mixer Brush work? 285

        Features of the Mixer Brush 285

    Brush Setting Panel 286

        Selecting brush settings 289

    Mixing colors 291

    Mixing colors with a Photograph 292

    Painting and combining colors using brush defaults 293

    Wetness control 295

    Load control 295

    Mix control 296

CHAPTER 11: WORKING WITH CAMERA RAW 297

    About camera raw files 297

    Processing files in Camera Raw 299

    Opening photos in Camera Raw from Photoshop 299

    Navigating the Camera Raw interface and knowing its tools 301

        The Camera Raw interface 301

    Making simple modifications in Camera Raw, such as exposure, contrast, and white balance 303

    Using the graded filter, radial filter, and adjusting brush in Camera Raw 305

    About the Camera Raw histogram 306

    Applying sharpening 307

    About adjusting color in Adobe Camera Raw 308

    About Camera Raw mask types 310

    Applying lens corrections and perspective tweaks in Camera Raw 311

    Working with settings and profiles in Camera Raw 312

Presets 312

Profiles 313

Combining Presets and Profiles 313

Syncing modifications across many pictures in Camera Raw 314

Using Camera Raw as a filter in Photoshop 315

Batch processing photographs in Camera Raw 316

Creating custom presets in Camera Raw 318

Retouching a portrait in Camera Raw 319

Saving Camera Raw modifications as new files 320

About saving files from Camera Raw to other formats 321

Tips and strategies for working successfully with Camera Raw in Photoshop. 322

CHAPTER 12: EDITING VIDEO 325

About the Timeline Panel 325

Creating a new video 326

Additional Tips & Tricks 328

Animating text with keyframes 330

Creating effects 331

Adding adjustment layers to video clips 332

Adding transitions 334

Types of Transitions 334

Animating a zoom effect 339

Animating a picture to generate a motion effect 340

Adding the Pan & Zoom effect 341

Adding audio 342

Muting undesired audio 343

Rendering video 344

CHAPTER 13: PREPARING FILES FOR THE WEB 345

Creating placeholders with the Frame tool 345
Adding graphics to a frame 346
Using layer groups to generate button graphics 347
Automating a multistep task 348
What are Photoshop Actions? 348
Benefits of automating chores with Actions 351
Examples of jobs that may be automated with Actions 352
Tips for generating successful Actions 352
Designing with artboards 353
    Tips for Designing using Artboards 354

CHAPTER 14: PRODUCING AND PRINTING CONSISTENT COLOR 357

Preparing files for printing 357
Zoom test 359
    Importance of Performing a Zoom Test 359
    Performing a Zoom Test 359
Interpreting the Results 360
Causes of Poor Image Quality 360
Tips for Improving Image Quality 361
About color management 361
    The Importance of Color Management in Photoshop and Why You Need It 362
    How Color Management Works in Photoshop 362
    Setting Up Color Management in Photoshop 362
About calibration and profiling 363
    Calibration 363
    Profiling 363
    Calibrating Your Monitor 364

Profiling Your Monitor 364

The RGB color mode..365

CMYK Color mode 366

Specifying color management defaults..366

Understanding Color Spaces 367

Choosing Working Spaces 367

Choosing Color Management Policies 368

  Specifying Other Color Settings 369

Identifying out-of-gamut colors...370

  Understanding Gamut..370

  Identifying Out-of-Gamut Colors 370

Proofing document colors on a monitor..372

  Bringing colors into the output gamut 374

Converting a picture to CMYK...376

Saving the picture as Photoshop PDF...377

Printing a CMYK picture from Photoshop..379

CHAPTER 15: EXPLORING NEURAL FILTERS 383

Understanding Neural Filters..383

Exploring the Neural Filters workspace 384

Output options 385

Additional Features 386

  PREVIEW CHANGES 386

  RESET..386

Restoring an ancient portrait picture...387

Adding color and depth blur 388

About Output Options in Neural Filters...389

Creating a more convincing composite 390

Improving Photoshop using your usage data and images 391
Common challenges and limits when using Neural Filters in Photoshop 392
Best practices when applying Neural Filters in Photoshop 393
Exploring third-party Neural Filters for Photoshop 395
    Topaz Labs AI Clear.. 395
    LuminarAI 395
    DxOPureRAW 395
    Skylum Aurora HDR 396
    ONI Photo RAW 396
    AI Gigapixel 396
Tips and techniques Photoshop 2023 396
    Select Colors from Anywhere 396
    Install Custom Photoshop Brushes 397
How to Create a Rain Texture 397
Create a Quick Light Bleed Effect 398
How to Use Blend If 399
How to Copy Layer Styles Quickly 400
    How to Create Multiple Stroke Effects on Text 400
    Make a Trendy Double Exposure Effect 400
    How to Merge Shapes 402
How to Paint Makeup 402
How to Make a Frequency Separation Photoshop Action 402
How to Create Chromatic Aberration 403
    Hide Layers Quickly 403
Extra Tips 404
    Keyboard Shortcuts 404
Customizing the Workspace 404
    Non-Destructive Editing with Adjustment Layers 404

- Smart Objects for Scaling and Transformations 404
- Content-Aware Fill 404
- Blend Modes 405
- Brush Customization 405
- Layer Masks for Seamless Edits 405
- Automating Tasks using Actions 405

Utilizing Photoshop Plugins 406

Utilizing Photoshop's Content-Aware Tools 406
- Utilizing Photoshop's Selection Tools 406
- Utilizing Photoshop's Healing Tools 406
- Utilizing Photoshop's Layer Styles 406

Utilizing Photoshop's 3D Tools 407

Frequently Asked Question 407
- What are layers in Photoshop? 407
- How can I remove the background from a photograph in Photoshop? 407
- Can I use Photoshop for digital painting? 407
- Is Photoshop just available on Windows? 407
- Can Photoshop restore blurry or damaged photos? 408
- Can Photoshop be used for site design? 408
- What is the difference between Photoshop and Adobe Lightroom? 408
- Can I use Photoshop on mobile devices? 408
- How can I build a panorama in Photoshop? 408
- Can Photoshop be used for 3D modeling and rendering? 409
- How do I erase red-eye in Photoshop? 409
- Can I generate animated GIFs with Photoshop? 409
- How can I resize or crop a picture in Photoshop? 409
- Is Photoshop adequate for professional photographers? 409
- Can I produce and edit videos with Photoshop? 409

What is the difference between Photoshop CC and Photoshop Elements? 410

Can Photoshop open and edit RAW files? 410

Is it possible to automate operations in Photoshop? 410

Can I interact with others in Photoshop? 410

Conclusion 410

ABOUT THE AUTHOR **412**

ABOUT ADOBE PHOTOSHOP 2023

Adobe Photoshop 2023 is the latest version of the famous image editing software developed by Adobe. It is a powerful application that helps users to create, edit, and alter pictures, graphics, and photos with precision and control. The software is extensively used by professionals and amateurs alike in a multitude of industries, including graphic design, photography, web design, and digital art.

Adobe Photoshop 2023 contains some powerful color correction and adjustment tools, strong selection and masking features, easy design and layout tools, 3D design features, and compatibility with a wide variety of file types. These key elements are merely some of the highlights of the program. In addition, there is a vast selection of advanced filters and effects included in the program, which may be used in images to make gorgeous visual effects and manipulations. Adobe Photoshop 2023 was intended to be incredibly adaptable and versatile, and it features an intuitive user interface that can be altered to better meet the requirements of certain users. Common design activities may be accomplished more rapidly, and procedures can be optimized with the help of the software's built-in templates and presets, which are included in a wide variety.

In overall, Adobe Photoshop 2023 is a tool that is both flexible and strong, and it may assist users in the development of amazing designs and pictures. Adobe Photoshop 2023 is a crucial tool that may assist you in bringing the quality of your work to the next level, regardless of whether you are a professional graphic designer or a photographer with a hobby.

What's new in this edition?

Create password-protected shareable links for your documents

With the most recent update to the Share for review process in Photoshop, you now can manage access to your public review links by specifying a password. This enables better collaboration and the sharing of opinions, while simultaneously providing more security. This guarantees that only those who have been invited to read your file may do so, and even then, only if they input the appropriate password. You are free to modify the password at any stage after it has been formed, or you may choose to do away with the need for a password entirely. Another feature that has been improved as part of the Share for review workflow is the fact that while you are in the process of generating a review link to send to other people, even if you shut the dialog box while the process is in progress, you will still be notified whether the link is successfully produced or if the process fails. This notification will occur regardless of whether you close the dialog box.

Snap Window support for Photoshop title bar available in the public app

With the 2023 release of the Photoshop version, snap your app windows on your Windows system in the main app, outside of the Beta app.

Faster and improved selections using the Object Selection tool

Your app performance is now significantly better with increased object identification and object refining. So go ahead and operate effortlessly with high-quality masks or obtain a more refined human and animal tagging experience.

Photo touch-up with smarter automatic features

The picture touch-up and re-touching tool is one of the most interesting new tools that have been incorporated. Using this application, you will be able to eradicate faults from your photographs in a fast and easy manner, as well as even skin tones and correct red eyes. It also boasts a capability that can repair old or damaged images, bringing them back to life with only a few clicks thanks to a neural net function. This feature is included.

Cropping

The content-aware crop tool is another one of the brand-new features. By automatically recognizing and saving the elements that are included in the shot, this tool enables you to crop your photographs without losing crucial information that is included inside the photograph. It also contains a feature that proposes various cropping possibilities for your picture, making it simpler than ever before to choose the one that has the most attractive composition.

Brush updates

The content-aware crop tool is another one of the brand-new features. By automatically identifying and saving the elements that are included in the image, this tool enables you to crop your photographs without losing crucial information that is included inside the snapshot. It also contains a function that proposes various cropping possibilities for your photo, making it simpler than ever before to select the one that has the most attractive composition.

Cloud-aided magic select tool

There is an upgrade to the magic select tool as well. You may utilize the function locally, which is faster but less accurate, or you can specify that you want to use the Adobe Cloud power and harness the newest version of their AI to detect things. If you have an Internet connection, the cloud option is advised, especially if you are dealing with the selection of hair, fur, or similar material around the boundaries of an object.

Neural filters to restore old photos

The neural filter to recover aged pictures is one of the most interesting new features of Adobe Photoshop 2023. This capability employs artificial intelligence to repair damaged or ancient images, bringing them back to life with only a few clicks. It is a terrific tool for mending ancient family images that have been damaged over time, or for recovering photos that were taken before the digital age. With only a few clicks, you can have your old images looking like new again. The neural filter may also aid to tone up and colorize photographs that have been captured in black and white exclusively. With only a few clicks, you can bring color back into your images, making them seem more alive and lifelike. This is a terrific tool for giving old black-and-white images a fresh lease on life.

Materials based on substance

Another intriguing part of Adobe Photoshop 2023 is the quantity of new material functions that have been introduced. With only a few clicks, you can apply realistic textures to your images, making them seem more lifelike than ever before.

The new material functions include:

- Stone
- Glass
- Wood
- Leather
- Fabric
- Metal

Each of these materials has its distinct texture and look, which may be utilized to improve your image in a variety of ways. The leather material, for example, may be utilized to lend an exquisite and classy touch to your images. The fabric material may be utilized to offer a feeling of realism and depth to your images, while the metal material can give your photos a sleek and polished aspect. The stone material may be utilized to lend a rustic and earthy vibe to your images, while the glass material can be used to produce amazing visual effects. With so many choices available, the sky's the limit when it comes to employing the new material features in Adobe Photoshop 2023.

WebP image format support

Support for the brand-new WebP image format has at long last been introduced to Adobe Photoshop 2023. This picture format is designed to offer greater compression than the more conventional JPEG and PNG image formats, which will result in lower file sizes and speedier load times. You may decrease the amount of space used up by pictures on your website by using the WebP image format, while at the same time presenting readers with images of good quality.

The WebP picture format is supported by a number of internet browsers, including Chrome, Firefox, Opera, and browsers for Android devices like Chrome, Firefox, and Android. If you are using one of these browsers, you may take advantage of the increased compression and speedier load rates given by the WebP image format. These features are accessible to you if you are using one of these browsers.

A new slider for the replace-sky feature

The replace-sky feature now includes a slider, which is one of the new features added in Adobe Photoshop 2023. The sky in your shots may be modified in terms of both the hue and its intensity using this slider, making it simple for you to acquire the style you desire for your images. You may modify the color and brightness of the sky to perfectly meet your tastes with simply a few mouse clicks. The "replace-sky" function is a great tool for allowing you to adjust the sky in any of your images. You may alter the color and saturation of the sky with simply a few clicks to fit your temperament or aesthetic preferences. The slider that is featured in the function makes it simple to get the ideal sky for your images, regardless of the preferences that you might have.

Text recognition

One of the new features in Adobe Photoshop 2023 is the text search option. This method helps you to quickly and simply discover the configuration settings that you are looking for. With just a few clicks, you can search through all of the options in Adobe Photoshop 2023 and locate the setting values that you require. The text search option is a useful tool for discovering configuration variables quickly and conveniently. With just a few clicks, you can search through all of the options in Adobe Photoshop 2023 and locate the setting values that you require. This tool is very handy if you are working with a complex or lengthy text. With the text search tool, it is easy to discover the configuration settings that you need without having to go through all the choices.

Content-based filler enables "AI" aid you to fill content gaps

Utilizing the content-based filler tool is a terrific approach to refill enormous sections quickly and efficiently with text or photographs. You may quickly and simply fill up vast portions of the page with text or pictures using the content-based filler tool. Flyers, posters, and other forms of materials that demand a considerable number of text or photographs may be simply made with the aid of this essential application. The tool for producing content-based filler is simple to use. You first need to determine the area that you want to fill, and then you may choose the sort of material that you want to employ in that space. The content-based filler tool will immediately begin to refill the space with the material that you have selected. Altering the content's size, color, and other elements is another way you may place your own mark on its display. With the aid of the content-based filler tool, you can simply and fast load big areas of your website with text and pictures. You will be able to generate flyers, posters, and other types of papers that need a big quantity of text or photographs with the help of this application.

New blur option: Live Gaussian Blur

You may give your photographs a more realistic appearance by using the live gaussian blur effect. You may quickly and simply generate realistic blur effects in your photographs with the live gaussian blur. Using this function is straightforward. You first need to specify the place that will be blurred, and then you may choose the type of blurring effect that will be applied. The live gaussian blur will immediately apply the blur effect that you have selected to the region that you have picked. Altering the blur's hue, size, and other attributes, in addition to other aspects of its appearance, is another one of the countless ways it may be altered. You may give your photographs a more realistic appearance by using the live gaussian blur effect. With this tool, you may rapidly and efficiently create visual effects that replicate the look of a real-world blur.

Live Shapes

Live Shapes is a new tool that makes it easier than ever to generate vector shapes in Photoshop. With this feature, you can now build and edit shapes with live previews, allowing you to see precisely how your changes will affect the final outcome. This makes it easy to produce accurate and professional-looking graphics, even if you're not a vector specialist.

Object Selection

Object Selection is another new function in Photoshop 2023 that makes it easier to select certain objects inside your photographs. With this tool, you can quickly and easily select items based on their form, color, or texture, allowing you to make more accurate alterations and adjustments.

Faster and enhanced selections with the Object Selection tool. Your app performance is now significantly better with increased object identification and object refining. So go ahead and operate effortlessly with high-quality masks or obtain a more sophisticated human and animal tagging experience.

Improved Performance

Finally, Adobe Photoshop 2023 also has several performance changes that make the software function quicker and more smoothly. This includes enhanced support for huge files, quicker loading speeds, and more effective use of your computer's resources.

Prerequisites

Before you begin using Adobe Photoshop 2023, you need to understand your computer and its operating system. Make sure that you know how to use the mouse and standard menus and commands, and also how to open, save, and close files. If you need to review this information, read the documentation for your Microsoft® Windows® PC or Apple® Mac® computer.

NOTE: The official version numbers of Adobe apps don't necessarily correlate with years because several existed before the year was part of the name. For example, Photoshop was released in 1990 as version 1, and the year did not appear in the name until Photoshop CC 2014, which was technically version 15.

Here, we will work with Adobe Photoshop and Bridge (occasionally however). So, you'll need Adobe Photoshop 2023 and Adobe Bridge 2023 installed on your PC.

The exact version number of the software is different than the year in the application name:

To identify the version of Photoshop that you are running, select **Help > System Info** and look at the first line (Adobe Photoshop Version).

To identify the version of Bridge that you are running, select **Help > About Bridge** (Windows) or **Adobe Bridge > About Bridge** (macOS) and look at the first line in the window that appears.

Requirements for Adobe Photoshop 2023

Windows

	Minimum	Recommended
Processor	Multicore Intel® or AMD processor (2 GHz or faster processor with SSE 4.2 or later) with 64-bit support	
Operating system	Windows 10 64-bit (version 22H2) or later; LTSC versions are not supported	
RAM	8 GB	16 GB or more
Graphics card	<ul><li>GPU with DirectX 12 (feature level 12_0 or later)</li><li>1.5 GB of GPU memory</li><li>GPUs less than 7 years old (update display drivers from the GPU manufacturer's website). Currently, we don't support testing on GPUs older than 7 years</li></ul>	<ul><li>GPU with DirectX 12 support (feature level 12_0 or later)</li><li>4 GB of GPU memory for 4k displays and greater</li></ul>
	See the Photoshop graphics processor (GPU) card FAQ	
Monitor resolution	1280 x 800 display at 100% UI scaling	1920 x 1080 display or greater at 100% UI scaling
Hard disk space	20 GB of available hard-disk space	100 GB of available hard disk space<ul><li>Fast internal SSD for app installation</li><li>Separate internal drive for scratch disks</li></ul>
Internet	Internet connection and registration are necessary for required software activation, validation of subscriptions, and access to online services †	

	Minimum	Recommended
Processor	ARM processor	
Operating system	Windows 10 ARM device running Windows 10 64-bit (version 20H2) or later	
RAM	8 GB	16 GB or more
Graphics card	4 GB of GPU memory	
All the other aspects for ARM are the same as Intel		

macOS

	Minimum	Recommended
Processor	Multicore Intel® or Apple Silicon processor (2 GHz or faster processor with SSE 4.2 or later) with 64-bit support	ARM-based Apple Silicon processor
Operating system	macOS Big Sur (version 11.0) or later	macOS Big Sur (version 13.4) if Photoshop is started on a system with an older OS Installation is blocked on v10.15.x
RAM	8 GB	16 GB or more
Graphics card	• GPU with Metal support • 1.5 GB of GPU memory	• GPU with Metal support • 4 GB of GPU memory for 4k displays and greater
	To find out if your computer supports Metal, see Mac computers that support Metal See the Photoshop graphics processor (GPU) card FAQ	
Monitor resolution	1280 x 800 display at 100% UI scaling	1920 x 1080 display or greater at 100% UI scaling
Hard disk space	20 GB of available hard-disk space	100 GB of available hard disk space • Fast internal SSD for app installation • Additional high-speed drive(s) or SSD to set up scratch disks
	Photoshop will not install on a volume that uses a case-sensitive file system	
Internet	Internet connection and registration are necessary for required software activation, membership validation, and access to online services †	

	Minimum	Recommended
Processor	ARM-based Apple Silicon processor	
Operating system	macOS Big Sur (version 11.2.2) or later	
RAM	8 GB	16 GB or more
All the other aspects for Apple Silicon are the same as Intel		

Our Take on the Official Photoshop System Requirements

Although the system requirements sound modest, there's more to it. It makes sense for Adobe to keep their minimum system requirements low, so their target audience is as big as possible. However, operating Adobe Photoshop on a PC that just fulfills the minimal guidelines is no joy, and you'll fast want your PC to be stronger.

Programs like Adobe Photoshop raise performance demand from your computer in proportion to the complexity and simultaneous amount of your activity. So, you might be able to start Photoshop on a minimum-specs PC and work on extremely low-complexity graphics, but that's about it. As soon as you wish to open numerous photographs or work on something a bit more difficult, your PC will grind to a standstill. Factors that raise performance requirements are Image and Canvas Dimensions, Resolution, number of layers, Smart Objects, and Bit Depth, to mention a few. To have a quick and responsive interface, you'll need the correct components for your machine.

Here's an overview of component specifications that directly affect Photoshop's performance:

CPU: A high-clocking CPU will handle Adobe Photoshop far better than a CPU with a moderate clock rate but many cores.

RAM: To prevent bottlenecks, obtain at least 16 GB of RAM.

GPU: Get a dedicated GPU for increased performance. We suggest an NVIDIA GTX or RTX GPU.

Although Adobe recommends that you only require 5GB of accessible hard drive space, you should have at least twice as much available since your operating system and any other applications you may be running may also need some extra hard disk space.

The usefulness of an internet connection is a major feature that is removed from Adobe's official list of System Requirements. Updates are implemented on Adobe's Creative Cloud every few months, and it is released online. Your ability to keep updated will be considerably hampered if you don't have a fast Internet connection.

Installing Photoshop, Adobe Bridge, and Adobe Camera Raw

Installing Photoshop

Step 1: Go to the Adobe website and sign into your account. Click on the "Download" button next to Photoshop 2023.

Step 2: Choose your operating system and language. Click on the "Download" button again. Wait for the download to finish.

Step 3: Open the downloaded file and follow the installation instructions.

Installing Adobe Bridge

To install Adobe Bridge, you can follow these steps:

Step 1: Purchase Adobe Creative Cloud

Before you can install Adobe Bridge, you will need to acquire a membership to Adobe Creative Cloud. Adobe provides various subscription levels for Creative Cloud, including a monthly or yearly membership.

Step 2: Download the Creative Cloud desktop app

After you have paid for Creative Cloud, you will need to download and set up the desktop program that comes with Creative Cloud. The maintenance of your subscription, as well as the downloading and installation of Adobe Bridge, will be handled by this application.

Step 3: Install Adobe Bridge

Installing Adobe Bridge requires that you first download and install the Creative Cloud desktop software. After you have done so, you can use that program to install Adobe Bridge. Simply run the software, and when you see a list of available programs, touch or click "Install" next to Bridge. The process of installation could take a few minutes or even longer, depending on the speed of your computer and the quality of your internet connection.

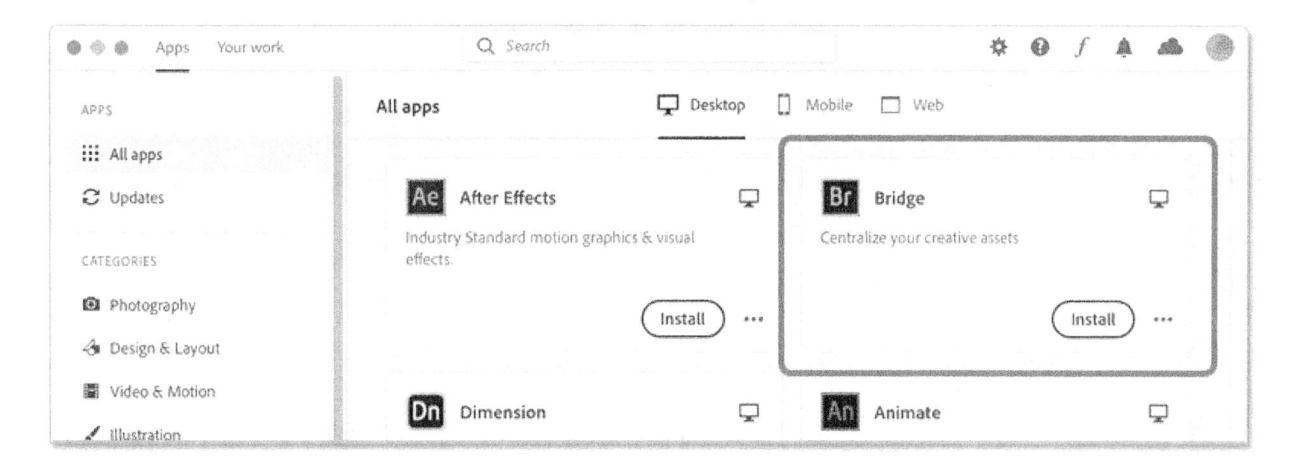

Step 4: Launch Adobe Bridge

Click the Open button when the installation procedure is done. You may start Adobe Bridge by locating the Bridge shortcut on your desktop or in your Start menu and then double-clicking it to open the software. Alternatively, you may open Adobe Bridge by putting "Adobe Bridge" into your Start menu search box. You may also run the Creative Cloud desktop software and navigate to the Bridge option under the drop-down menu of accessible apps.

Keep in mind that Adobe Bridge is an application for managing files that offers you the power to organize and show the media files you have. It is typically used in tandem with other programs offered via Adobe Creative Cloud, such as Photoshop or Premiere Pro. You may get adept at utilizing Adobe Bridge to handle your media files properly if you put in the appropriate amount of time and effort.

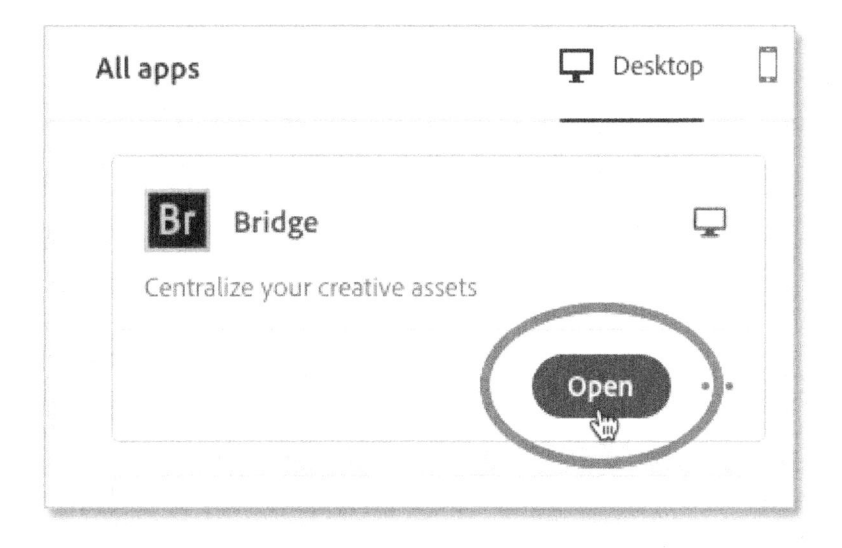

Installing Adobe Camera Raw

The plug-in known as Adobe Camera Raw is a component that may be downloaded and used with Adobe Photoshop. Because of this, you will first need to check that Photoshop is already installed on your computer before you can proceed with the installation of Camera Raw. You can install Photoshop by following the procedures that were provided before.

When you have done installing Photoshop, you will need to check for available updates to verify that you have the latest version of the Camera Raw application. Launch Photoshop, then go to the Help menu and click Updates. If there is an update for Camera Raw available, you may pick it and then install it by following the on-screen instructions. If there is no update for Camera Raw, or if you are installing Camera Raw for the first time, you may manually download and install it from the Adobe website. This is also the situation if there is no update available for Camera Raw. Visit the Camera Raw page on the Adobe website and pick the download link that corresponds to the operating system that you are running. You will need to restart Photoshop once you have completed the installation of Camera Raw to activate the plug-in.

After you have reopened Photoshop, you should be able to access Camera Raw to make modifications to your images and boost their quality. Keep in mind that Adobe Camera Raw is a formidable tool that allows you the opportunity to edit and improve your images with a high level of control and precision. When more advanced photo editing demands must be satisfied, it is commonly paired with Adobe Photoshop as the tool of choice. You may become skilled in utilizing Adobe Camera Raw to achieve outstanding outcomes with your images if you practice and devote yourself to be more educated about the application.

Installing fonts

Adding more fonts to your library in Photoshop will aid you in producing different designs and styles that stand out from the crowd. The process of installing fonts in Photoshop is uncomplicated and can be accomplished in just a few easy steps. The following instructions will lead you through the process of installing fonts in Photoshop:

Step 1: Download the Font File

Downloading the font file is the first step in the installation procedure for a typeface in Photoshop. You may obtain fonts from a broad number of websites, and some of them supply them for free while others demand a premium. After the font file has been properly downloaded, you should save it in a place on your computer where it can be immediately accessed.

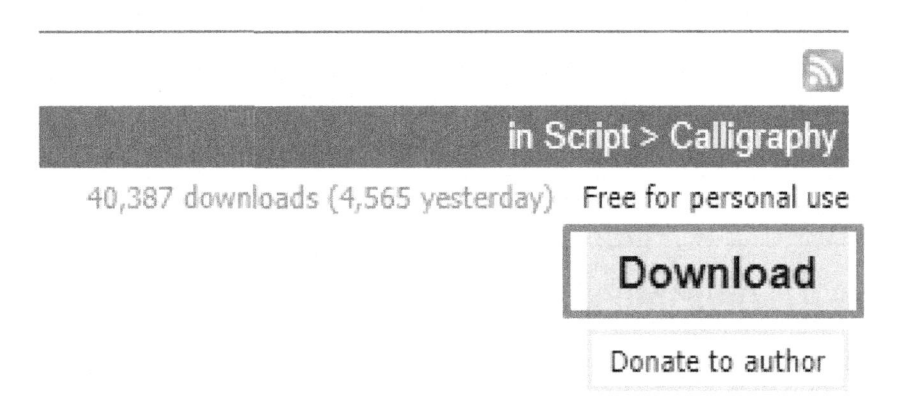

Step 2: Extract the Font File

You may need to extract multiple font files before you can install them as they have been archived in a compressed format such as ZIP or RAR. To extract the font file to a new folder, right-click on the file that was downloaded and select "Extract Files" from the context menu.

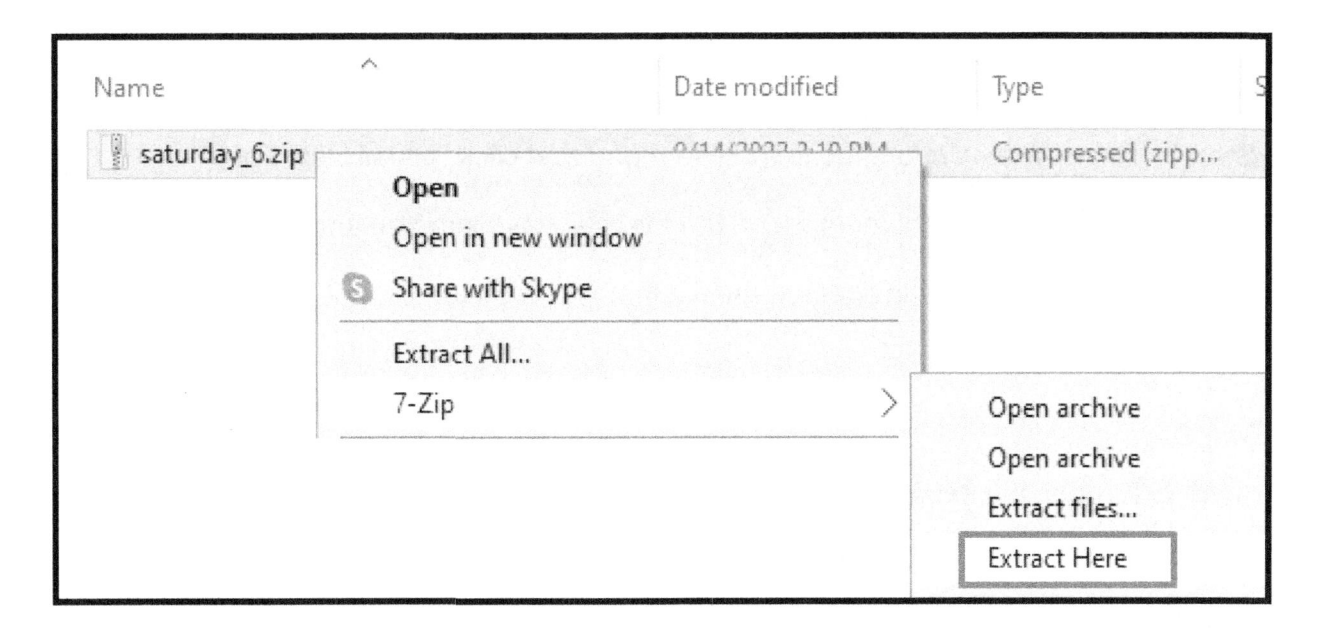

Step 3: Install the Font

When you have the font file extracted, you can then proceed to install it on your computer. The technique of installing fonts may alter based on the operating system that you use.

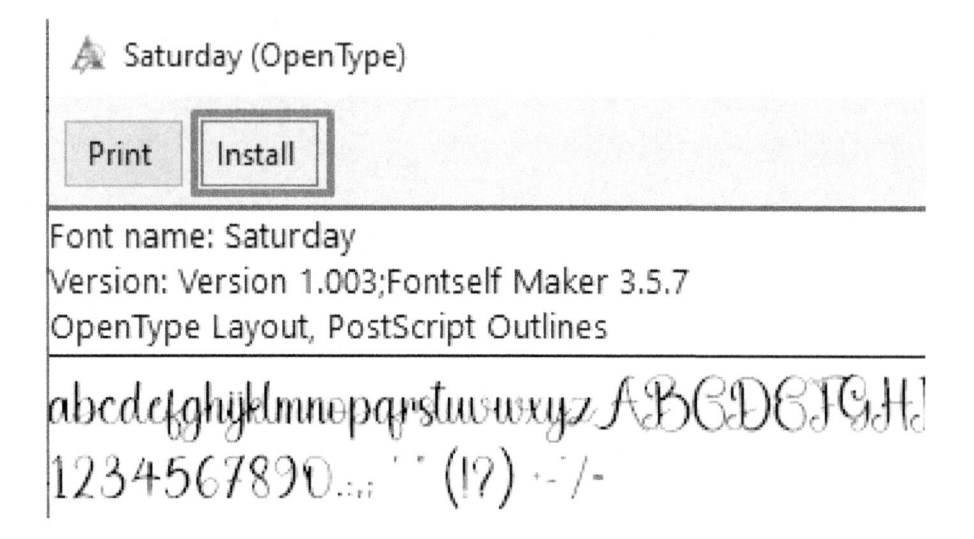

The following is a list of the steps for both Windows and Mac:

Windows

Step 1: Launch the Control Panel, and then navigate to "Appearance and Personalization."

Step 2: Make sure you select "Fonts."

Step 3: To install a new font, go to the File menu and click "Install New Font."

Step 4: Navigate to the folder in which the font file was extracted and double-click on it.

Step 5: To install a font, navigate to the file that you wish to use, and then click "Install."

MacOS

Step 1: To open the extracted font file in Font Book, just double-click on the file to extract it.

Step 2: In the Font Book window, locate the lower-right corner and search for the "Install Font" button.

Step 3: The font will be installed, and Photoshop will then be able to make it accessible for usage.

Step 4: Verify the Font is installed

After installing the font, you need to verify that it is available in Photoshop. Open Photoshop and create a new document. Select the Type tool from the toolbar on the left and click on the canvas to create a new text layer. In the Options bar at the top of the screen, click on the font dropdown option and look for the newly installed font. If it shows in the list, the font has been installed correctly.

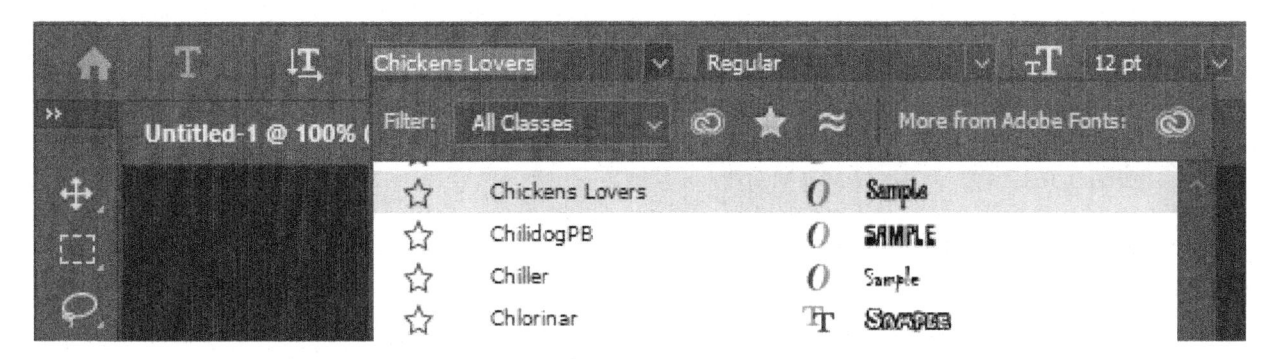

Starting Adobe Photoshop

Great! Once you have installed Adobe Photoshop, you can follow these steps to start using it:

Step 1: Launch Adobe Photoshop

You may open Adobe Photoshop by finding the Photoshop shortcut on your desktop or in your Start menu and then double-clicking it to start the software. If you don't have a desktop, you can look in your Start menu. You also have the option of launching the Creative Cloud desktop app on your computer and picking Photoshop from the list of apps that are accessible to you.

Step 2: Create a new document

After Adobe Photoshop has been opened, you may commence the construction of a new document by heading to the top menu bar, choosing "File," and then clicking the "New" option. This will bring up the New Document dialog box, in which you can make modifications to the document's settings including its size, resolution, and more.

Step 3: Open an existing document

If you already have a document that you want to work on, you may open it by going to the top menu and selecting "File" from the drop-down menu, and then clicking "Open." This will enable you to navigate through the files on your computer and select the file or document that you want to open.

Step 4: Familiarize yourself with the Photoshop interface

The interface of Photoshop can be frightening at first, but to work fast and successfully, it is necessary to get acquainted with the different panels and tools that are accessible in the application.

The Layers panel, the Tools panel, and the Properties panel are the three panels that are used the great majority of the time. You may also change the workspace to suit your requirements by rearranging the panels or generating more workplaces as needed.

Step 5: Start editing your document

After you have created or opened a project, you are ready to begin altering your document utilizing the various tools and functions that are available in Photoshop. You may begin modifying your document instantly. The scale of images, the inclusion of text, and the application of different filters and alterations are standard jobs. Keep in mind that Photoshop is a difficult tool that demands a lot of time and effort to learn. You may learn how to use Photoshop with the aid of a number of online resources, including those given by Adobe itself, such as tutorials and courses, as well as those supplied by third parties, such as online courses and lessons uploaded on YouTube. You may quickly become competent at using Photoshop to generate outstanding images and graphics if you put in the proper amount of practice and work.

Starting Adobe Photoshop online

It is normal practice to install Adobe Photoshop on a desktop computer; however, certain online versions of the application may be accessed via a web browser and used to edit images without the need to download and install any software.

Here is how you can get started with Adobe Photoshop online:

Launch Adobe Photoshop online by using your favorite web browser. You may access the online edition of Adobe Photoshop via the website for Adobe Creative Cloud; consequently, open your computer browser and continue to the website.

To utilize the online edition of Adobe Photoshop, you will need to sign into Adobe Creative Cloud. Sign into your Adobe account using the email address linked with your account and the password you set. You can set one up for free if you don't already have one.

After you have successfully logged in to Adobe Creative Cloud, go to the top of the page and click the "**Apps**" option. Clicking this link will take you to a list of all the Adobe programs that are presently accessible to you. Find Adobe Photoshop and then click "**Open**" from the menu that appears next to it. Your web browser will now open to the web-based version of Adobe Photoshop.

You may begin the editing process for your images when Adobe Photoshop has completed loading in your web browser. Because the desktop and online versions of Adobe Photoshop share many of the same tools and capabilities, you may use the online version of Photoshop to create and edit photographs in the same manner as you would using the desktop version.

The biggest benefit of Photoshop Online is that you may use this at the workplace or in the house where an internet connection is accessible. You don't need to be an expert or any programmer of IT to operate with it. You also don't need to install anything and therefore, your device is risk-free of viruses or malware. Another advantage is finding hundreds of photographs as you work on it and editing with your touch. It will save you time and you must follow some procedures to perform the task with it. In this way, you may use this program to shoot a group of images and share it with your friends and family. You may very simply use it on Computer or Laptop or even on the newest iPad. You can edit and manage your photographs on Photoshop Online. This replacement to Adobe Photoshop allows you to work from anywhere on the globe and not download and no need for space on your device.

Restoring default preferences

It's probable that over time, you've updated a variety of Photoshop settings and parameters to better fit the way you operate. On the other hand, there may come a point when you decide for several reasons that you wish to revert to the default selections. This can be because of performance problems, glitches, or perhaps just the desire to start from fresh. In these types of circumstances, resetting Photoshop to its factory settings might be a good remedy. You must realize that resetting the default preferences will remove all of your selections, including color settings, workspace layout, and general preferences before you proceed with the process of restoring the default settings. You will lose any modifications to the settings that you have made yourself. As a result of this, creating a backup of your unique settings and presets is a suggested best practice.

Here are the steps to restore the default preferences in Photoshop:

Step 1: Close Photoshop: Make sure to shut Photoshop if it is presently active. This is needed for the modifications to take effect.

Step 2: Start Photoshop by using the following combination of keys: When you open up Photoshop, make sure you keep the following keys pressed: Ctrl, Alt, and Shift (on Windows) or Command, Option, and Shift (on a Mac). Keep tapping these keys until the Photoshop launch is totally complete.

Step 3: Confirmation dialog: Once Photoshop has been run with the special keys held down, a dialog box will appear asking if you wish to erase the Adobe Photoshop Settings File and restore the default settings. This dialog box will show once Photoshop has been opened with the special keys kept down. Please read the letter attentively and be aware that once this action has been taken, it cannot be undone. Click the "Yes" button if you are convinced that you want to proceed.

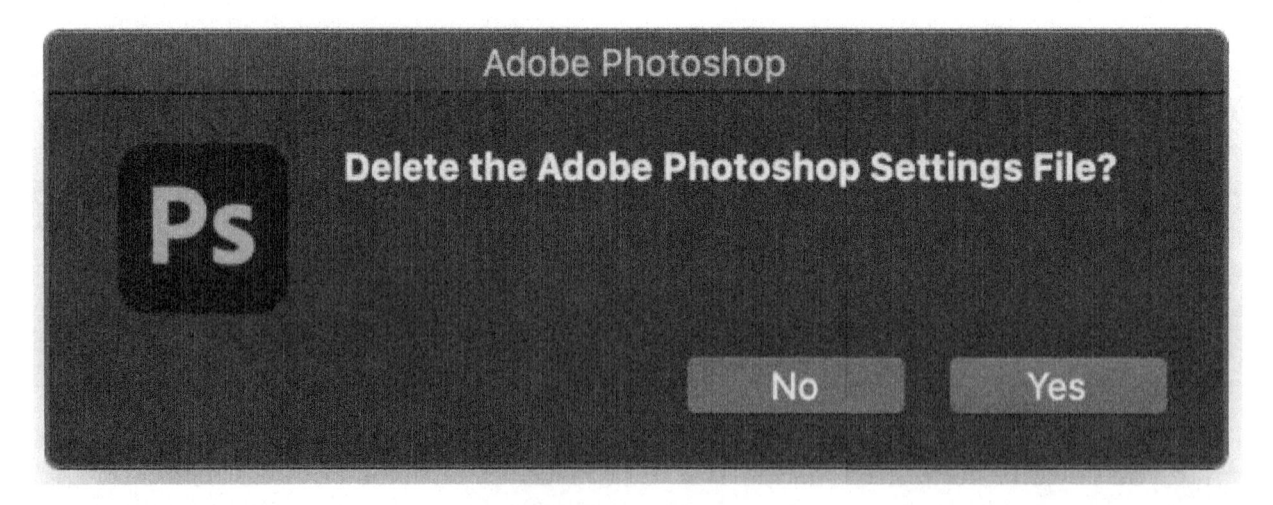

Step 4: Default preferences restored: Photoshop will launch with the default parameters and configurations. You will see that any edits you made in the past have been erased and are no longer available. The organization of the workspace, the settings for the tools, and any general preferences will all be returned to their initial states.

Step 5: Set up preferences: After you have successfully restored Photoshop to its factory defaults, you may continue customizing the application to match your individual requirements. Make any required modifications to the color settings, workspace layout, and other choices so that they correspond to the workflow you want.

Keep in mind that resetting the preferences to their original state is a powerful operation that has to be undertaken with care. It is highly advisable that you make a backup of your unique settings and presets before commencing. In addition, resetting Photoshop to its factory settings may not cure all of the difficulties you're encountering with the application, even if it does fix some of those problems. If you are having certain challenges, it may be good for you to examine extra procedures for troubleshooting or to seek help from the support resources or online forums given by Adobe. When you wish to start from scratch in Photoshop or repair certain problems, one step that might be beneficial is to reset the preferences to their factory values. You may quickly and simply return all of Photoshop's preferences and settings back to their factory defaults by following the instructions provided here. This will offer you a blank canvas on which to develop your ideas.

Additional resources

You may learn more about using Adobe Photoshop and increase your talents by reading the various additional materials that are accessible to you online.

The following are some examples:

Adobe's website: Adobe gives numerous distinct resources to aid you learn how to use Photoshop. These resources include lessons, courses, and forums where you may engage with other individuals who use Photoshop. You may acquire access to these documents by heading to the website for Adobe.

YouTube tutorials: There are a vast number of distinct Photoshop-related films that can be discovered on YouTube, and they span a broad array of topic areas. The bulk of these how-to instructions and videos were written by professional graphic designers and photographers who voluntarily contributed their skills and ideas for using the software.

Online courses: If you want more structured and in-depth education on how to use Photoshop, you may participate in one of the various programs that are given online. These workshops are generally given by seasoned industry specialists and may provide a full overview of a specific subject or set of methods.

Photoshop user groups: The Internet is home to a myriad of user groups and forums where you may engage with other individuals who use Photoshop, pose questions, and share your work. The Photoshop subreddit and the Photoshop Community on Behance are two examples of notable user communities for Photoshop.

Photoshop plugins: There are a great number of plugins and add-ons that are available for Photoshop. These might improve the functionality of the application or automate certain actions. Nik Collection by DxO, Topaz Labs, and Alien Skin Exposure are just a handful of the most well-known plugins available.

Keep in mind that the best way to become skilled with Photoshop is to practice and explore. You shouldn't be hesitant to try out new ideas and approaches, and you should continuously be learning new things and increasing your skill set. You may become competent in using Photoshop to generate outstanding images and graphics if you invest the time and effort necessary and remain persistent.

Launching New Plugins

To launch new plugins in Adobe Photoshop, follow these steps:

Install the plugin. The great majority of plugins come with an installation file, which you can frequently purchase from the website of the plugin's author. After the installation file has been downloaded, run it and then follow the on-screen directions to install the plugin.

Restart Photoshop: After the plugin has been properly installed, you will need to restart Photoshop to check that the plugin has been appropriately included.

Navigate to the plugin: After restarting Photoshop, browse to the plugin in the program's menu. It could be located in the "Extensions" menu or the "Filters" menu, depending on the plugin that you're using.

Launch the plugin: Click on the plugin to launch it. Some plugins may have a distinct interface that will open when opened, while others may function immediately within Photoshop.

Make use of the plugin: Once the plugin has been launched, you may make use of it by following the on-screen instructions. It is conceivable that to apply the effect to your photo, you will be forced to pick a specific layer or region of the image.

CHAPTER 1: GETTING STARTED

Starting to work in Adobe Photoshop

If you have never used Adobe Photoshop before, you may feel that the application is overwhelming at first. However, with little work and dedication, you may rapidly grasp the foundations of the application and become an experienced user. In this part, we will guide you through some of the core steps that are necessary to begin using Adobe Photoshop.

Understanding the Photoshop Interface

You must get accustomed with Photoshop's user interface before you can begin using the application. The workspace in Photoshop is made of a range of panels and tools, each of which may be utilized by the user to produce their artwork. By dragging and dropping panels, resizing them, and even designing your unique office, you may alter the workspace to match your requirements.

Creating a New Document

Go to the File menu and pick New to start a new document in Photoshop. From this option, you may alter the size of the document, as well as the resolution, color mode, and contents of the backdrop. The type of artwork that you wish to generate will dictate the settings that you pick. For instance, if you are designing a banner for your website, you may want to set the document size to 1200 by 600 pixels, and the resolution to 72 pixels/inch. This will help you to achieve the finest outcomes from your design.

Using Layers

One of the most significant components of Photoshop is its layering system. They enable you to work on various components of your artwork individually, which simplifies the process of editing and updating those aspects. Simply clicking the item labeled "Create a new layer" in the Layers panel will start the process of adding a new layer. Then, you may add numerous components to each layer, such as text, photographs, or shapes.

Adding Text To your Artwork

To add text to your artwork, go to the toolbar and choose the Type tool. Then, click on the area of your artwork where you would want to insert the text. After that, you may use the Character panel to input your text and pick the right font, size, color, and alignment for it. You may also add several effects to your text using the Layer Style tab. Some examples of these effects include drop shadows, bevels, and strokes.

Utilizing the Selection Tools

The use of selection tools helps you to isolate distinct aspects of your artwork, making it simpler for you to change and manipulate those elements. The Marquee, Lasso, and Magic Wand tools are the ones that are used for selecting the most commonly. To make use of these tools, first, choose the icon that corresponds to them in the toolbar, and then move your cursor over the location that you wish to choose.

Editing Images

The editing and enhancement of pictures are frequent uses for Photoshop. Adjusting the brightness, contrast, color balance, and saturation of your images may be done in Photoshop with the aid of the various tools and filters that are at your disposal. You may also erase distracting parts from your images, apply several effects, and even create composite pictures by blending several individual shots into a single image.

Working with Masks

Masks are yet another crucial component of Adobe Photoshop. They allow you the flexibility to hide or show off portions of your artwork without removing those components forever.

When dealing with difficult photographs or striving to establish a non-destructive workflow, masks are an extremely beneficial tool to have at your disposal. To build a mask, first, pick the layer that you want to mask, then go to the Layers panel and click on the option that reads "**Add Layer Mask**."

Using Filters

In Photoshop, filters are a powerful tool that can be used to apply several effects to your images and artwork to create a desired style. In Photoshop, you have access to a broad selection of filters, including Blur, Sharpen, Distort, and Stylize, amongst others. You may also design your customized filters by blending multiple effects in a single application.

Exporting Your Artwork

After you have completed the process of generating your artwork, you will need to export it in an appropriate format. To export your artwork, pick the format you wish to export it to from the drop-down option under the File menu, which is called Export. JPEG and PNG are the most generally used image formats for consumption on the web, but PDF is the most extensively used image file for use in print. The work area of Adobe Photoshop features menus, toolbars, and panels that offer you instant access to tools and choices for altering and adding components to your picture. These capabilities allow you to make modifications and add items more effectively. You may also enhance the functionality of the application by installing plug-ins, which are bits of third-party software.

Bitmapped digital photographs are images with a continuous tone that have been converted into a succession of small squares, or picture elements, called pixels. Most of your work in Photoshop will be done utilizing bitmapped digital pictures. You can also work with something called vector graphics, which are drawings constructed up of straight lines that preserve their clarity even when scaled up or down.

You may design your original artwork with Photoshop, or you can import photographs from a wide number of sources, including:

- Photographs from a digital camera or cell phone
- Stock photography, such as photographs from the Adobe Stock service
- Scans of images, transparencies, negatives, drawings, or other materials
- Captured video clips
- Artwork generated with drawing or painting programs

Starting Photoshop

To begin, you'll launch Adobe Photoshop and reset the default options.

To reset the default settings, click the Adobe Photoshop 2023 icon located on your Start menu (Windows) or the Launchpad on Dock (macOS). While doing so, concurrently hold down the Ctrl, Alt, and Shift keys (Windows) or the Command, Option, and Shift keys (macOS).

If you do not see Adobe Photoshop 2023, type Photoshop into the search box on the taskbar (Windows) or in Spotlight (macOS), and when the Adobe Photoshop 2023 application icon displays, click it and hit Enter or Return. If you do not find Adobe Photoshop 2023, put Photoshop into the search bar.

When prompted to confirm that you wish to erase the Adobe Photoshop Settings file, pick the Yes option when offered.

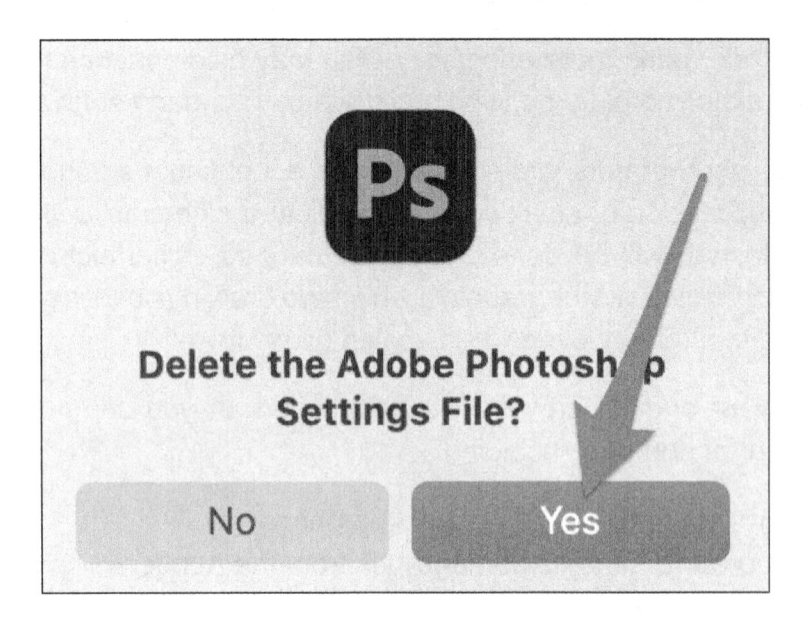

Using the Home screen

The Home screen in Adobe Photoshop is a useful and time-saving tool that gives simple access to previously used files, facilitates the creation of new files, and helps the user to learn about new features and content. When you run Photoshop, the first thing that shows is the **Home screen**, which may be changed to meet your tastes and requirements.

Accessing the Home Screen

Launch the software and wait for the splash screen to finish loading before attempting to enter the **Home screen** in Photoshop. On the first splash screen, the Photoshop logo and a loading progress meter are presented. As soon as the loading operation is done, you will be directed to the **Home screen.**

Navigating the Home Screen

You may access many features and information from the several regions that make up the **Home screen**.

These parts are as follows:

Home: This will lead you through how to operate the most recent version as well as tell you more about it. When you have visited at least one locally stored document, a recent section with previously opened documents will display at the bottom of the **Home screen**. This region will remain there until you close it.

Learn: This includes links to lessons that open in Photoshop, where the Learn panel guides you through the phases of a lesson that you follow using Photoshop itself. These lessons may be opened by clicking the "**Learn**" button.

Your Files: This displays all of the Photoshop Cloud Documents that you have generated, including ones that were crafted on mobile devices like an iPad.

Shared with You: This lists Cloud Documents that others have invited you to see by using the **File > Invite command**.

Lightroom Photos: This displays a list of images that have been synced to the Lightroom online photo storage connected with your Creative Cloud account (and not the Lightroom Classic local storage).

Deleted: This displays a list of Cloud Documents that you have destroyed if you change your mind and wish to retrieve them (this function is equivalent to the Recycle Bin or Trash icon present on the desktop of your PC). This list only contains things that are saved in the cloud, not files that have been deleted from Lightroom Photos or the local storage on your computer.

Photoshop looks for similar material in the Learn lessons about Photoshop as well as in Adobe Stock pictures when you click the Search button in the upper-right corner and type words. When a document is open, the Search symbol may also identify various actions and tools in Photoshop. Additionally, it can search for information in your **cloud synced Lightroom photographs**. For instance, search "**bird**" to discover all the cloud images in your Lightroom library that show birds. When you open a new document, the **Home screen** will disappear by itself, as this is the action that you are going to do next. You may visit the **Home screen** at any moment by touching the icon that looks like a home that is situated in the top-left corner of the application window.

Opening a document

Every user should be knowledgeable in Adobe Photoshop's basic feature of document opening. Opening a document is the starting stage in every process, whether initiating a new project, continuing an old one, or altering an image.

The essential steps to opening a document in Adobe Photoshop are described below.

Launching Adobe Photoshop

Launching Adobe Photoshop is the initial step in opening a file in it. Photoshop may be started by double-clicking on its desktop icon, picking it from the Start menu, or heading to the Applications folder.

Accessing the Open Dialog Box

Once Photoshop is open, you can reach the Open dialog box by clicking on the File menu and selecting Open or by using the keyboard shortcut **Ctrl + O** (Windows) or **Command + O** (Mac).

As an alternative, you may enter the enter dialog box by selecting the Open button on the **Home screen**, which opens when Photoshop is loaded. The Recent Files part of the **Home screen** is where you'll locate the Open button.

Selecting a Document

You may select the document you wish to open after you've reached the Open dialog box. The files and folders on your computer are presented in the Open dialog box. You may use the search box to hunt for a particular file or browse the directories to identify the one you want to open.

The File name field at the bottom of the Open dialog box reveals the name and file type of the selected file. To the right of the Open dialog box, there is a thumbnail preview of the file you may see.

Selecting Options

You may wish to make some tweaks to the document's opening procedure before you open it. You may adjust the document settings using several of the options that are accessible in the Open dialog box. By picking the right choice from the Mode drop-down box, for instance, you can decide to open the document in a particular color mode, such as **RGB** or **CMYK**. You may also opt to open the file as a **Smart Object**, which enables you to alter the photo without causing any damage. You can opt to open a document as a flattened picture or as a layered document if it has numerous layers. Make sure the Layers option is chosen in the Open dialog box to open the document as a layered document.

Opening the Document

To open the document in Adobe Photoshop after choosing it and making your selections, click the Open option. As soon as the file opens, you may start working on it in a new tab in the Photoshop workspace.

Opening Multiple Documents

You may open all the documents you need to work on simultaneously at once. Simply repeat the preceding steps for each document you want to open to accomplish this. Each document you open in Photoshop will appear on its tab when you open many files. The tabs may be changed by either clicking on them or by using the **Ctrl + Tab (Windows)** or **Command + Tab** (Mac) keyboard shortcut.

Opening Recent Documents

You may simply recover often used documents from the Recent Files area of the **Home screen** if you routinely work on the same ones. The most recently opened documents are presented in the Recent Files tab, and you may open a document in Photoshop by clicking on a thumbnail picture. As an alternative, you may access recent documents by selecting the Open Recent option under the File menu. You may pick one of the recently opened documents from a list that will display to open it in Photoshop. The menu bar and options bar at the top of the screen, the Tools panel on the left, and multiple active panels in the panel dock on the right make up Photoshop's default workspace. One or more document windows also appear when a document is open, and you may utilize the tabbed interface to see them all at once. Learning how to employ the tools and panels in one program, such as Photoshop, makes it easy to learn and use other applications, such as Adobe Illustrator® and Adobe InDesign®. The Photoshop work area on Windows and the Mac varies essentially in one way: Windows always shows Photoshop in a window that is on its own. On macOS, you may select whether to work with an application frame, which sets the Photoshop document windows and panels in a frame distinct from any other active programs. The navigation bar is the only portion of the application frame that is not within the Photoshop document frame. By default, the application frame is switched on; to turn it off, click **Window > Application Frame**.

Using the tools

A range of tools are available in Adobe Photos hop that may be used to edit and modify images in numerous ways. You may make lovely photographs and fulfill your creative ideas by employing these tools. It's vital to practice and experiment with these tools to master their features and restrictions to become effective at employing them.

Here are some of Photoshop's most popular tools along with instructions on how to utilize them:

1. Selection Tools

You may choose a certain portion of a photograph for change using selecting tools. The Marquee Tool, Lasso Tool, and Magic Wand Tool are just a handful of the selecting tools offered in Photoshop. Simply click and drag to build a selection around the area you wish to edit to apply these tools. You may also adjust your selection using keyboard shortcuts, such as holding down the Shift key to add to it or the Alt key to deduct from it.

2. Crop Tool

The Crop Tool is used to crop a photograph and erase undesirable areas from it. When you wish to crop an area, pick the Crop Tool from the tool bar on the left side of the screen and drag it there. The Crop Tool may also be used to correct a photo that is crooked or to adjust the aspect ratio of the image.

3. Healing Brush Tool

To erase blemishes, scratches, and other imperfections from a photo, use the Healing Brush Tool. Click on the area you wish to clone, and then pick the Healing Brush Tool from the toolbar on the left side of the screen. Next, click and drag over the location where you wish to get rid of the defect. A clone of the pixels in the surrounding region will replace the area when you use the healing brush tool.

4. Clone Stamp Tool

Like the Healing Brush Tool, the Clone Stamp Tool lets you clone a section of the picture and use it to paint over another portion of the image. Alt-click on the area you wish to clone after picking the Clone Stamp Tool from the toolbar on the left side of the screen. Next, drag your cursor over the area you wish to paint. The area will be replaced with a replica of the area you pick when you use the Clone Stamp Tool.

5. Brush Tool

Use the Brush Tool to add effects or color to a photograph. Select the Brush Tool from the tool bar on the left side of the screen to use it. Then, from the settings bar at the top of the screen, pick the brush size and style. Next, drag your cursor over the area you wish to paint or affect.

6. Gradient Tool

To produce a gradient of colors or tones in a photograph, use the gradient tool. Pick the Gradient Tool from the toolbar on the left side of the screen to activate it. Then, from the choices bar at the top of the screen, decide the sort of gradient you wish to use. Next, drag your cursor over the location to which you wish to apply the gradient after clicking.

7. Text Tool

Text may be added to a photograph using the Text Tool. Pick the Text Tool from the toolbar on the left side of the screen to begin using it. Then, from the choices bar at the top of the screen, select a font, size, and color. Next, insert your text by clicking on the area of the photo where you want to place it.

Selecting and using a tool from the Tools panel

The main area where you may access these tools is the Tools panel. Here are the steps for picking and utilizing a tool in Adobe Photoshop's Tools panel:

Step 1. You should run Adobe Photoshop and then pick the photo you want to edit.

Step 2. Find the Tools panel, which by default is positioned on the left side of the screen.

Step 3. To view the name and purpose of each tool, hover your cursor over it.

Step 4. By clicking on it, you may pick the tool you wish to use. The selected tool will be highlighted.

Step 5. To adjust the functionality of the instrument, update its parameters. The choices for the selected tool will be presented in the options bar, which is at the top of the screen.

Step 6. When required, utilize the tool by clicking and dragging on the picture canvas.

Step 7. Simply click on the new tool in the Tools menu to change it.

The Brush tool, Clone Stamp tool, Eraser tool, and Selection tools like the Marquee, lLasso, and Magic Wand tools are a few of the frequently used tools in Adobe Photoshop.

You can make gorgeous images and graphics in Adobe Photoshop by becoming adept with these tools.

Using the Zoom tool, for instance.

An essential function in Adobe Photoshop that enables you zoom in and out on a photograph is the zoom tool. While zooming out is useful for seeing the complete image or receiving a general perspective of your work, zooming in is handy when you need to focus on minutiae or make accurate alterations.

The symbol for the Zoom tool looks like a magnifying glass with a + sign inside it. To utilize the Zoom tool, just choose it from the Tools panel by clicking on its icon.

By clicking the left mouse button on a photo after picking the Zoom tool, you may zoom it. The picture will expand bigger with each click as the magnification rises.

To zoom out of the photo, you may alternatively click while holding down the Alt key (Option key on a Mac). The magnification will be lowered with each click, making the picture seem smaller. You may use the Zoom tool options bar to zoom in or out to a specific magnification level. The top of the screen's options bar reveals the settings for the presently chosen tool. A magnifying glass icon and a percentage number denoting the current magnification level are provided in the options bar for the Zoom tool. By inputting a specified percentage or by using the plus and minus buttons to modify the magnification level, you may change this amount.

The Zoom tool's ability to zoom in or out of a particular portion of the picture is another valuable function. To achieve this, click and drag over the location you want to zoom in on while holding down the Alt key (Option key on a Mac). To make it simpler to work on details or make accurate modifications, the picture will zoom in on the targeted spot. To generate more sophisticated effects, you may also combine the Zoom tool with other Adobe Photoshop tools. To ensure that your brush strokes are crisp and accurate, you may find it beneficial to zoom in on the region you are working on if you are using the Brush tool to paint a big section of the picture. Similarly, to this, you may need to zoom in to make sure you're replicating the proper section of the picture while using the Clone Stamp tool to remove an item from an image.

When using the Zoom tool, there are a few key considerations to ponder. First, it's vital to keep in mind that expanding a photograph does not genuinely enhance its resolution.

Instead, it just enlarges the picture, giving the appearance that it is bigger. It might be tough to work on an image that appears pixelated or indistinct when you zoom in too far. Working at a reasonable magnification level that enables you to see the details you desire without losing image quality is key to preventing this.

When working on a considerably expanded picture, it can be easy to lose context, which is another key point to bear in mind when using the Zoom tool. When you expand a photograph, you are basically viewing a single, small portion of the image. This can make it difficult to understand how your edits are affecting the image.

To prevent this, it's a good idea to sometimes zoom out to observe how your edits are affecting the full picture.

Sampling a color

When you need to match the color of an object or piece of text in a photograph or when you need to apply a specific hue in a creative project, sampling a color could be beneficial. Selecting the Eyedropper tool from the Tools panel is the first stage in the color sample procedure. The Tools panel, which is by default on the left side of the screen, is where you'll find the Eyedropper tool. The Eyedropper tool's icon resembles a dropper with a color swatch next to it. You may click on any section of the photo or document to sample the color after picking the Eyedropper tool. The Foreground color swatch in the Tools tab will show the color you tested. The current color that will be applied when you use paint or drawing tool is visible in the Foreground color swatch, which is at the bottom of the Tools panel.

You can sample colors outside of the document window by using the Eyedropper tool's options bar if you need to sample a color that isn't currently showing on the screen. The top of the screen's options bar reveals the settings for the presently chosen tool. The Eyedropper tool's options bar contains a magnifying glass icon, a dropdown menu for Sample Size, and a drop-down menu for Color Mode. You may specify the size of the region that the Eyedropper tool will sample from the Sample Size drop-down menu. Point Sample, which samples a single pixel at a time, is the default choice. You can pick 3x3 Average or 5x5 Average to sample an average color from a 3x3 or 5x5 pixel area, respectively, if you need to sample an average color from a greater region.

You may pick the color mode for the sampled color from the Color Mode drop-down box. RGB, the standard color style used for digital pictures, is the default choice. Nevertheless, you may also pick another color mode according to your requirements, such as CMYK, Lab, or Grayscale. The Eyedropper tool's ability to sample a color from a particular layer or channel in an image is another important function. You must click on the layer or channel in the Layers panel or the Channels panel while holding down the Ctrl key (Command on a Mac). Instead of sampling colors from the complete picture, this will merely do it from the layer or channel you have selected. Adobe Photo shop gives several tools for creating and managing colors in addition to sampling colors from photographs. The Color Picker is one such tool that enables you to pick a color by adjusting its hue, saturation, and brightness values. Click on the Foreground color Swatch in the Tools panel is clicked to access the Color Picker.

The Color Picker features sliders for hue, saturation, and brightness on the right and a color spectrum on the left. You may click on a color in the spectrum to pick it, or you can use the sliders to create a custom color. When a color has been picked, the Foreground color swatch will show it.

Working with tools and tool properties

It might be tough to know which tool to use and how to adjust its attributes to attain the desired outcome when there are so many distinct tools accessible. In this part, we'll look at the foundations of utilizing tools and tool settings in Adobe Photoshop.

By default, the Tools panel is on the left side of the screen and offers some tools grouped into sections such Selection, Painting, and Navigation. Simply click on a tool's icon in the Tools panel to choose it. Once a tool has been selected, its attributes can be altered in the options bar at the top of the screen. The parameters for the current tool are presented in the options bar, where you may alter them to achieve the outcome you desire.

For instance, you may adjust the Brush tool's attributes in the options bar to change its size, hardness, opacity, and flow if you've picked it from the Painting category.

How the brush stroke is applied to the picture is influenced by these features. The Hardness property governs how soft or hard the edges of the brush stroke are, while the Size parameter sets the diameter of the brush tip. While the Flow property determines how rapidly paint is applied as you drag the brush over the picture, the Opacity property governs how transparent the brush stroke is.

The Type tool is yet another that may be customized using characteristics. The font, size, color, and alignment of the text may all be altered using the options bar when using the Type tool to add text to an image. You may access extra settings by right-clicking on the canvas while using a tool in addition to modifying tool characteristics in the options bar. For instance, if you are using the Brush tool, you may access multiple brush presets, such as varied shapes or textures, by executing a right-click on the canvas.

The Properties panel, which may be entered by selecting Window > Properties from the menu bar, gives another method to get tool properties. In comparison to the choices bar, the Properties panel gives a greater range of controls and options for the presently chosen tool. For instance, the Properties panel will include options for the crop size, aspect ratio, and resolution if you have selected the Crop tool. Filters, layer properties, and other adjustments to your project may all be made using the attributes panel.

It's vital to note that certain tools have extra choices that are concealed from visibility in the Properties panel or options bar. When using the tool, you may access these settings by pressing and holding the Shift key. For instance, you may draw a straight line connecting two points on the canvas while using the Brush tool and holding down the Shift key. Understanding how to move between tools rapidly and efficiently is another key component of working with tools in Adobe Photoshop. Using keyboard shortcuts is one approach to achieve this. Keyboard shortcuts are key combinations that may be pushed to carry out a particular job, such as picking a tool or modifying its properties.

You may pick Help > Keyboard Shortcuts from the menu bar to view a list of keyboard shortcuts for each tool in Adobe Photoshop. This will bring up a dialog box with a set of keyboard shortcuts for each Photos hop tool. You may change the Tools panel so that it only contains the tools you use the most commonly in addition to keyboard shortcuts. Simply choose the Edit Tool bar by clicking on the three dots at the bottom of the Tools panel. You may then add, delete, or reorganize tools in the Tools panel using the dialog box that will be presented.

Setting the unit of measure

Setting the right unit of measurement for your project is vital when using Adobe Photoshop. The program measures and displays sizes and distances based on the unit of measure. You can assure your project's correctness and consistency by utilizing the right unit of measurement.

You can use Photoshop to set the unit of measurement by following these easy steps:

Step 1. Launch Photoshop and select **File > New** from the menu bar to start a new document.

Step 2. The New Document dialog box features a section labeled "**Units**." You may choose your desired unit of measurement in this section using the drop-down option. Pixels, inches, centimeters, millimeters, points, and picas are among the alternatives.

Step 3. Decide which unit of measurement is ideal for your project. For instance, you may wish to use pixels as the unit of measurement while constructing a website, while you could prefer to use inches or centimeters when generating a print page.

Step 4. In the same dialog box where you pick the unit of measurement, you may also adjust the document's width, height, and resolution. These characteristics will change based on the details of your project.

Step 5. Click "**Create**" to create a new document after adjusting the unit of measurement and other document choices.

If you have already created a document and need to change the unit of measure, you can do so by following these steps:

Step 1. In the menu bar, select **Image > Image Size**.

Step 2. The "**Document Size**" field is in the Image Size dialog box. You may choose your desired unit of measurement in this section using the drop-down option. The settings are the same as those in the dialog box for creating a new document.

Step 3. After picking the unit of measurement you wish to use, click "**OK**" to preserve your changes.

Regardless of the size or planned production of your project, you can assure accuracy and consistency by picking the correct unit of measurement. Setting the right unit of measurement is a vital stage in the design process, whether you are producing a modest symbol or a big banner. Furthermore, it's crucial to bear in mind that various design activities might call for employing distinct units of measurement, such as pixels for digital design and inches for print design. To assure the success of your project, make sure to utilize the right unit of measurement for each component.

Undoing actions in Photoshop

1. Undo and Redo Buttons

Using the undo and redo buttons is the easiest approach to undo activities in Photoshop. You can reach the undo button by tapping the shortcut keys **Ctrl + Z** (Windows) or **Command + Z** (Mac) or by choosing it from the top menu bar. This will undo anything you just did. The undo and redo buttons are near to each other, and the shortcut keys **Shift+ Ctrl + Z** (Windows) and **Shift+ Command+ Z** (Mac) may be used to swiftly access the redo button. The earlier action you undid will be undone again by this.

2. Step Backward/Forward

The Step Backward command in Photoshop may be used to undo several tasks. You can use this command to return to a given period in your editing history.

You may use the shortcut keys **Alt + Ctrl + Z** (Windows) or **Option + Command + Z** (Mac) to proceed to this command by selecting **Edit> Step Backward**. When you use this command, your editing history will progress by one step each time. The Step Forward command may be used to advance through your editing history. The same menu item or the shortcut key **Shift+ Ctrl + Z** (Windows) or **Shift+ Command+ Z** (Mac) may be used to access this command. You will advance in your editing history by doing this.

3. History Panel

You will see a full list of all the activities you've performed during your editing session in Photoshop's History panel. By clicking on the action, you wish to reverse, you may employ the History panel to undo activity. By selecting **Window > History**, you may access to the History panel. Click on the action you wish to reverse in the History pane. You'll be led back to that period in your editing history by hitting here. You may also travel back in time in the History panel by using the shortcut keys **Ctrl +Alt+ Z** (for Windows) or **Command+ Option+ Z** (for Mac).

4. Revert Command

You may use the Revert command to reverse all the alterations you've made to your photo from the previous time you saved it. This command will reopen the most recently saved version of your photo while quitting the current document without storing any adjustments. Go to File > Revert to utilize the Revert command.

5. Liquify Filter

You may apply the Reconstruct tool in Photoshop's Liquify effect to undo certain modifications that you've made to your photo. You can paint over the areas you want to undo using the Reconstruct tool. Click the Reconstruct button in the Liquify filter dialog box or use the shortcut key R to access the Reconstruct tool.

6. Using History States

Utilizing History States in Photoshop is another approach for redoing tasks. Using this approach, you may create a new state to your editing history that you can access to go back in time. Select New Snapshot under **Edit > Undo** to establish a new History State. The shortcut keys **Ctrl + Shift+ N** (Windows) and **Command + Shift+ N** (Mac) can also be used.

Once a new History State has been generated, you may employ it at any moment to go back to that point in your editing history. Go to the History panel and pick the state you want to revisit to view the History States.

More on Using the History Panel

You may retrieve any recent state of the picture generated during the current working session by utilizing the History panel. The new state of a photograph is added to the panel each time you alter it. Each of the steps is presented independently in the panel, for instance, if you choose, paint, and rotate a section of an image. The picture returns to its former condition when you pick one of the states, which was when the adjustment was initially done. Following that, you may start working. In Photo shop, you may produce a document from a state or snapshot by utilizing the History panel to delete photo states.

Use the History panel with the following in mind:

Because they don't influence a single picture, program-wide changes like those to panels, color settings, actions, and preferences don't display in the History panel.

The History section by default displays the previous 20 states. The quantity of remembered states may be adjusted by selecting an option under Preferences > Performance.

Older states are automatically destroyed to give Photoshop greater memory. Create a snapshot of the state to keep it for the length of your work session.

All states and snapshots from the previous working session are wiped from the panel if you close and reopen the document.

The top of the panel always shows a photograph of the document in its original condition.

Additional states are listed at the end of the list. Meaning that the oldest state is at the top and the newest is at the bottom of the list.

The tool or command used to alter the picture is listed next to each stage.

By default, when you choose a state, the states below it is darkened. This way you can quickly identify which modifications will be lost if you continue working from the specified state.

By default, picking a state and then changing the picture removes all states that follow it.

If you choose a state and then modify the picture, removing the states that came later, you may use the Undo command to undo the latest modification and restore the destroyed states.

By default, erasing a state deletes that state and those that came after it. If you pick the Allow Non-Linear History option, removing a state deletes only that state.

Revert to a previous image state

1. Do any of the following:

• Click the name of the state.

• Choose Step Forward or Step Backward from the History panel menu or the Edit menu to advance to the next or previous state.

Delete one or more image states

1. Do one of the following:

• Click the name of the state and pick erase from the History panel menu to erase that modification and any that occurred after it.

• Drag the state to the erase icon W to erase that modification and others that came after it.

• To delete the list of states from the History panel without affecting the image, pick Clear History from the panel menu. This option does not influence how much memory Photoshop uses.

• If you wish to erase all the states from the list without changing the picture, hold down **Alt** (Windows) or **Option** (Mac OS) and pick Clear History from the panel menu. Purging states is beneficial if Photoshop indicates that it is running low on memory as it eliminates the states from the Undo buffer and relieves memory. The order to Clear History cannot be reversed.

• To erase all open documents' lists of states, pick **Edit > Purge > Histories**. This action cannot be undone.

Create or replace a document with an image state

1. Do one of the following:

• Drag a state or snapshot onto the Create a New Document from Current State button in the History window. The history list for the freshly formed document has simply the Duplicate State entry.

• Click the Create a New Document from Current State button after picking a state or snapshot. Only the Duplicate State item can be discovered in the freshly produced document's history list.

• From the History panel menu, pick New Document after selecting a state or snapshot. Only the Duplicate State item can be discovered in the freshly produced document's history list.

• Drag a state onto an existing document.

Remember to build a new file for each state you save and save it in a distinct file if you wish to preserve one or more snapshots or picture states for use in a later editing session. Plan to open the other saved files as well when you reopen your primary file. You may recover the snapshots again from the History panel of the original picture by dragging each file's initial snapshot onto it.

Set history options

You may choose the maximum number of items to include in the History panel and configure additional variables to personalize the panel.

1. Choose History Options from the History panel menu.

2. Select an option:

Automatically Create First Snapshot

Automatically creates a snapshot of the initial state of the image when the document is opened.

Automatically Create New Snapshot When Saving

Generates a snapshot every time you save.

Allow Non-Linear History

Makes modifications to a specified state without removing the states that follow later. Normally, when you pick a state and alter the picture, all states that come after the selected one are removed. In this approach, the History panel may display a list of the editing steps in the order that they were made. By capturing states in a nonlinear fashion, you may choose a state, make a modification to the image, and remove just that state. The modification is inserted at the end of the list.

Show New Snapshot Dialog by Default

Forces Photoshop to ask you for snapshot names even when you utilize the buttons on the panel.

Make Layer Visibility Changes Undoable

This option is chosen by default. Turning layer visibility on or off is documented as a historical step. Deselect this option to omit layer visibility changes in historical stages.

Set Edit History Log options

You may need to maintain thorough notes of what's been done to a file in Photoshop, either for your records, client records, or legal considerations. The Edit History Log enables you retain a textual history of modifications made to a picture. You may access the Edit History Log information using Adobe Bridge or the File Info dialog box. You can opt to export the text to an external log file, or you can save the information in the metadata of modified files. Storing several editing processes in file metadata increases file size; such files may take longer than usual to open and save.

Note: If you need to confirm that the log file hasn't been tampered with, maintain the edit log in the file's meta data, and then use Adobe Acrobat to digitally sign the log file. By default, historical log data regarding each session is preserved as metadata included in the picture file. You may decide where the history log data is kept, and the amount of information provided in the history log.

Step 1. Choose **Edit > Preferences > General** (Windows) or **Photoshop > Preferences > General** (Mac OS).

Step 2. Click the History Log choice to turn from on to off or vice versa.

Step 3. For the Save Log Items To option, pick one of the following:

• **Metadata**: Saves the history log as metadata included in each file.

• **Text File:** Exports the history log to a text file. You are requested to name the text file and pick a place in which to save it.

• **Both:** Stores metadata in the file and makes a text file. Note: If you wish to store the text file in a different location or save another text file, click the Select button, decide where to save the text file, name the file if necessary, and click store.

Step 4. From the Edit Log Items menu, pick one of the following options:

• **Sessions Only:** Keeps a record of each time you start or exit Photoshop and each time you open and close files (each image's filename is included). Does not provide any information regarding alterations made to the file.

• **Concise:** Includes the text that appears in the History panel in addition to the Sessions information.

• **Detailed:** Includes the language that appears in the Actions panel in addition to the Concise information. If you require a comprehensive history of all modifications made to files, pick Detailed.

More about panels and panel locations

The panels in Photos hop are sturdy and adaptable. You wouldn't commonly need to view all the panels at once. They are grouped as a result, and many of the basic configurations' panels are left closed. The Window menu offers a comprehensive list of all panels. The names of the panels that are open and active in their panel groups are indicated by checkmarks.

By picking the panel's name from the Window menu, you may open a closed panel or shut an open one. By hitting the Tab key, all panels-including the tools panel and options bar-can be hidden at once. Press the Tab once again to open it again. NOTE: When panels are concealed, a thin vertical strip appears along the left or right side of the application frame. Hover the cursor across the strip to momentarily show the panels docked along that edge. When you employed the Layers and Swatches panels, you had previously used panels from the panel dock. Panels may be moved around the panel dock using drag and drop. This is perfect for large panels or ones you seldom use but want to keep nearby.

You can arrange panels in other ways as well:

• To transfer an entire panel group, drag that group's title bar to another position in the work area.

• To move a panel to another group, drag the panel tab into that panel group so that a blue highlight appears inside the group, and then press the mouse button.

• To dock a panel or panel group, drag the title bar or panel tab onto the top of the dock.

• To undock a panel or panel group so that it becomes a floating panel or panel group, drag its title bar or panel tab away from the dock.

Expanding and collapsing panels

You may resize panels to make more efficient use of the available screen real estate and to view fewer or more panel choices by moving the panel's border or by clicking to cycle between its preset sizes:

To convert open panels to icons, click the double arrow in the title bar of the dock or panel group. This will bring up the context menu. Simply clicking on the panel's icon or the double arrow will force it to expand.

You may modify the height of a panel by sliding the border at its bottom.

To alter the width of a dock, position the cursor on the left side of the dock until it transforms into an arrow with two heads. Next, drag to the left to make the dock broader or to the right to make it smaller.

To modify the size of a floating panel, slide the pointer over the panel's right, left, or bottom border until it transforms into an arrow with two heads, and then drag the edge to the left or right to make it larger or smaller. You may also move the corner to the bottom right in or out of its location.

Double-clicking a panel tab or panel title bar will allow you to collapse a panel group, making it so that just the dock header bar and the tabs are visible. Simply repeat the double-click operation to get back the larger view. Even when the panel collapses, the menu for the panel can still be accessible.

Certain panels, like the Character and Paragraph panels, cannot have their size modified, but you may still collapse them if you want to.

After collapsing a panel, you will note that the tabs for the other panels in the panel group, as well as the button for the panel menu, will continue to be visible.

Notes on Tools Panel and Option Bar

The Tools panel and the options bar are similar some of the other panels in the following respects:

TIP: Simply right-click the workspace icon in the top-right corner of the application window and pick the Reset Essentials option to revert the Essentials workspace back to its default setting.

You may relocate the Tools panel to a new spot in the work area by dragging its title bar with your mouse. You may transfer the choices bar to a new place by moving the grab bar positioned at the panel's extreme left end.

You may conceal the Tools panel and the options bar by using the commands that are in the Windows menu.

But the Tools panel and the choices bar don't support all the panel's features, and some of them aren't even available to use:

- The Tools panel and the options bar cannot be grouped with any other panels in the UI.
- The Tools panel and the options bar cannot be resized in any manner.
- The Tools panel and the options bar cannot be layered in the panel dock at this time.
- There are no panel menus linked with the Tools panel or the options bar.

At first look, the choices bar and the Properties panel might seem to be performing the same purpose; nonetheless, they are completely independent from one another. The choices bar provides settings for the active tool (the item that will be generated next), while the Properties panel contains settings for the active layer or document state (something that has already been created by you).

At times, the sheer variety of panels accessible in Photo shop might be frightening. As your expertise with Photoshop develops, you should give serious attention to conducting most of your work in the Properties panel. The Properties panel changes to present the choices that are most relevant to the item you have selected when you pick several various types of items. The document's choices are visible in the Properties panel even when nothing is chosen in the document. This can help you save some time.

For instance, if you choose a type layer, the Properties panel will show you choices for altering the layer (if you want to move or rotate it) as well as options for modifying the type itself (so that you may adjust more type features than can be accommodated in the options bar). Because of this, you won't need to use the Character or Transform panel very often, which will cut down on the amount of time you spend doing so.

If you want to utilize an option that is not as common, you may need to access a more specialized panel, but for many normal actions, what you want to conduct may already be available to you in the Properties panel. If you wish to use an option that is not as prevalent, you may need to enter a more specialist panel. It is advised that the Properties panel be always kept open if the available screen real estate is allowed.

CHAPTER 2: BASIC PHOTO CORRECTIONS

Strategy for retouching

Fixing imperfections and increasing an image's general quality are the aims of the operation known as "retouching," which is an integral aspect of the process of editing digital images. Although there is no generally applicable methodology to retouching, there are several key phases and approaches that may be applied to generate high-quality results.

An approach to editing images with Adobe Photoshop is as follows:

1. Start with a high-quality image

Beginning any photo editing procedure with a high-quality photograph is always the first order of business. Capturing the picture in this manner demands the use of a camera that has a high resolution as well as suitable light. Even the most advanced retouching procedures might fail if the photo you're working with is of low quality.

2. Analyze the image

After you have gotten a photo of outstanding quality, the following step is to carefully inspect it to establish what portions of it need altering. This includes evaluating the picture to discover any faults or imperfections that need to be repaired before going on to the next phase. Problems including pimples, wrinkles, uneven skin tone, and distracting objects in the backdrop are typically encountered while retouching.

3. Use the right tools

The second stage, after finding the locations that need retouching, is to determine the suitable tools to use for the retouching procedure. The Healing Brush, Clone Stamp, Patch Tool, and Liquify are just a handful of the many tools that may be used in Photoshop for retouching. It is crucial to pick the suitable instrument for the work at hand as each one comes with a distinct set of benefits and limitations.

For instance, the Healing Brush is wonderful for eradicating minor faults and imperfections, whereas the Clone Stamp is more suitable for usage on bigger regions of the face. The Patch Tool may be used to eliminate greater patches of imperfection and merge the surrounding pixels, while the Liquify tool can be used to bend and change minor portions of the picture. Both features are featured in the Photoshop editing software package.

4. Work non-destructively

It is necessary to act in a non-destructive manner while you are editing a photo. Before making any alterations, you should first make a duplicate of the original photo or a new layer over the existing one. You may make alterations to the photo in this manner without those changes being reflected in the original, and if needed, you can always revert to the original form of the image. Go to the **Layers panel** and click on the "**Create a new layer**" button when you are there. This will generate a new layer. The effect of this operation will be the construction of a new layer on top of the present one. After that, you can make alterations to this new layer without those modifications being mirrored in the original.

5. Use layer masks

Photoshop's layer masks are an exceptionally powerful tool that allows users the ability to selectively conceal, or display areas of a layer's contents. When altering a photo, layer masks may be used to selectively apply the modification to portions of the image that require it the most. Just select the layer you want to apply the mask to and then click the "Add layer mask" option accessible in the Layers panel. This will allow you to build a layer mask. After that, you may use the Brush tool to paint on the layer mask, concealing or displaying areas of the layer according to what the scenario calls for.

6. Use adjustment layers

Adjustment layers are yet another powerful tool that may be utilized in the retouching process inside Photoshop. You may make alterations to an image's color, brightness, and contrast without altering the original file by utilizing adjustment layers. Go to the Layers panel and click on the "Create new fill or adjustment layer" option. This will allow you to build an adjustment layer to your document. This will cause a dialogue box to open, in which you may pick the sort of adjustment layer you wish to apply, such as brightness/contrast or hue/saturation, among other possibilities. After that, you may make updates to the layer without those changes being mirrored in the primary picture.

Using Filters for retouching

In Adobe Photos software, filters are an incredibly helpful and effective tool that can be used for retouching. Image filters can be used to improve the quality of an image, get rid of distracting areas of the picture, and aid in producing a broad range of other creative effects.

The following is a list of popular filters that may be used throughout the retouching process:

1. Blur Filters

One may employ blur filters to either soften a picture or get rid of annoying parts. The Gaussian Blur filter is one of the most widely used blur filters, and it may be used to achieve an effect that is delicate and ethereal when correctly applied. To utilize the Gaussian Blur filter, go to the Filter menu and pick Blur followed by Gaussian Blur. Then, use the slider to change the degree of blurring until you obtain the result you desire.

2. Sharpen Filters

The utilization of sharpen filters may bring out the finer elements in a photograph and create the appearance that the image is crisper. The Unsharp Mask filter is one of the most widely used sharpen filters, and it may be applied to a photo to make it more distinct and distinct. To utilize the Unsharp Mask filter, go to the Filter menu and click Sharpen > Unsharp Mask. Then, use the sliders to finetune the amount of sharpness that is applied to the image.

3. Noise Reduction Filters

Graininess and other kinds of visual noise can be eliminated with the use of noise reduction filters. The Reduce Noise filter is a well-known noise reduction filter, and it may be used to meet the aim of generating an image that is immaculate and unbroken. To apply the Reduce Noise filter, go to the Filter menu, Select Noise, and then select Reduce Noise. Next, adjust the sliders so that the quantity of noise reduction meets your tastes.

4. Artistic Filters

Creative effects may be added to an image with the use of numerous creative filters. A painting-like effect may be obtained by utilizing the Oil Paint filter, which is one of the creative filters that is used the most commonly. To use the Oil Paint filter, go to the Filter menu, pick Stylize, and then select Oil Paint. Next, change the sliders until you obtain the outcome you desire.

5. Distortion Filters

A image can be stretched or deformed with the use of distortion filters. It is one of the distortion filters that is utilized the most commonly, and it may be used to rearrange specific parts of a picture.

The filter is named **"Liquify."** To apply the Liquify filter, click **Filter > Liquify** from the menu bar, and then edit the photo using the tools offered in the Liquify dialog box. When undertaking picture editing with filters, it is crucial to use them judiciously and to avoid going excessive with their application. The use of excessive filters can give a photograph an aspect that is artificial or fake, and it can reduce the quality of the image.

In addition to this, it is vital to apply filters in anon-destructive manner. This includes adding filters to a unique layer or utilizing adjustment layers so that you can always return to the primary photo if it is necessary. Create a new layer or adjustment layer, apply the filter to that layer, and then use layer masks to selectively apply the filter to selected portions of the photo.

This will allow you to apply filters in a non-destructive manner while dealing with photographs. Information: Some of the options you make while altering an image will be impacted by how you plan to employ the final output. If a photograph is going to be published in black and white on newsprint, for instance, the decisions you make about cropping and sharpening may be quite different from the ones you make if the image is going to be exhibited in full color on a web page. The **RGB** color mode is used for writing on the web, mobile devices, and desktop photo printing.

The CMYK color mode is used to prepare a picture for printing utilizing process colors.

The Grayscale color mode is used for printing in black and white. Other color modes are employed for printing in black and white or for other particular needs. You may also edit the pixel dimensions of a photograph using Photoshop to change the resolution. In general, you should expect to conduct most of your adjustments on a brand-new original photo of high resolution and quality.

After that, for specialized applications such as print or the web, you should make versions that are adjusted to match the unique demands of each of those media.

Resolution and image size

Resolution and picture size are two fundamental terms in digital photography that are closely connected yet pertain to various things. Both are crucial, yet resolution and picture size have separate implications.

When working with digital images, particularly when preparing them for printing or exhibition on various kinds of screens, it is vital to have a strong grasp of the ideas outlined here. Image resolution may be described as the number of pixels that are packed into one unit of measurement. Dots per inch (dpi) and pixels per inch (ppi) are the two units of measurement that are used the most commonly for resolution. Printed photographs are sometimes described to as having a DPI, whilst digital photos that are shown on screens often have a PPL When the resolution of an image is better, it shows that there are more pixels packed into each unit of measurement, which frequently results in a picture of superior quality that is clearer and more detailed.

On the other hand, the phrase "image size" refers to the actual measurements of a photograph, such as its width and height, which may be measured in inches, centimeters, or pixels. Image size can be measured in any of these units. The resolution of a photograph and the number of pixels that it comprises both contribute to the total size of the image. For illustrative purposes, an image with dimensions of 4 inches by 6 inches and a resolution of 300 dots per inch would have a pixel count of 1200 by 1800. When you are modifying a photo in Photoshop for a particular purpose, you need to make sure that the image has an acceptable quantity of pixels. Pixels are microscopic squares that describe an image and determine the quantity of information that it carries. You may establish this using the pixel dimensions, which relate to the number of pixels that run along the width and height of a picture.

To determine the total number of pixels in a photograph, merely multiply the width of the image in pixels by the height of the image in pixels. For example, a 1000 × 1000 pixel photograph includes 1,000,000 pixels (one megapixel), whereas a 2000 x 2000 pixel image has 4,000,000 pixels (four megapixels). Pixel measurements affect file size and upload/download time. In Photoshop, resolution refers to the number of pixels that are packed into a picture across a certain unit of length, such as pixels per inch (ppi).

NOTE: When referring to displays shown on computers and TVs, the word resolution frequently refers entirely to the size of the pixels (such as 1920 by 1080 pixels) and not the pixel density ratio (300 pixels per inch). In Photos hop, resolution is measured in pixels per inch rather than the size of individual pixels. Does changing the resolution of a file affect the amount of space it takes up? Only when the dimensions of the pixels are varied. For instance, the pixel measurements of a photograph that is 7 inches wide by 7 inches tall and has a resolution of 300 pixels per inch are 2100 by 2100. If you adjust either the size in inches or the ppi number (resolution), but leave the pixel dimensions the same, the file size will not change.

However, if you adjust the size in inches without changing the ppi number (or vice versa), the pixel dimensions will need to change, and the file size will also change proportionately. For instance, if the image's resolution is increased from 72 ppi to 7 × 7 inches while preserving the same number of pixels per inch, then the pixel dimensions must be extended to 504 x 504 pixels, and the file size will fall accordingly. The requirements for resolution fluctuate depending on the sort of output being generated. If a photograph has a ppi number that is less than 150 to 200, then it may be judged to have a low resolution. I f a picture has a ppi number that is more than 200, then it is often deemed to have a high resolution. This is because it can include enough information to make full advantage of the device resolution that is supplied by high-resolution (Retina/HiDPI) device displays and commercial or fine-art printers.

NOTE: The size of the file is governed by more than only the dimensions of the pixels themselves. Other aspects include the sort of file, the bit depth, the number of channels and layers, and the kind of compression utilized if the file is compressed.

The resolution that is perceived by human eyes is determined by a multitude of elements, including viewing distance and output technology; consequently, resolution demands are also impacted by these factors.

Because a laptop is seen from farther away than a smartphone, its display may seem to have the same high quality as a smartphone with a resolution of 3 60 pixels per inch (ppi). On the other hand, the resolution supplied by a high-end printing press or fi n e -art inkjet printer, which may be able to reproduce 300 ppi or even more, may not be sufficient for printing at 220 ppi. When seen from a distance of several hundred feet, a picture with a pixel density of merely fifty pixels per inch might give the impression of being sharp.

Your graphics may not need to match the device resolution of h i g h -resolution printers due to the way that display and output technology's function. For example, even if many professional printings plate setters and photo-quality inkjet printers have a device resolution of 2400 dots per inch (dpi) or more, the best image resolution to send to such devices may only be 200 to 360 ppi for photographs. This is because the greater the dpi value, the more detailed the printed image would be.

The dots created by the device are connected together to form greater halftone cells or inkjet dot patterns, which are responsible for the development of diverse tones and colors. In a similar vein, images for a smartphone display with 500 pixels per inch do not always need to be recorded at 500 ppi. You should enquire with your production team or the output service provider about the pixel dimensions or ppi value they want in the final photographs that you give, independent of the media you are working with. Follow the rules stated in this industry standard to calculate the necessary picture resolution for printing it on a press: The picture should have a ppi value that is between 1. 5 and 2 times greater than the halftone screen frequency (measured in lines per inch, or lpi) that the printer employs. For instance, if the picture is going to be made with a screen frequency of 133 lpi, then the image should be at a resolution of 200 ppi (133 multiplied by 1.5).

When dealing with pictures in Adobe Photoshop, you can utilize the Image Size dialog box to adjust the resolution as well as the size of the image. To enter this dialogue box, pick Image Size from the Image menu available in the Menu Bar at the top of the screen. You can locate the Image menu in the top-right area of the screen. By typing **Ctrl + Alt + I** (on Windows) or **Command + Option + I** (on Mac), we can also jump to the Image Size dialog box directly from the keyboard:

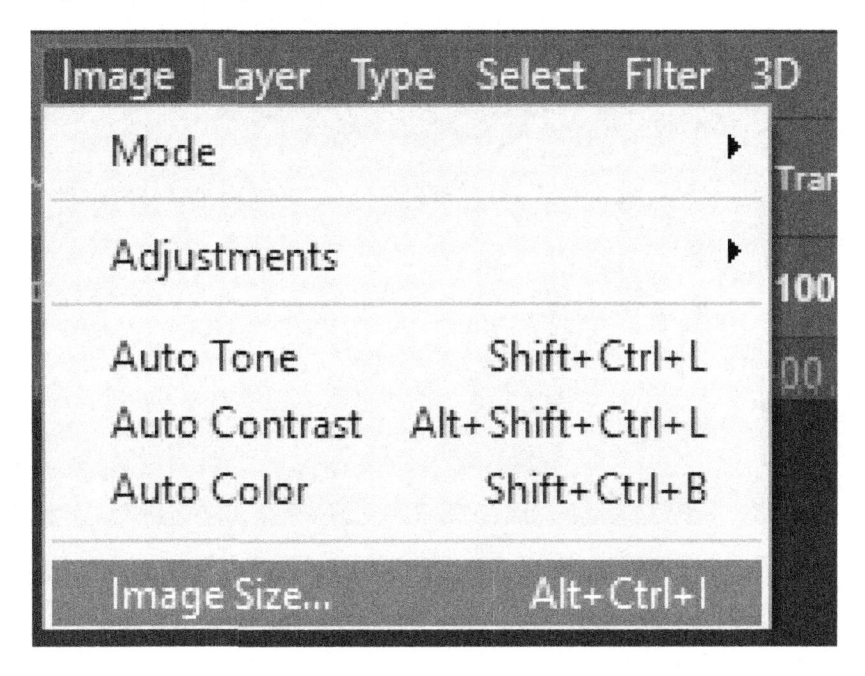

The Image Size dialog box, which has been streamlined and enhanced in Photoshop, will open when you click this button.

The real settings may be located along the right side of the page:

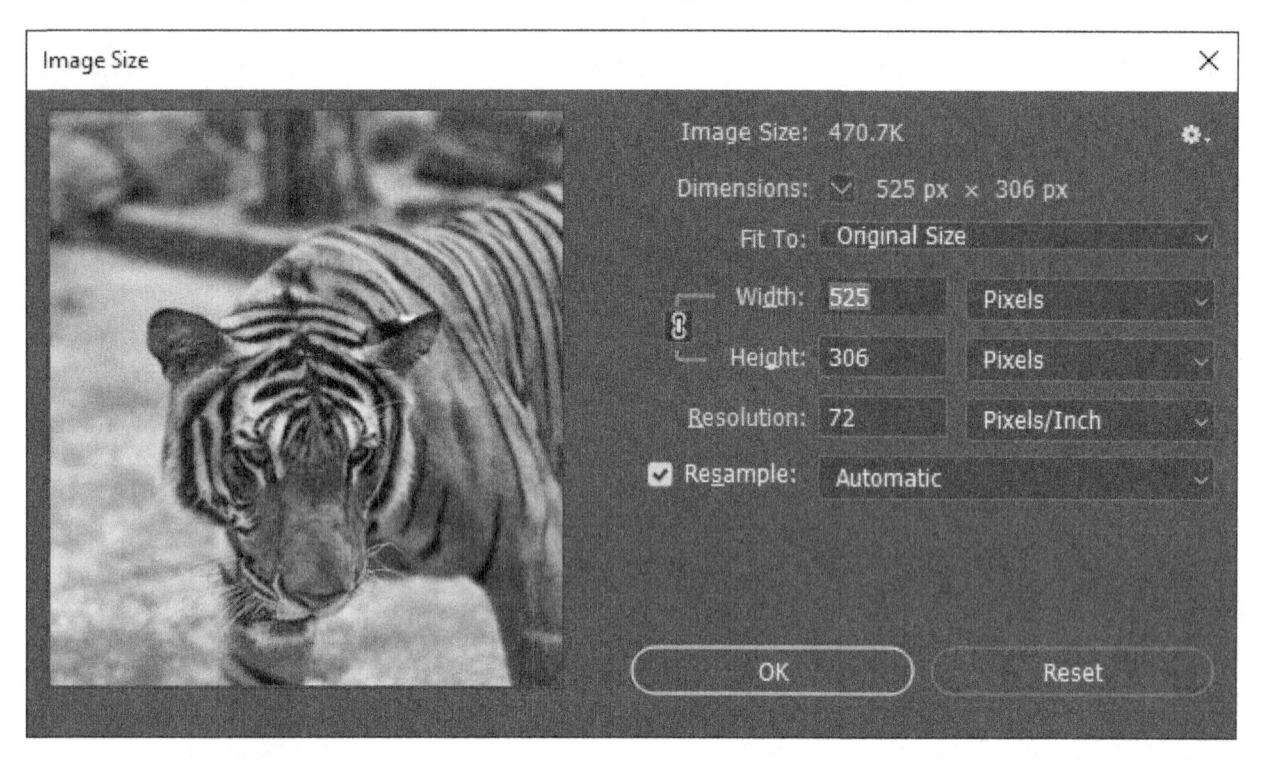

You may adjust the image's resolution, size, and other parameters in this area. When adjusting the size of a photograph, it is vital to keep the image's aspect ratio in mind to prevent the image from being distorted. When getting a photograph ready for printing, resolution, and size are both very vital considerations to take into account. Images that are going to be printed need to have a larger resolution than those that are going to be exhibited on screens, frequently between 300 and 600 dpi. Because printed images are seen up close, they need a significant quantity of information to look sharp and clear to the viewer. It is crucial to take into consideration the size of the print when deciding the proper resolution for a photograph that will be printed.

If you want to preserve the same degree of information in a bigger print, you will need a higher resolution than you would with a smaller print.

When it comes to digital photos that are exhibited on screens, the size of the image counts more than the quality. Images with a better resolution will not necessarily seem to have a higher quality as the common screen resolution is 72 pixels per inch (ppi). On the other hand, the size of the photo can alter how it is presented on various kinds of devices. For instance, a photograph that looks clear and sharp on the screen of a computer may appear blurry or pixelated when seen on a mobile device with a smaller screen.

Opening a file with Adobe Bridge

If Bridge isn't installed, the File > Browse in Bridge command in Photoshop will open the Creative Cloud desktop software, which will download and install Bridge.

After installation is complete, you can start Bridge.

Step 1. Start Photoshop, and then concurrently hold down **Ctrl + Alt + Shift** (Windows) or **Command + Option + Shift** (macOS) to reset the default settings.

Step 2. When prompted, click Yes to confirm that you wish to remove the Adobe Photoshop Settings file.

Step 3. Choose **File > Browse in Bridge**. If you're requested to enable the Photoshop extension in Bridge, choose **Yes** or **OK**.

NOTE: whether Bridge asks you whether you wish to import preferences from a previous version of Bridge, select Don't Show Again, and click No. Adobe Bridge launches, exposing a combination of panels, menus, and buttons.

Straightening and cropping the image in Photoshop

Image editing comprises of various distinct procedures, two of which are crucial and commonly used jointly to produce better alignment and composition in a photograph. These operations include straightening and cropping. In this part, we will go over the processes necessary to align and crop a photo in Adobe Photoshop.

Step 1: Open the Image

To begin, run Adobe Photoshop and load the photo that must be trimmed and straightened. You may accomplish this by choosing the photo from the file system on your computer after going to the File menu and selecting the Open option. You may also drag and drop the photo on Photoshop's workspace if you prefer.

Step 2: Straighten the Image

To remedy the crookedness of the picture, use the "Crop" tool from the toolbar that is placed on the left side of the display. Simply go to the settings bar at the very top of the screen and click the "Straighten" button. This will bring up a grid that you may use to straighten out the photo that you just brought up.

You may construct a reference by clicking and dragging a line across the horizon or any other straight edge that you want to employ. Photoshop will rotate the picture for you automatically so that it is aligned with the line. When you are pleased with the alignment of the picture, use the "Enter" key to execute the modification.

Step 3: Crop the Image

To crop the image, select the "Crop" tool from the toolbox again, and then click and drag over the area of the photo that you wish to keep. By moving the box's edges or corners, you may adjust the region that will be cropped from the image. You may also utilize the settings bar to create specific dimensions for the crop box or lock the aspect ratio of the crop. Both settings are accessible by clicking the relevant buttons on the options bar. When you are pleased with the crop, you may apply it by pressing the "Enter" key on your keyboard.

Step 4: Save the Image

After you have altered the image's orientation and cropped it, you can save it by selecting **File > Save or File > Save As** from the menu bar. Select an acceptable file type and location on your computer to save the photo, then click the "**Save**" button.

Some Pointers on Cropping and Straightening Images in Photoshop

To straighten the photo, use the "**Ruler**" tool. If the image does not have a clear horizon or straight edge, you may use the "**Ruler**" tool to construct a guide for straightening the image even if there is no obvious edge or horizon. To straighten an edge, go to the tool bar and pick the "**Ruler**" tool. Then, click and drag along the edge you wish to modify. The rotation may then be implemented by selecting **Image > Image Rotation > Arbitrary** from the menu.

Select the "**Delete Cropped Pixels**" option and click the "**Checkmark**" button: When you crop a photo, you should make sure that the "**Delete Cropped Pixels**" option in the options menu is ticked before you begin. This will result in the pixels that were cropped being eliminated, which will in turn make the photo file smaller.

Use the "**Content-Aware**" option when cropping a picture: When you crop an image, you may use the "**Content A-ware**" option in the options bar to automatically fill in the blank portions of the image with content that suits the surrounding region. This is a great tool when you are working with tiny photos. While doing so, the image's composition may be left intact, and the picture can still be cropped to the needed dimensions.

If you need to straighten the photo as well as crop it at the same time, you may use the **"Straighten and Crop"** option that is found in the options bar of the **"Crop"** tool. This will allow you to complete both activities at the same time. The photo will be aligned appropriately, and it will be cropped to have the same size and aspect ratio as the original image.

Adjusting the color and tone

Changing the color and tone of a picture is a vital stage in the process of editing images because it helps the editor to improve both the overall look of the photograph and the mood expressed by it. Adjusting the color and tone of an image may be done utilizing a broad number of tools and methods in Adobe Photoshop. Some of these tools and procedures include adjustment layers, curves, and levels. The following is a summary of some of the most frequent techniques of adjusting the color and tone in Photoshop documents.

Adjustment Layers

Adjustment layers are a handy tool in Photoshop that enable users to make nondestructive adjustments to the color and tone o f a picture. Adjustment layers may be found under the **"Color"** and **"Tone"** categories. Click the **"Create new fill or adjustment layer"** button at the bottom of the Layers panel to begin the process of generating an adjustment layer. Next, choose the sort of adjustment layer that you would want to employ from the drop-down option that displays.

When it comes to modifying color and tone, some of the most typical adjustment layers include the following:

Hue/Saturation: The Hue/Saturation adjustment layer allows you the power to modify the hue, saturation, and brightness of colors within the picture. This can assist in bringing out some hues while muting others at the same time.

Curves: By modifying a graph that displays the picture's brightness and contrast, you may vary the tonal range of the image with this adjustment layer. Curves are referred to as the **"curves"** adjustment layer. This can assist adjust the contrast of the picture, as well as for creating individual tonal modifications in select sections of the image.

Levels: By modifying the levels of the picture's shadows, mid-tones, and highlights with this adjustment layer, you may vary the brightness and contrast of the image. This can assist modify the exposure of the picture, as well as for making special modifications to the sections of the image that are the darkest and the brightest.

When you utilize adjustment layers, you may apply alterations to the picture that are quickly modified or erased later. These alterations are also reversible. You may also utilize layer masks to make alterations to select areas of the picture, such as deepening the shadows or brightening the highlights, depending on whichever element of the image you wish to edit.

Color Balance

The Color Balance tool is yet another important tool that can be used to adjust the color and tone of a photograph. With the aid of this tool, you'll be able to change the levels of the red, green, and blue channels to create a more attractive color balance in the picture. **Image > Adjustments > Color Balance** is where you'll locate the Color Balance tool if you wish to utilize it. You may then alter the levels of each channel by using the sliders, which are placed there. If the picture appears like it has too much blue in it, for instance, you may alter the levels of the red and green channels to make the colors look more balanced.

Selective Color

Another tool that may be used to adjust the hue as well as the tonal quality of select parts within a photograph is called Selective Color. Utilizing this tool, you will be able to adjust the intensities of colors, such as reds, yellows, and blues, as well as the intensities of black, white, and neutral tones contained in the picture. **Image > Adjustments > Selective Color** is where you'll find the Selective Color tool if you wish to utilize it. You may then use the sliders to vary the levels of that color by picking the color whose levels you wish to change and then utilizing those sliders. This can assist eliminate color casts from a photograph or accentuate colors already present in it.

Color Lookup

You may apply color-grading effects to a photo by utilizing a tool called Color Lookup, which is a relatively recent addition to Photoshop. This tool works by applying a 3 D LUT, commonly known as a Look Up Table, to the picture. The LUT makes modifications to the colors and tone of the image depending on the parameters that are in the LUT. **Image > Adjustments > Color Lookup** is where you'll find the Color Lookup tool if you wish to utilize it. You will then be offered a variety of pre-set LUTs, or you will have the opportunity to construct your LUT from scratch. The employment of color grading effects is a significant strategy that may be utilized to improve the ambiance and general style of an image. You may also employ layer masks to target sections of the photo while applying the Color Lookup effect.

Example: You'll use Curves and Levels adjustment layers to eliminate the color cast and modify the color and tone of the image. The Curves or Levels choices may appear sophisticated, but don't be afraid.

Step 1. In the Adjustments panel, click the Curves icon (first row, third button). This adds a Curves adjustment layer; its settings show in the Properties tab.

Step 2. Select the White Point tool on the left side of the Properties screen.

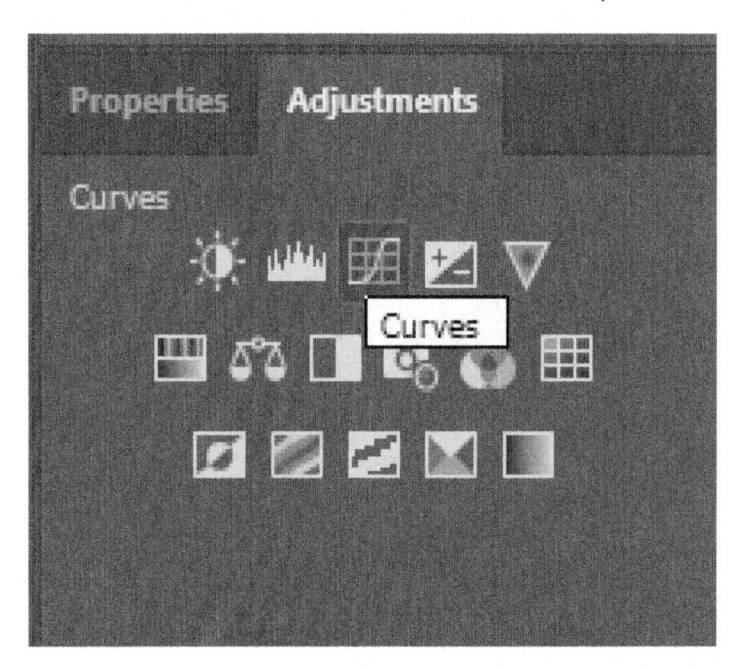

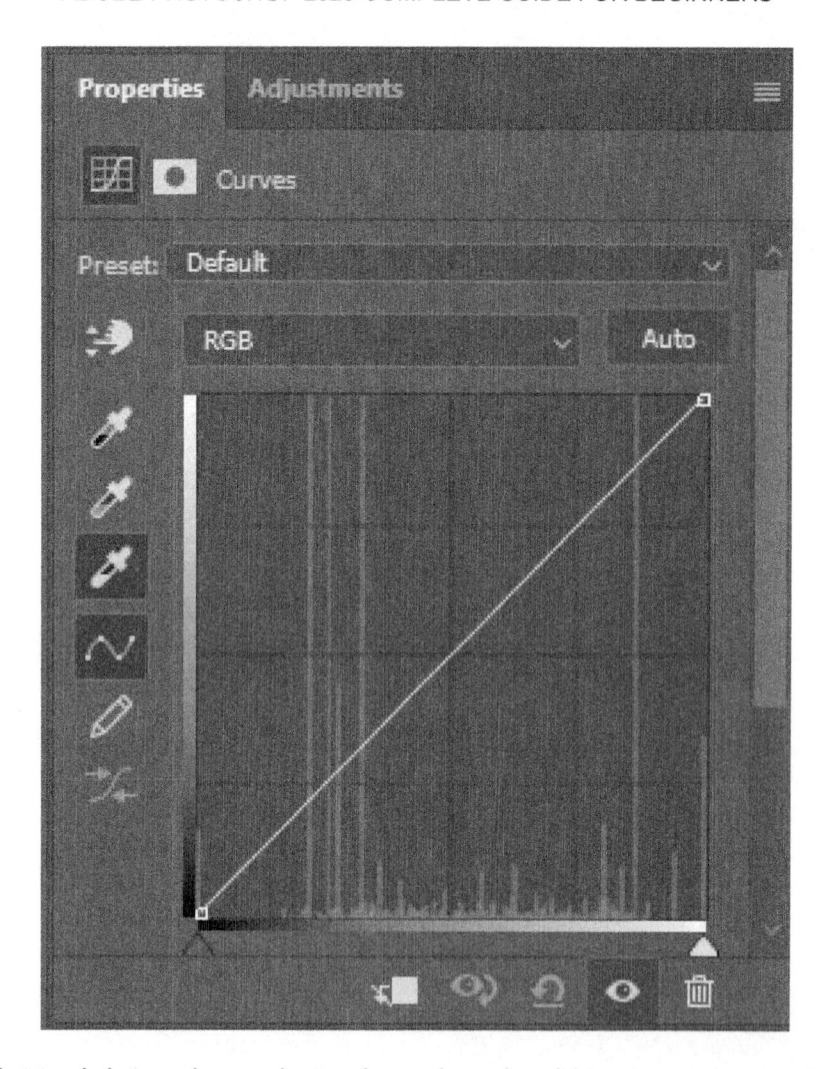

The White Point tool determines what color value should be turned a neutral white. Once determined, all other hues and tones adjust proportionately. When done correctly, this is a rapid approach to eliminate a color cast and adjust image brightness. To establish an exact white point, pick a region of the picture that should be the brightest neutral section of the image that has detail-not a blown-out area like the sun or a lamp and not a specular highlight such as a reflection of sunlight on chrome.

Step 3. Click a white color on the picture. Here, we click a white stripe on the tiger skin.

Clicking the white stripe with the White Point tool alters the color balance and brightness dependent on how far the sampled color is from neutral white, enhancing the image. Try clicking other white parts, such as the child's sailor outfit or sock, or a stripe on the woman's clothing. You'll often get the best-balanced outcome by clicking the region that was closest to neutral brilliant white in the actual world.

TIP: If you wish to know the color values of the pixels that the cursor is positioned on, they're presented in the Info panel (Window> Info). Now you'll utilize a Levels adjustment layer to modify the tone range of the image.

Step 4. In the Adjustments panel (if needed, click its tab to make it visible), click the Levels icon (first row, second button) to add a Levels adjustment layer.

NOTE: The color and tone modifications in this section are quite basic; it's easy to perform them all simply using Levels or Curves. Typically, Curves are utilized for modifications that are more specific or sophisticated. For both Curves and Levels, the Properties panel displays a histogram-a graph indicating the distribution of tonal values in the picture, from black on the left to white on the right.

For Levels, the left triangle under the histogram indicates the black point (the tonal level you want to set as the darkest in the image), the right triangle represents the white point (the tonal level you want to set as the lightest in the image), and the middle triangle represents the mid-tones.

Step 5. Drag the left triangle (black point) under the histogram to the right, where substantial shadow tones start to develop. Our value was 15. All tones less than 15 become black.

Step 6. Drag the center triangle a little to the right to modify the mid-tones. Our value was .90.

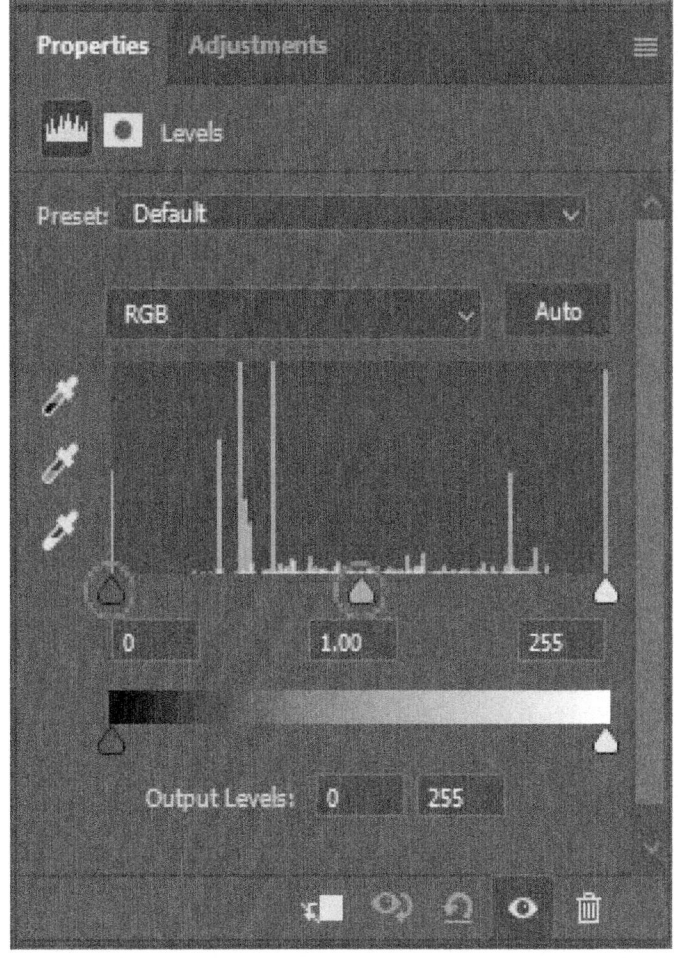

ADOBE PHOTOSHOP 2023 COMPLETE GUIDE FOR BEGINNERS

Now you'll. Flatten the image so it's simpler to deal with when you touch it up. Flattening an image blend all of its layers into the Background layer. Flatten only if you no longer require the flexibility of altering the modifications you previously performed using distinct layers. NOTE: Flattening also eliminates material hiding beyond the visible border of the canvas. For example, if you used the Crop tool with the Delete Cropped Pixels option disabled, flattening eliminates the concealed pixels that the Crop tool kept.

Step 7. Choose Layer > Flatten Image.

The adjustment layers mix with the Background layer.

The Spot Healing Brush tool

The Spot Healing Brush tool is a powerful tool in Adobe Photoshop that allows you to erase undesirable blemishes, scratches, and other flaws quickly and simply from a picture.

Getting Started

To begin utilizing the Spot Healing Brush tool in Adobe Photoshop, first, open the photo that needs to be modified in the software. The next step is to pick the Spot Healing Brush tool from the toolbar that is placed on the left side of the screen. The letter "J" is the shortcut key for accessing this tool. When you have the tool chosen, you may utilize the options bar at the top of the screen to adjust the brush's size, amount of hardness, and transparency.

Using the Spot Healing Brush Tool

To use the Spot Healing Brush tool, all you need to do is click on the section of the photo that needs to be changed. Photoshop will automatically inspect the pixels in the surrounding region and replace the selected area with a color that is sampled from the pixels in the surrounding area. This enables it simple to eradicate undesirable faults and other problems from the picture without having to pick and replace individual pixels one at a time manually. The Spot Healing Brush is most effective when used on blemishes or imperfections that range in size from microscopic to medium. You may consider utilizing Clone Stamp or Healing Brush tools instead if the area you are modifying spans a greater region and requires more precision editing. Example: Let's imagine you want to retouch a portrait shot using the Spot Healing Brush tool, and you have a photo of a person.

The following is an in-depth tour of the most effective approach to using the tool:

Step 1. Open the photo in Adobe Photoshop and pick the Spot Healing Brush tool from the toolbar on the left-hand side of the screen. Adjust the brush size, hardness, and opacity in the settings bar at the top of the screen. In the settings bar, open the Brush pop-up window, specify a brush with a Size of roughly 25 px and 100% Hardness, and make sure Content-Aware is chosen.

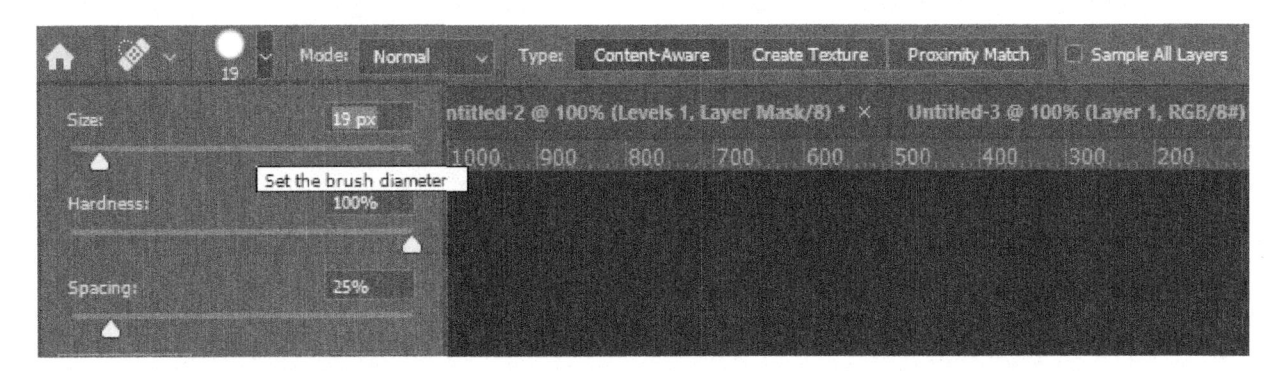

Step 2. Zoom in on the region you wish to retouch, such as a blemish on the subject's face.

Step 3. Click on the imperfection using the Spot Healing Brush tool. Photoshop will automatically evaluate the surrounding pixels and replace the imperfection with a sampled color from neighboring pixels.

Step 4. Continue to edit other defects or imperfections in the same manner. Use a tiny brush size for fine editing, then modify the hardness and opacity as required for a flawless blend.

Step 5. If you discover bigger regions that require more exact editing, go to the Clone Stamp or Healing Brush tools instead.

Step 6. Once you have completed editing, zoom out to examine the full photo and make any final modifications as needed.

Tips for Effective Use

The following are some tips that might help you utilize the Spot Healing Brush tool more effectively:

1. Use a tiny brush size: If you want to be more exact when identifying the place that has to be retouched, utilizing a tiny brush size is the way to go. When working on areas that comprise microscopic details, like the characteristics of the face or the hair, this is particularly vital to keep in mind.

2. Modify the brush's hardness: The brush's hardness will determine the degree to which the pixels in the selected region are sharply blended with those in the surrounding area. For softer mixing, use a lower hardness level.

3. Sample from neighboring pixels: When you are altering a region, it is vital to acquire a color sample from adjacent pixels that are comparable to the color of the surrounding area. This will aid to ensure that the pixels in the modified region blend in properly with those in the surrounding places.

4. Use numerous passes: When working on bigger or more intricate locations, you may need to make many runs with the Spot Healing Brush tool to acquire the outcome you desire. Be cautious and take your time to ensure that the region that was edited seems natural and does not stick out from the rest of the picture.

Advanced Techniques

You may build more intricate retouching effects by employing a range of other approaches in addition to the primary use of the Spot Healing Brush tool.

These approaches may be found in the extra panel. The following are some examples:

1. Removing bigger things: You may use the Content-Aware Fill feature to erase larger objects from a photo. This function is available in Adobe Photoshop. Because of this capability, you may choose the object and replace it with a sampled region drawn from adjoining pixels, all while keeping the texture and color of the surrounding area.

2. Fixing skin blemishes: You may use the Spot Healing Brush tool in conjunction with the Healing Brush tool or the Clone Stamp tool to repair skin flaws such as acne scars or other forms of scars. To begin, eliminate the flaw by utilizing the tool known as the Spot Healing Brush. After that, use the Healing Brush or the Clone Stamp tool to integrate the modified region with the texture and color of the surrounding skin to give it a more realistic appearance.

3. Editing hair: Use the Spot Healing Brush tool in combination with the Clone Stamp tool to retouch the hair. To begin, utilize the Spot Healing Brush tool to get rid of any wayward hairs or blemishes. The next step is to make use of the Clone Stamp tool to copy and paste individual strands of hair from surrounding spots to fill in any gaps or produce a more uniform appearance.

Applying a content-aware patch

Using Adobe Photoshop to retouch photographs may be a time-consuming task, particularly when it comes to deleting undesirable items or filling in gaps in the image.

The Content-Aware Patch tool is an exceptionally handy feature that offers you the ability to fast and undetectably extend or replace elements of an image. The steps necessary to utilize the Content-Aware Patch tool in Adobe Photoshop are explained below for your convenience.

Step 1: Select the Area to Be Patched

The first thing you'll need to do to install a content-aware patch is to identify the area of the system that needs to be addressed. You can make a selection around the object or location that you wish to repair by using any of the available selection tools. In this instance, the Lasso tool will be used to delineate the region that has to be corrected.

Step 2: Choose the Patch Tool

After you have made the selection, choose the Patch tool from the toolbar. The Patch tool is represented with an icon that looks like a patch or Band-Aid (0). Once you have picked the Patch tool, you will see various options in the options bar at the top of the screen. You may customize the size, hardness, and opacity of the tool from here.

Step 3: Drag the Selection to a Similar Area

After picking the place that has to be patched and using the Patch tool, it is time to drag the selection to a region in the picture that is pretty similar to the one you just chose. You should seek a zone that has a texture and color that is equivalent to the area that has to be fixed. If you want to patch a cloud that's in the center of a blue sky, for instance, you should seek a region of the sky that has a color and texture that's equivalent to the cloud.

Step 4: Apply the Patch

While the selection is still active, click and drag it to the position you have selected will serve as the replacement. The content-aware technology will automatically fix the region as soon as you let go of the mouse button in Photoshop. This operation could take as little as a few seconds or as much as a few minutes, depending on the intricacy of the picture and the size of the selection.

Step 5: Touch Up the Patch

After the patch has been stitched on, you might observe certain seams or imperfections in the region that have been corrected that were not there before. To make tiny tweaks to the patch, use the Spot Healing Brush tool and set the brush size so that it is just slightly bigger than the patch itself. After that, make use of the tool to mix the edges of the patch with the pixels that are around it.

It is vital to bear in mind that the Spot Healing Brush tool makes use of the same content-aware technology as the Patch tool. This implies that it will automatically sample and blend the pixels in the surrounding region to achieve a smooth output.

Step 6: Adjust the Patch Tool Settings

If the initial output did not meet your expectations, you may alter the parameters of the Patch tool in the options bar to make a more suitable end product. To achieve the best potential output for your photo, you may tweak the tool's size, mixing, and color adaptation settings.

Step 7: Apply the Patch to Complex Areas

You may need to employ the Clone Stamp or Healing Brush tools instead of the Content-Aware Patch tool to apply a content-aware patch to an area that is particularly intricate or textured. You may manually pick the pixels from the source and then apply them to the target area with the aid of these tools. To make use of these tools, choose them from the toolbar and then use the Alt key (on Windows) or the Option key (on Mac) to pick the pixels that will be used as the source. After that, apply the patch by painting over the appropriate place.

Repairing areas with the Clone Stamp tool

The Clone Stamp tool in Adobe Photoshop is one of the most helpful and adaptable tools available in that application. It provides you with the power to mend broken or faulty areas of a photograph by allowing you copy pixels from one region of the image and paste them into another part of the image. This program is particularly helpful for rescuing ancient photographs and editing photos that have been taken more recently.

Here are some instructions to utilize the Clone Stamp tool:

Step 1: Select the Clone Stamp tool

In the Tools panel, pick the Clone Stamp tool. You may also use the keyboard shortcut S to choose the tool.

Step 2: Choose the source location

To modify the source area, you need to click and hold the Alt (Windows) or Option (Mac) key pushed down. This will activate the cursor for the Clone Stamp tool, which will display as a target icon when it has been activated. Place the cursor on the part of the photo that you would want to utilize as the foundation for the cloning procedure. Simply making one click will choose the source location.

Step 3: Choose the brush size and hardness

You may change the size of the brush as well as its amount of abrasiveness by utilizing the Options bar at the very top of the screen. The size of the brush should be set such that it is slightly bigger than the region that has to be cloned. You may control the degree to which the edge is rounded by modifying the level of brush stiffness.

Step 4: Start cloning

When you are ready to begin cloning, drag the cursor to the region of the picture that needs to be corrected after first determining the brush size and then the amount of pressure it should have. To clone pixels from the source region to the target area, click and drag the mouse over the piece of the image that is damaged or faulty.

Step 5: Adjust the brush parameters

You may need to alter the brush parameters as you continue to clone. To clone little or enormous regions, for instance, you may need to alter the brush size by either increasing or lowering it.

Altering the degree to which the brush is stiff can also be done to vary the degree to which the edge is rounded.

Step 6: Blend the copied area

Use either the Smudge tool or the Blur tool to blend the freshly cloned region with the pixels in the surrounding area. These tools can aid smooth down the edges of the duplicated section and make it fit in more organically with the rest of the picture.

A few useful pointers while employing the Clone Stamp tool

1. Use a soft touch: When you clone, keep your hand light so that you don't produce noticeable repeated patterns in the picture.

2. Clone in tiny areas: Clone in small pieces at a time to prevent o v e r -cloning or producing unusual patterns in the picture. Clone little sections at a time.

4. Use several sources: If you want to prevent developing a pattern that repeats itself, you should always clone from numerous sources when you are working with difficult regions.

5. Avoid copying over essential details: Be cautious not to clone over vital aspects in the image, such as eyes, lips, or other key characteristics.

6. Preview often: You should make numerous previews of the findings by zooming in and out of the picture. You may use this to assess whether the duplicated region is blending in organically with the pixels surrounding it.

Sharpening the image

The last stage in the process of retouching a picture is to sharpen the image, which is something you may choose to accomplish. There are a few various techniques to sharpen a photo in Photoshop, but the Smart Sharpen effect gives the best control over the final look. Because sharpening might bring out artifacts, you should get rid of them before you start.

Step 1. Zoom in to roughly **400%** to notice the intricacies of the boy's outfit. The process of scanning generates artifacts such as the multicolored dots that you see.

Step 2. Navigate to the Filter menu and pick **Noise > Dust & Scratches**.

Step 3. In the dialog box named **"Dust & Scratches,"** retain the default settings of a Radius of **1 pixel** and a Threshold of **0**, and then click the **OK** button.

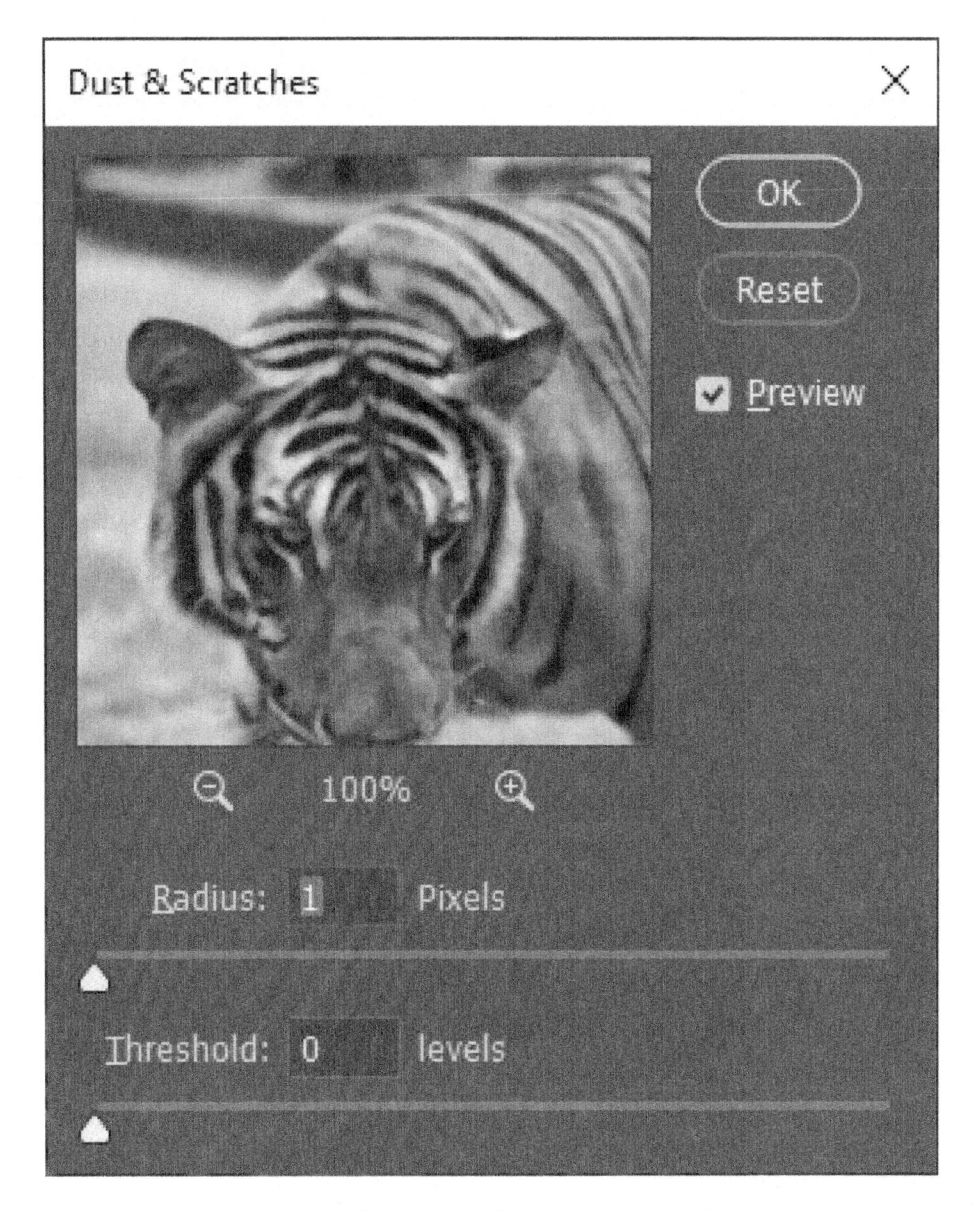

Step 4. Pay great attention to the visual detail when you make alterations to the Dust and Scratches choices. For instance, if you set the Threshold level to be too high, visual information that you would want to keep would be lost.

The value of the threshold shows how distinct the pixels must be before they are eliminated from consideration. The size of the zone that is searched for pixels with various attributes is governed by the Radius parameter. The default settings work extremely well for making very few color dots like the ones in this photo. You may go ahead and sharpen the picture now that the artifacts have been gone.

Step 5. Choose Filter> Sharpen> Smart Sharpen.

Step 6. In the Smart Sharpen dialog box, make sure that the Preview option is chosen so that you can see the impact of the adjustments you make to the parameters in the document window.

You may see various portions of the photo by moving your mouse within the preview window in the dialog box, or you can use the magnification buttons that are positioned below the thumbnail to zoom in and out of the image.

Step 7. In the Remove menu, make sure that the Lens Blur option is chosen.

TIP: The Preview option is present in a variety of dialog boxes, including the Smart Sharpen dialog box. Not only does it reveal the result in the dialog box, but it also displays it in the document window. You may compare the before-and-after views of the document using the settings that are now in effect by activating the Preview option. In the Smart Sharpen dialog box, you may select to eliminate Lens Blur, Gaussian Blur, or Motion Blur. The usage of Lens Blur leads to a more refined sharpening of details and a reduction in the appearance of sharpening halos. The contrast at the image's edges is boosted when the Gaussian Blur filter is employed. Motion Blur is a p o s t -processing filter that decreases the appearance of blur in images that was generated by either the movement of the camera or the subject being photographed.

Step 8. To sharpen the photo, adjust the Amount slider to roughly 60 percent.

Step 9. Adjust the slider for the Radius to roughly **1.5**. The value of the Radius parameter defines the number of surrounding pixels that contribute to the overall sharpness of the image. The Radius parameter should normally be adjusted in proportion to the resolution in most circumstances.

Step 10. When you are delighted with the results, you may apply the Smart Sharpen filter by clicking the **OK** button.

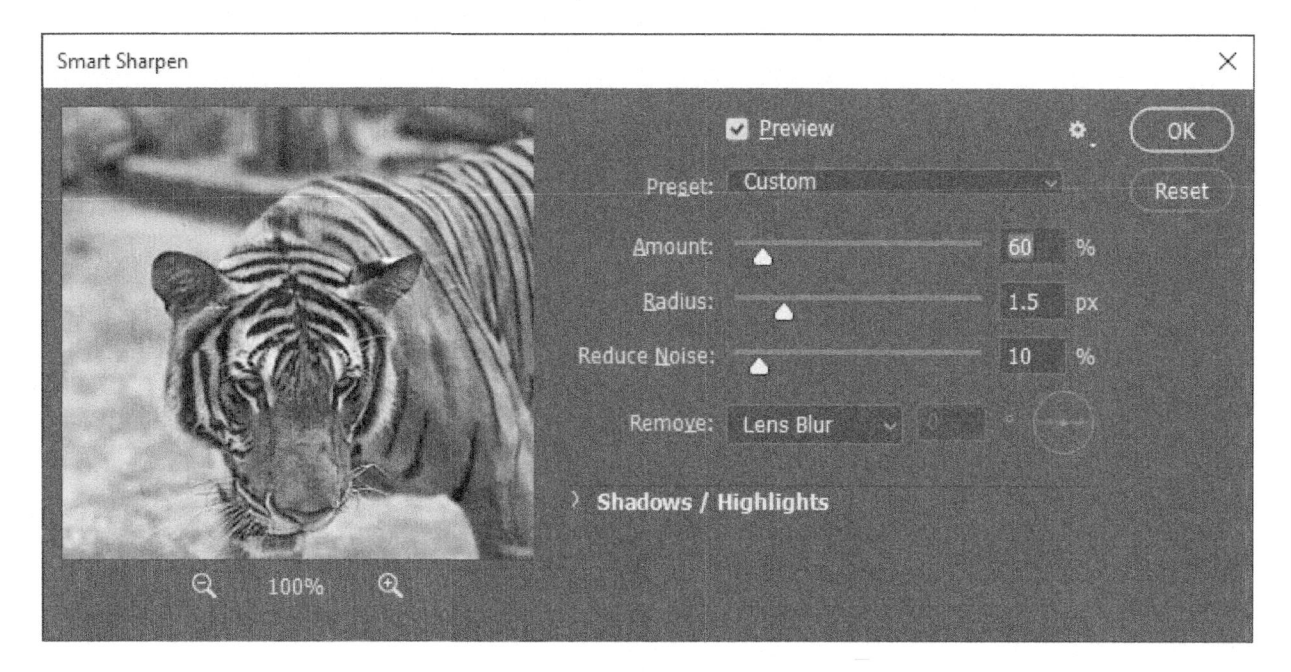

Step 11. Go to the "**File**" menu, choose "**Save**," and then exit the project file.

Your picture is now ready to be printed or shared with others.

CHAPTER 3: LAYER BASICS

About layers

Adobe Photoshop layers are an important component that offers you the flexibility to work on various areas of a picture. With layers, editing and modifying a photograph without affecting other areas of the image is easy. The backdrop layer is covered with a transparent sheet called a layer. A layer can be filled with photographs, text, shapes, and other design components that you can alter separately from the other layers. Picture it as if you were to stack transparent sheets on top of one another. You may independently move or alter each sheet, and each sheet can contain a different element. For a single photo, Photoshop lets you create several layers, each of which can have a distinct set of attributes like opacity, blending mode, and layer style. To make layers more manageable and tidier, you may also mix them.

How do Layers Work?

Layers operate by enabling you to isolate and modify sections of a photo without changing the overall composition. For instance, you may build a new layer and add text to it if you want to add text to a photo. In this technique, you may relocate or edit the text without disrupting the image's other features. The top layer is put on top of the layers below it in a stack of layers.

By rearranging the layers in the stack, you may vary their order. By choosing the eye symbol next to a layer in the Layers panel, you can simply show or conceal that layer.

How to Use Photoshop Layers

Creating a new Layer: Click the "**New Layer**" button found at the bottom of the Layers panel or use the keyboard shortcut **Shift + Ctrl + N** (for Windows) **or Shift + Command + N** (for Mac) to add a new layer. The backdrop layer will be changed with a brand-new one.

Renaming Layers: To maintain your file organized and comprehensible, it is always a good idea to rename your layers. Double-click the layer name in the Layers box and input a new name to rename it.

Changing Layer Order: Click and drag a layer to the proper location in the Layers panel to adjust its order. Alternatively, you may shift a layer up by hitting Command+ [on a Mac or Windows computer, and down by using **Ctrl + [** on a Windows computer.

Making Layer Opacity Adjustments: You may modify a layer's opacity to make it more transparent or opaque. To do this, select the layer in the Layers panel and modify the opacity using the Opacity slider at the panel's top.

Including Layer Styles: Layer Styles are effects that you may apply to modify the look of a layer. Select the layer in the Layers panel, then click the Layer Style button at the panel's bottom to create a layer style. You may pick from a range of layer styles, such as stroke, bevel and emboss, and drop shadow.

Grouping Layer: Layers may be maintained organized and made more manageable by grouping them. Layers may be grouped by choosing them and then clicking the Group Layers button on the Layers panel's bottom. Additionally, you may hit **Ctrl + G** on a PC or **Command + G** on a Mac.

There are one or more layers in every Photoshop file. Before adding text or artwork, all new layers in a photograph are transparent. Working with layers is like putting sections of a painting on translucent film that can be seen via an overhead projector: Editing, moving, and removing a single sheet has no effect on the other sheets. It is possible to view the whole composition when the sheets are layered. Certain file formats, like JPEG and GIF, do not support layers. You must save the images in Photoshop or TIFF file if you want to keep their layering. Additionally, certain color options, notably Bitmap and Indexed Color (under the **Image > Mode** submenu), do not support stacking.

Using the Layers panel

The Layers panel in Adobe Photoshop is an essential tool that allows you to deal with multiple layers in a picture. It's where you may examine, select, and alter layers to build more complicated and sophisticated designs.

Understanding the Layers Panel

In Photoshop, the Layers panel is on the right side of the screen. It gives a list of all the layers in an image coupled with information about their settings and features. The **'Layers'** tab in the **'Workspace'** area may be chosen to access the Layers panel, or you can use the keyboard shortcut **F7**.

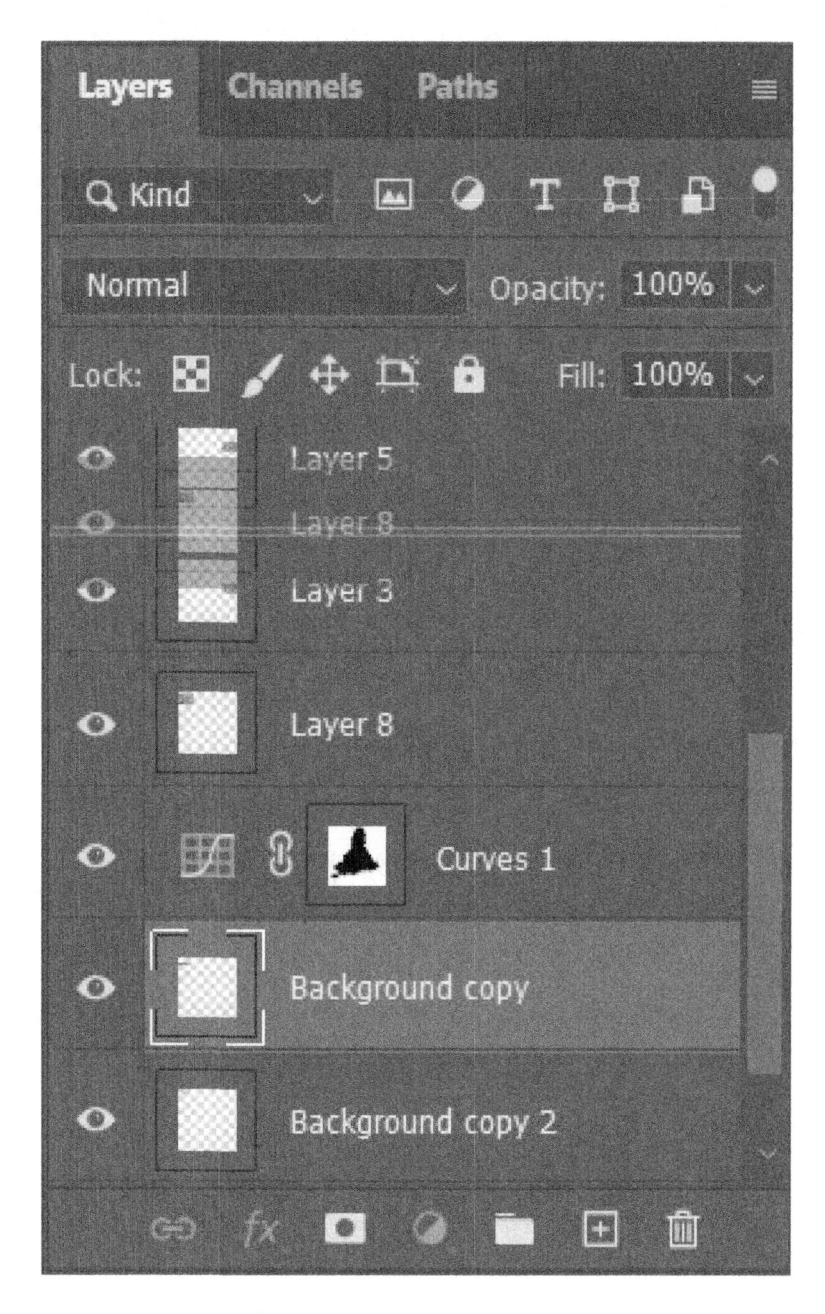

ADOBE PHOTOSHOP 2023 COMPLETE GUIDE FOR BEGINNERS

The top layer appears on top of the layers below it in the Layers panel, which depicts each layer as a different row. Each player's name is presented on the right, along with its visibility sign (an eye), and its lock icon, which is positioned on the left. You can reveal or conceal a layer using the visibility icon, and you may restrict unintended adjustments to a layer by using the lock sign.

Selecting Layers

Layer selection is as simple as clicking on a player's name in the Layers panel. You can modify the highlighted layer as required as it will be the chosen layer. Additionally, you may pick numerous layers by clicking on their names while holding down the Shift key.

Moving Layers

Layers may be relocated by simply clicking and dragging their names to a new spot in the Layers panel. The layer order, which defines how the layers look in the photo, will shift as a consequence. Alternatively, you may move a layer by hitting **Ctrl + [** on a computer running Windows or **Command + [** on a computer running Mac] to move it down, and **Ctrl +)** (Windows) or **Command +]** (Mac) to move it up.

Layer Properties

The Layers panel shows different settings and attributes for every layer, which you may alter to reach the desired outcome. These consist of:

Opacity: This influences a layer's transparency. By typing a value between O and 100 or using the Opacity slider at the top of the Layers panel, you may modify the opacity.

Blending Modes: These have an influence on how a layer communicates with layers below it. You may pick from a range of blending methods, including Multiply, Screen, Overlay, and more.

Layer Style: With this, you may offer layer effects like a drop shadow, bevel and emboss a stroke, and more.

Grouping Layers

To keep layers ordered and manageable, you may group layers in the Layers panel. To do this, pick the layers you wish to group, then click the **"Create a New Group"** button situated at the Layers panel's bottom. Additionally, you may hit **Ctrl + G** on a PC or **Command + G** on a Mac. The Layers panel provides thumbnails of the information on each layer as well as a list of all the layers that make up a picture. You may hide, inspect, move, delete, rename, and combine layers using the Layers panel. As you edit the layers, the layer thumbnails are automatically updated.

1. Select **Window > Layers** if the Layers panel is not showing in the work area.

From top to bottom, the Layers panel displays the following five layers for the file we're working with: Postage, Hawaii, Flower, Pineapple, and Background.

2. If the Background layer isn't already chosen, choose it to activate it. Take notice of the Background layer's layer icon and thumbnail:

The layer thumbnail, which is the small preview picture next to the layer name, may be hidden or resized using the context menu. To choose a thumbnail size, right-click (Windows) or control click (Mac OS) a thumbnail in the Layers panel to bring up the context menu.

3. The lock icon shows that the layer is protected from layer modifications. That's why the choices above the layer list are inaccessible. However, it's still possible to change the layer content itself, such as drawing on it.

4. The eye icon shows that the layer is visible in the document window. If you click the eye, the document window no longer displays that layer.

The postcard's photo must be provided as the initial stage in this project. The photo will initially be opened in Photoshop.

5. In Photoshop, select **File > Open**, scroll to the folder, and then double-click the file to open it.

The current file's layer information will be accessible in the Layers window.

About the background layer

The backdrop layer in Adobe Photoshop is a distinct layer that works as the framework for a picture. Photoshop automatically provides a backdrop layer that fills the complete canvas with a solid color when you create a new picture. Since the background layer is locked by default and always at the bottom of the layer stack, you cannot simply move or edit it. The backdrop layer varies from other layers in Photoshop in a few distinct ways. You cannot adjust its opacity, blending mode, or layer style, for instance. It also cannot be instantly erased or turned into a regular layer. Instead, before you can make any changes, you must first unlock the background layer and then adjust it from a normal layer.

The following are some of the main characteristics of Photoshop's background layer:

• **The layer stack always contains it at the bottom:** Photoshop automatically produces the backdrop layer and covers the complete canvas when you start a new project. The background layer cannot be added to, moved above, or moved below other layers in the layer stack.

• **It's locked by default:** The background layer is locked by default to avoid inadvertent modifications. The background layer cannot be directly moved or modified without first unlocking it.

• **Its opacity is fixed:** The background layer's opacity is always 100%. Although you can't directly edit its opacity, you may change the opacity of layers above the background layer to vary how visible it is.

• **It has a fixed mixing mode:** The background layer's blending mode is set to Normal by default, and you cannot directly adjust it.

• **Its editing opportunities are restricted:** It's normally advised to establish a new layer above the background layer and employ that layer to add any new objects to your image as the background layer is locked and has restricted modification possibilities.

The backdrop layer in Photoshop is an essential component of any photo, and any designer or editor must be aware with its properties and limits. The backdrop layer serves a critical purpose by giving your picture a firm basis and guaranteeing that your design is founded on a robust foundation, despite first seeming to be restricting.

Convert a background layer into a regular layer

Click the lock button next to the Background layer name. It converts to a default layer name. (Or double-click the Background layer, specify settings, then click OK.)

To transform an ordinary layer into a backdrop layer:

Step 1. Select a layer in the Layers panel.

Step 2. Choose **Layer >New> Background from Layer**.

Rearranging layers

In Adobe Photoshop, layer reordering is a critical stage in the editing and creative processes. You may pick which sections of your design are revealed on top of one another, modify the opacity of individual layers, and make elaborate compositions by rearranging your layers. You must employ Photoshop's Layers panel, where all of your layers are shown and structured, to reorganize them.

In Photoshop, you may reorganize layers using the following methods:

1. Drag and drop: Clicking and dragging the layer you wish to move in the Layers panel is one of the easiest techniques to rearrange layers. To move a layer in the layer stack, click on it and drag it up or down the list.

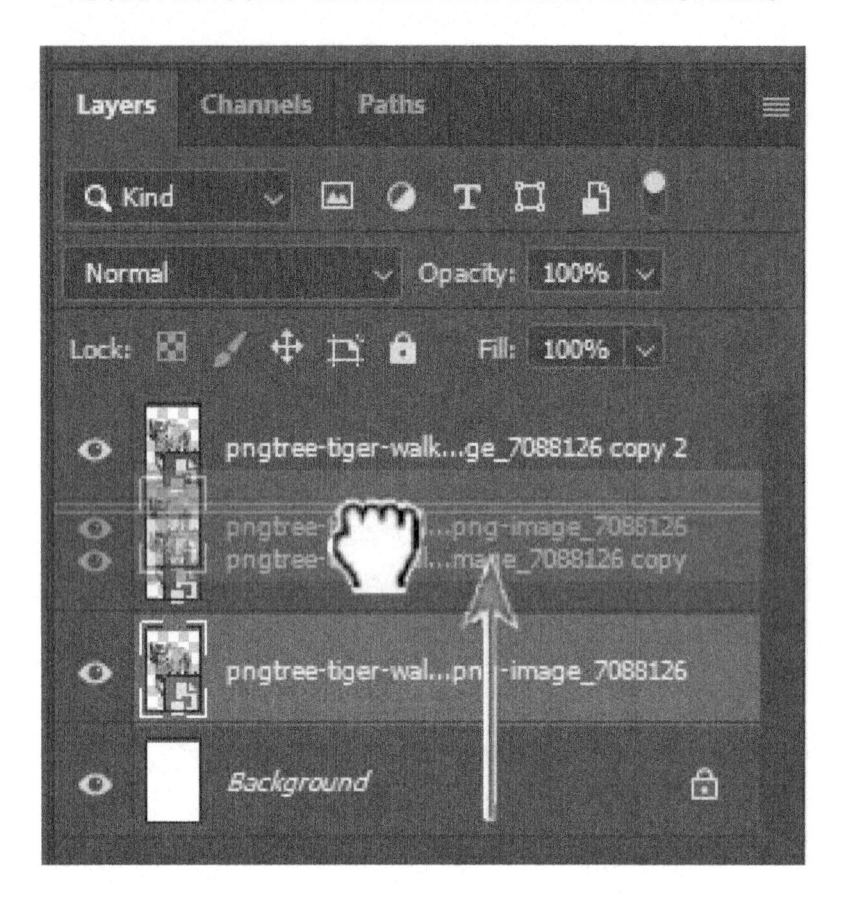

2. Use the Layer menu: The Layer menu is positioned at the top of the screen and may be used to reorganize layers. To access choices for moving layers up or down, bringing layers to the front or back, or rearranging the order of layers, go to Layer > Arrange.

3. Use keyboard shortcuts: Instead of clicking and dragging to fast move layers, you may use keyboard keys. Press **Ctrl + (** to move a layer down and **Ctrl + (** to move a layer up.

4. Group layers: You may group layers that must remain together by picking them in the Layers panel and then clicking the "New Group" button at the panel's bottom. When your layers are grouped, you may click and drag the group to move them all at once.

5. Make use of the Move tool: The Move tool is yet another option for shifting levels. Use the arrow keys on your keyboard to drag the layer you wish to move up, down, left, or right after choosing it.

6. Make use of the Auto-Select feature: You may make use of the Auto-Select function to move layers without first choosing them in the Layers panel. Select "**Auto Select**" from the options menu after selecting the Move tool. The layer that it is on will now be automatically picked by Photoshop when you click on an element in your picture. It's vital to examine the order of your layers and how they interact with one another while rearranging layers in Photoshop. Make sure an element is at the top of the layer stack if you want it to be noticed as layers at the top of the stack will show up in front of levels below it. To govern how transparent a layer is, you may also modify its opacity. To achieve this, pick the layer that needs to be modified, and then use the Layers panel's Opacity slider to modify its transparency.

Applying gradient to a layer

Your designs may enhance depth and dimension by employing a gradient that you can quickly apply to a layer in Photoshop.

A step-by-step instruction for applying a gradient to a layer is provided below:

Step 1: Create a new layer

By clicking the "**Create a new layer**" button located at the bottom of the Layers panel in Photoshop, start by generating a new layer. Additionally, you may hit "**Ctrl + Shift + N**" on a PC or "**Command + Shift + N**" on a Mac.

Step 2: Select the Gradient tool

Next, pick the Gradient tool from the toolbar on the left-hand side of the screen.

Step 3: Choose a gradient type

Select the gradient type you wish to use from the choices bar at the top of the screen. There are various distinct gradient sorts accessible in Photoshop, including linear, radial, angle, reflected, and diamond. Pick the one that best suits your design.

Step 4: Select the colors for your gradient

To pick your gradient colors, click on the color swatches in the options bar. By clicking on the color Swatch and picking a color from the Color Picker, you may pick from some preset colors or design your own colors.

Step 5: Apply the gradient

Click and drag the Gradient tool over the layer to apply the gradient after picking your colors and the Gradient tool. By moving the tool in various directions or making use of the choices in the options bar, you may adjust the gradient's angle, position, and length.

Step 6: Adjust the gradient using layer styles

You may apply layer styles to add effects like shadows, glows, and strokes to the gradient if you want to fi n e -tune it even further. Double-click the layer in the Layers panel and pick **"Layer Style"** from the menu to apply a layer style. From there, you may pick the style you wish to utilize and tweak its characteristics.

Step 7: Save your work

When you're pleased with your gradient, pick **File > Save or File > Save As** to save your work.

Tips for Applying Gradients in Photoshop

• **Play around with various gradient types:** Don' t be hesitant to experiment with numerous designs and angles to discover the gradient type that best matches your design since Photoshop supplies a huge choice of gradient sorts.

• **Use many gradients:** By combining several gradient layers and layer styles, you may build more sophisticated gradients. A more dynamic effect, for instance, can be obtained by utilizing a linear gradient on one layer and a radial gradient on another.

• **Adjust the opacity:** You may use the Opacity slider in the Layers panel to lessen the opacity of your gradient if it is too strong. You'll be able to generate a more muted impression by doing this.

• **Use layer masks:** You may use a layer mask to mask out the sections you don't want to include in a gradient if you merely want to apply it to a bit of a layer. Simply paint over the areas you wish to mask out using the Brush tool after applying a layer mask to your layer.

• **Create custom gradients:** Create your personal gradients by clicking on the gradient color swatches in the options bar and selecting **"New Gradient"** from the menu if you can't find the appropriate gradient from Photoshop's preset alternatives. The Gradient Editor may then be used to create a new gradient.

Duplicating a layer and adjusting the blending mode

In Adobe Photoshop, you may employ the powerful approach of duplicating a layer and adjusting its blending mode to achieve a broad range of effects and styles.

Here's how to duplicate a layer in Photoshop and adjust its blending mode:

1. Duplicate the layer: First, pick the layer in the Layers panel that you wish to duplicate. Next, pick "**Duplicate Layer**" from the context menu by executing a right-click on the layer. As an alternative, you may duplicate the layer by hitting **Ctrl +J** on a Windows or Mac computer.

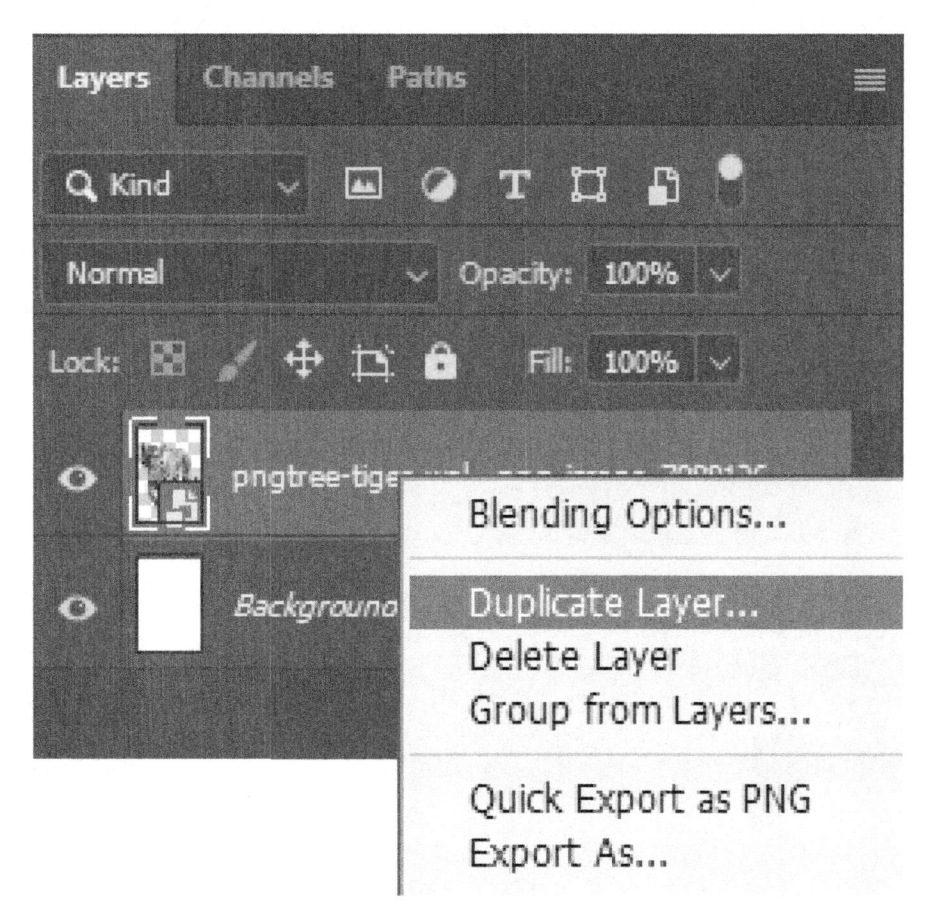

2. Modify the blending mode: While the duplicated layer is chosen, click the Blending Mode menu option at the top of the Layers panel to pick a different blending mode. You may apply a blending mode to the layer by clicking the dropdown menu. The blending mode governs how the duplicated layer's colors interact with those in the layers behind it.

Layers
Channels
Paths
Kind
Normal
Opacity: 100%
Lock:
Fill: 100%
pngtree-tiger-wal...png-image_7088126
Layer 1
Background

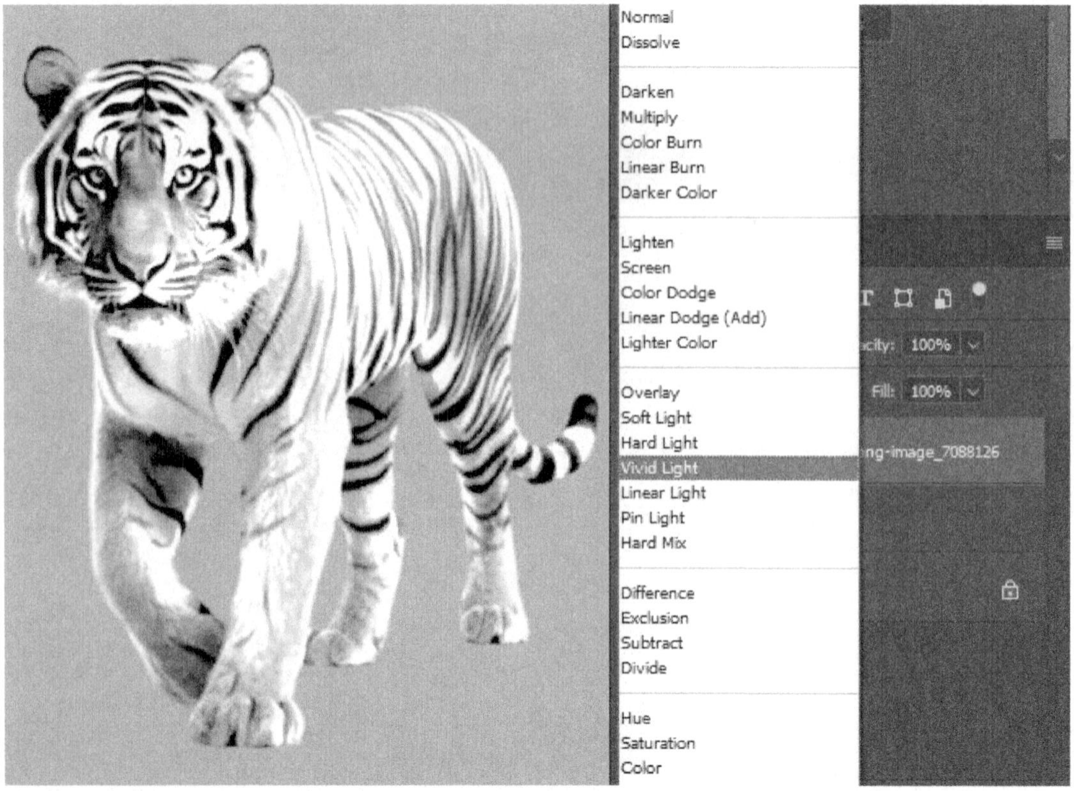
Normal
Dissolve
Darken
Multiply
Color Burn
Linear Burn
Darker Color
Lighten
Screen
Color Dodge
Linear Dodge (Add)
Lighter Color
Overlay
Soft Light
Hard Light
Vivid Light
Linear Light
Pin Light
Hard Mix
Difference
Exclusion
Subtract
Divide
Hue
Saturation
Color
100%
Fill: 100%

Photoshop's blend modes are a formidable tool that enables you merge the pixels of one layer with those of layers below it. You may achieve a large range of effects and styles in your designs by modifying the blending mode of a layer. An overview of a handful of Photoshop's blending modes is presented below:

Normal is the default blending mode, and it prevents pixels on the layer from being touched by pixels on layers below it.

Multiply: In this blending mode, the color values of the layer and the layers beneath it are multiplied. As a consequence, the picture gets darker and more contrasty.

Screen: With this blending mode, the layer's color values are merged with those of the layers beneath it. As a consequence, the picture gets brighter and less contrasty.

Overlay: To generate a high-contrast effect, this blending mode combines multiply and Screen blending techniques. Where the layer's color values are dark, they are multiplied, and where they are light, they are screened.

Soft Light: This blending option provides the layer with a delicate, diffused lighting effect. With less contrast than Overlay, it is equivalent.

Hard Light: This blending method has a sharper contrast than overlay yet is similar to it.

Color: Using this blending mode, the layer's hue and saturation are modified to adapt to the brightness of the layers below it.

Luminosity: When using this blending mode, the layer's brightness adapts to match the color and saturation of the layers below it.

Darken: This blending mode keeps the darker hue by comparing the layer's color values to those of the layers behind it.

Lighten: This blending mode keeps the lighter color by comparing the color values of the layer with the one below it.

Difference: This blending mode subtracts the layer's color values from the layer values below it.

Exclusion: This is a blending option that's equivalent to Difference but has less contrast.

Hue: This blending mode retains the layer's saturation and brightness while adjusting the layer's hue to match the layers below it.

Saturation: This blending mode retains the layer's hue and brightness while altering the layer's saturation to match the layers below it.

Color Dodge: By dividing the color values of the layers behind it by the layer's color values, this blending technique brightens the layer.

Color Bum: Using this blending mode, the layer is rendered darker by dividing its color values by those of the layers beneath it.

These are only a sample of the various blending options that Photoshop offers. You may generate a vast range of effects and styles in your designs by toying with various blending modes, from subtle color changes to dramatic, high-contrast photos.

3. Adjust the layer opacity: To fine-tune the effect after selecting a blending mode, you may wish to alter the layer opacity of the cloned layer. Use the Opacity slider in the Layers menu to achieve this. The layer may be made more transparent or opaque by sliding the slider to the left or right, accordingly. You may apply a number of effects to your designs by cloning a layer and adjusting its blending mode. For instance, you may duplicate a layer and use the Screen blending mode to achieve a glowing effect, or you might use the multiple blending mode to give your color pallet additional depth and richness.

This approach is incredibly helpful for adding overlays and textures to your designs. To blend a layer with the layer below, you may, for example, duplicate a layer, add a texture or pattern to it, and then set the blending mode to Overlay.

Resizing and rotating layers

You may adjust the size and orientation of layers in Adobe Photoshop to change the appearance of objects, text, and other visual components in your design. This lets you adjust the content's size, placement, and orientation to better suit your composition.

Using the Free Transform tool, which enables you to scale, skew, and distort a layer's content, you may resize a layer. This is how:

Step 1. In the Layers panel, select the layer you wish to enlarge.

Step 2. To access the **Free Transform** tool, pick **Edit > Free Transform** (or press **Ctrl + T** on a PC or **Command + T** on a Mac).

Step 3. To proportionately resize the layer, click and drag any of the corner handles of the bounding box.

Step 4. Hold down the Ctrl key (or the Command key on a Mac) and drag any of the corners handles to skew or distort the layer.

Step 5. To make the modification, hit **Enter** (or Return).

The Free Transform tool may also be used to rotate a layer, but it has a unique set of handles. This is how:

Step 1. In the Layers panel, select the layer you wish to rotate.

Step 2. To access the Free Transform tool, pick **Edit > Free Transform** (or press **Ctrl + T** on a PC or **Command + T** on a Mac).

Step 3. Move your cursor until a curving, double-headed arrow emerges beyond the enclosed box.

Step 4. To rotate the layer, click and drag the mouse.

Step 5. To make the modification, hit **Enter** (or Return).

Alternatively, you may precisely rotate a layer by using the rotate tool. This is how:

Step 1. In the Layers panel, pick the layer you wish to rotate.

Step 2. To activate the Rotate tool, click **Edit > Transform > Rotate** (or press **Ctrl + Shift+ R** on a PC or **Command + Shift + R** on a Mac).

Step 3. To rotate the layer, click and drag your mouse outside the bounding box.

Step 4. To make the modification, hit **Enter** (or Return).

You may also access other transformation tools like scale, skew, distortion, perspective, and warp by utilizing the menu choices under **Edit > transform**. You have better control over the visual components of your design because of the various ways in which each of these tools enables you to modify the content of a layer.

Layers can become pixelated or misshapen if you stretch them too much or rotate them at extreme angles, so take that in mind while extending and rotating them. Use high-resolution photographs whenever you can and aim to keep your edits within acceptable boundaries to prevent this.

Additionally, you may align several layers or spread them equally around your canvas by utilizing the Align and Distribute options located under the Layer menu. You may do this to build compositions that are more precise and well-balanced.

Using a filter to create artwork

The next step is to create a new layer without any artwork. (Adding blank sheets of clear film to a stack of images is equivalent to adding empty layers to a file.) Using a Photoshop effect, you'll extend this layer to add realistic-looking clouds to the sky.

Step 1. In the Layers panel, choose the Background layer to make it active, and then click the Create a New Layer button at the bottom of the Layers panel.

A new layer, dubbed Layer 1, arises. The layer has no content; thus, it does not influence the image. You may also build a new layer by choosing **Layer > New > Layer** or by choosing New Layer from the Layers panel menu.

Step 2. To rename the layer, double-click Layer 1, type Clouds, and then hit Enter or Return.

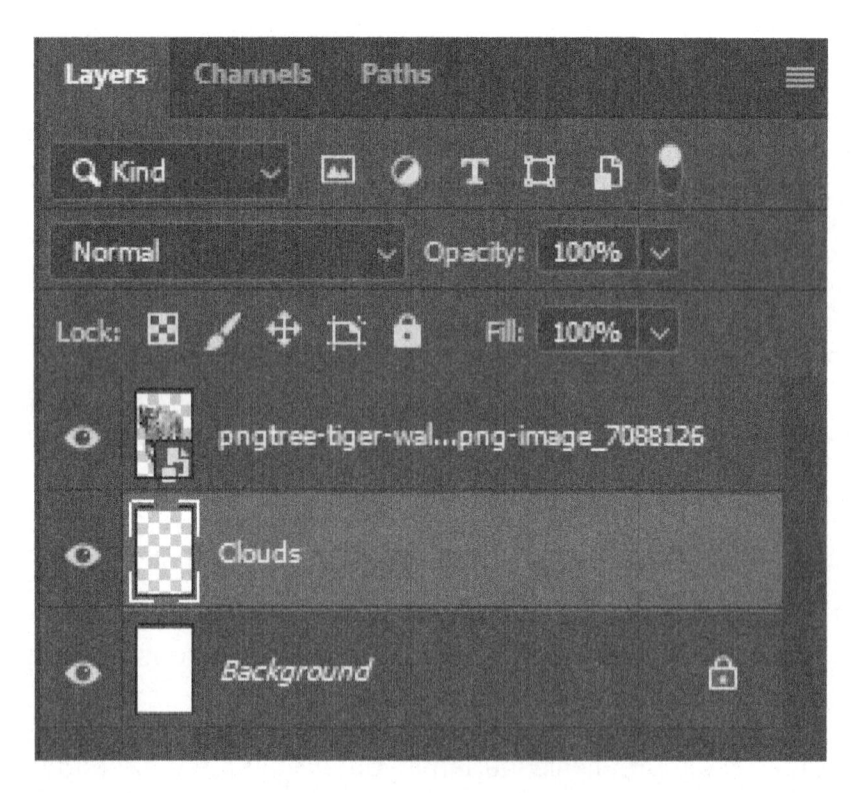

Step 3. Click the foreground color Swatch in the Tools panel, choose a sky-blue shade from the Color Picker, and then click **OK**. The following values were used to pick a color: **R=48, G=138, B= 174**. White continues to be the backdrop color.

Add the color to your Creative Cloud Libraries if you anticipate utilizing it consistently across a range of media. In the Swatches panel, make a swatch of the color, and then drag it to a library in the Libraries panel. Any Photoshop project you open now has access to that color.

Step 4. Pick **Filter > Render > Clouds** while the Clouds layer is still chosen.

Behind the photo are clouds that appear genuine.

Step 5. Select **Save > File**.

Adding Text

The inclusion of text is an important component of graphic design, and Adobe Photoshop offers several tools and options for achieving so. Photoshop makes it simple to add and edit text in your designs, whether you're constructing a logo, designing a poster, or adding explanations to your images. The Type tool in Photoshop can be in the toolbar on the left side of the screen and is used to add text to pictures.

The Type tool may be used to add text as seen below:

Step 1. From the toolbar, select the **Type tool**.

Step 2. To add a text box, click anywhere on the canvas.

Step 3. Fill in the text box with your material.

Step 4. Modify the text's font, size, color, and other settings using the options on the toolbar.

Step 5. To save your change, click the checkmark button in the choices window.

Once your text has been inserted, you may move it wherever on your canvas using the Move tool. Using the same tools and techniques as with any other layer in Photoshop, you may also resize, rotate, and make other changes to your text. Photos hop has various more text-editing options in addition to the Type tool. For instance, you may produce text that seems like a cutout in your photo by utilizing the Horizontal Type Mask tool.

This is how:

Step 1. From the toolbar, select the **Horizontal Type Mask tool**.

Step 2. To add a text box, click anywhere on the canvas.

Step 3. Fill in the text box with your material.

Step 4. Modify the text's font, size, color, and other settings using the options on the toolbar.

Step 5. To apply the text mask to your photo type **Enter** (or Return).

Additionally, you may produce vertical text that seems like a cutout in your photo by utilizing the Vertical Type Mask tool. Making text into a shape in Photoshop is an extra approach for working with text. This lets you modify the appearance of your text by applying numerous effects and transformations, such adding a gradient fill or a 3D effect.

How to turn text into a form is as follows:

Step 1. In the Layers panel, right-click on the layer that includes your text.

Step 2. From the context menu, select Convert to Shape.

Step 3. To alter the parameters for your form, such as the fill color, stroke, and other characteristics, use the choices on the toolbar.

The ability to create and edit text styles is one of Photoshop's most effective tools for working with text. To give your text a cohesive appearance and feel across your design, you may apply a text style, which is a set of formatting characteristics, to it.

Making a text style in Photoshop involves:

Step 1. Select the text layer you wish to use as the basis for your design.

Step 2. Click the **Create New Style** button in the Styles section.

Step 3. Give your style a name and select the parameters you wish to incorporate, such as font, size, color, and other features.

Step 4. Click **OK** to save your style.

Then, by picking the layer and clicking on your style in the Styles panel, you may apply your text style to any other text layer in your design.

Applying a layer style

Photoshop 's layer styles function is a useful tool for creating visual effects to your layers. With just a few clicks, layer styles help you easily apply a range of effects to your layers, such as glows, bevels, and drop shadows. Here, we'll look at adding layer styles and tweaking them to create the aesthetic you desire for your project.

To add a layer style to a layer in Photoshop, follow these steps:

Step 1. Select the layer you wish to apply the layer style to.

Step 2. In the Layers panel, click the Layer Style button (fx) at the bottom of the panel, and select the layer style you wish to apply from the drop-down menu.

Step 3. The Layer Style dialog box will open, enabling you to change the parameters for the selected layer style.

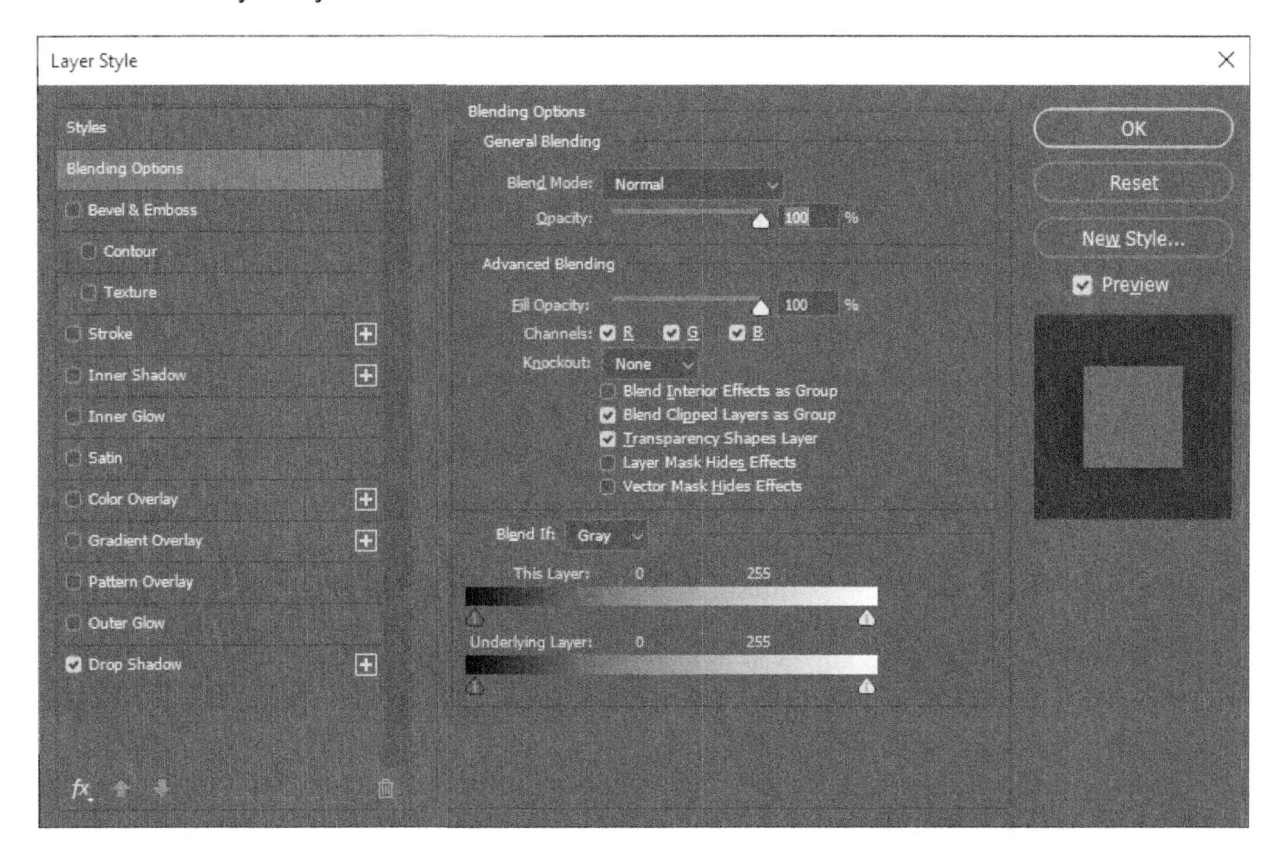

Step 4. After making the appropriate modifications, click **OK** to apply the layer style to your layer.

Let's take a deeper look at some of the most widely used layer styles and how to apply them.

1. Drop Shadow: This layer style adds a shadow to the layer beneath it. This effect is wonderful for providing depth and dimension to your project. The shadow's color, size, opacity, angle, and distance may all be modified.

2. Bevel & Emboss: This layer style provides your layer with a 3D effect. You may modify the size, depth, and angle of the effect by picking from a range of bevel and emboss styles, including Inner Bevel, Outer Bevel, and Pillow Emboss.

3. Inner Glow: The Inner Glow layer style gives your layer a slight gloss. This is a terrific effect for giving a glowing or backlit look. The glow's size, opacity, color, and blending mode may all be adjusted.

4. Outer Glow: The Outer Glow layer style gives your layer's edges a soft glow. This effect works great for generating halo or aura effects. The glow's size, opacity, color, and blending mode may all be adjusted.

5. Stroke: The Stroke layer style encircles your layer with a border. The stroke's location with the layer may be altered, as well as its size, color, and opacity.

Photoshop offers a large selection of other choices for customizing your layer styles in addition to these often-used ones, such as adding gradients, patterns, or distinctive textures to your effects.

You may also store your layer styles as presets, which allows you to effortlessly apply the same effects to other layers in your design. When adding layer styles, it is vital to think about the overall design of your project and how the effects will fit in with the rest of your components. This is especially critical if you plan to employ a lot of layer styles. The usage of an excessive number of layer styles or effects that are exceedingly intricate may soon become overwhelming or deflect attention from the core focus of your design.

It is often advisable to start with a simple effect and progressively alter the parameters until you get the desired appearance. If you are unclear of how to begin, it is often better to start with a simple effect. When it comes to creating visual effects to your layers in Photoshop, one of the most efficient methods to achieve so is by applying layer styles. You may produce patterns that appear like they were developed by a professional by familiarizing yourself with the numerous accessible options and playing with the various settings.

This will allow you to blend layer styles in different ways. Layer styles are a flexible tool that may aid you in fulfilling your design objectives in Photoshop, regardless of whether you are working on a project to create a logo, design a poster, or work on any other sort of project.

Using the Gradients panel

The Gradients panel in Photoshop is a powerful tool that enables you to create and apply gradient effects to your pictures and creations. You may locate this panel in the Edit menu. A gradient is a smooth transition between two or more colors that generates an effect that is aesthetically beautiful and visually intriguing. Your artwork may benefit from having depth, dimension, and texture added to it with the use of these tools, and they may be applied to a broad range of components, such as backgrounds, text, and shapes. In Photoshop, you may visit the Gradients panel by going to the Window menu and selecting "**Gradients**" (or by entering **Shift + Ctrl + G** on a PC or **Shift + Command + G** on a Mac). Alternatively, you can use the shorthand combination "**G**." The panel will open on the right side of the screen and give an option of numerous preset gradient settings. By pressing the "**Create New Gradient**" button available in the panel, you may build your very own unique gradients from the beginning.

Select the layer you wish to apply the gradient to, and then create a new layer style by clicking on the "**Layer Style**" button at the bottom of the Layers panel and choosing "**Gradient Overlay**." This will allow you to apply the gradient to the element in your design that you have selected. The Gradient Overlay dialog box will show up, offering you several modifications you may make to your gradient that you may make. By clicking on the gradient preview box inside the Gradient Overlay dialog box, you are permitted to pick the gradient that will be used for the overlay.

This will start the Gradient Editor, in which you may pick a gradient from the presets or construct a gradient from scratch according to your individual needs. You also may modify the opacity and blending mode of the gradient, as well as the angle and size of the gradient. The Gradients panel offers you access to a broad selection of different sorts of gradients that you may employ. Linear, radial, and angle gradients make up the bulk of all gradients found on the globe. While radial gradients transition in a circular pattern, linear gradients transition between hues in a straight line. Linear gradients are more prevalent. The transition from one angle to another in an angle gradient linearly takes place.

The Gradients panel may save and load gradient presets, which is another vital function of the panel. If you create a custom gradient that you wish to use again in the future, you can save it as a preset in the Gradient Editor by clicking on the "New" button and giving it a name. This will store it as a custom gradient preset. To load a preset, just click on the dropdown menu accessible in the Gradient Editor, and then choose the preset that you would want to employ. You are also able to construct and preserve gradient maps using the Gradients panel. Gradient maps are relatively like typical gradients; however, they are applied to an image as a map of tones rather than a color shift. The development of duotone effects and the adding of depth and contrast to your images are both feasible with this approach.

Adding an adjustment layer

Adjustments to color and tone may be applied to a picture by adding adjustment layers, which prevents the pixel values from being altered irrevocably. Because the adjustment layer is the only location the change takes effect, for instance, if you add a Color Balance adjustment layer to a photo, you may play with a range of colors without changing any other portions of the image. If you prefer to restore to the original pixel values, you may hide or wipe the adjustment layer. Adjustment layers are a handy tool for making non-destructive alterations to the color, tone, and saturation of a picture in Photoshop. Adjustment layers may be found in the Adjustment panel. An adjustment layer, as opposed to directly changing the pixels of a picture, alters the layer underlying it. This permits you to make alterations without permanently changing the image that you started with.

In Photoshop, you must first confirm that the Layers panel is visible before you can create an adjustment layer. You may reach the Layers panel by heading to the Window menu and choosing "**Layers**" (or by using the **F7** key on a PC or the **Command + F7** key on a Mac). Alternatively, you may enter the Layers panel by clicking the "**Layer**" button in the Layers palette. Click the "**Create new fill or adjustment layer**" button when the Layers panel has been opened. This button is situated at the bottom of the Layers panel. This button has the look of a circle that has been sliced in half, with one half being white and the other half being black.

There are various more adjustment layer choices available, such as **Brightness/Contrast**, **Levels**, **Curves**, and **Hue/Saturation**, which may be accessed in the menu that opens. Simply clicking on the **Hue/Saturation** adjustment layer type will allow you to pick the sort of adjustment layer you wish to create. The new adjustment layer will show up in the Layers panel at the top of the panel, immediately above the layer that it is affecting.

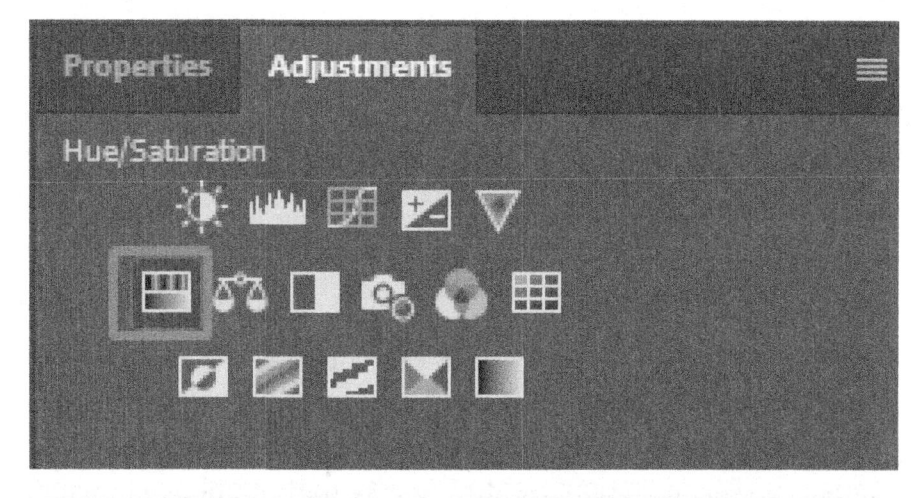

ADOBE PHOTOSHOP 2023 COMPLETE GUIDE FOR BEGINNERS

After you have added an adjustment layer, you may edit the adjustment parameters by double-clicking on the adjustment layer in the Layers panel. This will bring up a menu that allows you to pick from a range of alternatives. This will open the Properties panel, in which you may make adjustments to a range of characteristics concerning the adjustment layer. The precise choices that are accessible to you will alter depending on the kind of adjustment layer that you are working with; however, in general, you will have the ability to tweak the brightness, contrast, color balance, and saturation of the image.

Adjustment layers in Photoshop allow you the chance to make non-destructive modifications to your pictures, which is one of the program's most significant features. Instead of directly changing the image's pixels, an adjustment layer applies an adjustment to the layer beneath it. This is in contrast to the way that direct pixel editing works. This means that if you make a mistake or later decide that you want to modify the adjustment, you don't have to reverse a series of alterations to the picture itself; instead, you can merely delete or update the adjustment layer. This prevents you from having to repeat the adjustments. Adjustments may be made to select portions of the picture by making use of layer masks, which is yet another advantage of working with adjustment layers. You may selectively conceal or display portions of the adjustment layer by utilizing layer masks. This enables you to apply the modification to just the sections of the picture that require it, as opposed to applying it to the complete image. The **"Add layer mask"** button may be located at the bottom of the Layers panel. Clicking on this option will allow you to add a layer mask to an adjustment layer. By doing this, a white mask will be placed to the adjustment layer. After that, you may use the Brush tool to paint the mask with black to conceal portions of the adjustment, or you may paint the mask with white to reveal those regions.

You may make non-destructive modifications to your images using adjustment layers, but you can also utilize them to offer creative aspects to your pictures by employing them in unique ways. For instance, an image may be given a warm or cool tone by using a Color Balance adjustment layer, and a duotone effect can be generated by utilizing a Gradient Map adjustment layer. Both of these adjustment layers are present in Photoshop. Explore the characteristics of various adjustment layers by playing around with a selection of them to find how they could improve the images you've shot. You may make accurate alterations to your images by first generating an adjustment layer and then modifying the settings. This will prevent you from permanently changing the original. Adjustment layers are an important tool for any Photoshop user as they allow users to make alterations selectively via the use of layer masks and offer access to a broad range of creative effects.

Using an effect more than once in a layer style

Applying many instances of effects like strokes, glows, or shadows to a design element is a good approach for increasing visual impact to the component in question. Because you may apply several instances of an effect straight from inside the Layer Style dialog box, there is no need to duplicate layers to complete this work.

Step 1. Open a file.

Step 2. In the Layers panel, double-click the effect named Drop Shadow which is related with the HAWAII layer.

Step 3. In the effects list found on the l e f t -hand side of the Layer Style dialog box, click the plus button situated to the right of the Drop Shadow effect and then pick the second Drop Shadow effect from the list.

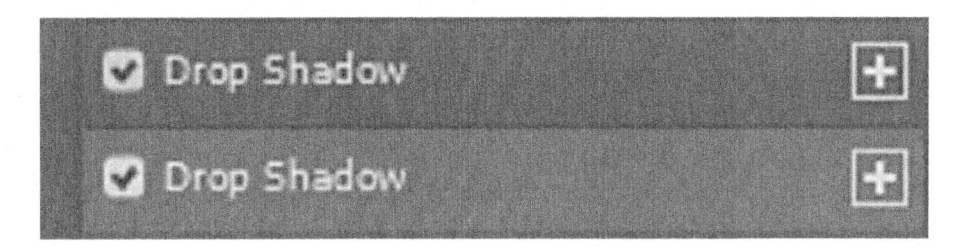

Step 4. You may make alterations to your second drop shadow, which includes modifying its color, size, and opacity.

Step 5. In the box called Drop Shadow choices, pick the color Swatch. Then, drag the cursor outside of the Layer Style dialog box so that it transforms into an eyedropper. Finally, click the bottom flower to experience the hue of its purple petals. After that, set the parameters for the Drop Shadow, and then click the OK button.

Updating layer effects

Stunning and complicated patterns may be made with the aid of Adobe Photoshop's layer effects in a number of various methods. You can give your designs additional dimension and depth by utilizing these effects, which enable you to add shadows, glows, bevels, and strokes to your layers, as well as a range of other aesthetic changes. Having said that, even after you have applied a layer effect to a layer, you might realize that you need to make some adjustments to it in the future. To our good fortune, the technique of adjusting the layer effects in Photos hop is a straightforward and basic one.

Here are the methods to update layer effects in Photoshop:

Step 1. Launch Photoshop and access the Layers panel by using the F7 key on your keyboard or selecting "**Layers**" from the Window menu.

Step 2. Choose the layer that includes the effect whose settings you wish to edit.

Step 3. In the Layers panel, to the right of the layer's name, you'll notice a "fx" sign. Double-click on this icon. This will start the dialog box for modifying the layer style.

Step 4. You will discover a list of effects that have been applied to the layer in the Layer Style dialog box. These effects have been applied to the layer. Simply click on the effect's name in the left-hand column to pick the one you wish to edit, and then click the "Update" button.

Step 5. Modify the settings of the effect to acquire the desired outcome. You may adjust the effect in a multitude of ways, including color, opacity, angle, and size.

Step 6. When you have completed making your edits, you may then dismiss the Layer Style dialog box by clicking the "**OK**" button, which will also apply the updated effect to the layer.

If you want to get rid of an effect altogether, you need to do nothing more complex than click on its name in the Layer Style dialog box and then drag it to the trash can icon at the bottom of the box.

Keeping your drawings up to date and making modifications as you go may be substantially assisted by using the update layer effects tool. It allows you to experiment with various effects and settings without needing you to repeat the procedure all over again. In addition, if you are working on a design project that will go through several revisions or versions, improving the layer effects could help you save a substantial amount of time and effort.

When updating the effects of a layer, one thing that is vital to bear in mind is that changes made to the look of one effect may modify the appearance of other effects that have been applied to the same layer. For instance, if you adjust the size or angle of a Bevel and Emboss effect, it may possibly alter the way that a Drop Shadow effect on the same layer appears. Be careful to give the adjustments you've made a full examination and make any required alterations to attain the anticipated effect.

Masking Objects in a Layer

You may selectively conceal or expose components of an image or layer by employing a process in Photoshop called masking, which includes placing items in a layer and then concealing or showing those objects.

This is how you can go about accomplishing it:

Step 1. Launch Photoshop, go to the file that you want to alter and choose the layer that has the element that you want to mask.

Step 2. In the Layers panel's lower-right corner, pick the **"Layer Mask"** button and click it. This will produce a layer mask for the selected layer that is white and relates to the layer you specify.

Step 3. Click on the layer mask's name in the Layers panel to pick it. When it gets selected, you will be able to know as it will have a white highlight surrounding it.

Step 4. Using the Brush tool, paint on the layer mask either with white to reveal areas of the layer or with black to conceal parts of the layer. You may also partly conceal or disclose areas of the layer by employing the different hues of gray that are available.

Step 5. Using the Eraser tool, delete areas of the layer mask to expose the layer that is behind it. A seamless transition between areas of the layer that are concealed and those that are visible may also be achieved with the aid of the Gradient tool.

Step 6. You may utilize the Properties panel to edit the layer masks by altering the density of the mask, the feathering of the mask, or any of the other choices.

Step 7. To remove the layer mask and reveal the whole layer once again, click on the thumbnail for the layer mask while holding down the Shift key. This will disable the layer mask.

Remember to save your modifications when you're done.

Harmonizer Filter

The harmonization filter seeks to match the tone and color of a layer to an underlying layer of your choice. Although still classified as a 'beta' filter, which indicates it's not entirely done yet; it's nevertheless a rapid and amazingly efficient approach to make photographs from disparate sources appear as though they belong together. Here's how it works.

Step 1. The Starting Images

This image of a woman, shot in a n indoor studio, is to be set against a background displaying seagulls on a rock at night. The first step is to remove the backdrop off the woman, which is readily performed with Photoshop's Select Subject function.

Step 2. The Background Removed

You can see how the lady layer seems utterly out of place in the backdrop when the studio layer is removed because she is too green and dazzling. **Curves or Levels** may be used to adjust her hue, but the new neural filter gives a more expedient choice.

Step 3. The Harmonization Filter

You may locate the Harmonization filter by clicking **Filter > Neural Filters**. Then, when the window opens, pick Harmonization by clicking the slider next to its name. You won't observe any instant difference, as the reference layer has yet to be picked.

Step 4. Choosing the Reference Image

From the pop-up pick a Layer menu, choose the layer you wish to establish as a reference. This will normally be the Background layer. After a few seconds, the target layer will be recolored to match the backdrop. Here, you can see how the colors have been modified to meet the bright blue backdrop; in addition, the layer has been darkened properly.

Step 5. Adjusting the Settings

The default options won't necessarily be the greatest final decision. Fortunately, Photoshop provides you with a significant degree of control over the product. Here, I've lowered the overall Strength of the impact significantly. I've also decreased the Saturation a touch and raised the Brightness.

Step 6. The Harmonized Result

The target layer will be cloned when you commit to the filter so you can always go back to the original if you want to. The new layer now matches the backdrop far more precisely, accomplishing in a matter of seconds what would have taken much longer with old approaches.

Step 7. A More Complex Scenario

The Harmonization filter brings you a long way toward your aim, but it isn't always a full answer. In this example, the identical cutout has been put against a warm sunset background. Once again, the woman is a terrible match for the scene: she's way too pale and under-saturated to appear like she belongs here.

Step 8. The Initial Harmonization

This is the outcome of running the Harmonization filter, after having changed the parameters somewhat. The lady is now a better tonal match for the backdrop, but she still doesn't appear as if she matches the place. Some additional effort is needed to accomplish the assignment.

Step 9. Create a Curves Adjustment

Choose **Layer > New Adjustment Layer > Curves** and tick the box to construct a Clipping Mask with the woman's layer so that it doesn't alter the backdrop. Drag down on the RGB curve to darken the layer. The impact is too powerful, but we'll improve it next.

Step 10. Mask the Adjustment Layer

Every Adjustment Layer comes with a built-in Layer Mask, and you may paint on here to disguise the effect. Choose a soft-edged brush, with Black as the foreground color, then drop the opacity of your brush to roughly 30%. As you paint over the left border of the layer, nearer the sunset, you'll hide the Curves effect here, to make her seem as though she is lighted from the side. Build up the bright-ness judiciously by painting over such parts many times.

Step 11. Finishing off

As a last phase, it helps to have a warm glow corning from the sun. Make a new layer, set to Hard Light mode, again utilizing the woman's layer as a Clipping Mask. Select a mid-orange from the sun, then paint this over the hair and the left side of the torso. Now it seems as if the sunshine is genuinely coloring the woman, situating her much more realistically in the environment.

Match Color Command

With the Match Color command, you may compare colors across numerous pictures, layers, or selections. Additionally, you may adjust an image's colors by altering the brightness, the color range, and the neutralization of a color cast. Only RGB mode is compatible with the Match Color command.

The pointer morphs into the Eyedropper tool when you do the Match Color command. To see the color pixel values in the Info panel while making edits to the picture, use the Eyedropper tool. As you execute the Match Color command, this panel informs you of any changes in color values. The Match Color command analyzes two pictures' colors, matching those in the source picture with those in the destination image. Match Color is handy when you want to match specified colors (like skin tones) in one picture to certain colors in another or when you want to make the colors in several pictures consistent. The Match Color command may also match colors across several layers inside a single picture in addition to matching colors between two photographs.

Match color between two photos

Step 1. (Optional) Choose one photo from the source and the target pictures.

• The Match Color command will match the overall Image statistics between photographs if you don't make a selection.

Step 2. Select **Image > Adjustments > Match Color** after making the chosen photo active.

• Make sure the layer you wish to apply the Match Color command to, is active if you want to apply it to a particular layer in the destination picture.

ADOBE PHOTOSHOP 2023 COMPLETE GUIDE FOR BEGINNERS

Step 3. Select the source picture whose colors you wish to match in the target image from the Source menu in the picture Statistics section of the Match Color dialog box. When you don't want to utilize another photo as a reference to calculate the color correction, pick None. When None is chosen, the source and destination pictures are identical.

• If needed, pick the layer from the source picture whose colors you wish to match using the Layer menu. To match the colors of all the layers in the source picture, you may also pick Merged from the Layer menu.

Step 4. Execute one or more of the following if you chose anything in the image:

If you're altering the complete target picture, check Ignore Selection When adjusting in the Destination image section. This option updates the complete target picture while ignoring the target image's selection.

If you generated a selection in the source picture and want to utilize the colors in the selection to compute the adjustment, click Use Selection in Source to compute Colors in the Image Statistics section. To compute the adjustment using the colors from the whole source picture instead of merely the selection in the source image, uncheck this option.

If you generated a selection in the target picture and want to use the colors in the selection to calculate the adjustment, click Use Selection in Target to Calculate Adjustment in the Image Statistics section. To compute the adjustment using the colors of the whole target picture and disregard the selection in the target image, uncheck this option.

Step 5. Choose the Neutralize option to rapidly eliminate a color cast from the target photo. As you make modifications, ensure the Preview option is chosen so that your picture updates.

Step 6. Slide the Luminance slider to modify the brightness of the target picture. You may also enter a value in the Luminance box. The default value is 100, the maximum value is 200, and the lowest value is 1.

Step 7. Use the Color Intensity slider to change the target image's color saturation. You could also put a number in the Color Intensity box. The default value is 100, the greatest number is 200, and the lowest value is 1 (which results in a grayscale image).

Step 8. Use the Fade slider to change the degree of alteration applied to the photo. Moving the slider to the right decreases the adjustment.

Step 9. Click OK to make changes.

Match color of two layers in the same picture

Step 1. (Optional) Align the colors of two layers in the same image. In the layer you wish to match, make a choice. Use this approach to match a color region (like the tones of skin on the face) from one layer to another.

The Match Color tool matches all the source layer's colors if you don't make a selection.

Step 2. Select **Image > Adjustments > Match Color** after making sure the layer you wish to target (make the color adjustment to) is active.

Step 3. Verify that the picture selected from the Source menu in the Image Statistics section of the Match Color dialog box matches the destination image.

Step 4. To pick the layer whose colors you wish to match, utilize the Layer menu. To match the colors from all the layers, you may also pick Merged from the Layer menu.

Step 5. Execute one or more of the following if you picked anything in the image:

If you're applying the adjustment to the complete target layer, click Ignore Selection When Applying Adjustment in the Destination Image section. This option applies the update to the whole target layer while ignoring the target layer's selection.

If you established a selection in the source picture and want to use the color in the selection to calculate the adjustment, click employ Selection in Source to Calculate Colors under picture Statistics. To compute the adjustment using the colors throughout the complete source layer, uncheck this option to disregard the source layer's selection.

To compute the adjustment using just the colors in the given region of the target layer, click Use Selection in Target to compute Adjustment under Image Statistics. To compute the adjustment using the colors of the complete target layer rather than the selection, uncheck this option.

Step 6. Choose the Neutralize option to automatically remove a color cast from the target layer. As you make modifications, ensure the Preview option is chosen so that your picture updates.

Step 7. Slide the Luminance slider to boost or reduce the brightness of the target layer. You could also provide a number in the Luminance field. The default value is 100, the maximum value is 200, and the lowest value is 1.

Step 8. Use the Color Intensity slider to alter the target layer's color pixel values. You could also put a number in the Color Intensity box. The default value is 100, the greatest number is 200, and the lowest value is 1 (which results in a grayscale image).

Step 9. Use the Fade slider to pick how much change was done to the photo. The amount of adjustment is lowered when the slider is pushed to the right.

Step 10. Press **OK** to make the changes.

Save and apply adjustments in the Match Color command

Click the Save Statistics button in the Image Statistics section of the Match Color dialog box. Give the settings a name and save them.

Click the Load Statistics button in the Image Statistics section of the Match Color dialog box. Find the saved settings file and load it.

Landscape Mixer Filter

The Landscape Mixer is a Neural Filter meant to assist us modify the environmental factors in our landscape photos-for example, we might cover a desert in snow or turn a bright, sunny day into a lovely sunset. But how well does it work? Let's find out!

Where to Find the Landscape Mixer

You can locate the Landscape Filter in the Neural Filters dialog. Click on the Filter menu and select **Neural Filters**. The Neural Filters panel will open. Locate the Landscape Mixer in the list (you may need to download the program if you haven't used it previously). Click on the switch to activate the filter and access the different features.

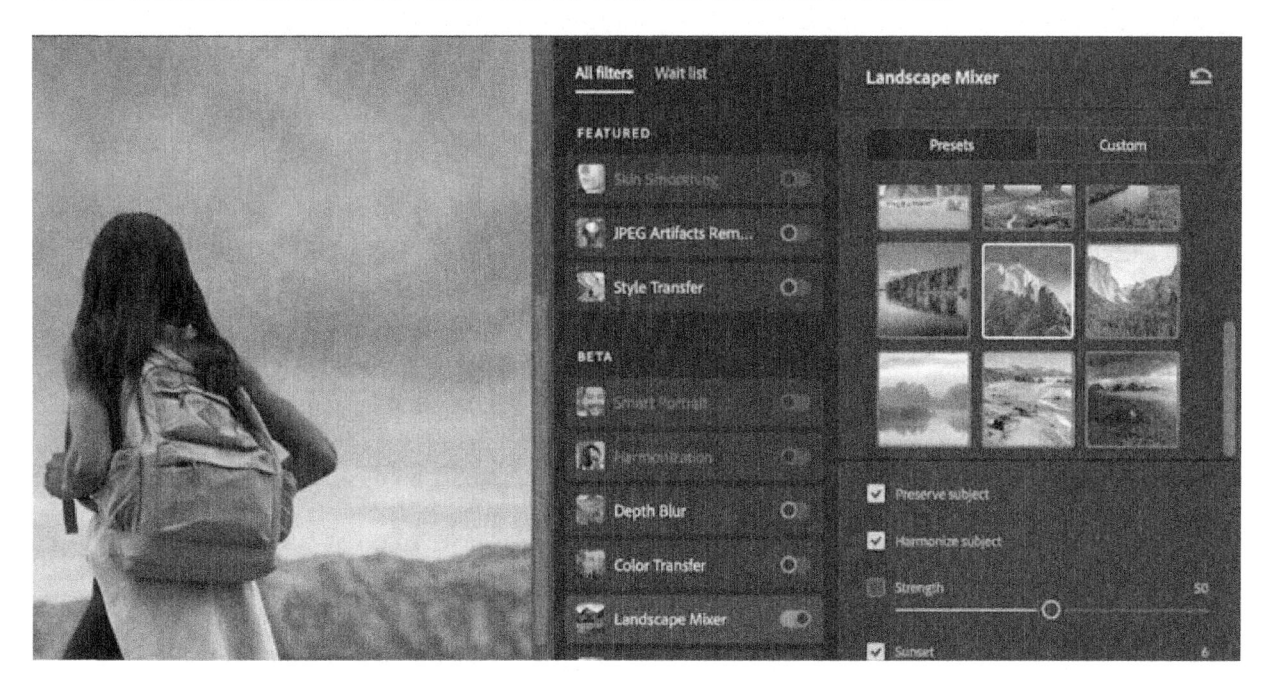

You may be shocked to realize exactly how easy the UI is. The Landscape Mixer delivers a selection of landscape types in the form of picture thumbnails. Clicking on one will immediately add that kind of landscape to your image (after some processing time).

Go through the list and try out the different effects. There are a ton of possibilities to try with! Some will focus more on the lighting in the image, such giving the appearance of a brilliant sunset. And some will modify elements of the terrain itself, like changing a desert into a meadow of green. The results are quite astounding! You will lose some quality and the additional textures cer-tainly aren't ideal, but this tool may be a big assistance if you're attempting to rapidly match a photo to another for a composite.

Creating a border from a selection

The addition of a border to an image or object can assist in calling attention to the focal point of the composition while also giving it a more polished appearance. Using only a few easy-to-under-stand tools and methods, you may quickly and simply construct a border around a selection in Adobe Photoshop.

The following are the processes that need to be performed to construct a border in Photoshop based on a selection:

Step 1. Launch Photoshop, load your image and use the marquee tool to form a selection around the portion of the photo that will act as the border. The Marquee or Lasso tools are just a couple examples of the choosing tools you may employ.

Step 2. When you are pleased with your selection, go to the Edit menu and click "**Stroke**." The Stroke dialog box will open as a result of clicking this.

Step 3. The Stroke dialog box allows you to specify the placement of the stroke, the color of the border, and the width of the border in pixels. You may also customize the width of the border. Additionally, you may choose whether the stroke should be drawn inside, outside, or in the Centre of the option.

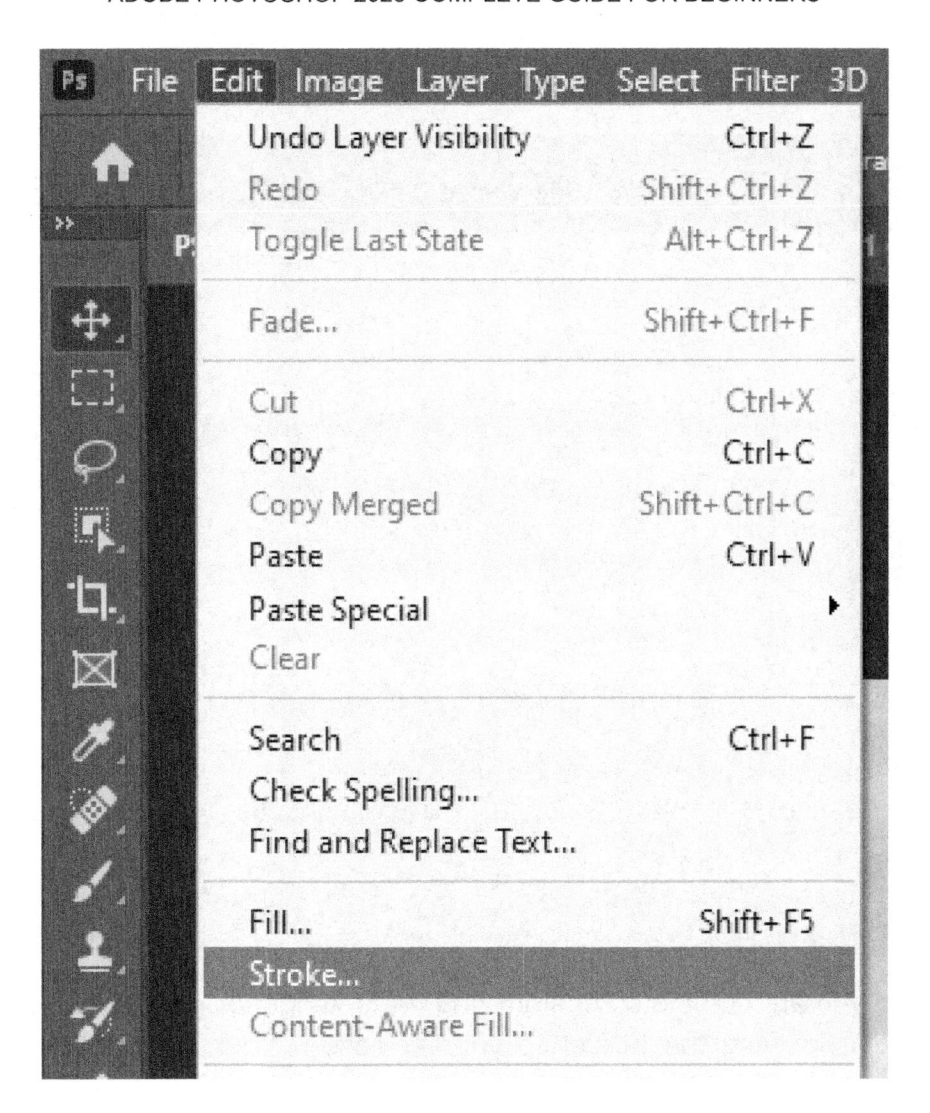

ADOBE PHOTOSHOP 2023 COMPLETE GUIDE FOR BEGINNERS

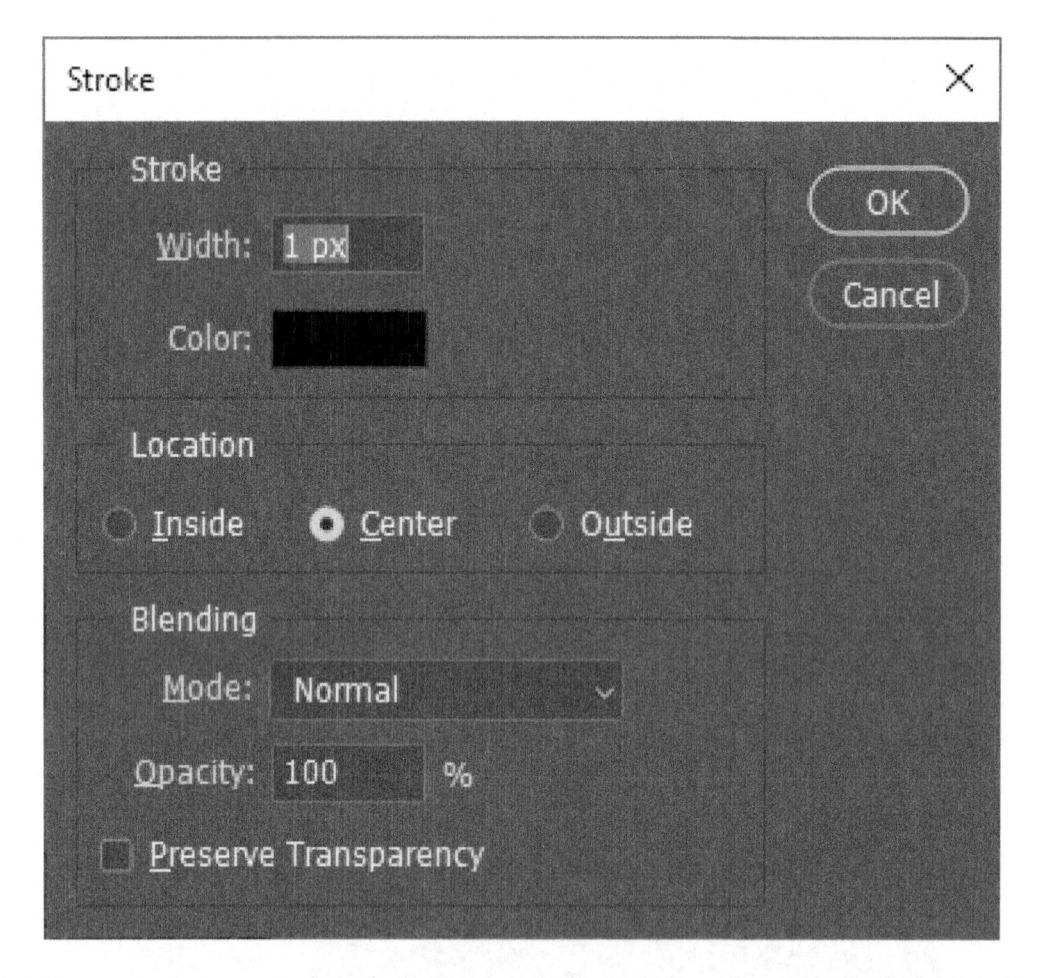

Step 4. When you are completed customizing the settings for the stroke, click the "**OK**" button to begin applying the border to your selection. Your option ought to now be enclosed by a border that complies with the color and width parameters that you picked previously.

Step 5. If you wish to further polish your border, you can utilize the Layer Style dialog box to apply additional effects to your stroke. This can be done if you want to further enhance your border. To achieve this, visit the Layer menu, click "**Layer Style**," and then pick "**Stroke**" from the drop-down menu that displays. This will start the dialog box for modifying the layer style.

Step 6. You may alter the size, color, and location of your stroke in the Layer Style dialog box. Additionally, you may apply extra effects like bevels, shadows, or glows to your stroke. Experiment with the different setting choices until you obtain the effect you desire.

Step 7. When you are pleased with the design of your border, close the **Layer Style** dialog box by clicking the "**OK**" button, and then apply the alterations to the selection you have made.

Your images may be edited and given a more professional appearance by making a border from a selection in Photoshop. This is a fast and straightforward approach to achieve this. To simply add a decorative touch or bring attention to a specific section of an image, or even to produce the sense of depth inside the picture, borders can be employed. By using the strategies explained above, you can make customized borders for your images that are customized to match your individual design needs and bring attention to them. You may also use other techniques to generate borders in Photoshop, such as utilizing the Rectangular Marquee tool to create a new layer with a specified size and then applying a stroke effect to that layer. These are just two examples of the various ways you can use to create borders in Photoshop. You may also construct a border around an object by making use of the Layer Mask tool, which does not have any effect on the underlying picture.

Layer Comps

Use layer comps to save and switch among design concepts

Switching between the various views of a multilayered photo file is as simple as clicking one button when utilizing the Layer Comps panel, which can be accessed by selecting **Window > Layer Comps**. A layer comp is nothing more than a snapshot of the settings in the Layers panel in their most recent form. Create a new layer comp if you wish to keep a certain mix of the properties of numerous layers. Then, you can fast analyze the two designs by switching from one layer comp to another. This will allow you to do so. When you want to display a number of diverse ways in which a design may be structured, you can highlight the brilliance of layer comps. After you've generated a few layer comps, you may assess the different design iterations without having to manually choose and deselect eye icons or make revisions in the Layers panel. Take for instance the fact that you are working on the layout of a brochure and developing it in both English and French at the same time. Within the same photo file, you may have the text written in French on one layer and the text written in English on another. To build two unique layer comps, you would first make the French layer visible, then make the English layer invisible, and last, in the Layer Comps panel, click the button labeled "**Create New Layer Comp**" to generate the first of your new layer comps.

Then, to construct an English layer comp, you would do the reverse, which is to make the English layer visible, make the French layer invisible, and click the box labeled "**Create New Layer Comp**." To see the various layer comps, click the Layer Comp box in the Layer Comps panel for each comp in turn. This will bring up the layer comp. When the design is still in flux or when you need to produce numerous variations of the same picture file, layer comps may be an immensely valuable tool to have. You may edit the visibility, placement, or appearance of one layer inside a layer comp, and then sync the layer comp to have that change replicated in all of the other layer comps. This is useful if certain elements of the layer comps need to remain consistent with one another.

Exercise

Step 1: Create a New Layer Comp

To begin the process of making a new Layer Comp, you will first need to enter the "**Layer Comps**" window. You may get to this by selecting Layer Comps from the Window menu in the software you're using.

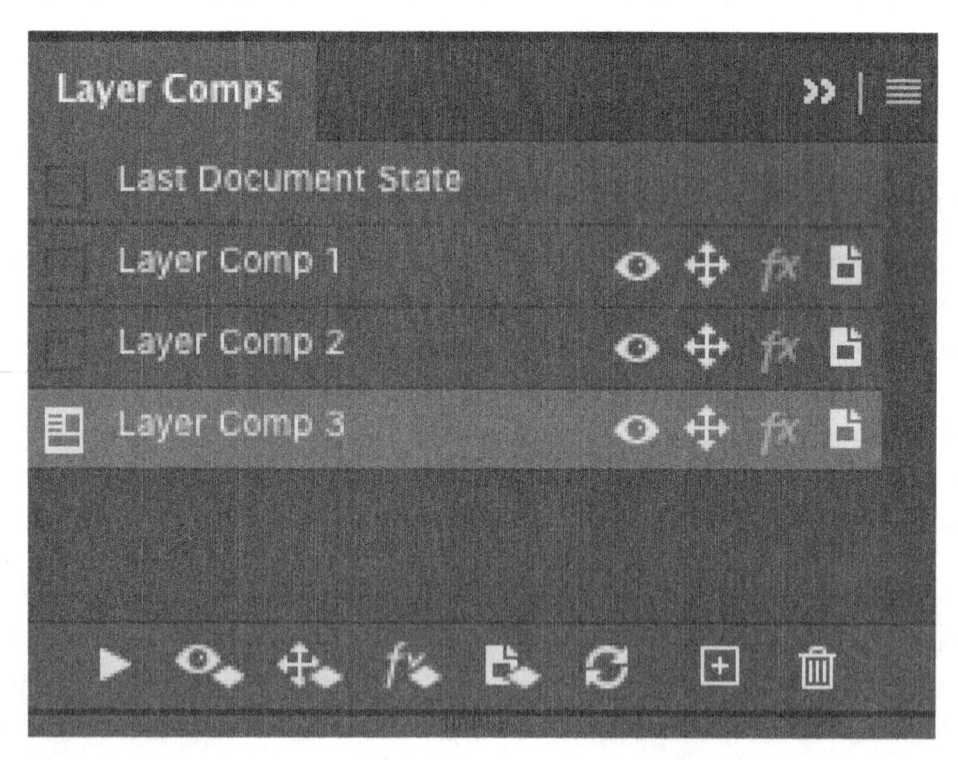

After you have visited the Layer Comps panel, you will find that there is a button titled "**New Layer Comp**" at the very bottom of the screen. To build a new Layer Comp, you may do so by clicking on this button.

Step 2: Choose Your Settings

You will be offered a dialog box to specify the parameters for your new Layer Comp anytime you create a new Layer Comp. This dialog box will be presented to you when you create a new Layer Comp.

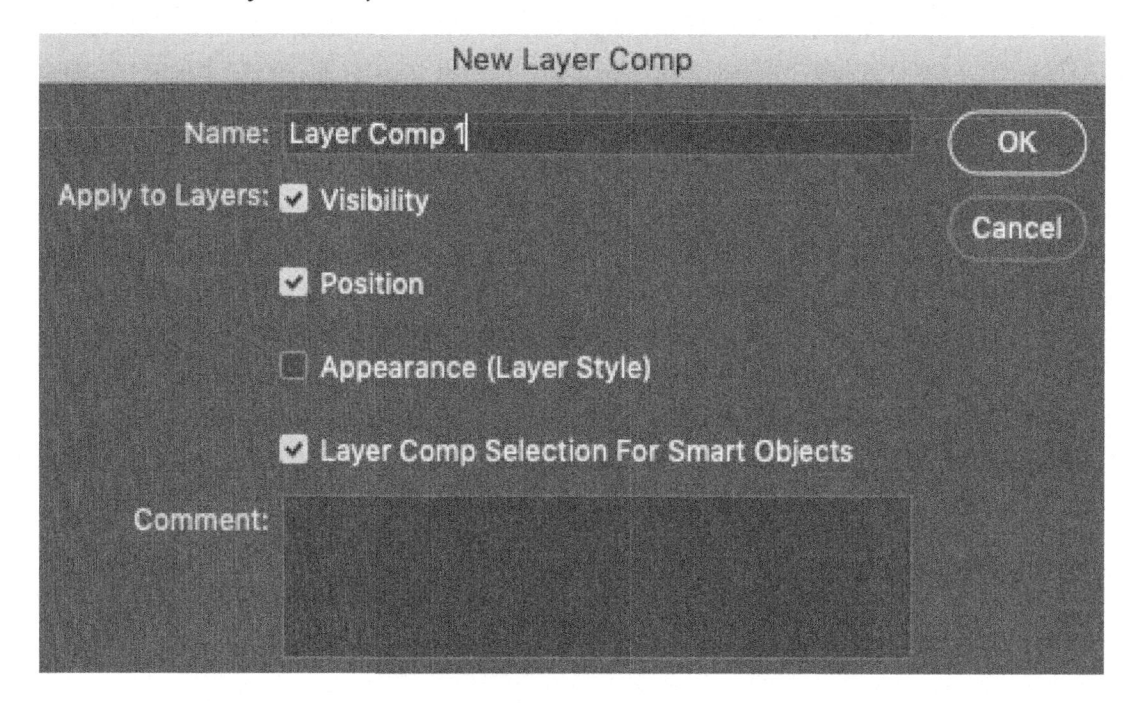

Here are the parameters you'll need to consider:

Name: Give your Layer Comp a name that is descriptive so that you can quickly remember it subsequently.

Visibility: This option lets you pick which layers and layer groups should be visible when the Layer Comp in question is active.

location: When this Layer Comp is active, you will have the opportunity to choose the location of the layers and layer groups in your design.

Appearance: When this Layer Comp is active, you will have the ability to customize the look of the layers and layer groups in your design.

Layer Comp Selection for Smart Objects: With this functionality, you may adjust the state of the Smart Object on a layer-by-layer basis without having to update the Smart Object itself.

Step 3: Save Your Layer Comp

After you have made your settings, hit **"OK"** to begin the process of establishing your new Layer Comp. The Layer Comp you just built will now be presented in the section titled Layer Comps.

If you decide to alter your design in any manner, you will be able to update your Layer Comp by utilizing the **"Update Layer Comp"** button that is accessible in the Layer Comps panel. This may be done by clicking on the button that reads **"Update Layer Comp."**

Step 4: Switch among Layer Comps

You may now shift between numerous design concepts by picking various Layer Comps in the Layer Comps tab once you have built a new Layer Comp. In addition, you may utilize the **"Previous Layer Comp"** and **"Next Layer Comp"** buttons to travel between your various Layer Comps more easily. If you want to examine how your design appears while numerous Layer Comps are active at the same time, you may use the **"New Document from Layer Comp"** button to build a new document that incorporates all of your presently active Layer Comps. This will allow you to view how your design appears when many Layer Comps are active at the same time.

Apply and view layer comps

Within the Layer Comp panel, perform any of the following:

To examine a layer comp, you first need to apply it. Click the **Apply Layer Comp** icon next to a selected comp.

To cycle through a view of all layer comps, utilize the Previous and Next buttons at the bottom of the panel. (To cycle through certain comparisons, first choose them.)

To restore the document to its state before you picked a layer comp, click the **Apply Layer Comp** icon next to **Last Document State** at the top of the panel.

Change and edit a layer comp

You are necessary to update a layer comp if its configuration is updated in any way.

Step 1. In the Layer Comps menu, pick the layer comp you wish to work with.

Step 2. Make tweaks to the layer's style, position, or visibility as appropriate. To record these updates, you may have to alter the parameters of the layer comp.

Step 3. To adjust your comp choices, go to the panel menu and choose Layer Comp options. Then, from the submenu that opens, choose additional choices to capture layer position and style.

Step 4. At the bottom of the window, you'll find a button titled Update Layer Comp. Click this button.

Clear layer comp warnings

Certain operations generate a condition where the layer comp can no longer be entirely restored. This happens when you delete a layer, combine a layer, or convert a layer to a backdrop. In such circumstances, a caution symbol hi displays next to the layer comp name.

Do one of the following:

Ignore the warning, which can lead to the deletion of one or more levels of protection. There is a potential that other saved parameters will be kept.

Perform an update on the compilation, which will cause you to lose any previously recorded settings but will bring the compilation up to date.

To see the notification that explains why the layer comp can't be restored correctly, click the icon that looks like a caution sign. Select the Clear option to get rid of the warning symbol while retaining the integrity of the other layers.

To open the pop-up menu where you may pick either the Clear Layer Comp Warning or the Clear All Layer Comp Warnings command, right-click (Windows) or control-click (Mac OS) on the warning icon. This will bring up the menu.

Delete a layer comp

Do one of the following:

While the layer comp is chosen in the Layer Comps panel, either click the Delete symbol situated inside the panel or pick Delete Layer Comp from the panel menu to delete the layer comp.

To remove it, drag it over to the trash can symbol on the panel.

Export layer comps

You may export layer compositions to separate files.

Choose **File > Export > Layer Comps** to Files and then choose the file format and specify the location.

Flattening and storing files

The process of flattening a picture in Photoshop entails merging all of the layers that are visible into a single layer. This is commonly done to minimize the size of the image or to prepare the picture suitable for output, such as printing or putting on the web. When a photograph is flattened, all of the layer styles, blending modes, and transparency effects are merged into a single layer. This can make the image simpler to manage than it was before. In Photoshop, you can flatten a photo by going to the Layer menu and selecting the Flatten Image option. Alternatively, you may right-click on any layer in the Layers panel and choose Flatten Image from the context menu.

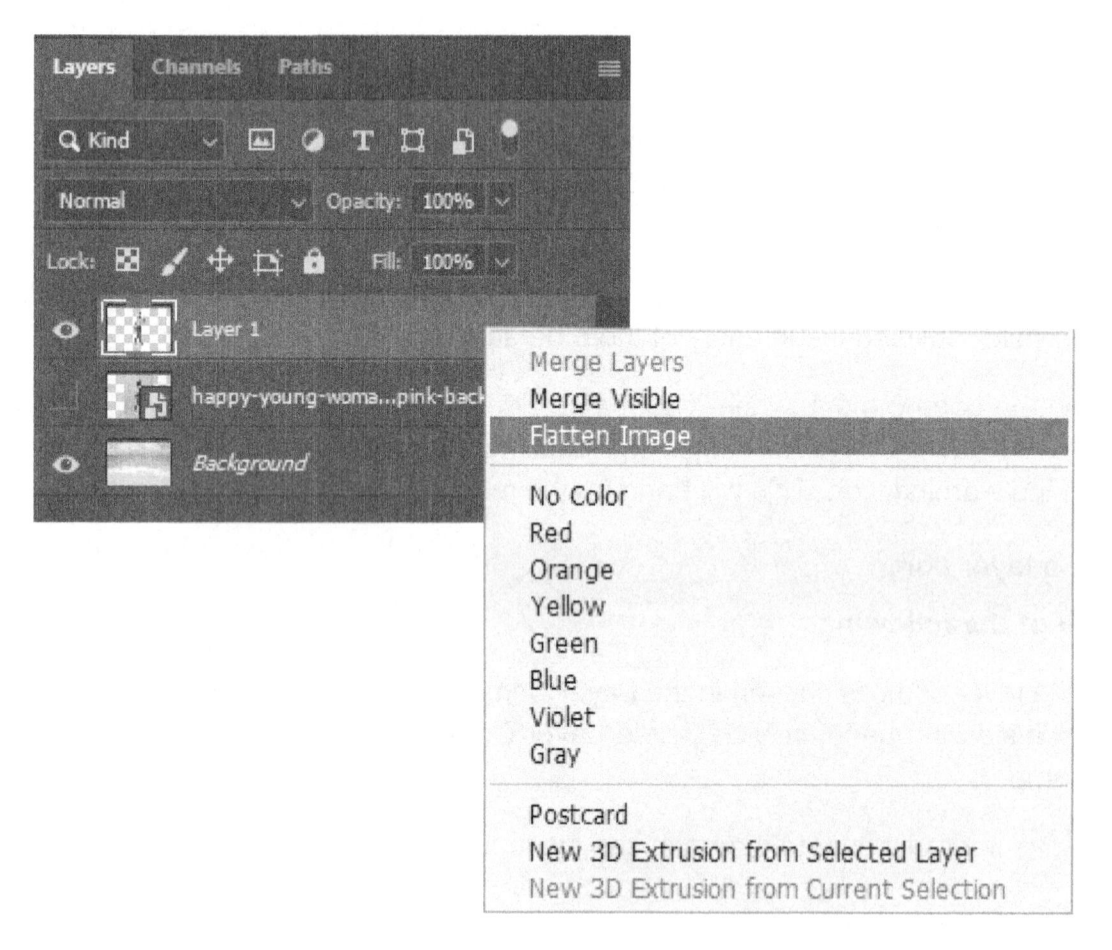

It is crucial to bear in mind that when you flatten a photo, you will no longer be able to make any more alterations to the individual layers inside the image. It is advised that before flattening the file, you first save a duplicate of the file with all of the layers intact. This is required if you need to retain the layers intact for future modification. After you have done flattening the photo, you can save it in various different file formats, depending on the requirements of your project. You might select to save the file as a JPEG or PNG file, for instance, if you are going to utilize it on the web once you have completed saving it. If you wish to print the photo, you should definitely save it as a high-resolution TIFF or PSD file before doing so.

You may save the file by heading to the File menu and selecting either Save or Save As from the drop-down menu. If you pick Save, Photoshop will save the file in the format it is presently using and will flatten all of the layers before doing so. If you click Save As from the file menu, you may pick a new file format and adjust various more parameters, such as the picture quality or the degree of compression that is employed. In addition to being able to save files and flatten them, Photoshop also gives users the opportunity to create and preserve presets for a broad number of file kinds and settings. You may, for instance, build a preset for storing JPEG photographs at a given quality level or for saving PNG files with transparency. Both of these are examples of typical usage for presets. Simply make your options in the Save As dialog box according to your preferences, and then use the Save Preset button to create a new preset.

Tip: When you flatten something, you always blend all of the layers into one. To combine just part of the layers in a file, first click the eye icons to conceal the levels that you do not want to merge, and then pick Combine Visible from the menu in the Layers panel to merge the layers that are still visible.

Zooming and scrolling using the Navigator panel

When working with a photo in Photos hop, it is vital to have a good view of the image and to be able to move around it without issue. The Navigator panel is one of the most crucial tools for accomplishing this work as it enables you to zoom in and out of your picture as well as scroll to various portions of it. In Photoshop, you can reach the Navigator panel by going to the Window menu and selecting the Navigator option.

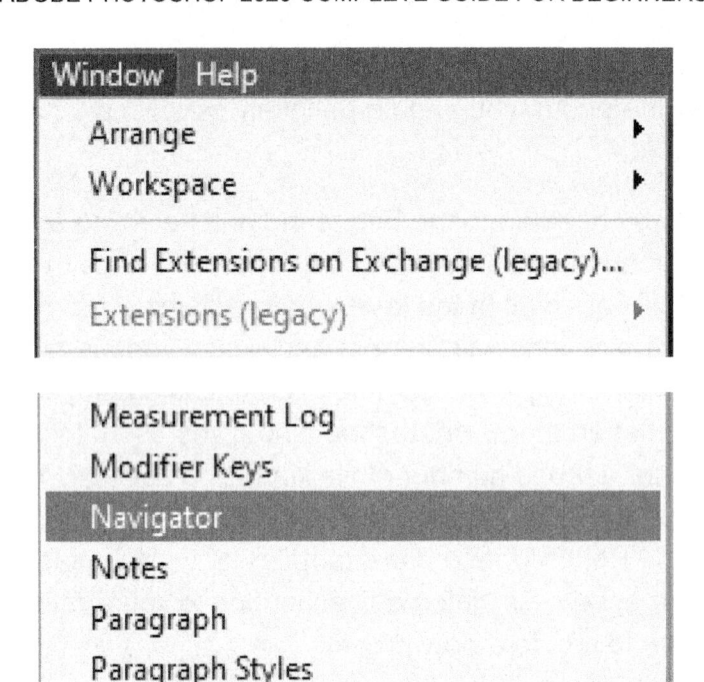

This will bring up a tiny window that provides a preview of your photo along with a rectangular box that represents the viewable section of the image. Clicking on this will bring up the viewable part of the image. You have the choice of utilizing the zoom slider that is situated at the bottom of the Navigator panel, or you may click on the plus (+) sign that is positioned at the bottom of the box and drag it to the right. Either approach will allow you to zoom in on the photo. This will force the photo to zoom in, which will result in it appearing bigger in the main window. You may use the zoom slider to zoom out, or you can click on the minus symbol (-) at the bottom of the box and drag it to the left. Both of these possibilities are located in the same area.

You may zoom in and out of an image using the mouse's scroll wheel or the plus and minus marks. Alternatively, you may use the shortcut keys on your keyboard. To enlarge a picture, you may do it by pressing the Ctrl key (on Windows) or the Command key (on Mac) in combination with the plus sign (+) key. To zoom out, click the Ctrl or Command key in combination with the negative sign (-) key on your computer. Use the Hand tool, which can be located in the toolbar on the left side of the screen, to move freely about the picture. This is yet another approach for navigating the picture. To use the Hand tool, first, click on the symbol representing the tool, and then click and drag anywhere on the picture to move it. When you are zoomed in on a given section of the image and wish to travel to a different area of the picture, this function may be incredibly beneficial.

When navigating around your image with the Navigator panel, it is crucial to bear in mind that this is only one of the tools accessible to you. Depending on your preferences and the way you generally operate, there are a range of other techniques to scroll, zoom in and out, and move about inside the picture. For instance, you may also use keyboard shortcuts to zoom in and out (such as Ctrl / Cmd +"+"or"-"), or you can use the zoom tool to pick a particular location to zoom in on. Both of these solutions are open to you.

Exploring design alternatives using Adobe Stock

Discovering fresh ideas and high-quality components for your design projects is made much simpler when you utilize Adobe Stock to study alternative design choices in Photoshop.

The following are some possible ways to take:

1. Searching for assets directly in Photoshop: You may search for assets straight inside Photoshop as Adobe Stock is integrated with Photoshop. This connection enables you to search for and license photographs without leaving the program. To do this, pick **"File"** from the menu bar, then click on **"Search Adobe Stock,"** and then begin your search.

2. Using the Libraries panel: The Libraries panel in Photoshop enables you to save and manage items such as photos, colors, and text styles. It also enables you to save and manage color palettes. You may also get assets from Adobe Stock from this panel by clicking on the **"Adobe Stock"** icon and looking through the available photographs.

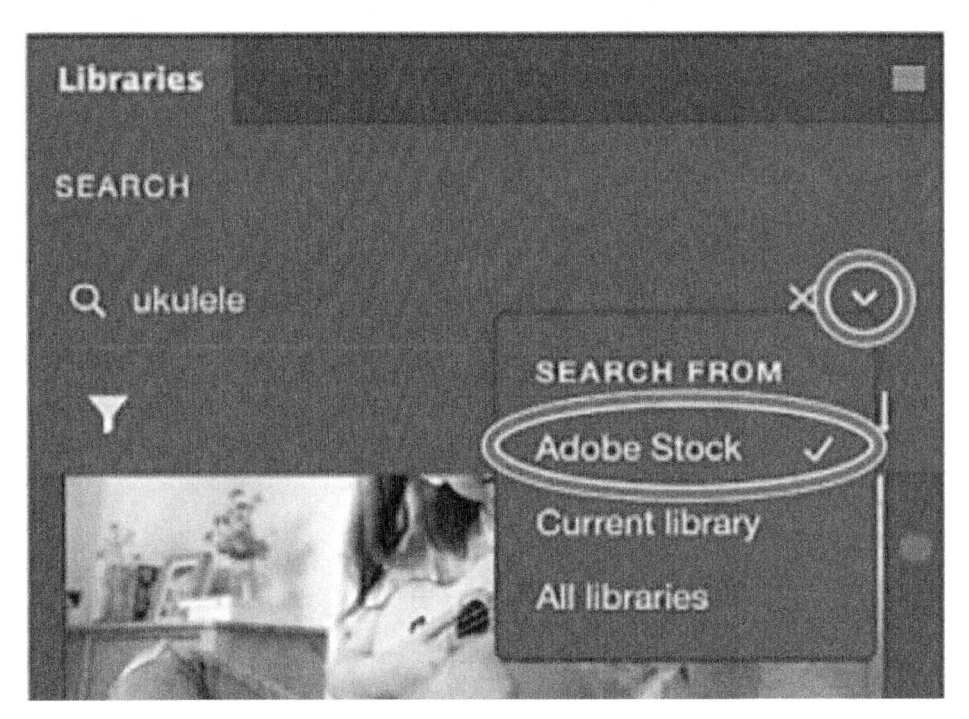

3. Trying out some various visual styles: Adobe Stock gives a huge range of photographs and graphics that may serve as a source of creativity for your design. You may experiment with a range of visual styles and uncover resources that match the subject matter of your project if you search for images using particular keywords or categories.

4. Customizing assets with Photoshop tools: Assets may be altered using Photoshop's capabilities once you have obtained a license for a photo from Adobe Stock. You may, for instance, modify the colors and tones of the picture by utilizing adjustment layers, or you can utilize selection tools to isolate particular portions of the image. Both of these op-tions are open to you.

5. The usage of templates: In addition, Adobe Stock gives a choice of templates that you may employ to aid you get your design project off the ground. You may search for tem-plates depending on their genre, such as brochures, flyers, or photos for social media, and then edit them to match your unique requirements.

Adobe Stock is a terrific tool that may aid you in exploring numerous design possibilities and locating resources of high quality to utilize in your projects. You can examine, license, and change photographs right from inside the software because of its integration with Photoshop. This helps you save time and streamlines your process.

CHAPTER 4: WORKING WITH SELECTIONS

About Selection and Selection Tools

The ability to isolate particular components of a picture is a crucial aspect of utilizing Adobe Photoshop for image manipulation, making it one of the program's most significant functions. You may remove backgrounds, build collages, and conduct other photo altering activities with the help of choices. In Photoshop, you have access to various distinct selection tools, each of which has a unique set of pros and downsides.

The following are some of the choosing tools that are utilized most commonly, as well as advice on how to apply them effectively:

1. Marquee tools

In Photoshop, the Marquee tools are the most fundamental selection tools accessible. The Marquee tools are a collection of selection tools that may be used in Adobe Photoshop to produce rectangular, elliptical, and single row/column selections. They may be initiated by either clicking on the Marquee tool icon in the Tools panel or by using the M key on your keyboard. You may find them under the section named Tools. The Elliptical Marquee tool is used to generate circular or oval possibilities, whereas the Rectangular Marquee tool is used t o construct rectangular selections. Both of these tools may be accessed under the Marquee menu. A single row or column of pixels can be chosen with the use of the Single Row Marquee tool or the Single Column Marquee tool, respectively.

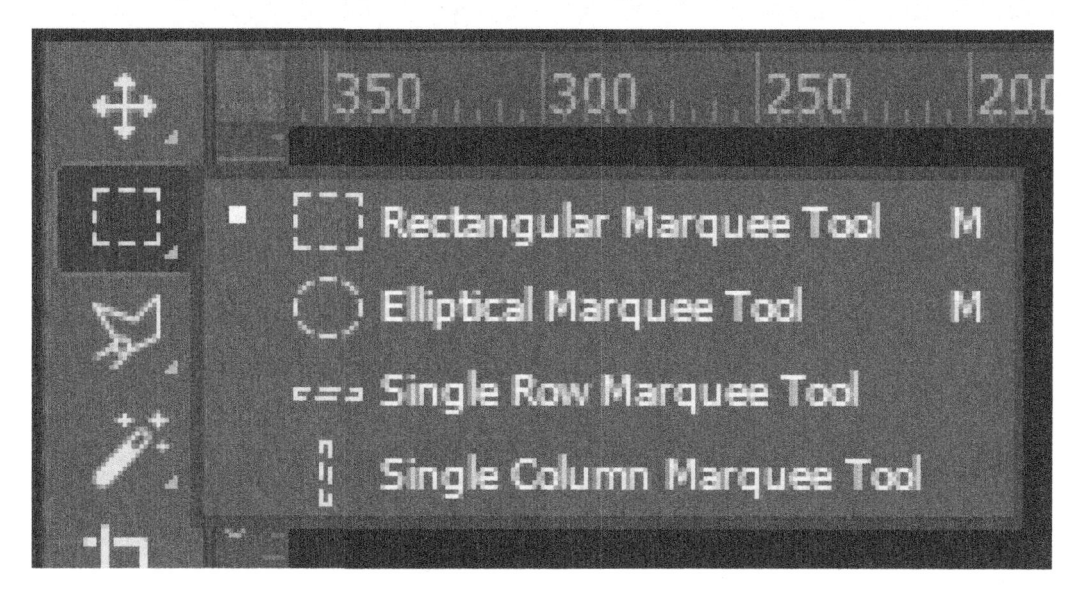

2. Lasso tools

The Lasso tools are freehand selection tools that help you make a selection around an area of a visual picture. These tools are located in the Selection group. There are three separate versions of lasso tools, the Lasso tool, the Magnetic Lasso tool, and the Polygonal Lasso tool. It is vital for you to manually draw the selection while using the Lasso tool as it is the most fundamental. You'll be able to make decisions with straight lines if you utilize the Polygonal Lasso tool, which needs you to click at specified spots all around the region you wish to choose. The Magnetic Lasso tool makes use of several anchor points so that it can automatically detect the edges of an item and snap to those edges.

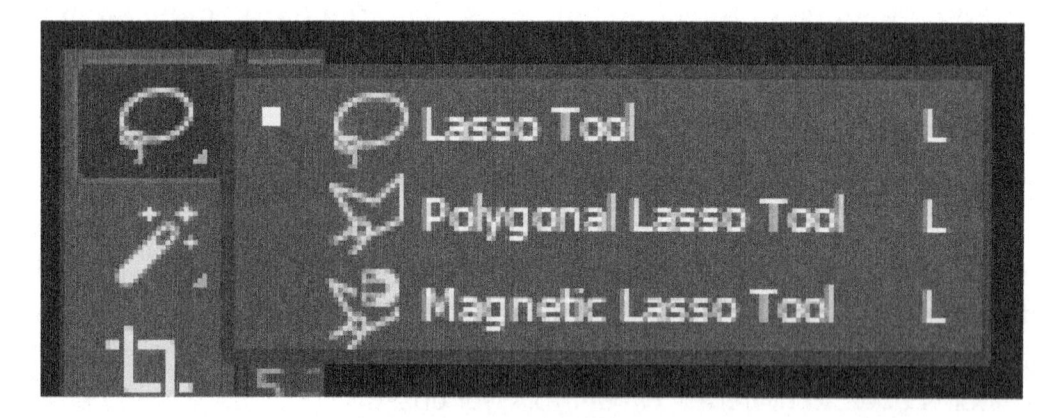

3. Magic Wand tool

The Magic Wand tool is a selection tool that enables you to choose all pixels within a given tolerance range that has a certain color or brightness. To employ this tool, you must first click on the region of the photo that you want to choose. Adobe Photoshop features an automatic selection tool that will choose any pixels that fall inside a defined tolerance range. To enlarge or shrink the range of colors that are selected, you can modify the tolerance level.

4. Quick Selection tool

The Quick Selection tool is an extremely powerful selection tool that helps you to identify complicated sections of an image swiftly and straightforwardly. To use this tool, just click and drag over the location you wish to choose, and the tool will handle the rest. Photoshop offers a tool that will automatically detect and pick pixels that have a color and texture that are similar to one another. You may create more specific selections by altering the brush size and the amount of its hardness.

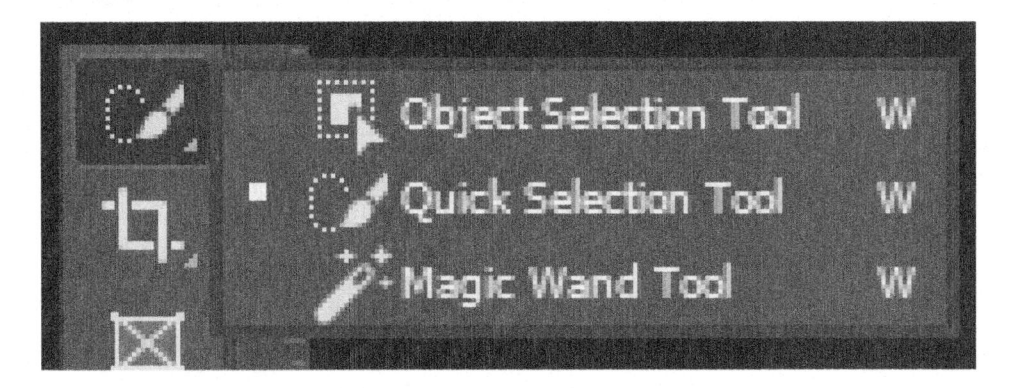

5. Select and Mask

You may further refine selections and get rid of background regions by utilizing the sophisticated Select and Mask tool in Photoshop, which is part of the application. This tool is very beneficial for choosing regions with intricate boundaries, such as hair or fur since it allows for more accurate control. To utilize this feature, first, build a selection using any of the various selection tools, and then go to the Options bar and click on the Select and Mask button. After that, you may employ the tools that are provided in the Select and Mask workspace to further refine your selection and get rid of undesirable backdrop regions.

6. Object Selection Tool

The goal of the Object Selection tool is to enable users to make selections in an image based on the items or subjects that are present in that picture. It achieves this by employing algorithms for machine learning and artificial intelligence so that it can automatically detect and pick items in a manner that is intelligent and correct.

Tips for Selection in Photoshop

Step 1. Make sure you're using the suitable tool for the task at hand: Each technique of choosing has its own set of pros and downsides. Utilize the tool that operates effectively for the location you wish to choose.

Step 2. Zoom in for increased accuracy: When picking options, it is beneficial to zoom in on the picture so that you can make more exact picks.

Step 3. Refine the edges: Make intricate choices more exact by utilizing the Select and Mask option, which also enables you get rid of ugly backdrop sections.

Step 4. Save selections: After you have made a selection, you should immediately save it as a selection or a layer mask so that you may readily edit it in the future.

Step 5. Experiment with various blending modes: You may generate some unique effects by playing with different blending modes and applying them to your choices.

Selecting and using the different selection tools available in Adobe Photoshop are key components of working with pictures. You can make more accurate selections and generate more effective alterations if you have a thorough knowledge of the various selection tools as well as their pros and limitations. You may become an expert in the art of selection in Photoshop with enough practice and experimentation, which will allow you to open up a world of creative possibilities.

Using cloud documents

Photoshop documents may grow fairly enormous, particularly when they incorporate high-resolution photographs that make significant use of layers. When working with documents that are kept online, uploading and downloading big file sizes takes more time, and if you have a restricted data plan, you may approach your data limit faster. You can edit online documents quickly and simply with Adobe Cloud Documents because they employ file formats that are intended expressly for network use. In the case of editing a Photoshop file as a cloud document, for instance, just the areas of the file that are touched by a change are delivered, rather than the whole file. If you use Photoshop on both a computer and an Apple iPad, and you save a photo as a cloud document, you'll find it on the **Home screen** of Photoshop on both devices, and it will always be updated with the most recent alterations you've made to it. When opposed to uploading a Photoshop file to a cloud-based fil e -sharing service, employing cloud documents can be a more time- and resource-effective solution. You may access a cloud document with only one click from the Photoshop Home interface. It will only upload the portions of a file that have been updated since it was last saved.

The usage of cloud documents is straightforward; all that is required of you is to save the document to the cloud documents service. After you have performed these steps, the name of the Photoshop project you are working on will be added with the ".psdc" filename extension to signal that it is now a cloud document, and you will be able to locate it in the cloud documents area of the Photoshop Home screen. Because the conversion to the PSDC format is done on autopilot, there is no need for you to give it any attention.

To open the photo file in Photoshop, double-click the Photoshop file thumbnail in Bridge. This will open up Photoshop. You have obtained the file from your local storage and opened it.

Go to the **"File"** menu, click **"Save As,"** and then select **"Save to Creative Cloud."** If the Save As dialog box displays, you should click the Save to Cloud Documents button before doing anything else.

If Photoshop provides a dialog box describing the difference between saving to Cloud Documents and saving on your local computer, click the Save to Cloud Documents option. This will conclude the lesson. **"Don't Show Again"** is another option you may choose, however if you reset Photoshop's settings, that option will be deselected.

Give the file a new name, and then click the Save button. The file is delivered to the place known as Cloud Documents. You may now see a cloud symbol before the filename in the document window tab, and the filename now ends in ".psdc".

You can also discover your cloud documents via the Creative Cloud app (mobile or desktop) and website, in the Your Files option in the Cloud Documents panel. The list may include cloud documents from other Adobe apps.

Close the document.

NOTE: Adobe Cloud papers are kept in a distinct online place than Creative Cloud Files or Creative Cloud Libraries. Now you'll open the cloud document. Again, this will be slightly different from opening a document from local storage.

In the Photoshop Home page, pick Your Files on the left side. It lists cloud documents you uploaded using your Adobe ID. You may also pick Home, where the recent list includes local and cloud documents you recently opened.

You may organize your cloud documents in folders on the server. When viewing Your Files on the Photoshop Home screen, click the folder icon towards the top to create a new folder.

If you wish to manage or remove a cloud document, click the document's ellipsis button in the Your Files list on the Photoshop Home screen, and pick Rename, remove, Make Available Offline Always, or Move.

Click the file you just saved. This downloads the file to your computer and opens it in Photoshop.

If you are working on a Photoshop Cloud Document (PSDC), how can you offer that file to a customer that demands a PSD file? You may achieve this by saving the document from the cloud to your local storage. Once again, the conversion is automated, which makes it simple and inconspicuous.

NOTE: You can't discover a cloud document on your computer by going through folders on your desktop; you see cloud documents on the Home screen in Photoshop. A cloud document is saved on Adobe servers and cached exclusively to your local storage. If you require a local copy of a cloud document, pick File > Save As and save it to your PC as stated to the left.

• Select **"Save As"** from the File menu. If you see a dialog box called Cloud Documents, click the Save On Your Computer link at the bottom to get to the more typical Save As dialog box. Take notice that the extension of the filename has been changed to .psd, as you are not storing this document to Cloud Documents but rather to the storage on your local device.

• Give the file a name and put it in the right location. You now have a copy in PSD format that is saved locally on your computer and can be disseminated and backed up in the normal manner (without the use of cloud services).

Using the Marquee Tools

The Marquee tools are:

• Rectangular Marquee tool

• Elliptical Marquee tool

• Single Row Marquee tools

• Single Column Marquee tool

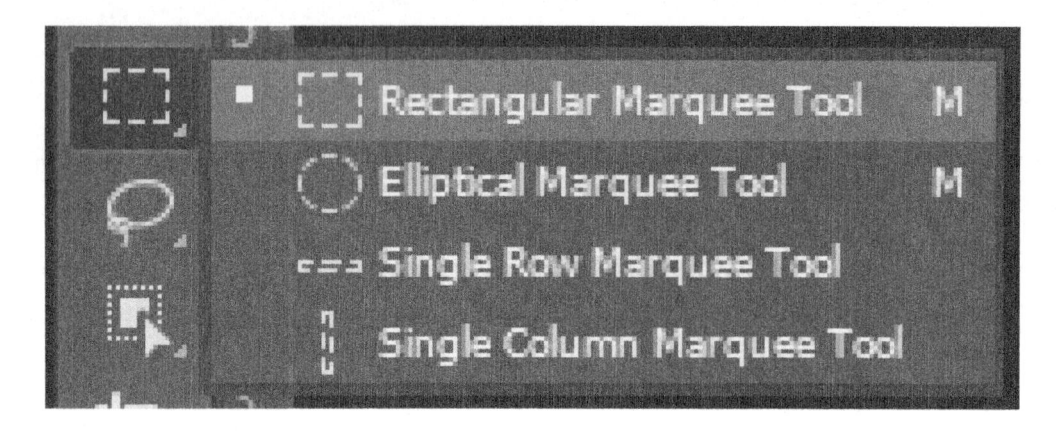

Rectangular Marquee tool

The Rectangular Marquee tool in Photoshop is a powerful selection tool that enables users to produce rectangular selections on a picture. Users may use this tool to crop a photograph. The tool may be used to a multitude of tasks, including cropping a photo, choosing a specified section of an image, or isolating a certain region of an image for additional editing. To employ the Rectangular Marquee tool in Photoshop, you will first need to open the photo that you want to change. After that, pick the Rectangular Marquee tool from the toolbar on the top. It is the tool represented by an icon in the form of a rectangle. T h e next step is to make a rectangle selection by clicking and dragging the cursor across the picture. You may alter the size of the selection by dragging the selection's sides or corners to make modifications. You may also maintain the selection's aspect ratio unchanged by holding down the Shift key while you move it. This will allow you to preserve the selection in its original dimensions.

After you have made the selection, you will have the option to execute a range of editing operations on the region that you have specified. You may, for instance, move the selection to a different area within the picture, apply a range of effects or modifications to the selection, or copy and paste the selection into a new layer or project. The technique of trimming a photograph is a frequent usage of the Rectangular Marquee tool. To accomplish this, first make a selection around the section of the photo that you wish to save, and then Select Crop from the picture menu in your editing software. Performing this step will lower the size of the picture to match that of the selection.

One further application for the Rectangular Marquee tool is to isolate a specified portion of a photograph for later modification. If you wanted to apply a particular effect or correction to a person's face in a group image, for instance, you would need to isolate that person's face first. To achieve this, first, use the Rectangular Marquee tool to draw a selection around the face, then copy and paste the selection into a new layer when you've done so. After that, you may apply any effects or alterations that you desire to the new layer without having those effects or adjustments impact the remainder of the photo. In addition to the fundamental Rectangular Marquee tool, Photoshop provides users with a range of other selection tools, including the Elliptical Marquee tool, the Single Row Marquee tool, and the Single Column Marquee tool. These tools may be found in the Tools menu. Users may pick various areas and shapes inside an image with more ease and precision due of the fact that each of these tools has its o w n set of specialized characteristics and capabilities.

Elliptical Marquee tool

You may generate a circular or elliptical selection of a segment of a photo with the aid of Adobe Photoshop's Elliptical Marquee tool, which is a sophisticated selection tool that's part of the application. This tool comes in quite helpful when it comes to the design of rounded forms or the choosing of round items like buttons or logos. When you initially pick the Elliptical Marquee tool, you will see a number of options in the top menu bar that enable you to adjust the size and form of your selection. You may accomplish this by moving the corner handles or dragging the center point of the selection. The following is a collection of useful ideas and instructions on how to utilize the Elliptical Marquee tool in Photoshop:

1. Creating a circular selection: To produce a selection in the shape of a circle that is perfectly round, press and hold the Shift key while dragging out the selection with the Elliptical Marquee tool. This confines the possibilities to a circular form that is exactly round.

2. Making an elliptical selection: To make an elliptical selection, use the Elliptical Marquee tool to move the selection outwards. This will provide elliptical selection.

Hold down the Shift key and drag one of the selection handles to the left or right to resize the ellipse. This will allow you to adjust the shape of the ellipse.

3. Feathering the selection: This entails lowering the sharpness of the selection's boundaries so that it merges in more naturally with the backdrop. To feather the selection, go to **Select > Feather** menu item and choose a value in the range of 1 to 100 pixels.

4. Inverting the selection: There may be situations when you need to choose the backdrop rather than the foreground. To achieve this, either go to the **Select > Inverse** menu item on your computer's menu bar or use the keyboard shortcut **Ctrl + Shift + I** (Windows) or **Command + Shift + I** (Mac).

5. Utilizing the Marquee tool for various shapes: In Photoshop, the Elliptical Marquee tool is only one of the countless distinct kinds of Marquee tools. The Rectangular Marquee tool may be used to make choices that are either square or rectangular. The Single Row Marquee tool and the Single Column Marquee tool, on the other hand, may be used to pick one row or column of pixels at a time.

6. Adding to or removing from the selection: You can add to the selection by holding down the Shift key while making a new selection. This will allow you to add more things to the selection. If you create a new selection while simultaneously holding down the Alt key (on Windows) or the Option key (on Mac), you can reduce the size of the existing selection.

7. Duplicating the selection: When you have done making a selection using the Elliptical Marquee tool, you can duplicate it onto a new layer by selecting **Layer > New > Layer via Copy** from the menu bar or by using the keyboard shortcut **Ctrl + J** (Windows) or **Command + J** (Mac).

8. Moving the selection: Once you have generated a selection using the Elliptical Marquee tool, you can move it around the canvas by using the Move tool or by hitting the arrow keys on your keyboard.

9. Applying effects to the selection: After you have generated a selection using the Elliptical Marquee tool, you can then apply a range of effects to it including blur, color correction, and filters. The effect may be applied by simply selecting it from the applicable menu or dialog box.

10. Saving the selection: Once you have produced a selection using the Elliptical Marquee tool, you may save it as a new selection for later use. Pick Select > Save Selection, and then give the selection a name before storing it. After that, whenever you wish to load the selection, you may do so by going to Select > Load Selection and picking the selection from the list that displays.

The Elliptical Marquee tool in Adobe Photoshop is a strong and handy tool that enables you to produce circular or elliptical selections in your pictures. To conclude, this tool allows you to generate circular or elliptical selections in your photographs. You may swiftly create proper selections and add a number of effects to them to generate amazing consequences in your images if you learn the various approaches and possibilities that are accessible with this application and make use of all of its capabilities.

Single Row Marquee tool

One of the selection tools that may be utilized in Adobe Photoshop is referred to as the

Single Row Marquee tool. It allows you the opportunity to make a selection on a photo that is contained inside a single row, either horizontally or vertically. This tool is highly helpful for picking certain areas of an image that are only one pixel wide or for cropping a given row of pixels in an image.

Additionally, this tool may be used to pick certain portions of a picture that are only one pixel tall. To begin utilizing the Single Row Marquee tool in Photoshop, you will first need to open the photo that you want to change. After that, pick the Single Row Marquee tool from the tool bar on the left. It is the tool represented by an icon consisting of a single horizontal line.

Next, click on the photo to indicate where you want to begin the selection, either vertically or horizontally, and then drag the mouse across the image to produce a row selection that is one pixel wide. If you need to pick several rows or columns, you can simply repeat the method by making a new selection for each row or column as needed. This will allow you to pick numerous rows or columns at once. After you have made the selection, you will have the option to execute a range of editing operations on the region that you have specified. You may, for instance, move the selection to a different area within the picture, apply a range of effects or modifications to the selection, or copy and paste the selection into a new layer or project. The Single Row Marquee tool is typically used to crop a single row of pixels inside a photograph. To achieve this, first use the Single Row Marquee tool to construct a selection around the row of pixels, and then go to the Image menu and click the Crop option. Performing this step will lower the size of the picture to match that of the selection.

The Single Row Marquee tool may also be used to choose particular sections of a photograph that are just one pixel wide. This is one of its numerous uses. You may, for instance, need to pick a single pixel line of text to move it to a different region of the picture or apply a certain effect to it. To achieve this, first, use the Single Row Marquee tool to produce a selection that spans the row that is one pixel wide, and then copy and paste the selection into a new layer. After that, you may apply any effects or alterations that you desire to the new layer without having those effects or adjustments impact the remainder of the photo. Photoshop provides users with a range of selection tools, including the Rectangular Marquee tool, the Elliptical Marquee tool, and the Single Column Marquee tool, in addition to the Single Row Marquee tool. Users may pick various areas and shapes inside an image with more ease and precision due to the fact that each of these tools has its own set of specialized characteristics and functions.

Single Column Marquee tool

The Single Column Marquee tool in Adobe Photoshop is a selection tool that enables you to produce precise vertical selections of an image that are just one pixel wide. This tool is highly handy for making narrow strips inside a picture that have a predefined width, as well as for choosing a certain column of pixels for editing reasons. When you initially pick the Single Column Marquee tool, you will see a number of options in the top menu bar that enable you to adjust the size and form of your selection. You may accomplish this by moving the corner handles or dragging the corners of the marquee.

The following is a collection of some useful advice and suggestions concerning the usage of the Single Column Marquee tool in Photoshop:

1. Creating a single-column selection: Simply click on the border of the photo where you want the column to begin, and then drag the selection tool down to the bottom of the image to produce a selection of a single column. The width of the selection may be adjusted at this stage by dragging the selection handles to the left or right of the screen.

2. Converting a rectangular selection to a single column selection: If you already have a rectangular selection and want to change it into a selection of a single column, all you have to do is select the Single Column Marquee tool and click on the edge of the rectangular selection where you want the column to begin. The rectangle selection will then be modified. After that, to make the single-column selection, you may drag the selection tool down to the bottom of the picture.

3. Feathering the selection: This entails lowering the sharpness of the selection's boundaries so that it merges in more naturally with the backdrop. To feather the selection, go to the **Select > Feather** menu item and choose a value in the range of 1 to 100 pixels.

4. Inverting the selection: There may be situations when you need to choose the backdrop rather than the foreground. To achieve this, either go to the **Select > Inverse** menu item on your computer's menu bar or use the keyboard shortcut **Ctrl + Shift + I** (Windows) or **Command + Shift + I** (Mac).

5. Adding to or removing from the selection: You may add to the selection by holding down the Shift key while making a new selection. This will allow you to add more things to the selection. If you create a new selection while simultaneously holding down the Alt key (on Windows) or the Option key (on Mac), you can reduce the size of the existing selection.

6. Duplicating the selection: After you have made a selection using the Single Column

Marquee tool, you can replicate it onto a new layer by going to Layer> New > Layer via Copy or by using the keyboard shortcut **Ctrl + J** (Windows) or **Command+ J** (Mac). Alternatively, you may use the shortcut **Ctrl+ J** (Windows) or **Command+ J** (Mac).

7. Moving the selection: Once you have generated a selection using the Single Column Marquee tool, you can move it across the canvas by using the Move tool or by hitting the arrow keys on your keyboard. This step is optional.

8. Applying effects to the selection: After you have made a selection using the Single Column Marquee tool, you can then apply a range of effects to it including blur, color correction, or filters. The effect may be applied by simply selecting it from the applicable menu or dialog box.

9. storing the selection: When you have done making a selection using the Single Column Marquee tool, you have the option of storing it as a new selection that you may use in the future. Pick **Select > Save Selection**, and then give the selection a name before storing it. After that, whenever you wish to load the selection, you may do so by going to **Select > Load Selection** and picking the selection from the list that displays.

The Single Column Marquee tool in Adobe Photoshop is an accurate and convenient tool that enables you to produce vertical selections in your pictures that are just one pixel wide. You may swiftly create precise selections and add a range of effects to them to generate amazing consequences in your images if you learn the various approaches and possibilities that are accessible with this application and make use of all of its capabilities.

Using the Magic Wand tool

Using the Magic Wand tool, you may choose pixels that have a given hue or range of colors. It is especially beneficial in circumstances when the color or tone of the place that you wish to choose shows out clearly against its background. The Tolerance option sets the range of tonal levels that the Magic Wand tool will choose, beginning with the pixel that is presently chosen.

A tolerance value of 32, which is the default, will pick the color you click in addition to 32 shades lighter and 32 shades darker of that color. Try boosting the value of the Tolerance attribute if the Magic Wand tool isn't picking the whole region that you want it to. If the tool picks too many things, consider reducing the value of the Tolerance parameter.

Step 1. Select the Zoom tool in the Tools panel, and then zoom in so that you can view the full sand dollar in detail.

Step 2. Select the Magic Wand tool, buried under the Object Selection tool.

Step 3. In the settings bar, validate that the Tolerance value is 32. This number defines the range of colors the wand chooses.

Step 4. Click the Magic Wand tool on the red backdrop outside the sand dollar.

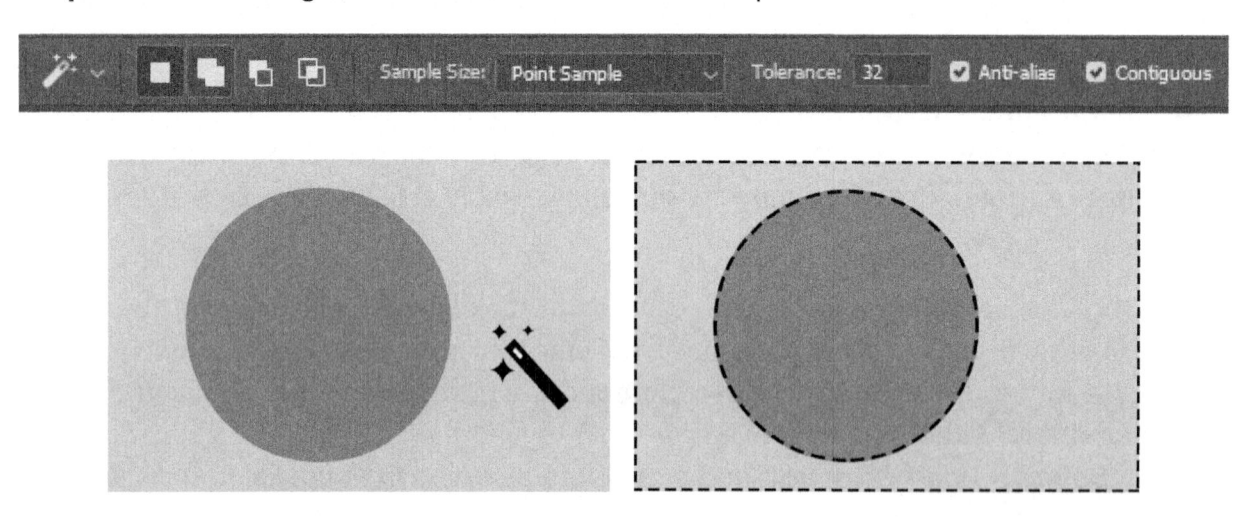

Because all of the colors in the background are near enough to the pixel you clicked (within the 32 levels set in the Tolerance option), the Magic Wand tool accurately picked the red back-ground. This is because the Tolerance option allows for up to 3 2 levels. However, the shell is the component that we are interested in, so let's begin again.

TIP: If a selection is made using the Magic Wand tool takes up an excessive number of identical colors outside of the region you want to choose, you could try selecting the Contiguous option accessible in the options bar.

Step 5. Pick Select > Deselect.

Step 6. Place the Magic Wand tool on the sand dollar, and then click.

Pay particular attention to the moving marquis that serves as a selection and appears over the sand dollar. If this was a faultless choice, the marquee that tells which objects have been picked would precisely follow the rim of the sand dollar.

However, be aware that some of the interior areas of the sand dollar exhibit selection marquees. This is because the colors of these places vary from the color you clicked by more than 32 levels, which is the value for the tolerance. Because it does not cover all of the interior color selections, the selection that is presently being utilized is useless.

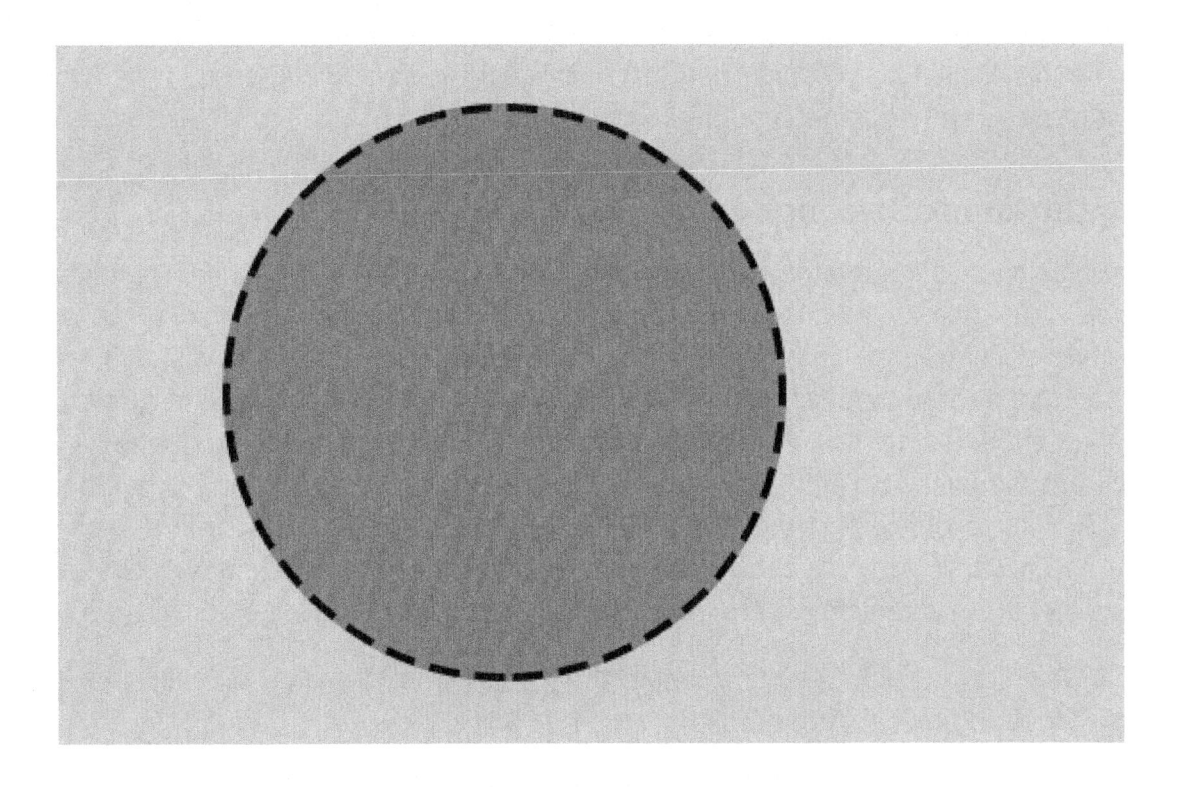

When you wish to choose a topic that is typically the same color and value as the backdrop, against a decently solid background, you can frequently handle this problem by boosting the value of the Tolerance option. However, the possibility that a large Tolerance number might also chose unwanted regions of the backdrop grows in proportion to the intricacy of the subject or background. When presented with a circumstance like this one, it is advised that you make use of an alternate selection tool, such as the Quick Selection tool. You'll do that next, but before you do, let's wipe away the option that's currently active.

Step 7. Choose **Select > Deselect**.

The backdrop of an image may be erased from a photograph using the Magic Wand tool, which is a common application of that tool. To achieve this, you will first need to choose the backdrop color by using the Magic Wand tool. The next step is to invert the selection by going to the choose menu and selecting the Inverse option. This will choose the object rather than the background. After that, you may copy the selection, then paste it into a new layer or document, after which you can apply a different backdrop or effect. Altering the color of a particular location inside an image is yet another use for the Magic Wand tool. To achieve this, you will first need to choose the section of the image whose color you wish to modify by using the Magic Wand tool. The next step is to choose

Hue/Saturation under Adjustments after going to the Image menu and selecting Adjustments. After that, you may edit the color of the selected region by modifying the hue, saturation, and brightness of the color.

Using the Quick Selection tool

Simply clicking or dragging the Quick Selection tool inside a topic forces the tool to seek the subject's edges as it looks for those edges. You may adjust the selection by adding or deleting sections of it until you have precisely the region that you wish. The Quick Selection tool performs better than the Magic Wand tool because it is more aware of the substance of the picture and does not depend solely on color similarity to make its picks. Try utilizing the Quick Selection tool to see if it performs a better job of picking the sand dollar. TIP: Take notice that the Quick Selection tool seeks for a topic in the direction outward from where you click or drag the tool, whereas the Object Selection tool searches for a subject in the direction inward from where you drag that tool's selection area.

Step 1. Select the Quick Selection tool in the Tools panel. It's grouped with the Object Selection tool and Magic Wand tool.

Step 2. Select Enhance Edge in the options bar.

By selecting the Enhance Edge option, you should be able to make a selection of greater quality, with edges that are more accurate to the object. When you utilize Enhance Edge, you might notice a slight delay if you are running on a system that is particularly slow or very old.

Step 3. Click or drag within the image (do not cross over into the background).

If the Quick Selection tool contains regions that are not part of the topic, you can remove undesirable areas from the selection by clicking or dragging over them while holding down the Alt (Windows) or Option (macOS) key. This will delete the undesirable sections from the selection. That is the shortcut that you may use to pick the icon labeled "Subtract from Selection" in the options bar. The Quick Selection tool evaluates what material is most likely connected with the region where you clicked or dragged and then identifies the complete edge automatically, picking the entire sand dollar in the process. Because it is so basic, the Quick Selection tool can rapidly pick out the sand dollar for attention. If the Quick Selection tool does not quickly finish the selection for you, you may manually finish it by clicking or dragging over the places you wish to include in the selection.

Moving a specified area

One of the most significant parts of photo editing in Adobe Photoshop is the ability to relocate to a selected region. Users may rearrange things, make tweaks to composition, and create one of -a-kind image arrangements due to the flexibility to manipulate a selection. A chosen location in Photoshop may be moved using a number of tools, such as the Move tool, the Arrow keys, and the Transform tools. These tools are all accessible via the Edit menu. To move a selected area using the Move tool, first choose the area you wish to move using any of the selection tools that are available in Photoshop, such as the Lasso tool, the Magic Wand tool, or the Rectangular Marquee tool. Next, choose the region you wish to relocate using the relocate tool. Finally, move the chosen region using the Move tool. After the selection has been made, go to the toolbar and choose the Move tool from the menu. It is the instrument represented by the picture of an arrow with four heads.

The next step is to click and drag the region that has been selected to transfer it to the new spot. You may also move the selection in step-by-step increments by using the arrow keys found on your keyboard. When using the arrow keys to move the selection, pressing the Shift key at the same time will move the selection in greater increments. You can utilize the Transform tools if you need to resize or rotate the chosen region when you are moving it. Simply utilizing the keyboard shortcut Ctrl +T (Windows) or Command +T (Mac) will allow you to access the tools that belong to the Transform category. Alternatively, you may go to the Edit menu and pick Transform from there. This will enable the Transform controls around the selected region, enabling you to resize and rotate it after it has been selected.

When you are in the Transform mode, you may move the selected region by clicking and dragging inside the Transform controls. When you are in the Transform mode, you may also use the arrow keys on your keyboard to move the selection in gradually smaller amounts. In addition to the Move tool and the other tools in the Transform category, Photoshop includes additional tools, such as the Content-Aware Move tool and the Puppet Warp tool, which may be used to move particular areas. The information-Aware Move tool is great for photo retouching and editing as it enables users to move selected parts while automatically filling in the surrounding region with information that is equivalent to the moved selection. Because it allows users the opportunity to distort and warp chosen areas in some distinct ways, the Puppet Warp tool is suitable for the development of o n e -o f -a-kind, aesthetic effects. It is vital to keep in mind the layer structure of your picture anytime you move a defined location around in your image. When you move a selection on a layer that has parts of transparency, the layer below it will be seen, but when you move a selection on a layer that has a solid background color, all that will happen is that the selection will be moved on top of the background.

Using the Object Selection tool

Users may pick things inside a photograph in a rapid and exact manner using the Object Selection tool, especially when working with circumstances that are intricate and crowded. To employ the Object Selection tool in Photoshop, you will first need to open the photo that you want to change. After that, pick the Object Selection tool from the toolbar at the top of the screen. The tool may be distinguished by its icon, which resembles a rectangle with a dashed line around it.

Next, pick the object you wish to deal with by clicking and dragging the item Selection tool over it. The tool will recognize and pick the object automatically as long as it is positioned inside the limits of the rectangle. You may make adjustments to the selection by dragging the handles around the object. This allows you to adjust the sizes of the selection as well as its placement.

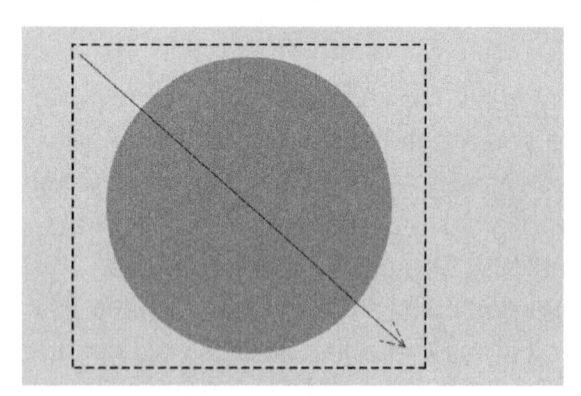

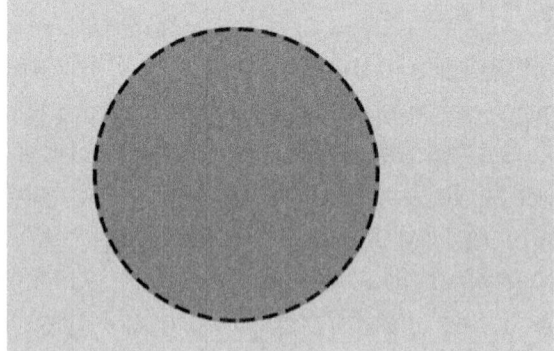

The capacity of the Object Selection tool to discriminate between the numerous sorts of items that may be discovered in an image is one of its most essential characteristics. For instance, if a photo includes both people and automobiles, the item Selection tool may detect and pick each object independently, allowing for more accurate editing. This is made feasible by the fact that the tool may pick numerous things at once. The Object

Selection tool not only enables users to choose items from inside a photograph, but it also provides them the opportunity to further refine their selections. You may utilize the Select and Mask option, for instance, to change the bounds of the selection. Additionally, you may use the lasso tool or the brush tool to either add to or take away from the selection.

The ability of the Object Selection tool to automatically pick various items inside an image is yet another vital feature that it delivers. To achieve this, you will need to utilize the Object Selection tool, which can be accessible by clicking and dragging it over various things inside the photo. You'll be able to execute mass tweaks or modifications quickly and rapidly owing to the tool's capacity to instantly detect and choose any item in the scene.

The Object Selection tool also includes various choices and configurations, all of which may be modified to match the requirements of a specific project. You may alter the tool's brush size and hardness, for instance, which might be handy when picking things with varying degrees of intricacy and complexity. Additionally, the tool's brush color may be modified. The "Snap to Edges" feature is yet another handy option that can be found on the Object Selection tool. This feature enables the tool to instantly snap to the boundaries of items in a photograph, which makes it much simpler to pick intricate lines and shapes.

Manipulating Selections

Selections can be moved, relocated even as they are being made, and even copied by the user. In this part, you will explore numerous strategies for modifying choices. The bulk of these approaches apply to any selection; but, in this case, you will use them using the Elliptical Marquee tool, which enables you to choose accurate ovals or circles. The addition of modifier keys, which may save you time and lessen the number of arm movements you need to complete, is one of the most beneficial things you will find in this area.

Repositioning a selection marquee while creating it

It might be challenging to pick ellipses and rectangles at the same time. Sometimes the options may not be centered properly, or the width-to-height ratio won't be the appropriate match for what you desire. During this assignment, you will uncover tactics such as two important keyboard-mouse combinations that might make your work in Photoshop simpler. These tactics can be highly beneficial. Be sure to carefully follow the directions when you carry out this exercise, and don't forget to keep the mouse button or any other relevant keys pressed the whole time. If you unintentionally let go of the mouse button at the incorrect moment, you need merely complete the exercise all over again from the very first step.

Here, we are dealing with a dish of shells.

Step 1. Click the plate of shells at the bottom of the document window after selecting the Zoom tool, and then zoom in to at least **100%** view (use **200%** view if the complete plate of shells can still fit in the document window on your screen).

Step 2. Choose the **Elliptical Marquee** tool, which is nestled away under the Rectangular Marquee tool.

Step 3. Position the pointer over the photo, and then while holding down the left mouse button, slide the cursor in a diagonal way across the oval plate to make a selection.

It is not an issue if the form of the plate that you have picked does not match it yet.

NOTE: You do not have to include every pixel on the plate of shells; nevertheless, the selection should be the form of the plate and should comfortably include the shells. If you unintentionally release the mouse button while creating the selection, you will need to construct the selection again. In the great majority of situations, including the current one, the new choice takes the place of the previous one.

Step 4. While using the left mouse button, retain pressure on the space bar and continue to move the selection. You are now changing the selection rather than resizing it as you did previously. Adjust the selection so that it is positioned so that i t is more closely aligned with the plate.

Step 5. With great care, release the spacebar (but do not remove the mouse button) and continue to drag while striving to make the size and form of the selection correspond as nearly as possible to the oval plate of shells. If it is needed to do so, hit and hold the space bar once again, and then use your mouse to slide the selection marquee into position around the plate of shells.

TIP: Other drawing tools in Photoshop, such as the shape tools and the Pen tool, may also benefit from the strategy of sketching while holding down the spacebar to change the design while it is being generated.

Step 6. When you are convinced that the selection border is in the proper position, you may let go of the mouse button.

Step 7. Select **View > Fit on Screen** or use the slider in the Navigator panel to lower the zoom view so that you can see all of the objects in the document window. Alternatively, you may pick **View > Zoom Out** to see more of the items.

Moving selected pixels using a keyboard shortcut

Now you'll utilize a keyboard shortcut to move the selected pixels onto the shadow box. The shortcut temporarily transforms the current tool to the Move tool, so you don't need to pick it from the Tools panel.

Step 1. If the plate of shells is still not picked, repeat the preceding exercise to choose it.

Step 2. With the Elliptical Marquee tool chosen in the Tools panel, hit Ctrl (Windows) or Command (macOS) and hover the cursor within the selection. Continue to hold down the key for the following step.

NOTE: In step 2, if you try to move the pixels but Photoshop shows an alert reading "Could not use the Move tool because the layer is locked," make sure you start dragging by locating the pointer within the selection. The pointer icon now incorporates a pair of scissors, suggesting that the selection will be cut from its present place.

Step 3. While continuing to hold down the Ctrl or Command key, move the plate of shells onto the region of the shadow box labeled "C." (You'll use another approach to nudge the oval plate into the exact place in a minute.)

Step 4. Release the mouse button and the key, but don't deselect the picture.

Moving a selection using the arrow keys

You may make modest modifications to the location of selected pixels by using the arrow keys. You can shift the selection in increments of 1 pixel or 10 pixels. If a selection becomes deselected accidently, choose **Select > Reselect**. When a selection tool is active in the Tools panel, the arrow keys nudge the selection boundary, but not the contents. When the Move tool is active, the arrow keys move both the selection boundary and its contents. You'll use the arrow keys to nudge the plate of shells. Before you begin, make sure the picture is still chosen in the document window.

Step 1. Select the Move tool and hit the Up Arrow key on your keyboard a few times to move the oval higher.

Notice that each time you touch the arrow key, the picture travels 1 pixel. Experiment by pushing the other arrow keys to see how they influence the selection.

Step 2. Hold down the Shift key as you press an arrow key.

When you hold down the Shift key, the selected pixels move 10 pixels every time you hit an arrow key. Selection edges, guidelines, and other visible elements that aren't genuine objects are termed extras, therefore another approach to conceal the selection edges is to uncheck the **View > Extras** menu or hit its keyboard shortcut**, Ctrl + H** (Windows) or **Command + H** (macOS).

Sometimes the selection marquee might distract you while you make revisions. You can conceal the margins of a selection momentarily without really deselecting it and then show the selection boundary once you've done the edits.

Step 3. Choose **View > Show > Selection Edges** to deselect the command, concealing the selection boundary around the picture.

Step 4. Use the arrow keys to move the picture until it's positioned over the silhouette so that there's a shadow on the left and bottom of the plate. Then click **View > Show > Selection Edges** to display the selection boundary again.

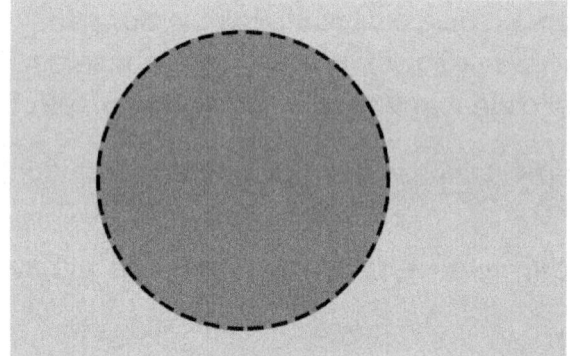

Step 5. Choose **Select > Deselect** or press **Ctrl + D** (Windows) or **Command + D** (macOS).

Step 6. Choose **File > Save** to save your work thus far.

Selecting with the lasso tools

Photoshop contains three lasso tools:

• The Lasso tool.

• The Polygonal Lasso tool.

• The Magnetic Lasso tool.

• The Lasso tool.

The Lasso tool

One of the core selection tools in Adobe Photoshop is the lasso, which is typically used to pick out irregular objects or shapes in a photograph. Using the tool, you may click and drag all around the thing you wish to choose to generate freeform choices.

Basic Selection: Simply choose the Lasso tool from the toolbar, click and hold down the mouse button at the beginning of the selection, and then draw a circle around the object while continuing to hold down the mouse button. Release the mouse button to stop the selection when you've returned to your original starting position.

Straight Edge Lasso: While using the Lasso tool to make a selection, hold down the Alt (Windows) or Option (Mac) key. You may continue to utilize the Lasso tool while making segments of straight lines by doing.

Magnetic Lasso: This automated selection tool allows you to make selections around an item by automatically snagging to its edge. Click and hold down the Lasso tool button in the toolbar, then choose the Magnetic Lasso tool to utilize it. The tool will begin to snap to the edge of the item as you move it around once you click once on the edge of the thing you wish to pick.

Adding to a Selection: To add to an existing selection, just hold down the Shift key while using the Lasso tool. This will allow you to add to the selection without deselecting the region you have already picked.

Subtracting from a Selection: Hold down the Alt (Windows) or Option (Mac) key when using the Lasso tool to delete items from an existing selection. By doing this, you'll be able to eliminate areas from the selection without deselecting the ones you've already chosen.

Feathering choices: By feathering your selections, you may give them smoother borders that will make it simpler to incorporate them into the background of the picture. Choose the Feather option from the Select menu and the required quantity of feathering to apply to a selection.

Intersecting Selections: While holding down the Shift key, you may use the Lasso tool to create a circle around the location where two selections intersect. By doing this, a selection will be produced that only contains the regions where the two selections overlap.

Copying and Pasting Selections: Selections may be copied and pasted by choosing **Edit > Copy (Ctrl + C)** on a computer running Windows or Command +C on (Mac) and Edit> Paste (Ctrl+ Von a computer running Mac) after making a selection using the Lasso tool.

Saving Selections: By choosing the Save Selection option from the Select menu, you may store selections for later use. By doing this, you may recover the selection again later even after Photoshop or the photo has been closed.

The Polygonal Lasso tool

With the aid of straight lines formed between points, the Polygonal Lasso tool in Adobe Photoshop enables you generate perfect selections in your pictures. It is especially effective for picking out items with strange forms, including the outlines of structures, products, or letters.

Here are some suggestions and strategies for utilizing Photoshop's Polygonal Lasso tool:

1. Creating a selection: Using the Polygonal Lasso tool, click on the edge of the item you want to pick, and then drag the mouse along the edge, clicking each time you wish to adjust the direction of the selection. Click on the beginning point to close the choice when you've reached the end.

2. Adding to a selection: To increase a selection, click the edge of the object you wish to include in the selection while holding down the Shift key. The Polygonal Lasso tool may then be used to keep adding points to the selection.

3. Subtracting from a selection: To take away from a selection, click on the edge of the object you wish to remove from the selection while holding down the Alt (Windows) or Option (Mac) key. The Polygonal Lasso tool may then be used to continue deleting points from the selection.

4. Editing the selection: Click on the selection using the Polygonal Lasso tool to activate the selection boundary. This will allow you to adjust the option. Then, you may delete a point by using the Delete or Backspace key, or you can erase a piece of the selection by hitting the Alt or Option keys on a Mac or Windows computer.

5. Feathering the selection: Feathering the selection softens the edges, allowing it to merge in with the background more naturally. Go to **Select > Feather** and choose a value between 1 and 100 pixels to feather the selection.

6. Intersecting selections: Holding down the Shift key while using the Polygonal Lasso tool to generate the initial selection will allow you to only choose the region where two options intersect. Create the second selection by holding down the Shift and Alt keys (Windows) or the Shift and Option keys (Mac). The region where the two selections overlap will be the final selection.

7. Copying and pasting a selection: A selection may be copied and pasted once it has been generated with the Polygonal Lasso tool by selecting **Edit > Copy** or by using the **Ctrl + C** (Windows) or **Command + C** (Mac) keyboard shortcut. The selection may then be pasted into a new layer or document by selecting **Edit > Paste** or by using the **Ctrl + V** (Windows) or **Command + V** (Mac) keyboard shortcut.

8. Saving the selection: After using the **Polygonal Lasso tool** to produce a selection, you may store it as a new selection for later use. Give it a name by selecting Save Selection under Select. The selection may then be loaded at any time by selecting it from the list under **Select > Load Selection**.

The Magnetic Lasso tool

In Adobe Photoshop, the Magnetic Lasso tool is a sophisticated selection tool that enables users to create perfect selections of complicated objects and forms. It is a modified version of the normal Lasso tool, which lets users generate freehand selections by clicking and dragging all around an image's topic or region. To make perfect selections, though, you may utilize the Magnetic Lasso tool, which employs edge detecting technology to automatically determine the limits of the thing you're choosing. Open the photo you wish to edit in Photoshop before beginning to employ the Magnetic Lasso tool. Pick the Magnetic Lasso tool from the toolbar after that. After picking the Magnetic Lasso tool, you may alter its parameters to fit your individual requirements.

You may alter certain parameters in the options bar, including **"Width," "Contrast,"** and **"Frequency."** The Magnetic Lasso tool's **"Width"** option affects how big the detecting zone is. When identifying an object's bounds, Photoshop will investigate more pixels the wider the width. The Magnetic Lasso tool's **"Contrast"** setting sets how much contrast it will seek while recognizing edges. To attain the maximum effects, you may need to adjust this choice if the object you're picking doesn't stand out substantially from its surroundings. The **"Frequency"** option affects how often anchor points are put along the specified line by the Magnetic Lasso tool. A more accurate selection is produced when more anchor points are added with higher frequency. But it can also slow down the choosing process.

Once the settings are how you wish them to be, click and drag the Magnetic Lasso tool over the object or location you want to pick. The tool will automatically recognize the object's edges as you move it and snap the selection line to those edges. You may manually add anchor points by clicking along the selection line if the Magnetic Lasso tool is having problems detecting the object's edges. By hitting the Delete key while the Magnetic Lasso tool is chosen, you may also delete anchor points. Once a selection is complete, you may use it for a range of operations, including copying, cutting, and adjusting an object's color, brightness, or contrast.

Rotating a selection

One may quickly rotate a selection in Adobe Photoshop by following a few straightforward steps. Rotating a selection can help you generate a specific aesthetic or shift an object's placement in your picture whether you're dealing with a rectangle or freeform selection.

To rotate a selection in Photoshop, follow these steps:

Step 1. By clicking on the layer in the Layers panel that includes the area or object you wish to rotate; the layer will be selected. Be cautious to pick the proper layer if you have several ones.

Step 2. Make a selection around the item or region you wish to rotate in Photoshop using a selection tool, such as the Rectangular Marquee tool or the Lasso tool. An ever-moving dashed line will be utilized to accentuate the option.

Step 3. After selecting your pick, click **Transform > Rotate** from the Edit menu. The Transform tool may also be utilized by using the **Ctrl + T** or **Cmd + T** keyboard keys on Windows or Mac, respectively.

Step 4. You will see a bounding box with handles around your selection. To rotate the selection, click and drag one of the handles. It may be rotated in any direction you wish.

Step 5. Holding down the Shift key while sliding the handle will limit the rotation to 45-degree increments.

Step 6. Click and drag within the enclosed box to reposition the selection while rotating it.

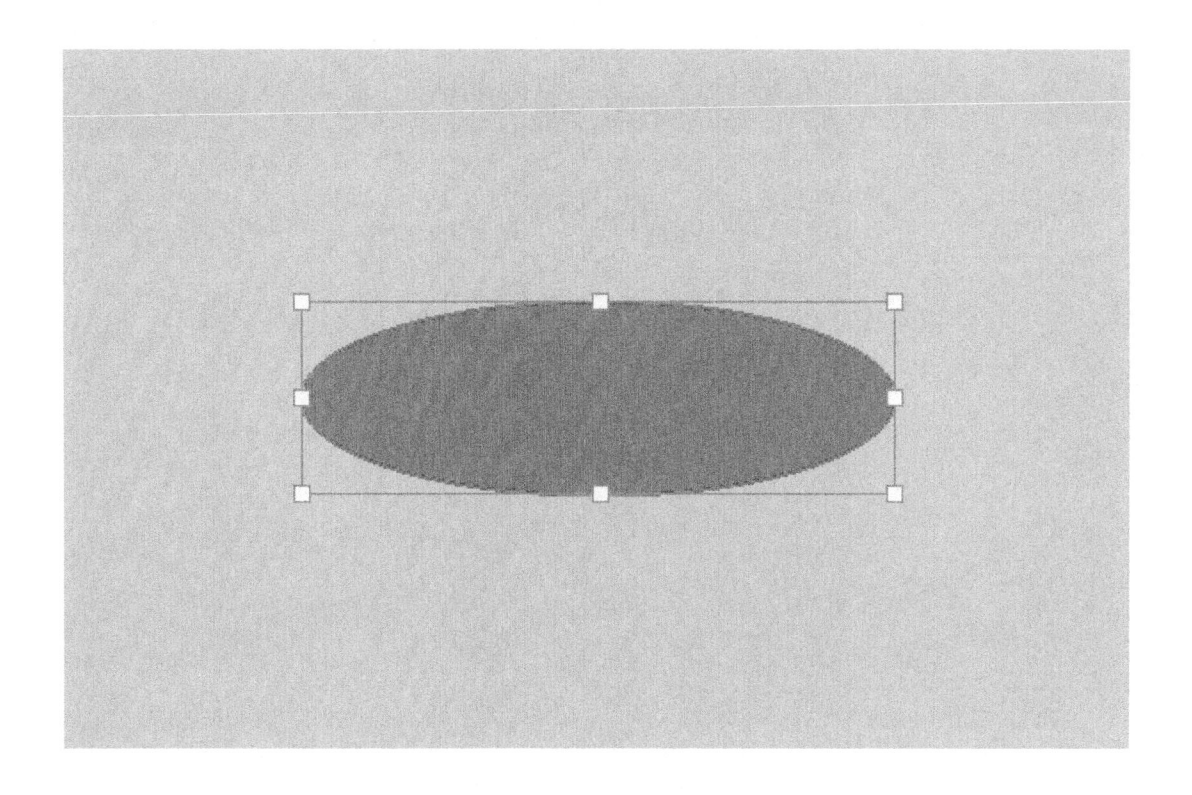

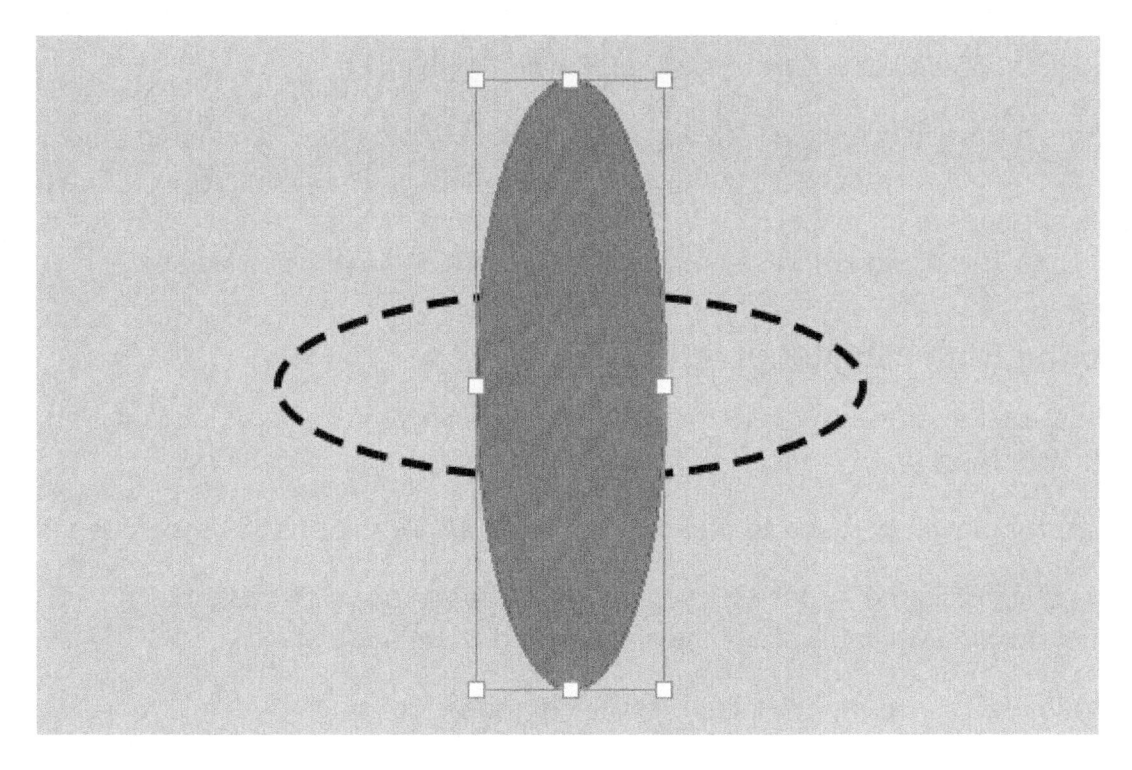

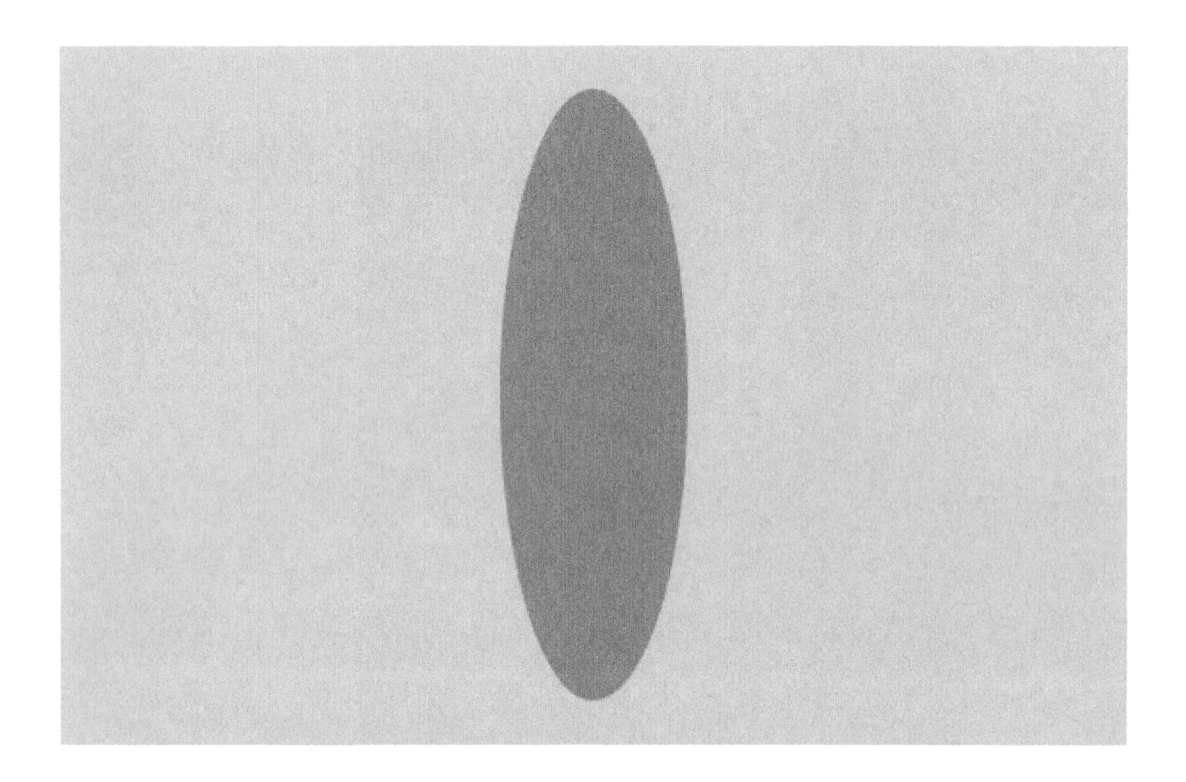

Step 7. Press Enter or Return to transform, turning the selection to the desired angle.

Step 8. Deselect the selection by selecting Deselect from the Select menu or by using the **Ctrl + D** (Windows) or **Cmd + D** (Mac) keyboard shortcut.

That's it. You've just completed rotating a selection in Photoshop. Remember that rotating a selection might vary the way your picture is put together, so you should experiment with various positions and perspectives to achieve the optimum effect. Additionally, be sure to regularly save your work in case you need to go back and make corrections.

Selecting from a center point

In certain cases, drawing a selection from an object's center point makes it simpler to construct elliptical or rectangular choices.

This approach will be used to pick the screw head for the shadow box corners.

Step 1. By utilizing the **Zoom** tool, you may enlarge the photo by roughly 300%. Ensure that your document window can show the whole picture head.

Step 2. In the Tools panel, pick the Elliptical Marquee tool.

Step 3. Place the cursor roughly in the image's middle.

Step 4. After clicking, start dragging. Then, as you drag the selection to the edge of the picture, hold down the **Alt** (Windows) or **Option** (MacOS) key while doing so. The selection is positioned in the center of its commencement point.

TIP: Shift should be held as you drag to choose a complete circle. To pick a perfect square, hold down Shift while dragging the Rectangular Marquee tool.

Step 5. Release the mouse button first, then **Alt** or **Option** (and the Shift key if you used it), when the complete image head has been selected.

Step 6. Reposition the selection border if needed. Select the screw once more if you mistakenly released the **Alt** or **Option** key before releasing the mouse button.

Resizing and copying a selection

Ensure that the photo is selected before you start.

• To make the complete picture fit inside the document window, click **View > Fit on Screen**.

• From the Tools panel, pick the Move tool.

• Within the photo selection, position the pointer.

The selection will be cut from its existing spot and transported to the new location when you drag it, as demonstrated by the pointer transforming into an arrow with a pair of scissors.

• Drag the photo into the shadow box's lower-right corner.

• Select Scale under **Edit >Transform**. Around the selection, a bounding box appears.

TIP: Hold on to the Control key to briefly switch off snapping to magenta Smart Guides when dragging if the photo won't move or resize smoothly, seeming as though it has "gotten stuck."

By deselecting the **View > Show > Smart Guides** instruction, you may deactivate them permanently.

• When the photo is roughly 40% of its original size or little enough to fit on the shadow box frame, slide one of the corner points inward. The selection marquee resizes along with the object as you modify its size. Both immediately resize accordingly.

- To finish the change and delete the transformation bounding box, hit Enter or Return.

- After resizing the photo, use the relocate tool to relocate it such that it is in the corner of the shadow box frame. As you drag the corner handle of a transformation bounding box, hold down the Shift key if you don't want to preserve the original proportions while scaling.

- Leaving the picture selected, choose **File > Save** to save your work.

Moving and duplicating a selection concurrently

In Adobe Photoshop, you may save a ton of time and labor by moving and duplicating a selection at the same time, particularly if you need to copy an object or region more than once inside the same picture. This procedure comprises duplicating the selection and moving it to another area. To move and replicate a selection concurrently in Photoshop, follow these steps:

- Make a selection around the item or location you wish to reproduce and move using one of Photoshop's selection tools, such as the Rectangular Marquee tool or the Lasso tool.

- Once you've made your decision, use the Edit menu option Copy or the keyboard shortcut **Ctrl+ C** on a computer running Windows or **Cmd + C** on a Mac to copy the selection to the clipboard.

- To paste the copied selection onto a new layer, click Paste from the Edit menu once again or use the **Ctrl+ V** or **Cmd + V** keyboard commands on a Mac or Windows computer, respectively.

- Use the transfer tool (shortcut: **V**) to transfer the selection to its new spot while the new layer is chosen. To move the selection about the canvas, click and drag it.

- Move the selection to duplicate while continuing to press the Alt key (Windows) or Option key (Mac). The Move tool cursor will have a+ symbol next to it to signal that you are duplicating the selection.

- Release the mouse button and then release the Alt or Option key. You will now have two identical copies of the selection in your picture.

- Repeat this method as many times as needed to make more copies.

That's it. Now with Photoshop, you have successfully moved and duplicated a selection at the same time. If you need to reproduce an object or location inside the same picture, this approach can help you save a ton of time. Remember that this strategy is ideal with selections that have a defined form and color as more elaborate selections might need more changes. Additionally, be sure to regularly save your work in case you need to go back and make corrections.

Copying selections

You may copy selections as you drag them around within or between photographs by using the Move tool, or you can use commands from the Edit menu to copy and move choices. Because it doesn't employ the clipboard, the Move tool takes less memory. Copy Numerous copy-and-paste options are available in Photoshop under the Edit menu:

This operation copies the current layer's chosen region to the clipboard.

Copy Merged: This operation combines all of the visible layers in the given region into a single copy.

Paste: This pastes the contents of the clipboard in the image's center. When you paste something into another photo, it generates a new layer. Additionally, Photoshop provides specialist pasting options under the **Edit > Paste Special** submenu to give you extra possibilities in specific circumstances:

Paste without Formatting: This option pastes text devoid of any font or size formatting that may have been applied when it was copied. It guarantees that text transferred from another application or document is formatted to match a text layer in Photoshop.

Paste in Place: Using this option, clipboard content is put where it was in the original picture rather than in the document's center.

Paste Into: This copies material from the clipboard into the presently chosen region of the same or a different image. The region outside the source selection is turned into a layer mask and the source selection is transferred onto a new layer.

Paste Outside: This option is identical to Paste Into, with the exception that Photoshop pastes information outside the current selection while converting the region within the selection into a layer mask. When you paste data across two pages with varied pixel measurements, it might seem to modify size. This is so that information transferred into a document with varied pixel dimensions preserves its original pixel dimensions. A pasted selection can be resized, but if it is extended, the picture quality may decrease.

Cropping a picture

The simplest yet vital stage of picture editing is cropping an image. Enhancing a picture's composition or calling attention to particular components includes picking and choosing elements of the image. Cropping is a fundamental method for generating better and more interesting images, and it is commonly employed in a number of circumstances, from professional photography to social media postings. There are a multitude of cropping tools and methods available in Adobe Photoshop, each with unique pros and downsides. The following tutorials will teach you how to crop a photo in Photoshop using various tools and methods:

How to Use the Crop Tool

The easiest and most flexible tool in Photoshop for cropping a photograph is the Crop tool. This is how to apply it:

Step 1: Launch Photoshop and open the photo you wish to crop.

Step 2: From the toolbar on the left side of the screen, pick the Crop tool. Alternatively, you may hit C on the keyboard.

Step 3: Drag the mouse to make a rectangular selection of the place you wish to preserve in the photo. The selection's border will be trimmed.

Step 4: Drag the selection box's handles to adjust the selection's size and placement. Additionally, you may modify the selection's aspect ratio by dragging a handle while using the Shift key.

Step 5: Press Enter or Return to crop the photo once you've positioned the selection where you want it.

Step 6: Press the Esc key or click the Cancel button in the Options bar i f you wish to cancel the crop.

Step 7: Select the Crop tool once again and update the selection as required if you wish to tweak the crop after it has been applied. To apply the updated crop, click Enter or Return.

How to utilize the Crop Presets

The Crop tool presets may be used to crop a photograph to a given aspect ratio. This is how:

From the toolbar on the left side of the screen, pick the Crop tool.

From the Preset dropdown menu in the Options bar at the top of the screen, pick the chosen aspect ratio.

Drag the mouse to make a rectangular selection of the region you wish to preserve in the photo. The selection's border will be trimmed.

Drag the selection box's handles to adjust the selection's size and placement.

Press Enter or Return to crop the photo once you've positioned the selection where you want it.

Using the Content-Aware Crop

A n useful feature that allows you automatically fill in the blanks left by cropping a photo is the Content-Aware Crop tool. This is how to apply it:

Step 1: From the toolbar on the left side of the screen, pick the Crop tool.

Step 2: Click and drag on the image to create a rectangle selection of the area you wish to preserve. The region outside the selection will be clipped.

Step 3: From the Crop dropdown option in the Options bar at the top of the screen, pick Content-Aware.

Step 4: Drag the selection box's handles to adjust the selection's size and placement.

Step 5: Press Enter or Return to crop the photo once you've positioned the selection where you want it. By leveraging neighboring content, Photoshop will automatically fill in the holes left by the crop.

Using the Perspective Crop

The Perspective Crop tool may be used to crop an image while adjusting its perspective. This is how:

Step 1: Launch Photoshop and open the photo you wish to crop.

Step 2: From the toolbar on the left side of the screen, pick the Perspective Crop tool. Alternatively, you may press the keys Shift and C simultaneously until the Perspective Crop icon displays.

Step 3: Drag the mouse to make a rectangular selection of the place you wish to preserve in the photo. The region that requires perspective adjustment should be included in the selection.

Step 4: Modify the selection box's corners to suit the viewpoint of the photo. You may accomplish this by dragging each selection box corner until it lines up with the appropriate corner of the scene or object.

Step 5: Press Enter or Return to crop the photo after adjusting the selection box's corners to meet the image's viewpoint.

Step 6: You may use the regular Crop tool to make extra crop modifications if desired. From the toolbar, choose the Crop tool, then modify the selection box as appropriate.

Useful advice for the Perspective Crop tool

Incorporate as much of the picture as you can into the selection box when using the perspective crop tool. By doing this, you'll make sure you have enough area to shift the image's viewpoint and crop it without missing any vital characteristics.

Watch wary for excessive perspective correction. Just enough to make the picture seem more natural and straight, but not so much that it appears distorted or unnatural, should be done to the selection box's edges.

If you're having problems modifying the selection box's corners, try zooming in on the photo for more specific modifications. The perspective of the picture may also be further adjusted by utilizing the Perspective Warp tool. To match the grid with the perspective of the picture, simply use the Perspective Warp tool from the toolbar. Using the Perspective Crop tool to crop an image, this technique can be handy for more detailed adjustments or for refining the perspective.

CHAPTER 5: QUICK FIXES

Getting started

Certain photographs may not require a tedious makeover in Photos hop employing the program's more sophisticated features. When you've gotten the hang of Photoshop, it's remarkable how swiftly you can enhance a photo. The key is to be aware of what is and is not achievable, as well as how to locate the resources you need. Beginning your work in Photoshop with Quick fixes is a wonderful approach for making uncomplicated alterations to your images and enhancing the general quality of those photographs.

Here are some suggestions for getting started:

1. Open your picture: The first thing you need to do is start Photoshop and open the image you want to edit. You may accomplish this by navigating to the "File" menu, selecting the "**Open**" option, and selecting the photo file from your computer.

2. Use the quick repairs tools: Photoshop offers various quick-fix tools that, with just a few clicks, may help you boost the quality of your images. Tools such as Crop, Straighten, and Auto Tone are covered in this category. Click the "**Quick**" tab situated in the tool bar to gain access to these many options.

3. Crop your image: The Crop tool helps you to eliminate unwanted portions of your photo so that you can concentrate on the most crucial aspects of the composition. To make the adjustments take effect, you must first choose the Crop tool, and then drag the image's edges to form a new composition, and then click the **Enter** key.

4. Straighten your image: If you find that your photo is skewed in any manner, you may straighten it by using the Straighten tool. Select the Straighten tool in Photoshop, then click and drag along a line in the photo, either horizontally or vertically, and Photoshop will automatically straighten the shot for you.

5. Adjust brightness and contrast: You may use the Auto Tone tool to automatically modify the brightness and contrast of the image if the shot you took is either too dark or too bright. You may also manually modify the settings by making use of the Brightness/Contrast tool that's accessible.

6. Remove imperfections: The tool known as the Spot Healing Brush may aid you in erasing blemishes, scars, and other faults from the images you have shot. Simply pick the tool, click, and drag it over the region that you wish to eliminate, and Photoshop will seamlessly blend the lost pixels into the surrounding ones.

7. Save your change: Once you have finished your fast repair and are satisfied with the outcome, be sure to save your change. You may do this by selecting **"File"**> **"Save"** or **"File"** > **"Save As"** and deciding on a new name for the file that you wish to save.

In general, utilizing Photoshop's fast fixes to enhance your photographs is a superb technique to upgrade them quickly and easily. You can crop, straighten, modify the brightness and contrast, and get rid of faults with only a few straightforward tools and approaches, and it only takes a few clicks to achieve all those things.

Improving a picture

A snapshot is a tool in Photoshop that enables you take a temporary photo of your work. This picture acts as a backup so that you can always go back to the original version of your file.

Improving an image is a regular duty for many designers and photographers since it provides them with the opportunity to refine their art and make any required improvements. In Pho-toshop, you may increase the quality of an image in several ways, including by modifying the color, brightness, and contrast. In the following, we shall discuss these strategies in greater depth.

Adjusting Color

Color correction is one of the most regularly used techniques for increasing the quality of an image. In Photoshop, you may achieve this with the aid of the Hue/Saturation tool. You have more control over the image's color balance owing to the Hue/Saturation tool, which enables you to make modifications to the image's hue, saturation, and brightness levels.

To make use of the Hue/Saturation tool, go to the Image menu, click on Adjustments, and then choose Hue/Saturation from the drop-down menu that displays. You will see a dialog box arise, which will allow you to make modifications to the sliders to vary the color of the photo.

Adjusting Brightness and Contrast

Adjusting the brightness and contrast of an image is yet another approach for boosting its quality. You may accomplish this aim by utilizing the Brightness/Contrast tool in Photoshop. You have additional control over the image's exposure owing to the

Brightness/Contrast tool, which enables you to make adjustments to the image's brightness as well as its contrast. Access the Brightness/Contrast tool by navigating to the Image menu, clicking on Adjustments, and then selecting Brightness/Contrast from the drop-down menu that displays. You will see a dialog box that provides you the opportunity to alter the brightness and contrast of the picture by using the sliders inside the box.

Using Curves

Utilizing Curves is yet another way that may be utilized to improve a photograph. You may adjust the tonal range of the photo by using the Curves tool, which offers you more control over the image's shadows, mid-tones, and highlights. You may utilize the Curves tool by going to the Image menu, choosing Adjustments, and then clicking on the Curves option that displays. It will bring up a dialogue window where you may make modifications to the curve to modify the tone range of the picture.

Using Levels

An image can be enhanced in still another method utilizing the Levels tool. You have more control over the shadows, mid-tones, and highlights of the picture when you use the Levels tool, which enables you to modify the tonal range of the image. To utilize the Levels tool, go to the Image menu, click the Adjustments submenu, and then select Levels from the list of available options. You will see a dialog box open, and you will be able to make adjustments to the image's tonal range by altering the sliders inside the window.

Sharpening the Image

A snapshot may be improved in several ways, one of which is by sharpening the picture. You may generate the appearance that an image is more distinct and distinct by utilizing the Sharpen tool to sharpen the edges of the picture. Go to the Filter menu, then choose Sharpen from the drop-down menu, and lastly, click on the Sharpen button to employ the Sharpen tool. You will see a dialog box open, inside which you may make modifications to the sliders to sharpen the photo.

Correcting the eye

When shooting humans or animals in dimly light locations with a flash, one of the most frequent complications that develop is the appearance of red eyeballs in the subject's eyes. When the light from the flash reaches the retina of the eye, it causes it to bounce back into the camera as a reddish tint. To one's relief, Adobe Photoshop provides a quick and reliable way for re-moving red eyes from photographic photos.

The following measures need to be done to correct red eye in Photoshop:

Step 1. Open the picture in Photoshop: Launch Photoshop and open the photo by heading to the File menu and picking Open from the drop -down menu. Alternatively, you may run Photoshop by dragging and dropping the picture file into the workspace.

Step 2. Zoom in on the eyes: Using the Zoom tool, you may zoom in on the subject's eyes and magnify them to a larger degree. You need to get a good look at the red eyes, so move closer.

Step 3. Choose the Red Eye Tool: In the Tools panel, choose the Red Eye Tool from the available options. If the tool is not easily evident, you may acquire access to the Red Eye Tool by clicking and holding on the Spot Healing Brush Tool.

Step 4. Adjust the tool settings: Adjust the tool parameters by heading to the Options bar and making the appropriate adjustments there. The Pupil Size, as well as the Darken Amount, may both be ad-justed. The amount of darkness may be modified to suit your preferences, and a greater pupil size will be necessary for eyes that are already very large.

Step 5. Click on the red eye: Position the Red Eye Tool over the Centre of the red eye, and then click once to make a selection. As the tool darkens the region, you should observe the red color progressively fade away. You may have to click more than once to achieve the outcome you want.

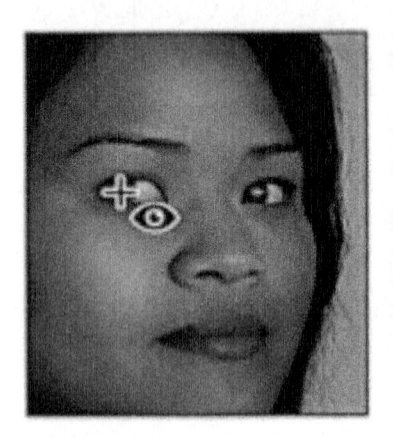

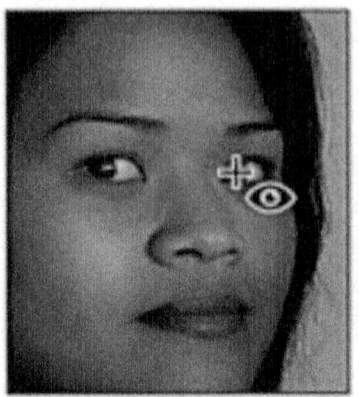

Step 6. Repeat the procedure for the second eye. Once again, repeat the process with the opposite eye, this time zooming in closer and making any required modifications to the tool settings.

Step 7. Save the picture: When you have completed making the necessary edits, you should save the image by navigating to the main menu and choosing **File > Save** or **Save As**.

Tips for fixing red eye

If the **Red Eye Tool** does not effectively correct the redness, you may try manually modifying it with the **Clone Stamp Tool** or the **Healing Brush Tool** instead.

Take care not to darken the area an excessive amount, as doing so might create the appearance that the eye is not real.

If you are working with a portrait that involves more than one subject, make sure to address the red eye condition for each individual in the photograph separately.

The appearance of your images may be considerably enhanced by utilizing Photoshop's quick and user-friendly red eye correction tool, which can also eradicate the problem. You can lessen the redness in the eyes and create the appearance that they are natural and healthy with only a few clicks of the Red Eye Tool.

Brightening an Image

When editing images, one of the most basic chores is to brighten a picture. This is particularly crucial if the image is underexposed or appears overly dark. You are in luck as Adobe Photo-shop comes loaded with a range of tools and methods that enable you to brighten a photo while also accentuating its features and colors.

Method 1: Adjusting Brightness/Contrast

A photograph can be brightened in Photoshop using the **Brightness/Contrast** adjustment, which is both the fastest and easiest approach to accomplish so. This adjustment may be accessible via the Image menu or by using the **Ctrl + Shift+ B** (or **Cmd +Shift + B** on Mac) keys on your keyboard. With this upgrade, you'll be able to make global changes to the brightness and contrast of the full picture.

This is how you can go about accomplishing it:

Step 1. Launch Photoshop, navigate to the photo and make a duplicate of the layer by clicking **Ctrl + J** (or **Cmd + J** on a Mac).

Step 2. Simply picking the cloned layer needs you to click on it.

Step 3. Navigate to the Image menu, and then click **Adjustments**, then

Brightness/Contrast.

Step 4. To make the picture brighter, adjust the **Brightness** slider to the right on the picture **Adjustment** window.

Step 5. If the image's contrast has to be adjusted, utilize the **Contrast** slider to make the needed modifications.

Step 6. To save the changes, click the **OK** button.

Method 2: Using Levels

Adjusting an image's levels with the Levels adjustment is another essential function that allows you control over an image's brightness and contrast. In contrast to the **Brightness/Contrast** adjustment, the Levels adjustment enables you to make individual modifications to the brightness, contrast, and color balance of the picture.

This is how you can put it to use:

Step 1. Launch Photoshop and make a duplicate of the layer you're presently working on.

Step 2. Simply picking the cloned layer needs you to click on it.

Step 3. Navigate to the Image menu and pick **Adjustments > Levels**.

Step 4. In the **Levels** dialog box, you will see a histogram that depicts the image's tonal range. This range is indicated by the number of levels.

Step 5. To brighten the picture, drag the middle slider (the one that appears like it's composed of gray) to the left.

Step 6. If needed, use the white and black slides to make modifications to the image's highlights and shadows.

Step 7. To save the changes, click the **OK** button.

Method 3: Using Curves

The Curves adjustment is a more advanced tool that allows you additional control over how exactly you may tweak the brightness and contrast of a photograph. You may vary the levels of bright-ness and contrast of particular tonal ranges within the picture by utilizing the Curves adjustment.

This is how you can put it to use:

Step 1. Launch **Photoshop** and make a duplicate of the layer you're now working on.

Step 2. Simply picking the cloned layer needs you to click on it.

Step 3. Navigate to the **Curves** tab under the Image's **Adjustments** menu.

Step 4. In the **Curves** dialog box, you will observe a diagonal line that indicates the image's tonal range. This line is positioned in the center of the box.

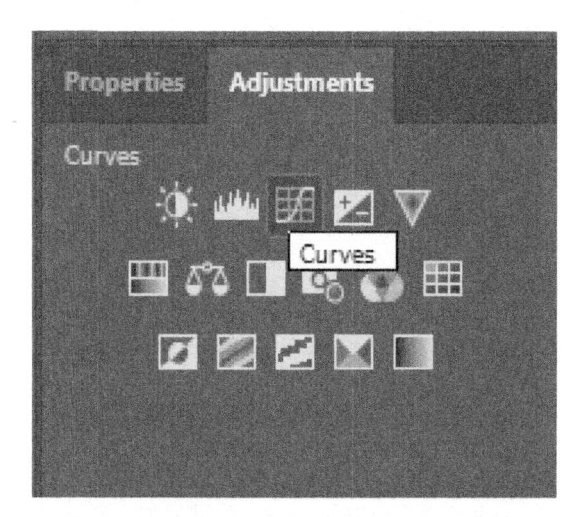

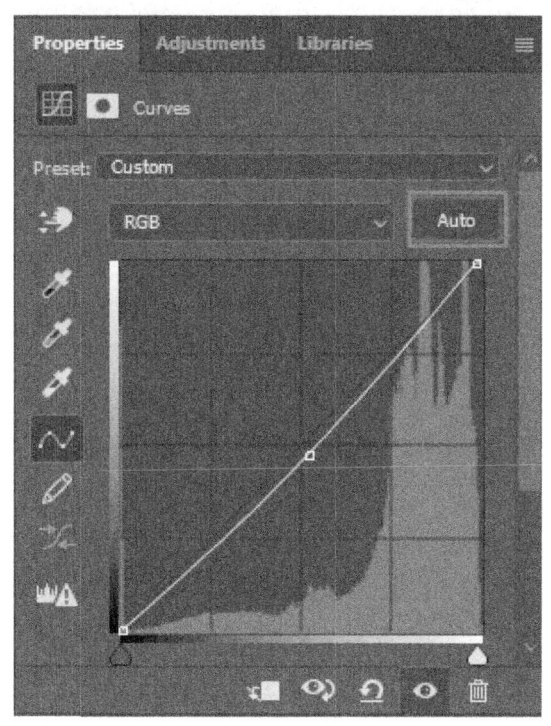

Step 5. To make the picture brighter, click in the center of the line and then drag it to the top of the screen.

Step 6. If desired, you may set more points on the line and then adjust those points to fine-tune the image's brightness and contrast.

Step 7. To save the changes, click the **OK** button.

Method 4: Using the Dodge Tool

You may deliberately brighten portions of a photograph by using a brush called the Dodge Tool. This tool offers you the ability. This tool is quite helpful when you want to brighten certain portions of the picture, such as the highlights or the mid-tones, and it lets you to do so selectively.

This is how you can put it to use:

Step 1. Launch Photoshop and make a duplicate of the layer you're now working on.

Step 2. Simply picking the cloned layer needs you to click on it.

Step 3. Make a selection in the toolbar for the **Dodge Tool**.

Step 4. Choose Highlights or Midtones for the Range in the choices bar at the top of the screen, depending on the sections of the image you wish to make brighter.

Step 5. Reduce the value of the Exposure slider to somewhere between 10 and 20 percent.

Step 6. Make the areas you wish to brighten brighter by using the Dodge Tool to paint over them.

Step 7. You may fine-tune the look by tweaking the Exposure setting or changing the size of the brush if desired.

Adjusting face features using Liquify

You may modify the form and look of a range of things, including facial features, with the aid of the powerful Liquify tool that is included in Adobe Photoshop. You may edit elements of an image to acquire the impression you desire by pushing, tugging, and twisting them with the aid of Liquidity. In this section, we will concentrate on making alterations to facial attributes using Liquify.

Step 1: Open the Image

To get started, run Photoshop, and pick the photo you wish to modify from the file menu. It is crucial to make certain that the image is of great quality, that the subject's face is in sharp focus, and that the subject's eyes are pointed squarely ahead.

Step 2: Duplicate the Layer

The layer should then be copied by tapping the **Ctrl + J** (Windows) or **Command + J** (Mac) keys simultaneously. This step is vital because it generates a duplicate of the original image layer, which may subsequently be modified without having any effect on the photo that was initially loaded.

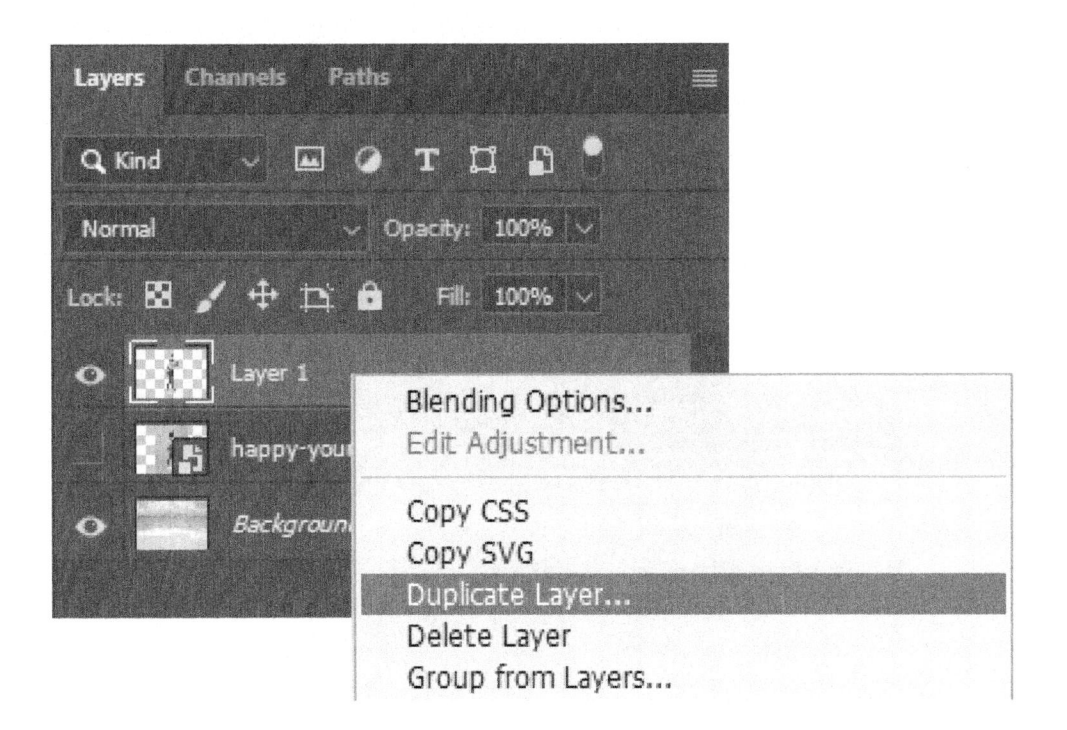

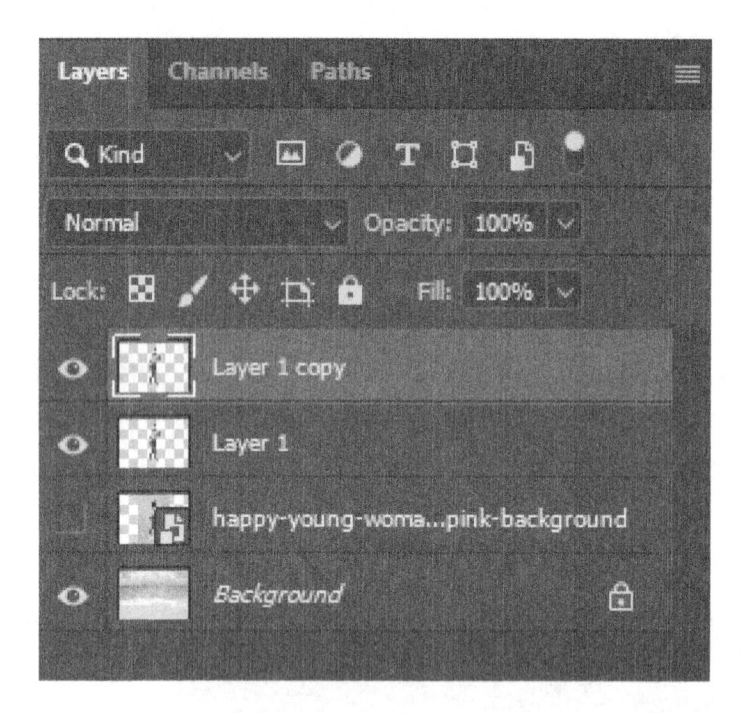

Step 3: Access Liquify Tool

To use the Liquify tool, either go to the Filter menu and choose Liquify from the drop-down menu or use the keyboard shortcut **Ctrl +Shift+ X** (Windows) or **Command+ Shift + X** (Mac).

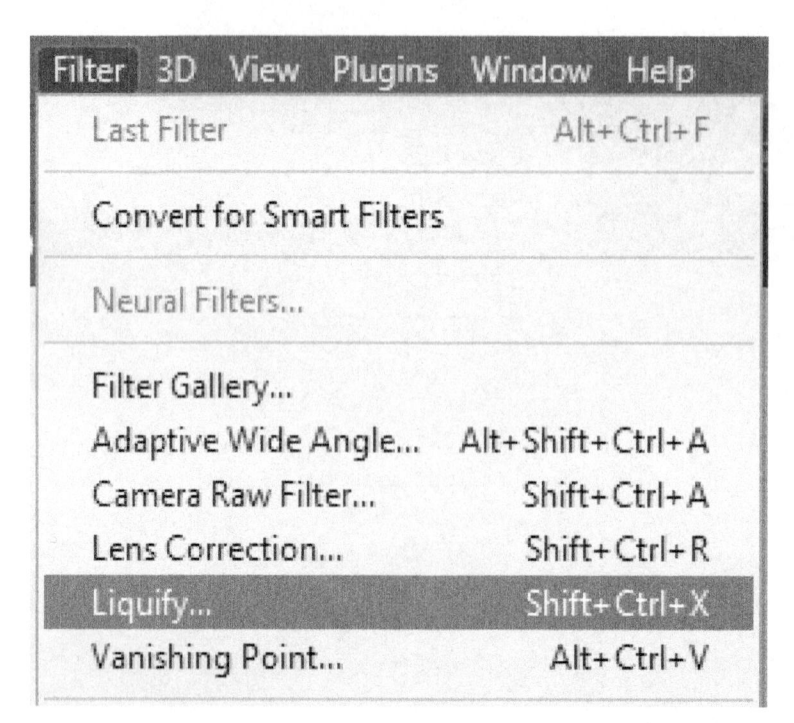

You will discover several tools on the left-hand side of this interface and choices for manipulating those tools on the right.

We'll know now how each tool works.

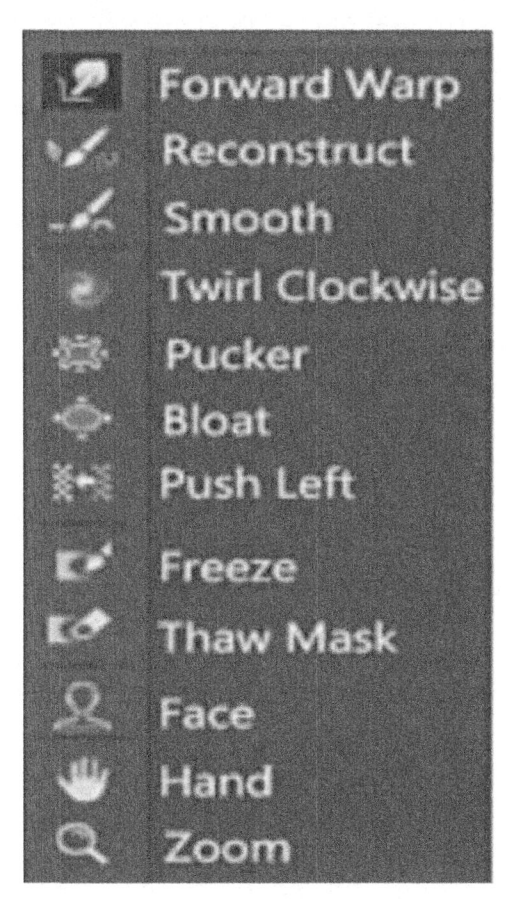

- Forward Warp
- Reconstruct
- Smooth
- Twirl Clockwise
- Pucker
- Bloat
- Push Left
- Freeze
- Thaw Mask
- Face
- Hand
- Zoom

Forward Warp Tool: This tool pushes forward a certain section of a picture. To utilize a tool, first, pick it, and then click the component you wish to alter, and then drag it to the correct spot. Because this tool allows you to push specific components, you may use it to increase or reduce the size of any area of an image.

Reconstruct Tool: You don't need to worry if you screw up any part of the picture since this tool will help you undo anything that you've done improperly. Get the tool from the drawer in the panel. After that, you will need to click and drag on the portion that you wish to restore. The original state will be restored little by bit, and everything will fall back into place as it does so.

Smooth Tool: The rough corners of an image can be smoothed with the aid of this tool. You may use this tool to smooth out sections of the picture that have straight angles if you need a curve to be put elsewhere in the image where it presently has a straight angle.

This tool also aids in fine-tuning any location that has been edited by the user.

Twirl Clockwise Tool: Take this tool, then click and hold it held down at any position across the picture. This utility will carry out its duties precisely as indicated. It will rotate the pixels in a counterclockwise manner. Additionally, this might contribute to distortion. Simply clicking the alt button on your keyboard will change the direction to an anti-clock-wise spin, after which you may continue to use the tool in the same manner as previously.

Pucker Tool: This tool brings everything that is on the edges closer to the center of the screen. If you chose the tool, then click and hold it in a given spot, it will bring every-thing that is on the periphery of the circle into the center. If you hit Alt in this circumstance, the shift will proceed in the other way, which will extend the center out toward the edges.

The Bloat Tool: This is the polar opposite of its counterpart, the Pucker Tool. The pixels are pushed outside from the center of the image as a result of employing the bloat tool. When you click on the location you wish to work on, the pixels in the Centre will be dragged outward toward the edges. When you hit the Alt button, it will return you back to the Pucker Tool, and the pixels will travel in the opposite direction from what they were moving before.

Push Left Tool: This device can press both left and right, despite its name indicates pressing left. To relocate an area, first grasp the tool, and then drag any section of it to the left. This will cause the area to migrate. If you drag it to the right, it will relocate the area to the right where it is presently positioned. That's all there is to it!

Freeze Tool: The Freeze tool accomplishes precisely what its name implies it would achieve. Imagine that you have to brush a specific spot, but you don't want to touch any of the other regions. Simply pick the "freeze" option, and then choose the section of the map that you wish to remain unchanged. Now is the time to focus on the other components without any concern. Access to the given site will not be provided.

Thaw Mask Tool: Once again, this is the tool that is the polar opposite of the freezer tool. If there is an area of the map that you require access to but is frozen by the freeze tool, you may use the thaw tool and click on the section to unlock it. This will allow you to continue working there. Simply tapping the Alt button on your keyboard, you may switch be-tween the Freeze Tool and the Thaw Tool.

Face Tool: The Face Tool in Photoshop is incredibly helpful. The bulk of the time, fashion photographers will utilize this accessory. This can recognize the face as well as individual sections of the face, such as the forehead, eyes, nose, lips, and chin, automatically from an image. You may make adjustments to any aspect of the face by using the face tool, and you can also give the face any shape you desire. You need to be aware of the industry beauty standard to operate this tool in a manner that is suitable for a professional context. It is crucial to grasp which type of eyes or nose would be lovely or how your consumer wants these traits to be in case it varies.

Hand Tool: You may move the picture in any way by using the hand tool, including up, down, left, and right. When the photo is zoomed in, you will often notice it being employed. Zoom Tool: The picture will be enlarged, precisely as it states it will be. If you pick the tool and then click anywhere on the image, the outcome will be an enlarged version of the photo.

To zoom out, click on the photo while simultaneously hitting the Alt button on your computer.

You can also zoom in and out of the image by using the keyboard commands "**Control +**" and "**Control -.**"

Control Other Options

Using the choices that are presented to you on the right-hand side of the liquify window, you may have total control over the picture that you are working with.

The following is a list of the possible options that you will see there:

Brush Tool Options

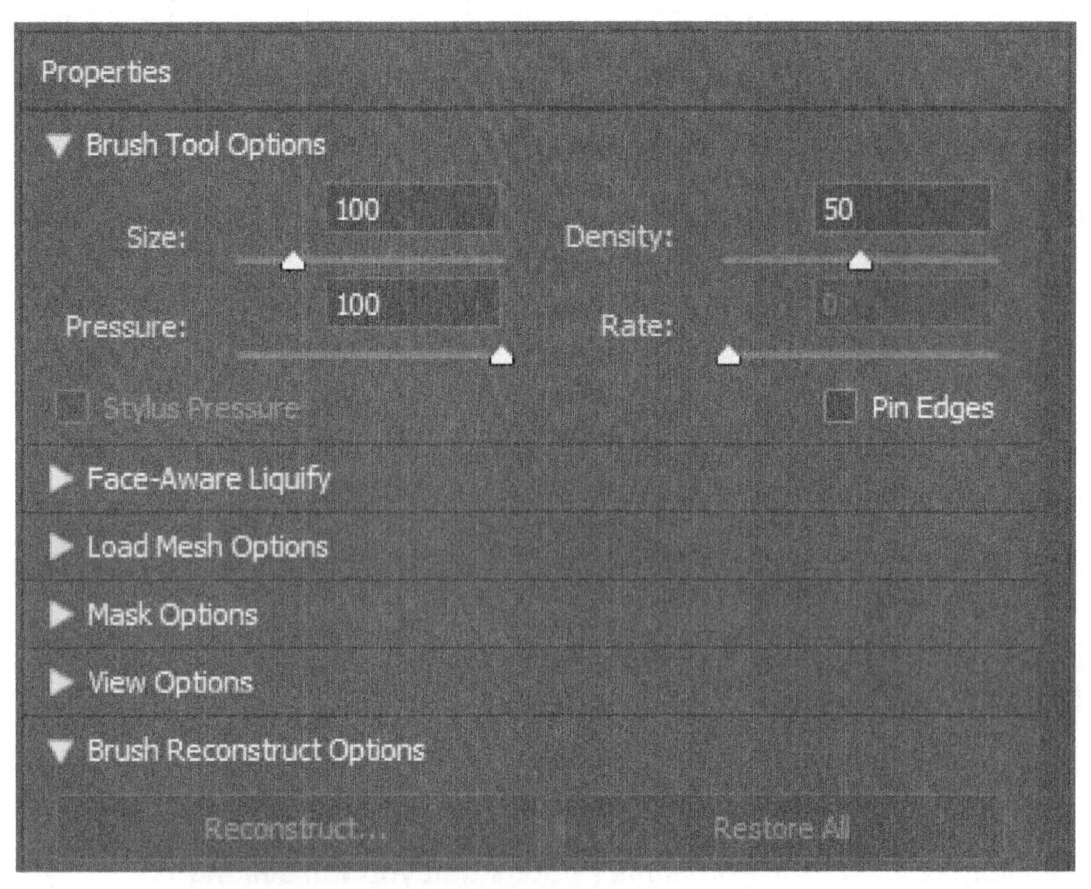

Size: The dimensions of the region you wish to operate on are decided by this element. To modify the size of the brush, just move the slider. Altering the size may also be achieved by simply entering in the new number or by clicking the corresponding bracket keys on the keyboard.

Density: This is the option that governs how tough or simple it is to utilize the brush. If the number is bigger, the edge will be more severe, and if it is lower, the edge will be milder.

Pressure: The amount of pressure you apply to the brush impacts how soon your work is done. If you use higher pressure, the tool will modify the region swiftly; if you apply less pressure, the filter will have a more subtle influence on the picture. The less pressure you apply to the brush, the more control you'll have over the picture you're working on.

Rate: The functioning of this tool is identical to that of the Brush Pressure tool. However, this option is particularly beneficial for those tools that execute their operations even when the cursor is not moved or dragged.

Face-Aware Liquify

You will have the possibility to examine individual choices such as Eyes, Nose, Mouth, and Face Shape when you look under the Face-Aware Liquify Tool. You'll discover extra tweaking possibili-ties for the face beneath each of the offered options. For the eyes, Photoshop gives the option to adjust the distance, size, height, and breadth of the eyes. For the mouth, Photoshop gives the option to adjust the smile, top lip, and lower lip. There are extra opportunities to modify the form of the chin and jawline. In the end, Photoshop allows you entire control over how the face looks by allowing you to make any alterations you can envision. In addition to this, there are further choices to Load Mesh, View, Mask, and Reconstruct Brushes. Depending on your requirements, you can use these choices. To see the modification you've made, go to View > Options and click the box next to Show Backdrop.

Using the tool

Here, we're going to modify an image utilizing the Liquify Tool.

As we've previously demonstrated how to open the file and the tool, we're moving directly to the Face Tool. After opening Face Tool, go to the Face-Aware Liquify on the right side.

First, we'll start on the forehead. It appears pretty enormous, thus lowering it just a bit.

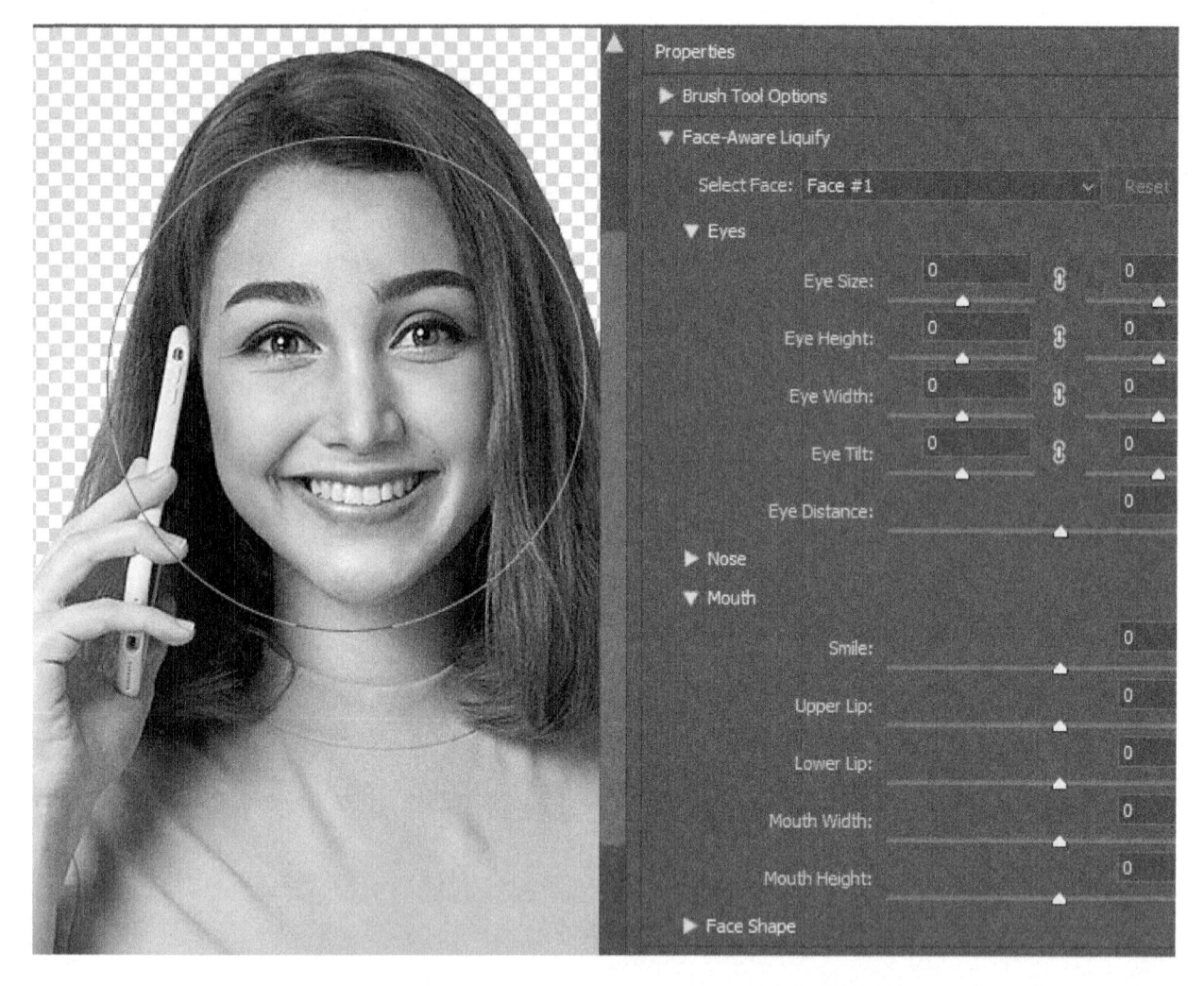

Now, moving to the eyes. Let's make these eyeballs a little bit larger.

We can lessen the smile size as well as it can look broader.

The rest of the pieces are **OK** with what they are. So, we'll conclude here. It's best not to destroy the image in the means of making it better.

Save the Image: Once you have made the necessary edits, click **OK** to apply the changes to the picture. Make care you save the image by going to **File > Save** or using the keyboard shortcut **Ctrl + S** (Windows) or **Command + S** (Mac).

Fine-Tune: If required, you may continue to fine-tune the image by repeating the Liquify procedure on the copied layer until you are pleased with the outcome.

To become an expert at utilizing the Liquify Tool, you will need to put in some practice. To keep the image's natural aspect while changing it, you will need to have a strong sense of manipulation. Your image might have a more polished and professional appearance if you employ this tool appropriately. You should now hopefully be aware of various beneficial applications for this formidable feature. However, there is no reason to resist exploring and finding out how it may also be utilized in imaginative ways. In the end, how you apply the liquify effect in Photoshop is totally based on your preferences.

Blurring around a Subject

A frequent practice employed in photography and design, blurring the area surrounding a subject attracts the viewer's attention to the topic while simultaneously smoothing out the backdrop. You can make your subject stand out and generate a photo that is more aesthetically beautiful by employing this easy and efficient method. Developing a narrow depth of field, sometimes known as blurring the background, is a method that can be performed by a variety of means, including the employment of a wide aperture, the acquisition of a specialist lens, or the use of post-pro-cessing techniques. In this part, we will explore a range of tactics, such as how to make use of the Blur Gallery, the Gaussian Blur filter, and the Lens Blur filter.

Before we get started, it is vital to bear in mind that blurring the region surrounding a topic works most successfully when the subject itself is in clear focus and the background is typically uniform. In addition to this, it is vital to make certain that the subject is well-defined and does not have any fuzzy or fuzzy-edged parts. You may need to apply selection tools to isolate the subject before blurring it, particularly if the subject's edges are not very well-defined.

Method 1: Using the Blur Gallery

The Blur Gallery in Photoshop is a helpful tool that gives several possibilities for the production of various forms of blurs. These blurs include Field Blur, Iris Blur, and Tilt-Shift Blur. The final effect may be customized to a considerable extent since these blurs can be applied to either the complete picture or to only portions of the image.

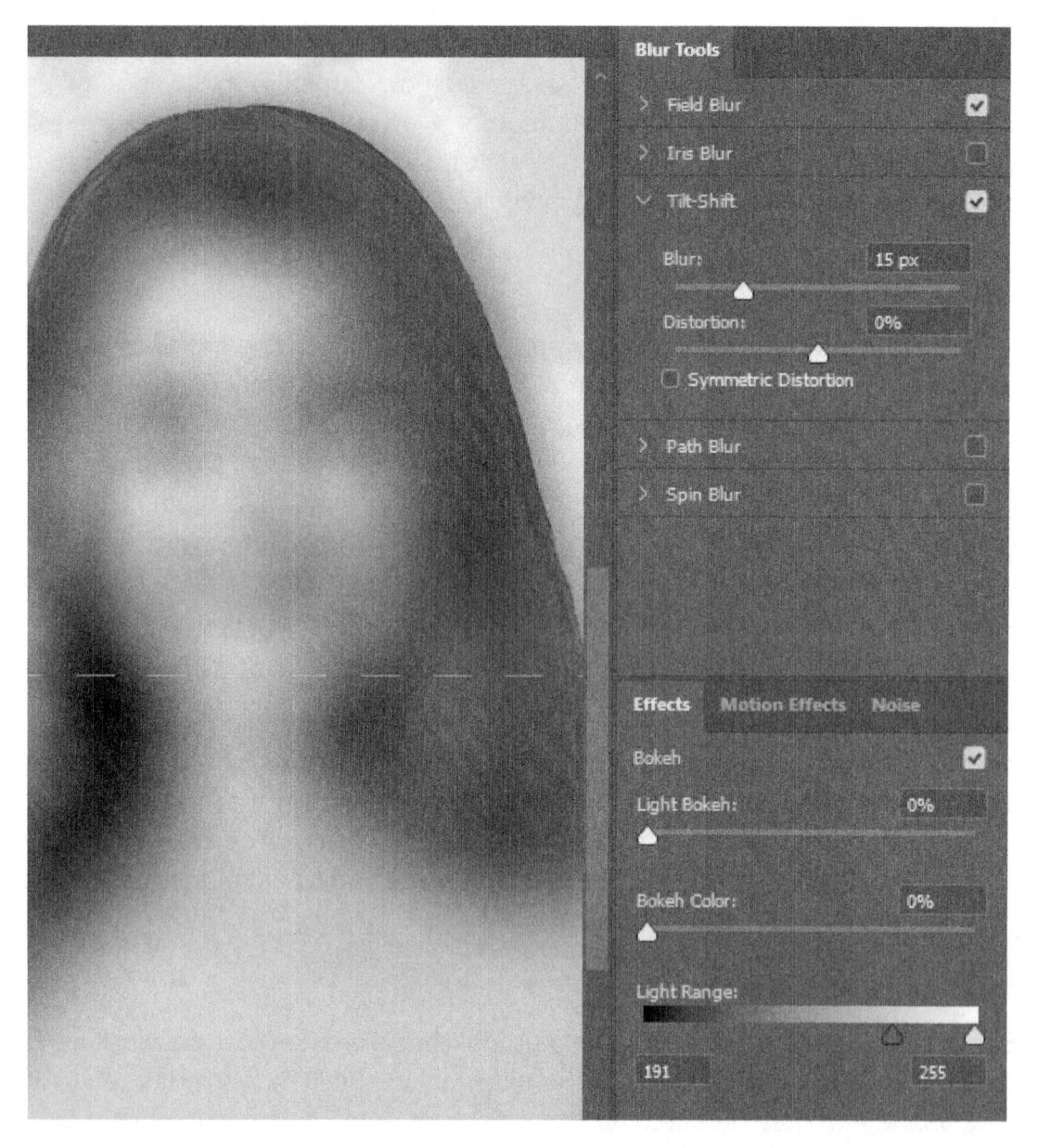

To utilize the Blur Gallery, first pick the layer that is home to the photo you want to blur, and then go to the Filter menu and choose Blur Gallery from the drop-down menu. After that, pick the kind of blur you want to apply to the image, and then change the parameters until you obtain the effect you desire. You may enhance both the regions that are in focus and the sections that are fuzzy by utilizing the tools in the Blur toolbox. The Blur Gallery contains five various forms of interactive blurs: the Field Blur, the Iris Blur, the Tilt-Shift Blur, and the Path Blur. Each one has on-image capabilities for selecting blurring motion, in addition to an initial blur pin. By clicking on the photo, you may make more blur pins. You have the option of adding just one blur or a mixture of blurs, and both the path blur and the spin blur can have a strobe effect added to them.

Field Blur: This applies a gradient blur to areas of the picture, with the definition of those regions being decided by the pins that you construct and the settings that you supply for each pin. When you initially activate Field Blur, a symbol that appears like a pin is positioned in the center of the picture. You may modify the blur's position relative to that point by moving the blur handle or inputting a value into the **Blur Tools box**. Alternatively, you may relocate the pin to a different position by dragging it.

Tilt-Shift: This duplicates a photo that was acquired with a tilt-shift lens, which generates an image with an incredibly narrow depth of focus and places the focal point in the distant. This blur delineates a plane of clarity, which then progressively transforms into a blur farther out. You may generate the illusion of pictures of small things by utilizing this effect.

Iris Blur: This is a feature that gradually blurs anything that is not inside the focus ring. To acquire the correct level of iris blur, play around with the ellipse handles, feather handles, and blur amount settings. A shallow depth-of-field blur effect may be created in a relatively short length of time with this approach.

Spin Blur: This is a form of radial blur that is stated in degrees. By holding down Alt or Option while clicking and dragging, you may change the rotation point, edit the ellipse's size and form, and vary the blur angle. In the Blur Tools window, you can also specify the blur angle. There can be an overlap between multiple spin blurs. The spinning of propellers, wheels, or gears may be more clearly depicted with the assistance of this blur effect.

Path Blur: This is a tool that allows you to make motion blurs along routes that you design. You have control over the blur's shape as well as its intensity.

When you apply a Path Blur for the first time, a default path will appear. Simply move the end point by dragging it. To adjust the curve, you must first click the center point and then drag. Simply click the icon to add more curve points. The directional arrow on the route depicts the movement of the blur. A form or a route with numerous points may also be constructed by you. The local motion blurs are defined by blur shapes, which are equivalent to camera shake. The speed of each route blur may be changed using the slider called **"Speed"** accessible in the Blur Tools panel. The Centered Blur option assures that the blurred shape for every pixel is centered on that pixel, which results in motion blurs that have a more stable sensation. If you want the mo-tion to seem more fluid, deselecting this option will accomplish that purpose. If you wanted to display the blurs generated by individual animal legs moving in various directions, you might give each leg its distinct instance of the Path Blur filter. Some blur types include extra choices in the Effects tab, where you set the bokeh parameters to customize the look of blurred areas. Light Bokeh enhances the blurring sections; Bokeh Color adds more vibrant colors to highlight areas that aren't blown out to white; Light Range determines the range of tones that the settings effect.

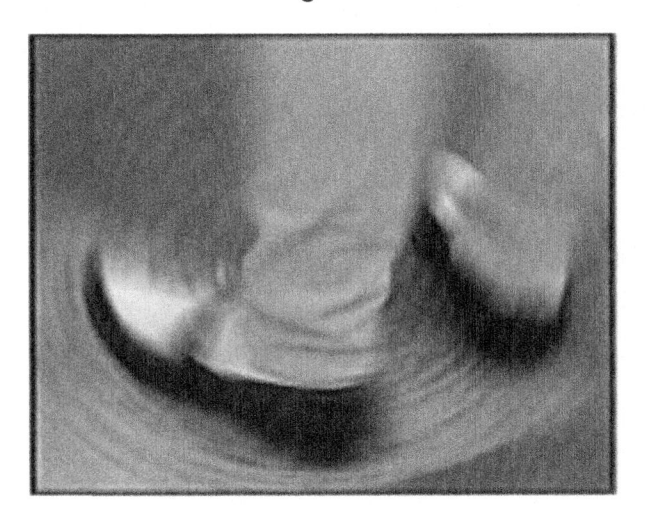

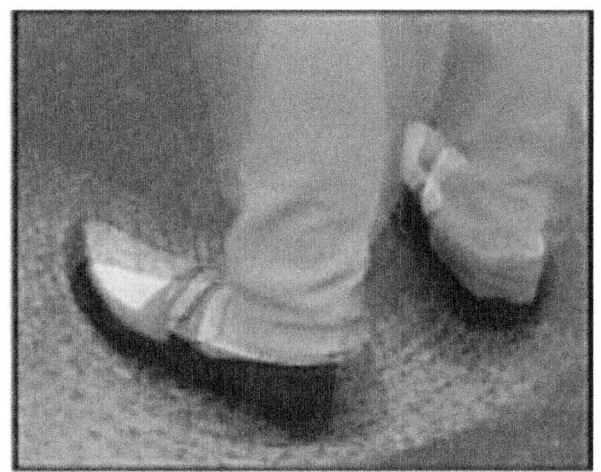

Spin and path blurring may both have a strobe effect applied to them. By selecting the Motion Effects tab, you may bring its panel to the front of the screen. The degree of blur that appears between flash exposures may be controlled using the Strobe Strength slider. A setting of 0% removes the strobe effect, while a value of 100% enables the whole strobe effect with extremely min-imal blur. The number of exposures is governed by the employment of strobe flashes.

Method 2: Using the Gaussian Blur Filter

The Gaussian Blur filter is an easy and fast approach for blurring the background surrounding a subject in an image. First, choose the layer that includes the photo you wish to blur, and then click **Ctrl + J** (or **Command + J** on a Mac) to duplicate the layer. Next, pick the layer that contains the picture you wish to blur. After that, choose the cloned layer from the list, then go to the Filter menu and pick Gaussian Blur from there.

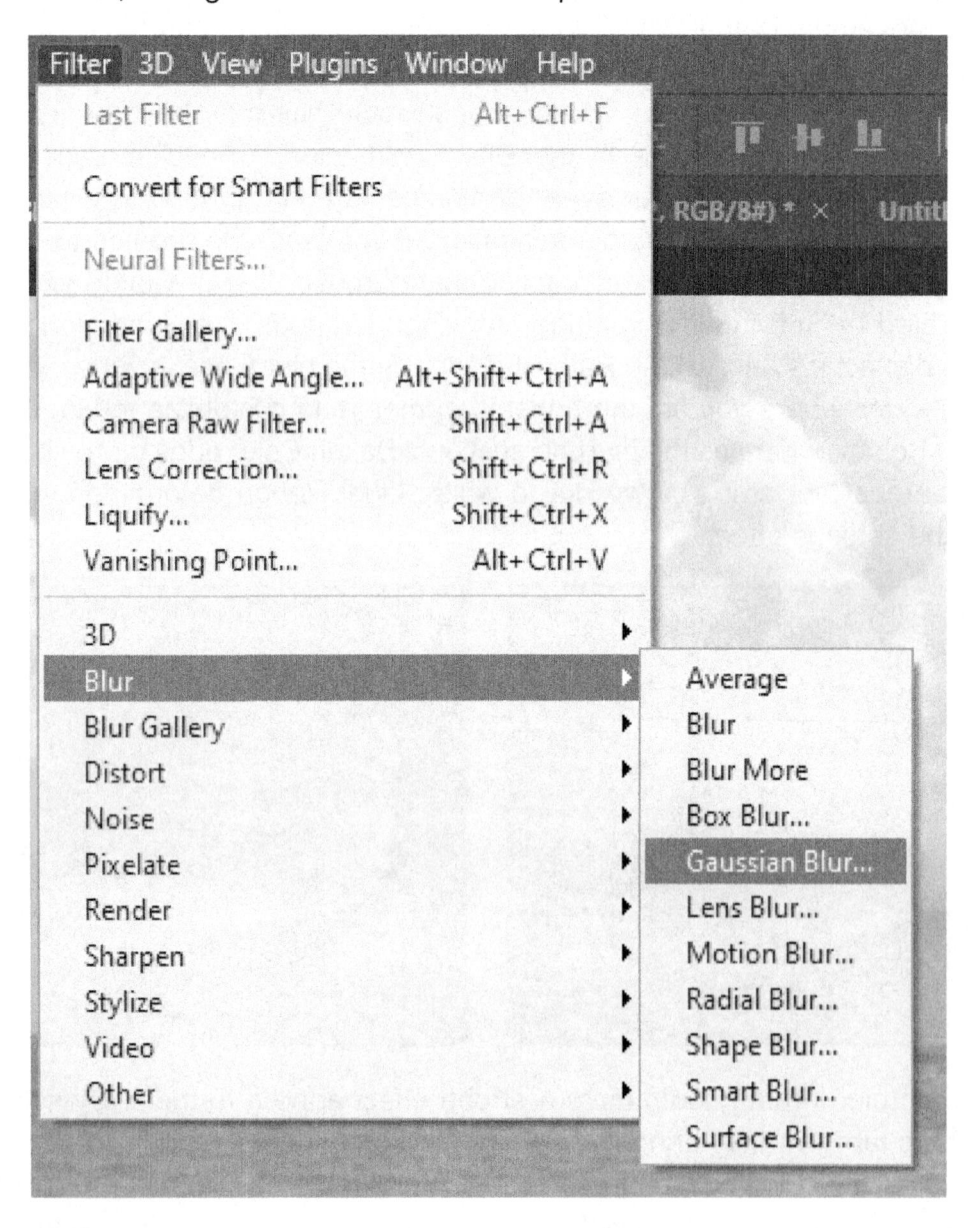

Adjust the radius slider inside the **Gaussian Blur** dialog box until the amount of blurring that you desire is obtained. You may also employ the preview pane to evaluate how the blurring will affect the photo before applying it. When you are pleased with the effect, you may apply the blur by pressing the **OK** button.

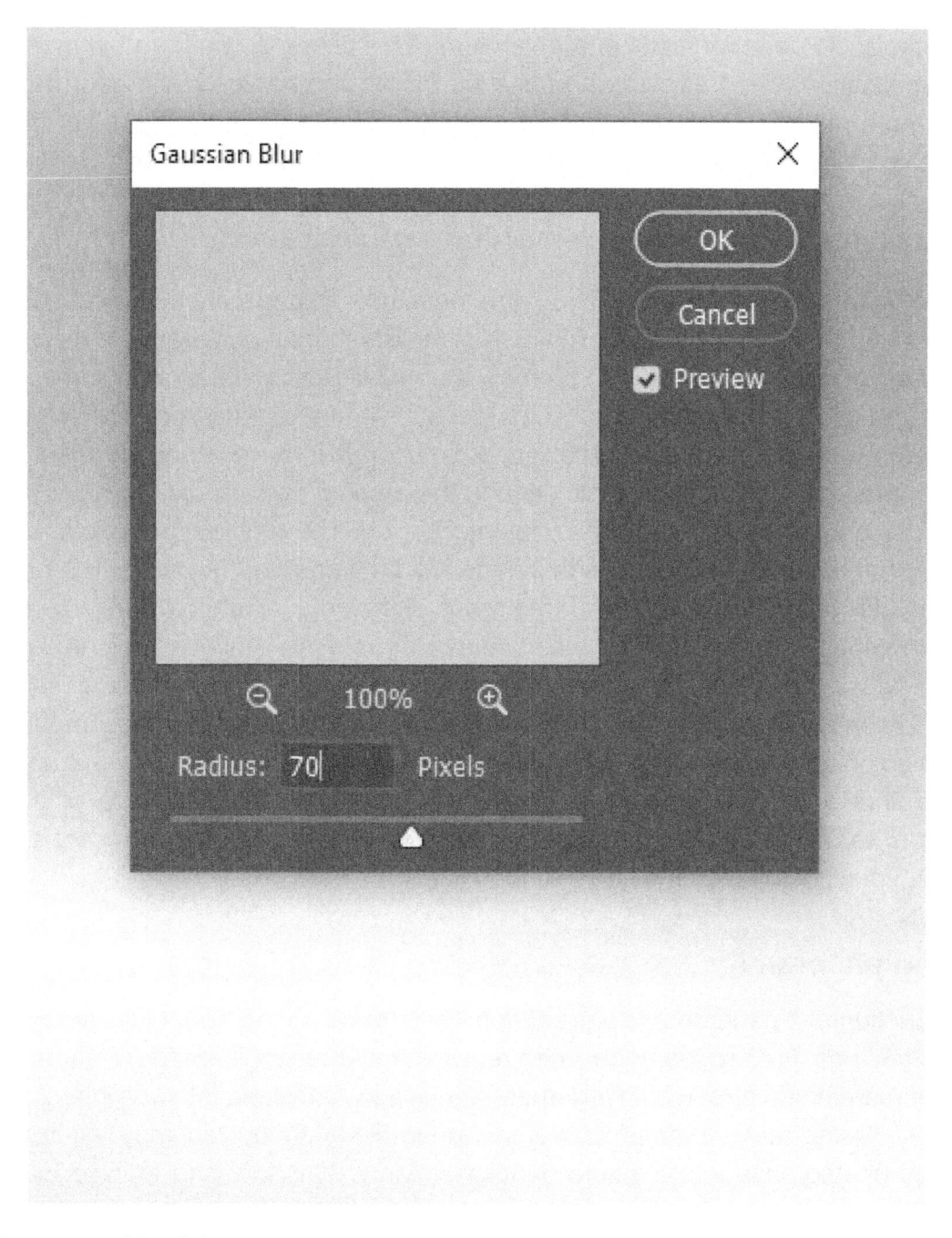

Click the **Layer Mask** button at the bottom of the Layers panel to add a layer mask to the copied layer. You may mask off topic by using a delicate brush with the foreground color set to black. This will allow you to view the original layer that is underneath. Make any required modifications to the opacity of the cloned layer to acquire the effect you desire.

Method 3: Using the Lens Blur Filter

The Lens Blur filter is a more advanced way for blurring around a subject that enables you to imitate the depth of focus of a given lens. This filter may be found in most picture editing applications. This strategy needs a bit more preparation, but it can give results that are more realistic and detailed. Before applying the **Lens Blur** effect, you must first duplicate the layer that is presently displaying the photo you wish to blur. Next, build a layer mask on the duplicate layer, and using a delicate brush, remove the subject from the mask so that the original layer, which is beneath, can be seen.

Next, pick **Filter > Blur > Lens Blur** from the menu bar. To generate the effect you desire, open the Lens Blur dialog box, pick Alpha 1 as the depth map channel, and then alter the other values as appropriate. The depth map channel is responsible for choosing whether areas of the picture are crisp and which sections have a hazy look. After you have modified the parameters to your preference, select **OK** to begin applying the Lens Blur filter. You may fine-tune the effect by altering the amount of transparency (or opacity) of the duplicated layer as desired. Additional Information: The visible digital picture noise or film grain that is present in the original image will be smoothed away when a blur effect is applied; still, the mismatch between the areas of the original and blurred pictures might create the appearance that the blur was added artificially. You may restore noise or grain using the Noise tab, which will allow blurry sections of the picture to more closely match parts of the image that are not blurry. You should begin by changing the Amount slider, and then go on to the other Noise elements to replicate the original grain's characteristics. If the original has perceptible color noise, you should boost the value of the Color parameter, and if you need to equalize the noise level in the highlights in contrast to the shadows, you should lower the value of the Highlights parameter.

Creating panoramic

The production of a panorama is a great approach for capturing beautiful vistas of nature or urban settings that are too huge to be represented in a single image. Panoramas are visuals that are made by stitching together various different shots into a single continuous panoramic. Using the Photomerge tool in Adobe Photoshop, you may stitch together numerous photographs into a single panoramic view. This tool can automatically align multiple images taken from different perspectives and stitch them together to make a panorama.

Here are the steps to build a panorama in Photoshop:

Step 1: Capture the photos

The first thing you need to do to build a panorama is to take the photographs that will be utilized to create it. It is crucial to retain the camera in a fixed position and overlap each photograph by roughly thirty percent to produce a smooth outcome when stitching together the photos. You will have a higher level of control over the final picture if you capture the pictures in RAW format.

Step 2: Open Photoshop and go to **File > Automate > Photomerge**

After you have shot the photographs, start Photoshop and go to the File menu, then click Automate, and lastly Photomerge. You may choose the images in a variety of various ways, depending on your desire, in the Photomerge dialog box. You may pick from a range of file formats, including documents and folders.

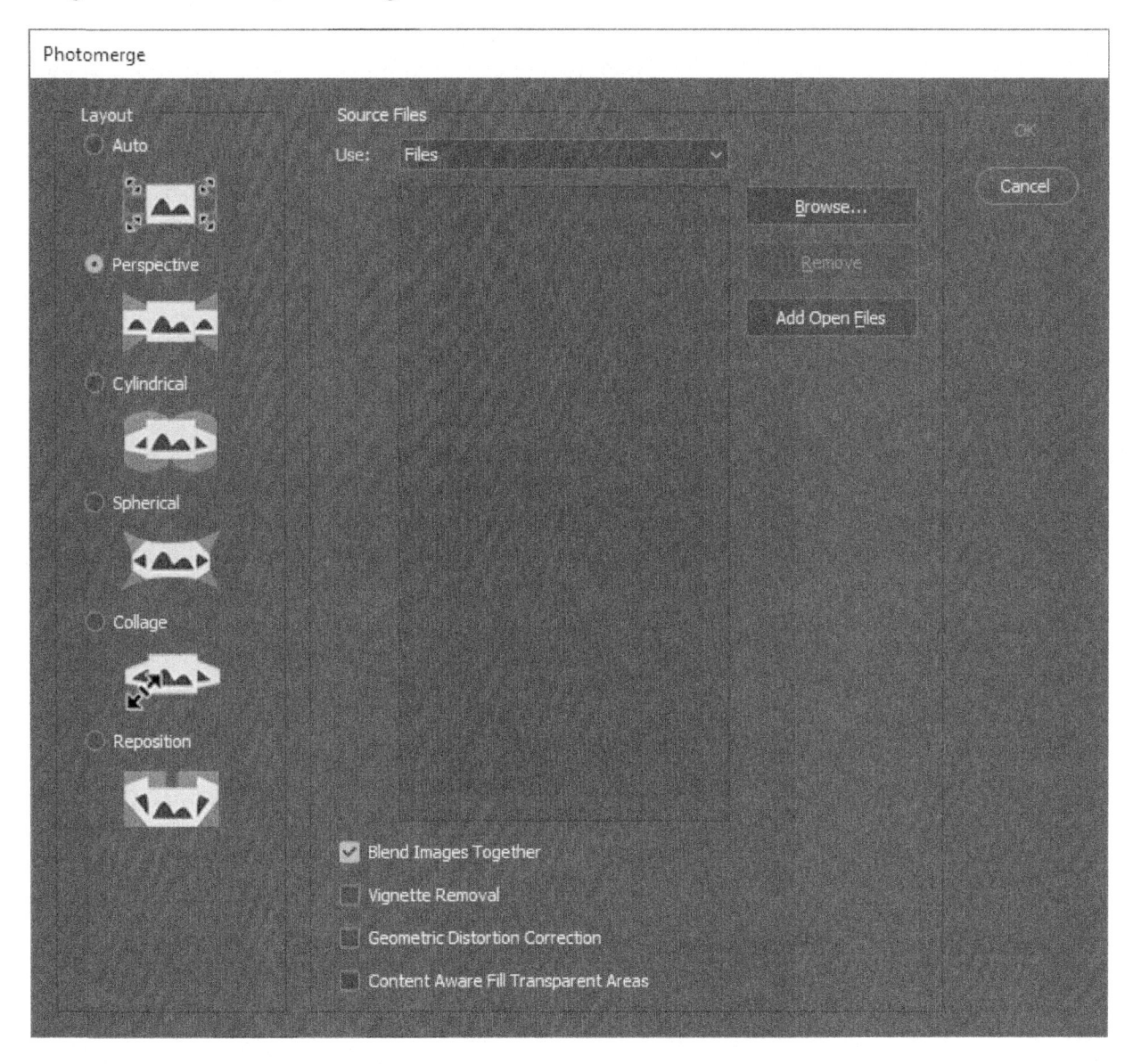

Blend photos combine photos depending on the ideal boundaries between them, instead of making a plain rectangular merge. Vignette Removal helps maintain constant brightness when merg-ing photos that are darker at their borders. Geometric Distortion Correction adjusts for barrel, pincushion, or fish-eye distortion. Content-Aware Fill Transparent spaces automati-cally patches the vacant spaces between the merged picture borders and the sides of the canvas. Photoshop is used to make an image of a panorama. Due to the complexity of the technique, you may need to wait a few seconds while Photoshop does its thing. When it is done, the full scene will be visible in the document window and the Layers panel will have five separate layers. The initial four photographs that you select to work with are located on the bottom four tiers.

Photoshop was able to find the sections of the pictures that overlapped with one another, align them, and make any required modifications to the angles. The top layer is a single panoramic picture that has been blended from all of the photographs that you chose, together with previously empty parts that have been filled in by Content-Aware Fill. The name of this layer contains the term "(merged)" in it. The selection brings focus to specific geographical locations.

NOTE: When utilizing Photomerge with a big number of pictures or images with massive pixel sizes, the procedure will take longer time. Photomerge functions faster on computers that are either more modern or have a bigger quantity of RAM.

Step 3: Select the photos and click OK

To choose the images that will be included in the panorama, pick the "Browse" option and then click it. After you have determined which pictures to utilize, you can next choose the layout choice that works best with those images. You may pick from various different layout options, including Cylindrical, Auto, and Perspective. The "Auto" mode is highly recommended as it will automatically determine the layout that fits best with your photographs.

Step 4: Merge the pictures

After you have picked the pictures to merge and the layout, you may begin to combine the images by clicking the "OK" button. The images may be loaded into Photo-shop, where the computer will automatically align them and blend them to generate the panoramic. This method can take a few minutes, depending on the number of images that you have picked and the size of the files that you have selected to work with.

Step 5: Crop and modify the panoramic

When you have done building the panorama, you may discover that some areas of it need to be trimmed or altered. Make adjustments to the exposure and color using the adjustment layers after you have cropped the edges of the panorama with the Crop tool.

Step 6: Save and export the panoramic

In the end, you should either export the panorama as a JPEG or TIFF file or save the panoramic as a Photoshop document (.psd). You may also print the panorama directly from Photoshop, or you can share it on other social networking networks.

Getting the best results with Photomerge

If you know you're intending to construct a panorama when you take your images, keep the following rules in mind to achieve the greatest result:

TIP: If you want to produce panoramas of interiors or with things near to the camera, spinning a camera by hand or on a tripod may generate parallax issues where items don't line up. You may avoid such inaccuracies by utilizing a tripod attachment (also termed a nodal slide) that accurately spins the camera around the entry pupil of the exact lens you use.

• Overlap photos by 15% to 40%: Sufficient overlap helps Photomerge blend edges cleanly. Over 50% overlap won't help and makes you take too many shots.

• Use a constant focal length: If you use a zoom lens, keep the focal length the same for all the photographs in the panoramic.

• Stay level: Keep the horizon at the same vertical position in each frame to avoid a slanted panorama. If your camera has a level indication in the viewfinder, utilize it.

• Use a tripod if possible: You'll get the greatest results if the camera is at the same height for each shot. A tripod with a rotating head makes that easier.

• Take the images from the same position: If you're not using a tripod with a rotating head, attempt to stay in the same position while you take the photos so that they are shot from the same viewpoint.

• Avoid lenses that cause creative distortion: They can interfere with Photomerge. (The Auto option does compensate for photographs you shoot with fisheye lenses.)

• Use the same exposure and aperture: Images merge more smoothly if the exposure is constant between frames; auto-exposure may generate unexpected exposure variances. Using the same aperture setting provides constant depth of field.

Try alternative layout options: If you don't like the results, try again with a different layout choice. Often, Auto makes the proper choice, but sometimes you'll get a better image with one of the other alternatives.

Filling Empty Areas When Cropping in Adobe Photoshop

In Adobe Photoshop, one of the most fundamental methods called "cropping," enables you to eliminate distracting areas of a photo so that you can concentrate on the most essential components of your design. When you crop an image, though, you often finish up with blank parts or missing details, both of which can throw off the visual balance of the picture as a whole. Photoshop provides a broad selection of tools and methodologies, which may be used to fill in the vacant spots in a seamless manner. When cropping a picture in Adobe Photoshop, there are a few various methods you may fill in any blank areas that may be left behind.

1. Content-Aware Fill: This is one of the most powerful tools that were added to Photoshop, and it was one of the first features to be introduced. This function leverages complex algo-rithms to analyze the pixels in its immediate environment to intelligently fill up any blank spots with visually acceptable content. To utilize Content-Aware Fill, all you need to do is pick the Crop tool, then draw the area that you want to crop, and then right-click anywhere within the selection. If you pick "Content-aware" from the option that appears when you right-click an image in Photoshop, the application will automatically analyze the picture and fill in any blank spots. Simple backdrops or regions with repeated patterns are great candidates for this strategy because of how successfully it works.

2. Utilizing the Clone Stamp Tool: This is another quick way for filling empty sections when cropping photos. It allows you the option to manually sample pixels from one section of the picture and clone them onto another portion of the image. Simply pick the "Clone Stamp" tool from the toolbar or click the "S" key on your keyboard to use it. Adjust the size of the brush so that it matches with the area that you want to fill, and while holding down the Alt key, click on a source area that has a texture and color that is relatively close to the one you want to duplicate. The next step is to let go of the Alt key and click or drag the brush over the open region to gradually fill it in with the sampled pixels. When using the Clone Stamp tool, you need to pay special attention to the details to create a seamless blend.

3. Healing Brush Tool: The Healing Brush tool is a valuable tool that not only helps fill empty parts in a picture but also removes faults in the image. When working with little empty spaces or when you wish to maintain the texture and features of the region around you, this tool comes in extremely helpful. Choose the Healing Brush tool from the tool bar or use the "**J**" key on your keyboard to use it. After making any required modifications to the brush size and hardness, press and hold the Alt key, and then click on an area to take a sample from. When you let go of the Alt key and paint over the empty region, Photoshop will automatically blend the sampled pixels with the pixels that are surrounding them, beautifully filling in the space that was before blank.

4. The Patch tool: This is a mix of the Clone Stamp and Healing Brush tools. It was made by merging these two tools. It allows you the option to pick a specified section, even the blank space, and then replace the pixels in that region with pixels taken from another portion of the picture. This tool performs exceptionally effectively when used in more difficult places that have irregular shapes or textures. You may use the Patch tool by either picking it from the toolbar or using the "**J**" key on your keyboard. Make sure that the region you wish to utilize as a source is included in the selection that you make around the space by drawing a selection around it. The next step is to click and drag the selection to a source region that has a texture and color that is comparable to the one you want to use to fill in the gap. When you let go of the mouse button, Photoshop will automatically blend and fill the area that has been selected with the sampled pixels.

5. Fill with Color or material: In simpler circumstances, when the unoccupied sections have a color or texture that is continuous throughout, you can select to fill the empty gaps with a solid color or material. If you want to fill an empty area with a given color, first choose the area using any of the available selection tools (such as the Rectangular Marquee tool), and then use the color picker to select the color you want to use. After that, go to the **Edit > Fill** menu item, pick "**Color**" from the Contents drop-down menu, and then click the **OK** button. You also have the op-tion of selecting "**Content-Aware**" from the **Fill** dialog box in Photoshop, which will force the software to automatically develop content that is customized to the surrounding region.

Correcting image distortion

When shooting photographs, one of the most prevalent difficulties that might develop is image distortion. This is especially true when using wide-angle lenses or photographing from an awkward angle. When an image is warped, straight lines might look curved, creating the sense that the picture has been stretched or twisted. You will be able to enhance the overall look of your images and generate a more realistic and exact portrayal of the subject matter by making use of the various tools that Adobe Photoshop provides to correct image distortion.

Lens Correction Filter

The Lens Correction filter is a powerful tool that may automatically correct distortion, chromatic aberration, and vignetting that are created by specific lenses. These difficulties can arise while using specific lenses. To apply this filter, you will first need to load your photo in Photoshop, then go to the Filter menu, choose Lens Correction, then click the "**Custom**" option. Choose your camera and lens combination from the drop-down options that are offered under the "**Lens Profile**" section of the program. The distortion will be automatically corrected by the filter, and you can use the sliders to fine-tune the correction once it has been applied. It is probable that the Lens Correction filter is not the ideal solution for repairing more intricate distortion problems as it is both a fast and simple way to repair distortion for specific lenses. Common faults that can be produced by camera lenses, such as barrel and pincushion distortion, chromatic aberration, and vignetting, can be addressed with a filter known as the Lens Correction filter. The phrase "panel distortion" refers to a lens imperfection that causes straight lines in an image to bend outward toward the picture's boundaries. Pincushion distortion is the reverse phenomenon, causing straight lines to bend inward. Chromatic aberration appears as a color fringe at the margins of picture objects. Vignetting happens when the margins of a picture, typically the corners, are darker than the center.

TIP: If you capture photographs using a camera option that saves raw files, the Optics panel of the Adobe Camera Raw plug-in module (which is used for processing raw images in Photoshop and Bridge) will give you with settings that are extremely equivalent to those used by professional photographers.

The existence of these defects in various lenses could vary depending on the focal length or the f-stop setting. The Lens Correction filter may be used to apply settings that are suited to the camera, lens, and focal length that were utilized during the production of the picture that was shot. Additionally, the filter may rotate an image or correct the perspective shift that happens when an image is acquired with the camera inclined vertically or horizontally. Adjusting these parameters using the grid that comes integrated into the filter is both simpler and more exact than doing it with the Transform command.

Transform Tool

The Transform tool is a versatile feature that enables users to manually modify the perspective of a picture, reducing distortion and making sure that lines are aligned appropriately. To employ the Transform tool, first, pick the photo you wish to change, then go to the change menu and click on Transform > Perspective. To make modifications to the perspective, drag the corners or borders of the bounding box, and make use of the guidelines or grid to ensure that lines are generated in a straight way. The skew and tilt distortions may both be rectified with the use of the Transform tool, which can also be used to correct other sorts of distortion.

Warp Tool

Another strong feature that may be used to repair distortion by manually adjusting the form of an image is the Warp tool, which can be found in the Edit menu. To employ the Warp tool, first, pick the photo you wish to change, then go to the change menu and click on the Warp option. Make sure that the lines in the picture are straight and that the overall appearance is natural by altering the shape of the image using the control points. When it comes to fixing distortion in photographs that have irregular forms or difficult views, the Warp tool may be a very beneficial tool to apply.

Liquify Tool

You may repair distortion in a photo by pushing or pulling pixels in various directions using the Liquify tool, which is a complex feature that offers you the power to manipulate the pixels in an image. To use the Liquify tool, first, pick the photo you wish to alter, then go to the Filter menu and click on Liquify. Adjusting the size, density, and pressure of the brush can be done with the tools on the left-hand side of the interface while editing the pixels in the picture may be done using the tools on the right-hand side. The Liquify tool may be a highly use-ful tool for correcting distortion, but its utilization asks for a more advanced degree of both ability and knowledge.

Adaptive Wide-Angle Filter

The Adaptive Wide-Angle filter is a specific piece of gear that may reduce distortion in images that were acquired using wide-angle lenses. To apply this filter to your photo, first, choose it, then go to the Filter menu and click Adaptive Wide Angle. If you use the tool to draw lines around the limits of items that should look straight, then the filter will automati-cally correct the perspective and repair any distortion that may have happened. The Adaptive Wide-Angle filter is a potent tool for correcting distortion in wide-angle images; yet, it is probable that it is not acceptable for usage with other kinds of distortion.

Extending depth of field

The phrase **"depth of field"** refers to the range of distances in a photograph that are clear enough to be deemed visible, with objects at varying distances looking to be in focus. If you want to make a dramatic impression or call attention to a specific topic, employing a tight depth of focus might be useful. On the other side, there are situations when you may want to enhance the depth of field in a picture to make sure that more items are in focus. Because the depth of field, or the range of distances that may be brought into focus, is occasionally limited in an image, it is frequently essential to select whether to concentrate on the image's foreground or backdrop. You can take a series of shots with the focus set along the range of distances you want to look sharp if you want a bigger range of distances to be in focus (more depth of field), but it isn't attainable due to the limits of the equipment or the location. You may merge the pho-tographs in Photoshop by employing a method that is known as focus stacking in some circles. You will get one picture that has the combined depth of field of the photographs in the collection. It is advised that you use a tripod to keep the camera stable to assist the perfect alignment of the images that will be required. On the other hand, if you can consistently frame your photographs and get them aligned, you may be able to create acceptable results with a handheld camera.

Many various ways may be utilized in Adobe Photoshop to boost the depth of field in the images that you have taken.

1. Focus Stacking: Focus stacking means capturing numerous images of the same subject, each of which has a separate point of focus, and then combining those photographs into a single photo-graph in which everything looks to be in focus. To employ the focus stacking tool in Photoshop, you must first open all of the photographs that you wish to stack. After that, pick Load Files into Stack by heading to the File menu and choosing Scripts. Select all of the photographs that you want to stack in the dialogue box, and then make sure the option labeled "Attempt to Automati-cally Align Source Images" is selected. After the photographs have been loaded, go to Edit> Auto-Blend Layers and pick the "Stack Images" option from the drop-down menu. Photoshop will automatically blend the photographs, generating a single picture in which everything is in sharp focus.

2. Utilizing Gaussian Blur and Masking: This is yet another way that may be used to widen the depth of field in a shot. The photo layer is duplicated, then a Gaussian blur is added to the top layer, and finally, the blurred areas are masked off so that the crisp portions that are underneath may be seen. To use this approach, first, make a copy of the layer you wish to work on, and then go to the Filter menu and pick the Gaussian Blur option for the top layer (Filter> Blur> Gaussian Blur). Next, apply a layer mask to the top layer, and using the brush tool, paint over the sections of the picture that you wish to stay sharp. This will expose the sections of the image that were once sharp on the layer behind it.

3. Smart Objects and Blur Filters: The employment of **"Smart Objects"** and **"Blur Filters"** is another strategy that may be utilized to great benefit to boost the perceived depth of field inside a photograph. To use this approach, you must first turn your photo layer into a smart object by right-clicking on the layer and choosing "**Convert to Smart Object**." After that, pick **Filter > Blur Gallery > Field Blur** from the menu at the top of your screen. You can achieve a deeper depth of field in the photo by utilizing the Field Blur panel, where you can alter both the degree of blurring and the distribution of that blurring. You may also blur some sections of the photo by using the "**Add Pin**" tool, which is found in the Tools menu.

4. High Pass Filter: Finally, you may brighten certain sections of a photo by using the High Pass filter. This will extend the perceived depth of field. To implement this function, first make a duplicate of the layer that you wish to work on, and then click **"Other"** from the filter menu and select **"High Pass"** from the drop-down menu that displays. Create a sharpened effect by first setting the radius to a value that makes the edges of the objects in the picture seem sharp, and then changing the blending mode of the layer to either **"Overlay"** or **"Soft Light**." This will re-sult in the items appearing sharper and more in focus than they originally were.

Removing objects with Content-Aware Fill

The process of eliminating undesirable items from images may be both time-consuming and tedious. However, the Content-Aware Fill tool provided in Adobe Photoshop may make this procedure simpler and more successful. You may remove items from your photographs in a smooth manner with the aid of a clever tool called Content-Aware Fill. This tool uses the pix-els in the surrounding area to fill in the voids left by the eliminated items.

Here's how to use Content-Aware Fill to eliminate things from your photos:

Step 1: Open your image in Photoshop and pick the object you wish to delete using the **Lasso**, **Marquee**, or **Magic Wand tool**.

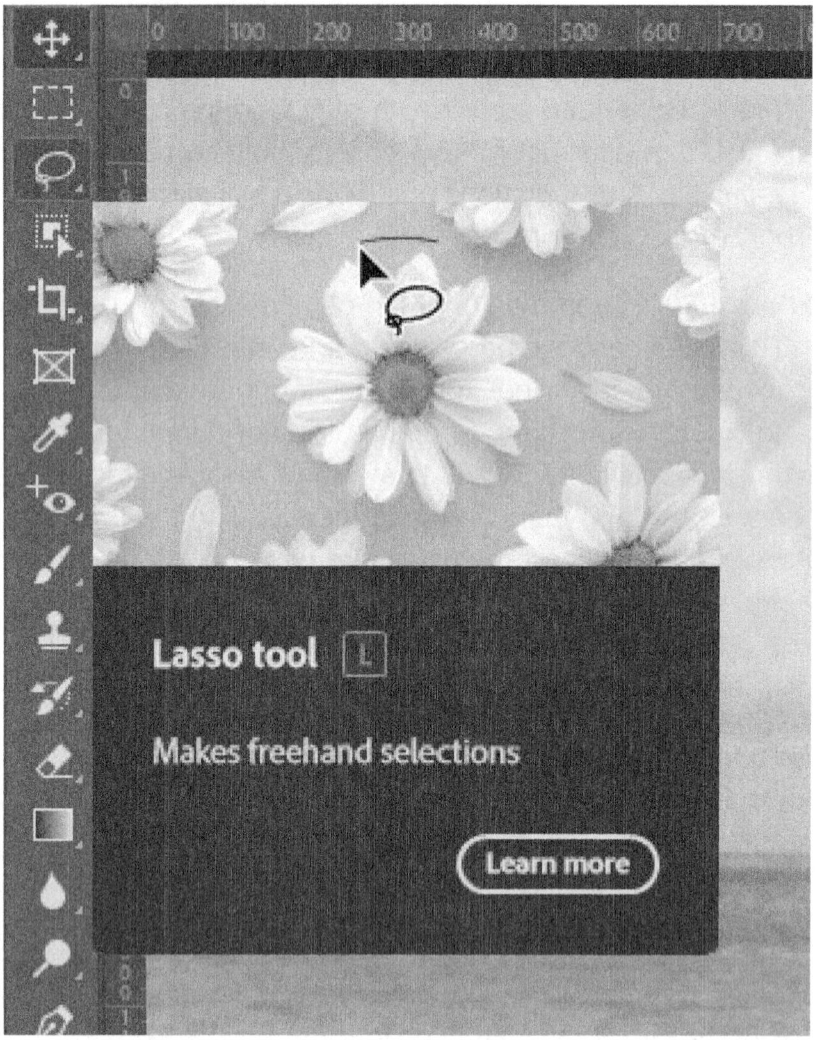
Lasso tool
L
Makes freehand selections
Learn more

Step 2: Once you have made your selection, go to **Edit > Fill** or use the keyboard shortcut **Shift + F5** to fill in the selected area.

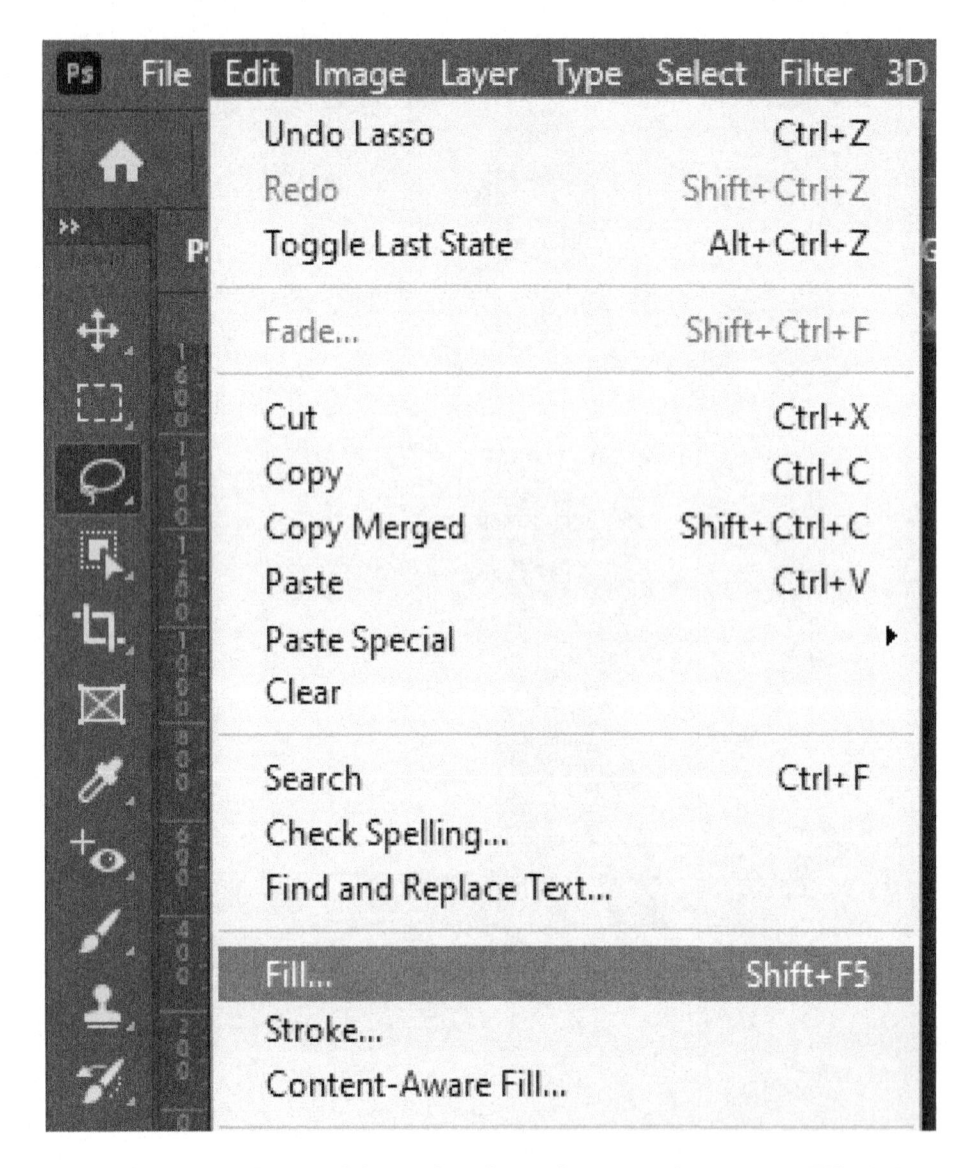

Step 3: Choose "**Content-Aware**" from the drop-down option in the Fill dialogue box, and then click the **OK** button.

Step 4: After evaluating the pixels in the surrounding region, Photoshop will now fill in the area that was chosen with a new texture that is consistent with the surrounding area.

Step 5: If you are not pleased with the results, you can alter the parameters in the **Content-Aware Fill** box. To acquire the best possible results, you may change the parameters for the Sampling Area, Output parameters, and Color Adaptation using this panel.

Step 6: When you are content with the way things turned out, click the "**OK**" button to save the alterations to your photo.

Here are some pointers for utilizing Content-Aware Fill effectively:

1. Use a tiny selection area: Content-Aware Fill functions most successfully when applied to relatively small items. If you make an effort to get rid of a massive thing, the repercussions may not turn out as well.

2. Use several selections: If you have a vast item that you wish to get rid of, consider generating many selections and then filling each one in individually. This will offer you more control over the removal procedure. This can aid you in getting more positive outcomes.

3. Use the Spot Healing Brush Tool: If you have little defects or blemishes that you wish to eliminate, consider utilizing the Spot Healing Brush tool instead of Content-Aware Fill. The Spot Heal-ing Brush tool is meant to eliminate minor imperfections without leaving any evidence behind.

4. Experiment with the options: The Content-Aware Fill panel provides you the flexibility to adjust the settings for the Sampling Area, Output parameters, and Color Adaptation. Try out different combinations of these choices to find what works best for you.

Adjusting perspective in a photograph

A vital talent for photographers and graphic designers alike is the ability to modify the perspective of a picture. Changing the orientation of a photograph is what this technique includes. This may be done to achieve a composition that is more visually attractive or to rectify distortion produced by the lens of the camera. When shooting architecture, landscapes, or interiors, where straight lines and angles are crucial, altering the perspective may be a highly helpful technique to employ. Adobe Photoshop is one of the most generally used picture editing applications, and it is packed with certain essential capabilities that make it simple and quick to make alterations to the perspective of an image. The following is a list of some of the ways and tools that may be used in Adobe Photoshop to make alterations to the perspective of a photograph.

Perspective Crop Tool

A relatively recent addition to Photoshop, the Perspective Crop tool allows users to make adjustments to an image's perspective by cropping select sections of the picture. It provides you the option to build a crop box around the area of the photo that you wish to adjust, and then you can vary the perspective of the image by altering the corners of the crop box.

To use the Perspective Crop tool:

Step 1: Select the Crop tool from the toolbar.

Step 2: In the choices bar at the top of the screen, pick the Perspective Crop tool.

Step 3: Draw a crop box around the region of the image you wish to modify.

Step 4: Use the knobs on the corners of the crop box to alter the perspective of the image.

Step 5: Press "**Enter**" to apply the adjustments and crop the image.

The Perspective Crop tool helps handle sophisticated perspective challenges, such as those generated by shooting from a low angle or utilizing wide-angle lenses. Because it retains the image's original proportions, it is also beneficial for maintaining the image's original quality, which is a function of sustaining the image's integrity.

Transform Tool

The Transform tool is a simple tool for changing perspective in Photoshop. It lets you distort, skew, or scale an image to modify its viewpoint.

To use the Transform tool:

Step 1: Open the image you wish to alter in Photoshop.

Step 2: Click on "**Edit**" in the top menu, then pick "**Transform**" and "**Perspective**."

Step 3: You will see a bounding box around the image with handles on the corners and sides. Drag the handles to alter the perspective of the image.

Step 4: Press the "**Enter**" key to apply the change.

The perspective of an entire picture or a single piece of an image can be adjusted with the use of the transform tool. It may also be used to adjust the image's size and orientation. How-ever, it may not be the ideal tool for retaining the quality of the original picture or addressing intricate perspective problems.

Transformations with the Content-Aware Move tool

A thistle may be copied using the Content-Aware Move tool in just a few simple steps, blending in with the backdrop without sticking out as an exact clone of the original. We are dealing with a sample of thistle here.

Step 1. Open the Thistle file.

Step 2. Select the Content-Aware Move tool (grouped with the healing brush and Red Eye tools).

Step 3. In the settings bar, pick Extend from the Mode menu. Choosing Extend duplicates the thistle; if you simply want to reposition the single thistle, you will pick Move.

Step 4. With the Content-Aware Move tool, create a selection around the thistle, with a margin big enough to include a bit of the grass surrounding it.

Step 5. Drag the pick to the left, then place it in the vacant space of grass.

Step 6. Right-click (Windows) or **Control-click** (macOS) the dragged thistle and pick Flip Horizontal.

Step 7. Drag the top-left transformation handle to make the thistle smaller. If you think the copy of the thistle should be farther from the original, put the pointer inside the transformation rectangle and drag the thistle copy slightly to the left.

Step 8. Press Enter or Return to apply the modifications. Leave the content selected so you may alter the Structure and Color choices in the choices box to optimize how the new thistle integrates with the backdrop.

Step 9. Choose **Select > Deselect**, save your changes, and close the document.

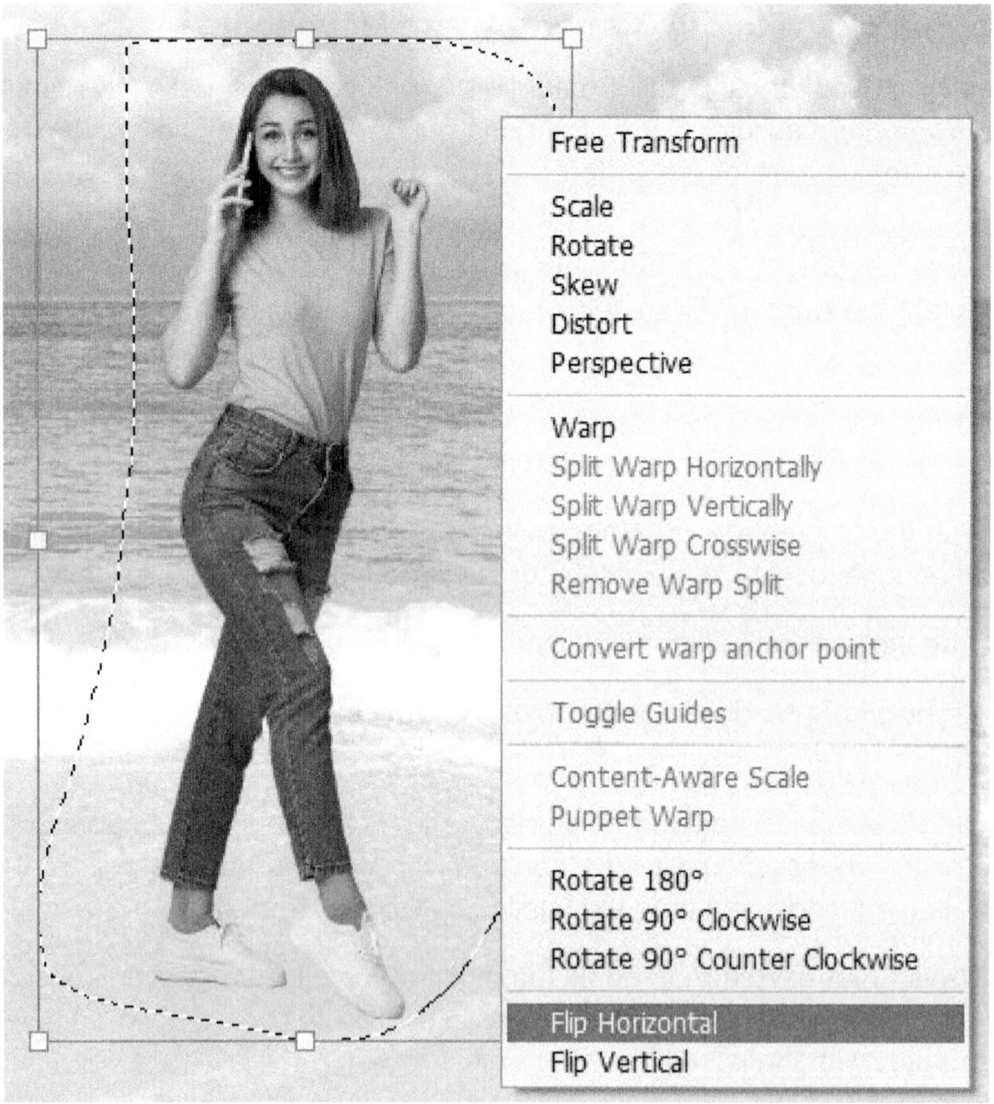
Free Transform
Scale
Rotate
Skew
Distort
Perspective
Warp
Split Warp Horizontally
Split Warp Vertically
Split Warp Crosswise
Remove Warp Split
Convert warp anchor point
Toggle Guides
Content-Aware Scale
Puppet Warp
Rotate 180°
Rotate 90° Clockwise
Rotate 90° Counter Clockwise
Flip Horizontal
Flip Vertical

Tips for utilizing the Content-Aware Move tool

1. Use a High-Quality Image

When working with high-quality photographs that have well-defined borders, the Content-Aware Move tool works the best. It is likely that the tool will not produce the results you desire if you are working with a photograph that is low quality or is unclear. Always employ photographs of good quality with well-defined borders to guarantee that the product operates as it was created to.

2. Adjust the Brush Size

When working with the Content-Aware Move tool, it is vital to alter the brush size so that it coincides with the particular item that you are editing. You may modify the size of the brush by using the left and right bracket keys. When working on smaller items, start with a lower brush size, then work your way up to a higher brush size as you work on larger objects. Because of this, you'll be able to make more exact selections and avoid choosing unwanted sections of the image by accident.

3. Use the Lasso Tool

When used in tandem with the Content-Aware Move tool, the Lasso tool is a terrific tool to have at your disposal. Make a more exact selection of the region surrounding the object you wish to move by making use of the Lasso tool. This will assist in guaranteeing that you do not select unwanted spots by accident and that the stuff you are shifting is documented accurately.

4. Use the Clone Stamp Tool

If the Content-Aware Move tool does not give the results you want, you may try using the Clone Stamp tool to manually fill in the gap left behind after relocating the object. This can be done if the Content-Aware Move tool does not give the results you require. This can be especially beneficial for more involved photographs when the automatic fill process does not perform as it was designed to.

5. Use Multiple Layers

When working with a photo using the Content-Aware Move tool, it is usually advantageous to create numerous layers. This helps guarantee that crucial sections of the picture are not erroneously erased. You should establish a new layer for each object that you wish to move, and you should always make sure that you are working on the proper layer. This will aid to guarantee that you don't accidentally delete important sections of the image and that you may quickly make improvements or rectify blunders if you do create them.

6. Practice, Practice, Practice

It takes work to become skilled with any of Photoshop's tools, and the Content-Aware Move tool is no exception. To acquire a better knowledge of how the tool works, attempt using it in a range of different photographs and try moving items to a variety of various positions. The more you use the tool, the more familiar you will get with it, which will lead to superior outcomes as you continue to make use of it.

7. Keep the Surrounding Area in Mind

It is necessary to take into mind the local surroundings if utilizing the Content-Aware relocate tool to relocate an object. Check to check that the relocation of the item to its new place does not result in any visual distractions or an imbalance in the picture. Make alterations to the composition of the picture by making use of the tool but verify that the finished output is aestheti-cally pleasing and has a feeling of balance.

8. Consider Using Masks

If you are working with a difficult image, you may want to think about applying masks so that you may make more accurate alterations and increase your selection. Masks enable you to make a selection that is based on a particular portion of the picture, which may be advantageous for creating more precise changes and preventing inadvertent adjustments to other sections of the image. You may make a selection based on a certain section of the image by applying masks.

9. Experiment with Different Settings

The Content-Aware Move tool includes a broad selection of parameters that users may tweak to achieve a variety of varied effects. Experiment with the different settings, such as the Patch Adaptation and Color Adaptation choices, to determine which combination provides your picture the greatest prospective outcomes. Experiment with a range of settings and assess the outcomes to deter-mine which one's suit most effectively to your requirements.

CHAPTER 6: MASKS AND CHANNELS

Working with masks and channels

A digital picture is an opaque rectangle once it has been recovered from the camera. To combine a piece of that picture with others, you must first conceal the areas of the image that are not the topic of the combination. You may even determine that just specified areas of a layer should have an adjustment layer or filter applied to them. The usage of a mask, which is a technique to in-dicate areas of a layer as translucent, is the method that is advocated for attaining both of these purposes.

TIP: The usage of masks is akin to putting masking tape on windowpanes or wall trim before painting a house: the areas that are masked are shielded from having their appear-ance changed.

Because it is reversible, utilizing a mask is a more helpful alternative than removing superfluous areas of a layer. For instance, if you realize that you mistakenly cut off part of the topic, employing a mask will allow you to recover the region that was trimmed so that you may fix your error. An image can have color channels as well as alpha channels, which allow retain and reuse choices as well as indicate translucent zones for an entire document. Alpha channels can be discovered in photographs. When trying to paint or draw a mask or channel edge that exactly follows a non-sharp border of a subject, such as fuzzy hair, it might be challenging to produce a satisfactory outcome. Adobe Photoshop offers numerous automated features that can aid you in fast making complicated selections and masks.

About Masks and Channels

Masks and channels are two significant features in Adobe Photoshop that enable users to produce accurate selections, adjust specified sections of a picture, and alter the transparency and opacity of an image. These capabilities allow Adobe Photoshop to be an exceptionally flexible application. In this part, we will explore the principles of masks and channels, including the dis-tinctions between the two and the various purposes for each.

Masks in Photoshop

In Adobe Photoshop, a mask is a non-destructive approach to alter a picture. It lets users construct a selection, or "**mask**," around a specified portion of a picture, which may subsequently be altered without impacting other areas of the image. In Photoshop, there are two separate types of masks to choose from: vector masks and layer masks. The brush tool or one of the other selection tools may be used to make layer masks, which can subsequently be used to apply to individual layers. Utilizing the pen tool, vector masks may be applied to vector forms and can be built from scratch.

In Photoshop, the most widely used sort of mask is called a layer mask. The "**Add Layer Mask**" button may be located at the bottom of the Layers panel. After picking the layer you wish to mask, you may then click on the button to generate the mask. After the mask has been formed, you may make a selection around the region that you wish to mask by using the brush tool or one of the other selection tools. Editing a mask can be done with the brush tool, which enables the user to add or delete areas from the mask, or using the selection tools, which allow the user to design a whole new mask. Masks may be saved and applied to additional layers, which makes it straightforward to create alterations that are uniform across several levels.

Channels in Photoshop

Channels arc another key feature accessible in Photos hop that offers users the power to adjust the opacity as well as the transparency of a picture. A image in Photoshop is made up of four channels: the red channel, the green channel, the blue channel, and the alpha channel. The alpha channel contains information about the transparency of the picture, in contrast to the red, green, and blue channels, which store information about the color of the image. The Channel Mixer is a piece of software that enables users to make changes to the levels of each channel to acquire the desired effect. Channels can be adjusted using this program. For instance, users may achieve a retro, sepia-toned effect by adjusting the intensities of the red and blue channels in the channel mix. In Photoshop, the construction of selections may also be achieved via the employment of channels. Users may make a selection depending on the contrast of the picture by choosing a channel and then using the Levels tool to modify the contrast. This strategy is especially effective for identifying portions that have a significant contrast, such as text or line art.

Differences between Masks and Channels

Although users of either masks or channels may make precise selections and alter particular portions of a picture, there are important contrasts between the two types of editing tools. The construction of non-destructive adjustments in a picture is performed via the usage of masks. They make it feasible for users to form a selection around a given region of a photograph and then edit that part of the image without influencing any other sections of the image. Masks are a highly valuable tool for conducting intricate edits, including erasing a backdrop from an image or adjusting the exposure of a certain region of the photo. On the other hand, channels are what are utilized to govern the opacity as well as the transparency of an image. They make it possible for users to modify the levels of each channel to create the aesthetic that they want, such as a vintage or sepia-toned impression. Channels may be quite beneficial when it comes to making correct selections dependent on the contrast of a picture, such as choosing text or line art. Channels may be found in most image editing systems.

Applications of Masks and Channels

In Adobe Photoshop, the employment of masks and channels may be observed in a broad range of various scenarios. The following are some examples of frequent applications:

1. Photo Retouching: When it comes to photo retouching, masks, and channels are two of the most crucial tools. Users may eliminate flaws, modify the exposure, and make other modifications without impact-ing other areas of the photo by applying masks to create precise selections around selected regions of the image. Channels may be used to produce precise selections based on contrast, which makes it simple to zero in on particular portions of a picture for the sake of editing.

2. Graphic Design: In graphic design, masks and channels are highly essential tools to have at your disposal. Designers may produce sophisticated composites, adjust colors and contrast, and add text and graphic elements to selected aspects of a photograph without influencing other parts of the image by applying masks to generate precise selections around certain regions of the image. Because channels can be used to produce specific selections based on contrast, it is a breeze to zero in on certain portions of a photo for editing or making translucent effects.

3. Fine Art Photography: Masks and channels are two tools that are highly vital for fine art photographers to have. Photographers may carefully modify contrast and exposure, construct dynamic black-and-white conver-sions, and apply filters and effects to specified sections of a photo by employing masks to create exact selections around those regions. Channels may be used to create specific choices based on contrast, which makes it straightforward to adjust just particular sections of a picture and to achieve one-of-a-kind color and tone effects.

4. Web Design: Web designers can profit from the utilization of masks and channels as essential tools. Designers may design sophisticated layouts, add textures and patterns, and adjust colors and contrast without impacting other sections of the picture by applying masks to produce accurate selections around specified areas of an image. Because channels can be used to produce specific selections based on contrast, it is a breeze to zero in on certain portions of a photo for editing or making translucent effects.

5. Print Design: Masks and channels are extra tools that print designers cannot live without. Designers may design elaborate layouts, adjust colors and contrast, and apply filters and effects to specified portions of a picture by creating accurate selections around those regions using masks. This permits them to do so without affecting any other parts of the image. Channels may be used to create specific choices based on contrast, which makes it straightforward to adjust just particular sections of a picture and to achieve one-of-a-kind color and tone effects.

Alpha channels, fast masks, clipping masks, layer masks, vector masks-what's the difference?

It's merely multiple variants of the same concept: an image overlay that allows you determine whether sections of a layer are visible or transparent by adjusting the quantity of white, black, and gray areas in the picture.

Determine which choice is ideal for you by familiarizing yourself with the following important distinctions:

Masks not only decide which sections of a layer are shown but also which parts of your adjustments are visible. This is because masks indicate which sections of a layer are visible. For instance, if you paint on a masked layer using the Brush tool, the brush strokes will only be seen on the areas of the layer that are not masked (those that are white).

One of the visible components of a color picture is kept in what is known as a color channel. An RGB image, for instance, comprises of three separate color channels: red, green, and blue.

A selection is kept in the form of a grayscale image in an alpha channel. Alpha channels are different from layers and color channels and exist on their own. Alpha channels can be converted to and from choices as well as paths. An alpha channel is a technique for some file formats, such as PNG, to designate areas of an image that are transparent in a manner that is recognized by other applications.

In Photoshop, a layer mask is an alpha channel that is connected with a certain layer. This channel regulates which aspects of the layer are shown and which portions are buried.

When you paint black in it, it shows as a white thumbnail next to the layer thumbnail in the Layers panel; an outline around the layer mask thumbnail indicates that it's chosen.

A vector mask is a layer mask that is not comprised of pixels but rather resolution-independent vector objects. It is handy in cases when having accurate control over the mask edges is more crucial than being able to update the mask using a brush. You may build vector masks by following the directions on the Layer > Vector Mask submenu and using the pen or form tools, accordingly.

When one-layer masks another layer, a clipping mask is formed as a consequence. In the layer list, the thumbnail preview of a clipped layer seems sunken, and an arrow heading to the layer below it is presented at a right angle. The name of the base layer that was cut is marked in bold.

The tonal contrast of a color channel, such as the green channel in an RGB image, is used to construct a mask known as a channel mask. This style of mask may be applied to a picture. The creation of channel masks is a key step in the implementation of increasingly advanced masking, color correction, and sharpening procedures. For instance, the border between the sky and the trees might be seen most clearly in the blue channel.

A Quick mask is a temporary mask that you construct to constrain painting or other alterations to a particular region of a layer. You may make a quick mask by clicking the **"Add Quick Mask"** button. It's a selection in pixel form; rather than altering the selection marquee, you use painting tools to build a fast mask instead.

Using Select and Mask and Select Subject

In the domains of graphic design, picture editing, and compositing, one of the most frequent jobs is picking and deleting topics from pictures. The technique may be simplified and made more accurate with the help of two strong tools that are provided with Adobe Photoshop. These tools are titled Select and Mask and Select Subject. These technologies make use of advanced algorithms to automatically distinguish and segregate items from the backdrop. As a result, users are given the chance to fine-tune their selections and extract subjects with higher precision. Let's study the most efficient approach to put these tools to work.

Select and Mask

The Select and Mask tool in Photoshop is a strong and adaptable software that enables users to undertake comprehensive selection and refinement operations. It offers a large number of tools and alternatives to assist customers to gain accurate outcomes by refining their decisions.

The following is a rundown on how to employ Select and Mask:

Step 1. Launch Adobe Photoshop and put the photo you wish to alter into the application.

Step 2. Using any of the available selection tools (such as the Quick Selection Tool or the Lasso Tool), construct a rough selection around the topic.

Step 3. While preserving the initial selection as the active one, go to the choose menu and pick the Select and Mask option.

Step 4. The Select and Mask workspace will emerge, presenting the photo along with a range of tools and choices for further editing the image.

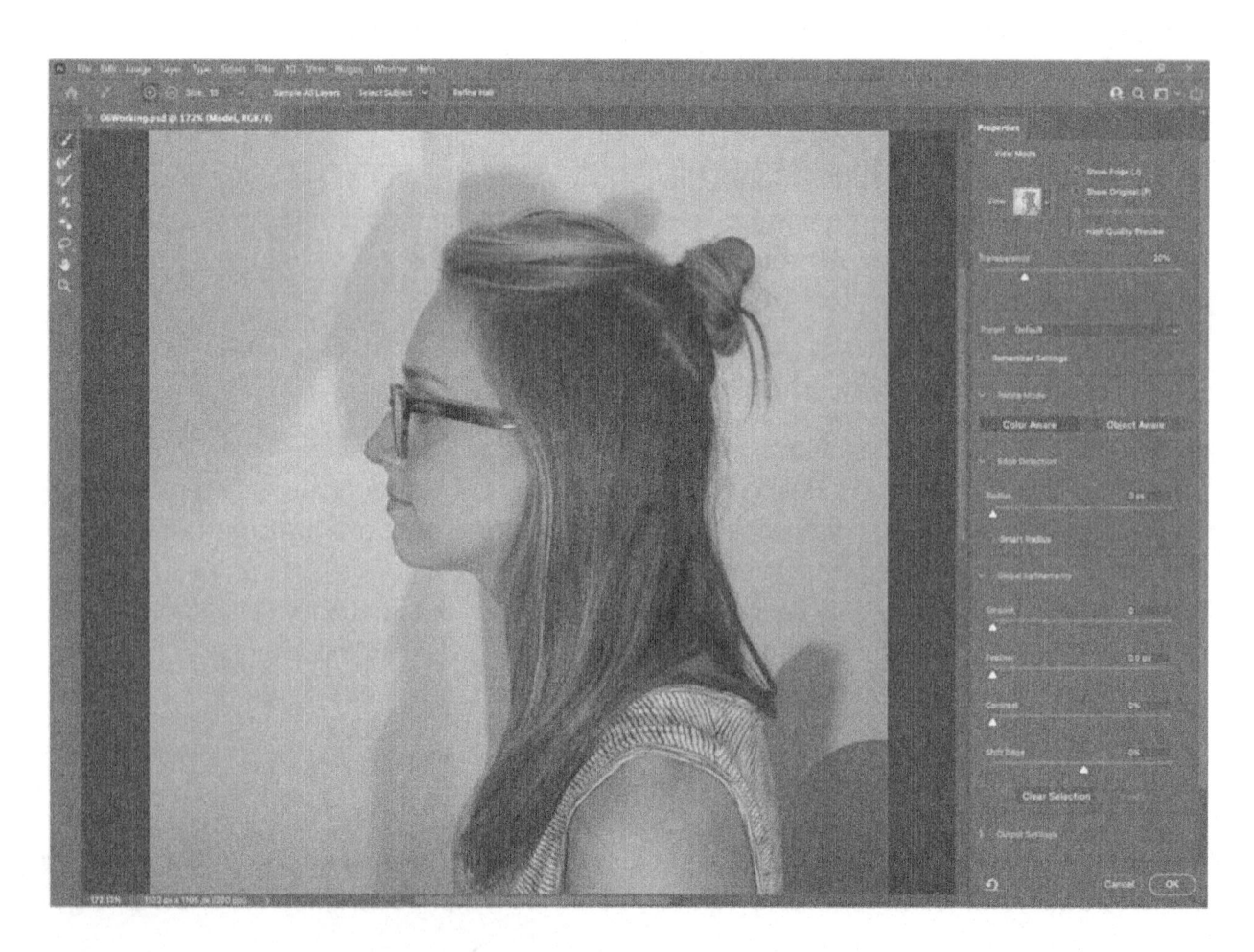

Step 5. To acquire the necessary amount of detail in the selection edges, you may use either the Quick Selection Tool or the Refine Edge Brush Tool You may add or delete areas from the selection with the aid of the Quick Selection Tool, while the Refine Edge Brush Tool enables you to paint around the edges to acquire a more accurate degree of refinement.

Step 6. To acquire a more accurate result with the selection, utilize the sliders contained in the Properties tab. Among the various adjustments are the improvement of edge detection, the smoothing of the edges, the alteration of the contrast, and more. Experiment with different combinations of these settings to determine what works best.

Step 7. You may receive a preview of the selection by picking numerous display choices (such as Overlay, On White, or Black), which will allow you to see how the topic appears against a range of backdrops. In the View Mode section of the Properties panel, select the View menu, and then choose Overlay from the list of available options. In place of the checkerboard pattern observed earlier on onion skin, the masked zone now appears as a shade of red that is only partially opaque. It is trustworthy since nothing has been concealed as of yet.

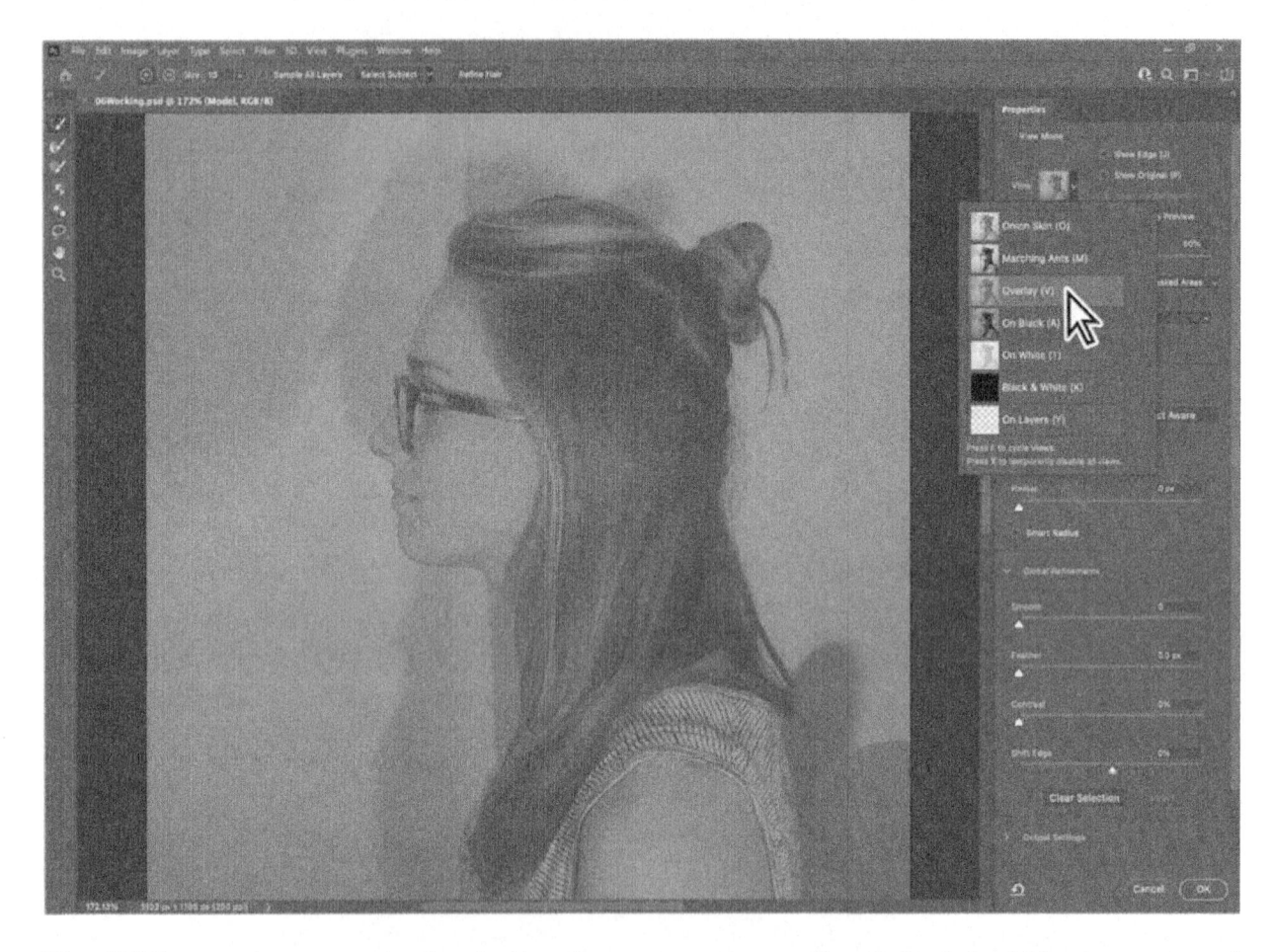

Tip: While you have a selection tool active, you may use the Select And Mask command by clicking the Select And Mask button placed in the options bar. Previously, you would have needed to locate the command in the submenu. Simply hitting the F key will allow you to toggle between the View Modes in a whirlwind. When you view the game in a number of settings, you are better able to discover errors in the selecting process that may not be so evident in other modes. You may observe the mask more clearly over a range of backdrops by utilizing the various observe Modes, which are offered for your convenience. In this instance, the red overlay will make it simpler to notice missing patches and boundaries where loose hair isn't totally covered. This is because the red overlay is translucent.

Step 8. Click the Select Subject button that is situated in the choices bar.

NOTE. You may decide where the selection will be processed by using the drop-down list provided in the Select Subject button. It's likely that implementing a more comprehensive machine learn-ing model on a more powerful distant computer will provide better results when using cloud processing. Typically, processes on your device will take less time. You may make this alteration permanent in the Image Processing section of the Preferences dialog box. Changing this parameter only affects the picture following the one you are now seeing.

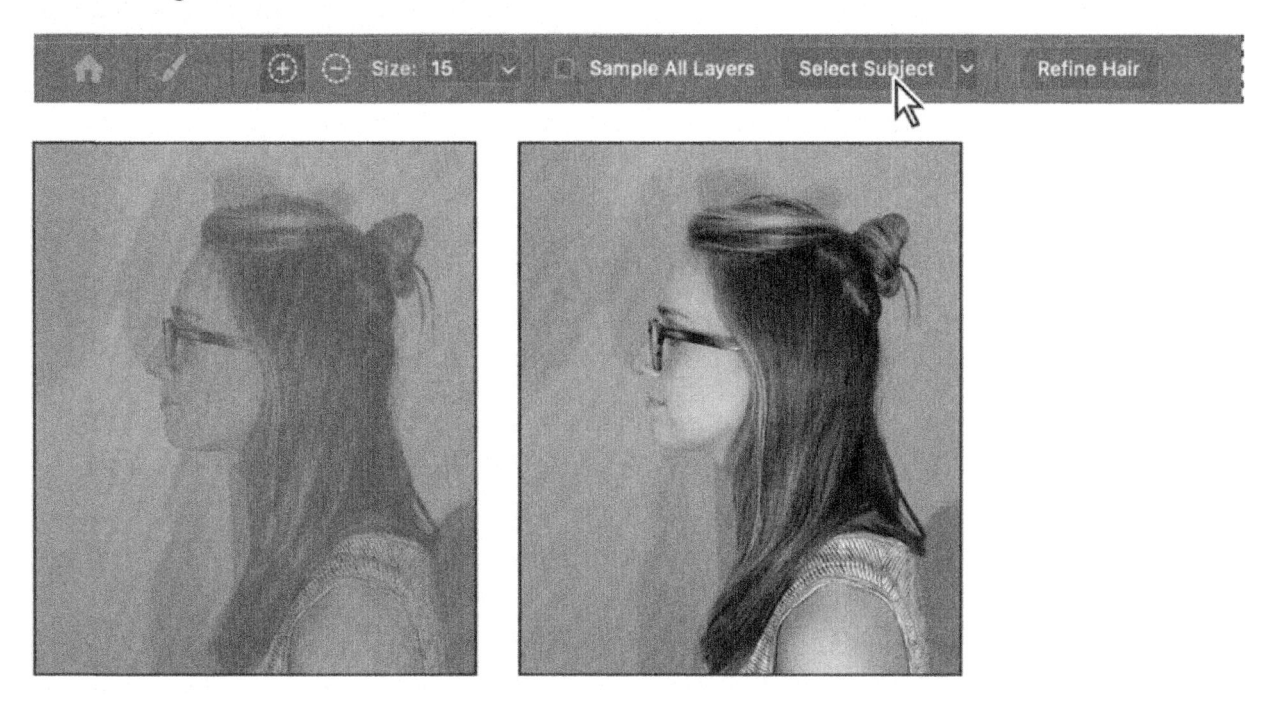

The Select Subject function is taught to detect common topics of an image, such as people, animals, and objects, and then produces a selection for them using cutting-edge machine learning technology. This procedure takes place before the photograph is even taken. Although the selection may not be optimal, it is typically near enough for you to be able to modify it in a clear and practical manner utilizing additional selection methods.

Step 9. Click the View option in the View Mode section of the Properties panel and pick Black & White. This View Mode helps make the mask edge easier to see.

TIP: You don't have to be in the Select and Mask dialog box to use the Select > Subject command. It's available even when a selection tool is not active. Also, it's OK to use Select Subject first and then enter Select and Mask to narrow the selection.

Step 10. In the Properties window, expand the Refine Mode if needed, then select Color Aware. If a notice displays, click **OK**. The mask edge changes.

The two Refine Modes read possible subject edges differently. Color Aware may work effectively on basic backdrops like the one in this experiment. Object Aware may perform better on more complicated backdrops. If you wish to compare the two results, choose **Edit > Toggle Last State** to move between them.

Step 11. Click the View option in the **View Mode** section of the Properties panel and pick Overlay to better compare the edge to the actual picture.

Notice that there are a few spots over the chest that were overlooked by Select Subject. You may quickly add them to the selection using the Quick Selection tool.

Step 12. Make sure the Quick Selection tool is chosen. In the settings bar, set up a brush with a size of 15 px.

Step 13. Drag the Quick Selection tool over the missed regions (without extending into the background) to add the missed areas to the selection. Notice that the Quick Selection tool fills in the selection as it recognizes content borders, so you don't have to be accurate. It's acceptable if you release the mouse button and drag it more than once.

Where you drag tells the Quick Selection tool which parts should be exposed and are not part of the mask. Do not drag the Quick Selection tool over or past the model's edge to the backdrop, because this instructs the Quick Selection tool to include part of the background in the mask, and you don't want that. If you mistakenly add undesirable regions to the mask, either pick modification > Undo or reverse the modification by drawing over it with the Quick Selection tool in Subtract mode. To activate Subtract mode for the Quick Selection tool, click the Subtract from Selection icon in the options bar.

As you move the Quick Selection tool over the model, the overlay fades from the regions that you are designating to be shown. Don't stress about absolute perfection at this time.

Step 14. Once you are pleased with the selection and refinement, click **OK** to make the changes.

Tips for Using Select and Mask and Select Subject

1. Refine the edges: To generate edges that are smooth and precise, you may utilize the refinement tools in Select and Mask, such as the Refine Edge Brush Tool and the Feather slider.

2. Use different view modes: Try out a range of view modes in Select and Mask, such as Overlay, On White, and Black, to evaluate the accuracy of the selection in relation to a variety of backdrops.

3. Combine with additional selection tools: If using Select Subject by itself does not offer an accurate selection, you can begin by using Select Subject, and then use additional selection tools, such as the Quick Selection Tool or the Pen Tool, to further refine the selection.

4. Understand limits. While the Select and Mask and Select Subject tools are powerful, it is likely that they may not always make faultless choices. This is particularly true when working with intricate photographs or detailed objects. In circumstances like these, more manual refinement with the use of additional selection tools might be necessary.

5. Practice and experiment: Get accustomed with the tools by working on a number of different images. Investigate the different parameters and choices available to gain a better grasp of how they impact the overall quality of the selection. Experimentation is the best approach to acquire adept with these tools as various alterations may need to be performed for different photos.

Getting better and faster outcomes with Select and Mask

When dealing with Select and Mask, it is necessary to apply separate tools for picture portions that should be seen, parts that should be totally masked, and edges that should be partly masked (such as fuzzy dog hair).

This is because Select and Mask treat these three sorts of picture portions extremely differently. Take a look at these suggestions:

• The Select Subject button can be a rapid approach to generate an initial selection.

• The Quick Selection tool is handy for fast touching up a selection created by Select Subject or for establishing an initial selection. As you drag it, it employs edge detection technology to locate mask edges automatically. Don't drag it on or over a mask edge; keep it entirely inside (in Add mode) or outside (in Subtract mode) the regions that should be exposed.

• Use the Brush, Lasso, or Polygonal Lasso tool to paint or create solid mask edges manually (without making use of any automatic edge detection). This may be done by painting on or sketching them. Additionally, they offer an Add mode for marking exposed zones and a Subtract mode for designating veiled sections. Both of these modalities can be used interchangeably.

• If you wish to temporarily employ a tool in Subtract mode, you may do so by holding down the Alt (Windows) or Option (macOS) key while using the tool. This will prevent you from having to switch between Add and Subtract modes using the toolbar. • Dragging the Refine Edge Brush across the edges of the mask where there are intricate transitions, such as hair, will assist improve the mask along those borders. Do not drag the Refine

Edge brush over any spots that have to have their masks entirely removed or their exposes totally shown.

• It is not required to finish all of your options inside the Select and Mask window. For instance, if you had already made a selection using another tool such as Color Range, you should keep that selection active and then click Select > Select and Mask in the options bar to tidy up the mask. This will delete undesired parts from the selection.

Creating a quick mask

Making choices in Adobe Photoshop based on locations that have been painted or edited may be achieved simply and swiftly by using the fast mask option. When you need to make a rapid selection of an area that has difficult or irregular borders, this approach is quite beneficial since it allows you to do it more accurately. Working more quickly and efficiently in Photoshop is achievable with the aid of fast masks, which may speed up your workflow.

Here's how to construct a simple mask:

Step 1: Open your image

The first step is to open the image you wish to change in Photoshop. You may either open an existing file or create a new one.

Step 2: Activate Quick Mask mode

After you have opened your photo, you can engage the Quick Mask mode by either clicking the "**Q**" key on your keyboard or selecting the "**Quick Mask**" button that is found in the Toolbar.

Both of these solutions are open to you. When you switch on the Quick Mask mode, your image will be changed into a grayscale overlay, and the sections of the picture that are not covered by the mask will be colored red.

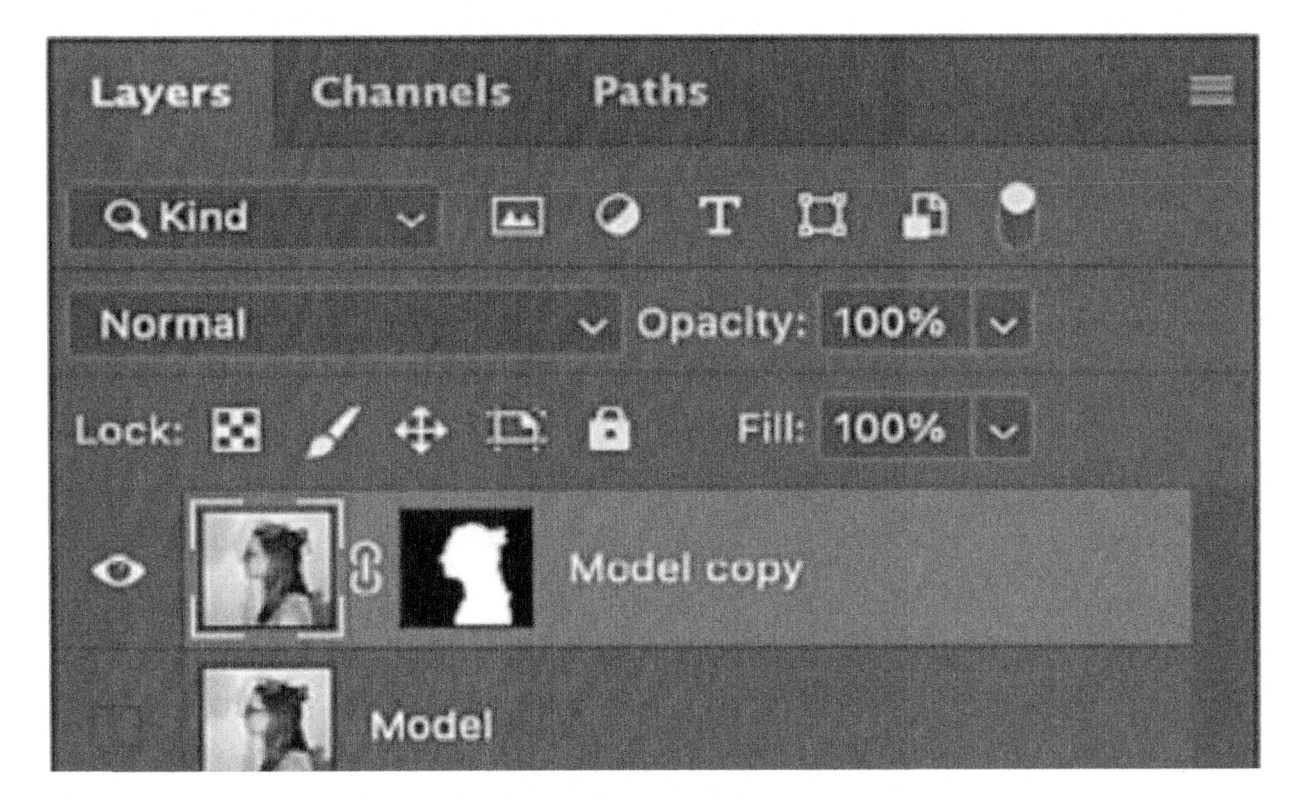

Step 3: Use the Brush tool

After that, go to the Toolbar and pick the Brush tool from there. In the settings bar at the top of the screen, you may modify the size of the brush, as well as its amount of hardness and trans-parency. Pick a brush size that correlates well with the dimensions of the region you wish to pick. Check the options bar and make sure Normal is chosen for the mode. Launch the pop-up window for the Brush tool and pick a small brush with a diameter of 13 pixels and a Hardness setting of 100 percent. To dismiss the panel, click anywhere outside of it.

Step 4: Paint over the area you want to select Paint over the region you want to pick while the Brush tool is chosen in your tool bar. If you wish to add to the selection, make sure that the color white is picked for the foreground of the selection. If you wish to delete anything from the selection, make sure that the black color is selected as the foreground color. Red will be utilized to emphasize the place that you will be paint-ing over. Right now, we are painting the earpieces of the glasses frame.

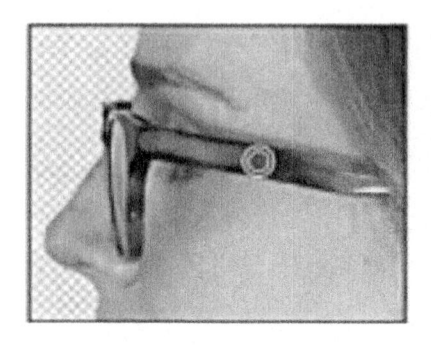

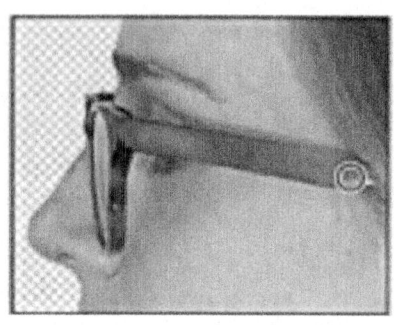

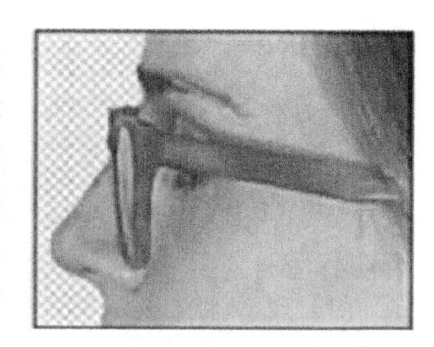

When you utilize Photos hop's Quick Mask mode, the red overlay is perceived as a grayscale mask by the software; the varied shades of gray reflect variable degrees of mask transparency.

When working in Quick Mask mode with a painting or editing tool, it is necessary to keep the following rules in mind:

When you paint with black, you add to the mask, which is the red overlay, and you are taking away from the targeted region.

Painting with white will remove the mask and add to the area that has been selected.

Painting with gray or lower opacity adds sections of the mask that are semitransparent, whereas deeper tones are more transparent and consequently less masked.

Step 5: Refine the mask

After you have painted the location that you wish to choose, you can next make any needed alterations to the mask. You may use the Eraser tool to remove sections that were painted in error, or you can use the Brush tool to paint over parts that were missed. Both of these tools are featured in the Tools menu. You may also access the Quick Mask Mode by clicking the Edit in Standard Mode button, which is placed in the same position. When you quit the Quick Mask mode, the Quick Mask is transformed into a selection instead.

To choose the region that was previously masked, go to the pick menu and choose Inverse. If you do not save the selection as an alpha channel (Select> Save Selection), it will be lost as soon as the region is deselected. If you do wish to keep the pick for future usage, save it as an alpha channel.

Select **"Image"** > **"Adjustments"** > **"Hue/Saturation"** from the menu. Without first generating an adjustment layer, the commands listed in the Adjustments menu have a direct influence on the pixels in the image. Change the Hue setting in the dialog box titled

"**Hue/Saturation**" to + 70. The fresh hue of green entirely covers the rim of the spectacles. Select the OK button.

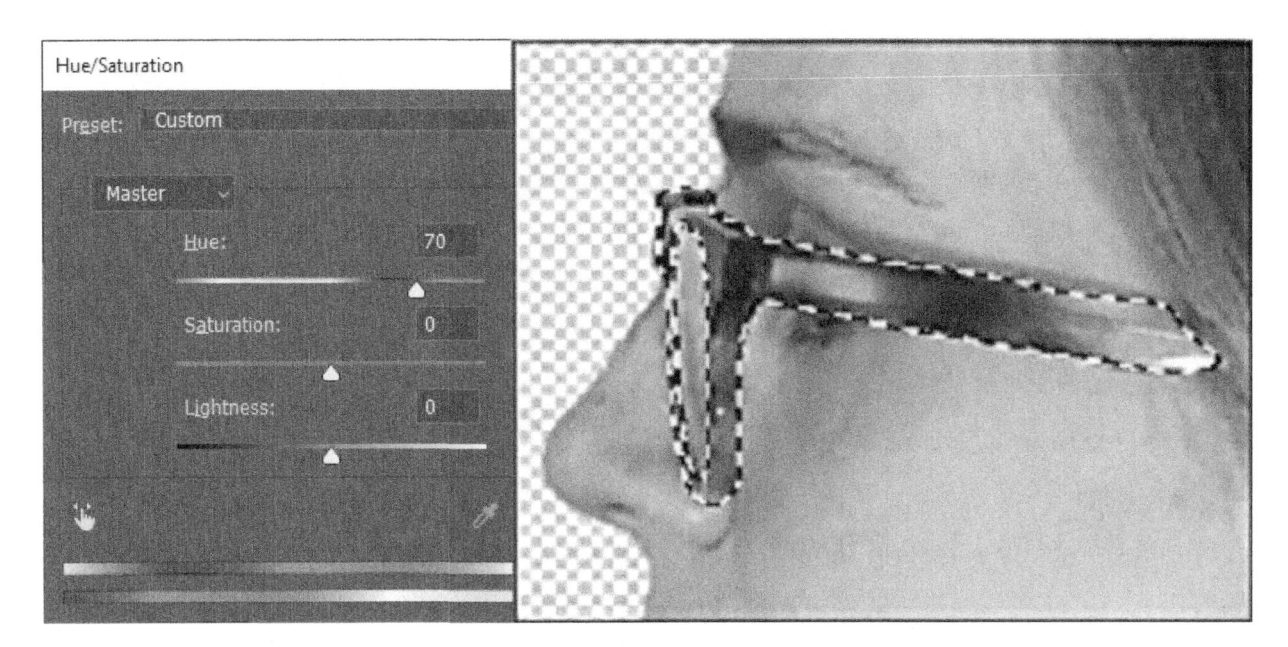

Click **Select > Deselect**.

Step 6: Exit Quick Mask mode

When you are done making your decision, you can exit the Quick Mask mode by either entering the "**Q**" key on your keyboard or selecting the "**Quick Mask**" button that is placed in the Tool-bar. After making your pick, the picture will restore to its former color, and you will be able to see your selection.

Step 7: Apply the selection

You can utilize your option for any reason you see fit now that you have made it. You may, for instance, employ it to make adjustments to the chosen region, or you can copy and paste it into another layer. Another purpose for it would be to generate a selection.

Tips for utilizing Quick Mask mode

• Use a brush with rounded edges to produce a more seamless selection.

• If you make a mistake during painting, you may hit the "**X**" key on your keyboard to flip between the foreground and background colors. These are some useful suggestions for employing the Quick Mask mode.

• You may further reduce your options by utilizing the tool known as "**Refine Edge**," which allows you to do things like smooth out rough edges or change the edge radius.

Manipulating a picture with Puppet Warp

Adobe Photoshop offers a capability called Puppet Warp that lets users change some parts of a picture by first pinning those aspects down and then dragging and warping the other components of the image around the pinned-down aspects. It is a wonderful tool for achieving more dramatic effects, such as modifying the contour of a person's body, as well as for making more subtle adjustments to the arrangement of an object inside an image.

How to use Puppet Warp

Step 1: Open your image

Launch Photoshop and pick the photo you wish to alter from the file menu. You may accomplish this by selecting **"File"** from the top menu bar, and then selecting **"Open."**

Step 2: Duplicate the layer

The next step is to build a clone of the layer so that you can make changes to it without the updates showing up on the original picture. To accomplish this, go to the Layers panel found on the right-hand side of the screen, click on the layer that you want to duplicate, and then drag it down to the "New Layer" button placed at the bottom of the panel. You may also right-click on the layer and pick "Duplicate Layer" from the context menu.

Step 3: Select the Puppet Warp tool

Make a selection in the toolbar that is displayed on the left side of the screen to utilize the Puppet Warp tool. It resembles a pushpin with a twisted wire attached to the top of it.

Step 4: Add pins

The Puppet Warp tool allows you to add pins to the locations that you wish to modify by simply clicking on such places. There is no limit to the number of pins that can be added. When you add a pin, it will function as an anchor, maintaining that area of the picture in its present location. Please hit the **Alt** key (on Windows) or the **Option** key (on macOS). A broader circle emerges around the pin, and next to it, a curving double arrow seems to be pointing in the same direction.

Maintain the Alt or Option key press while you drag the pointer to rotate the region of the picture in the opposite direction. In the settings bar, you may check out the angle of rotation; if you wish to rotate the head back 170 degrees, enter that value there. You mustn't mistakenly delete the pin by alt-clicking or option-clicking the dot itself.

Step 5: Move the pins

After you have put your pins in, you may move them using the Puppet Warp tool by clicking on them and dragging them in the desired direction. The remainder of the picture will warp around them as you move them, giving you the effect, you wish to accomplish.

Step 6: Fine-tune the warp

If you need to make more precise alterations, you may fine-tune the warp by utilizing the choices that are found in the toolbar that is placed at the top of the screen. You may, for instance, adjust the expansion of the mesh, which affects how far the warp extends out from the pins, or you can vary the density of the mesh, which defines the number of anchor points that are available for warping. Both of these criteria affect the number of anchor points.

Step 7: Apply the warp

After you have adjusted the warp to your desire, you may activate it by either hitting the Enter key on your computer or clicking the checkbox found in the options bar. By doing so, the mod-ifications will be committed, and a new layer will be produced with the twisted picture.

Tips for using Puppet Warp

1. Use as few pins as feasible. When you employ additional pins, the warp will grow more sophisticated, and it will be more challenging to retain control of it.

2. Use the grid to help guide your warp. You will be able to see where the anchor points are positioned owing to the grid, which might be of aid in ensuring that you are accurately warping the picture.

3. Be patient. Be patient and take your time when you learn how to utilize Puppet Warp since it might take some time to get the hang of it.

4. Experiment with different impacts. It is possible to generate a large variety of effects using Puppet Warp, from tiny adjustments to severe distortions; consequently, you should not be hesitant to explore with it.

Using an alpha channel to create a shadow

Channels allow you to access particular types of information, similar to how distinct layers in a photograph carry different forms of data. Grayscale photographs are preserved in the alpha channels when choices are made. Channels of color information are used to contain data on each color in a picture; for instance, a red, green, and blue (RGB) image will always comprise red, green, blue, and composite channels. If you want to avoid getting channels and layers confused, just think of channels as containing an image's color and selection information, and think of layers as storing painting, shapes, text, and other content. This will help you avoid getting them confused. To construct a shadow, first, you will make a selection of the sections of the picture layer that are trans-parent, and then on a separate layer, you will fill that selection with black.

Because the selection is going to be modified to produce the shadow, you should immediately save the selection in its present form as an alpha channel so that you may load it back in if required at a later time.

Step 1. In the Layers panel, click the layer thumbnail icon for the photo layer while holding down the Control key (Windows) or the Command key (macOS). The region that was dis-guised has been picked.

Step 2. Choose **Select > Save Selection**. Make sure that the New channel is selected in the Save Selection dialog box before you save the selection. After that, given the channel the name Model Outline, and then click the OK button.

There are no fresh advancements in either the Layers panel or the document window. On the other side, the Channels panel now includes an extra channel with the name Model Outline. The option is still accessible for selection. Tip: Now that the initial selection contour of the model has been kept as an alpha channel, you may reuse that selection at any time by using the **Select > Load Selection** command in Photoshop. You may even load that pick from another project.

Step 3. At the very bottom of the Layers window, you'll notice a button called "**Create a New Layer**." Click this button. Put the shadow where you want it to be below the photo of the model by dragging the new layer below the one holding the image. To rename the new layer, double-click on its name, and then pick "**Shadow**" from the drop-down menu.

There are a few distinct picture file formats that allow the user the option to save an alpha channel along with the image document. Photos hop will produce an alpha channel for the composite picture if you pick this option. This channel will comprise all of the sections of the image that are not occupied by an opaque pixel.

Step 4. While still having the Shadow layer selected, go to the selection menu and pick the Select and Mask option. This action loads the selection that is presently being utilized into the Select and Mask task area.

Step 5. In the View Mode section of the Properties panel, pick On Black from the View menu to turn the backdrop black.

Step 6. In the box named "**Global Refinements**," change the Shift Edge slider so that it reads + 36%.

Step 7. Go to the area under "**Output Settings**," make sure that "**Selection**" is chosen from the "**Output** To" menu, and then click the "**OK**" button.

Step 8. Select Fill under the Edit menu. Select "**Black**" from the "**Contents**" option displayed in the Fill dialog box, and then click the "**OK**" button.

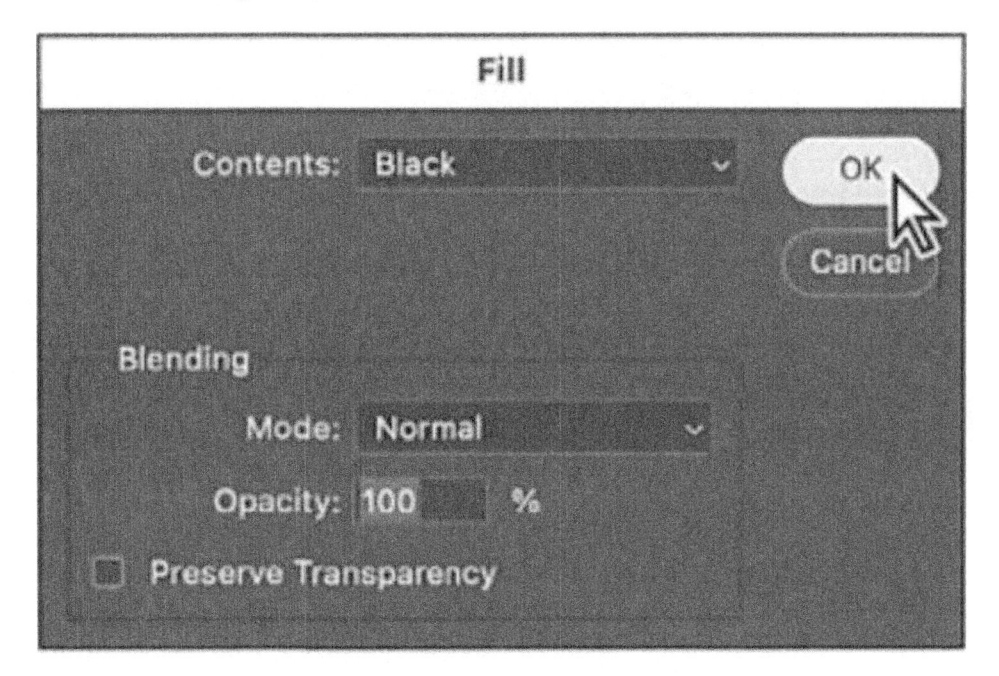

On the Shadow layer, the model's outline is viewed as being filled in with a dark hue. Because a person's shadow is not frequently as dark as the person who throws it, the opacity of the layer must be adjusted.

Step 9. In the Layers panel, lower the opacity of the layer to 30%.

The placement of the shadow is similar to that of the photograph, which implies that it cannot be seen. You are going to relocate it.

Step 10. To clear the selection, select it first, and then select Deselect from the menu.

Step 11. Select **Edit > Transform > Rotate** from the menu bar. You may manually rotate the shadow, or you can put -15 degrees into the rotate box in the options bar. The shadow should then be relocated to the left, or the number 545 should be typed into the X field in the options bar. To commit the transformation, either click the button labeled "**Commit Transform**" in the options bar or hit Enter or Return on your keyboard.

Step 12. To save your work thus far, go to the **File** menu and click **Save**.

Creating a pattern for the background

When seeking to add texture and aesthetic appeal to a photograph, one regular strategy that is employed is to develop a pattern for the backdrop of the image. Adobe Photoshop provides users with several tools, such as the Pattern Stamp tool, the Define Pattern command, and the Pattern Overlay layer style, with which they may produce customized patterns.

In this part, we will go over the processes necessary to build a pattern that may be utilized as the backdrop of your photo.

Step 1: Choose a base picture

The selection of a base photo to serve as the blueprint for the pattern you will ultimately produce is the first stage in the pattern-making process. You may use whichever photo you like as long as it has a texture or pattern that appeals to you. You may, for instance, pick a photo of a brick wall, a piece of fabric, or a natural texture such as bark or leaves to use as your background.

Step 2: Duplicate the picture

After that, you need to make a copy of the photo so that you may make modifications to the copy without harming the original. To achieve this, open the Layers panel and then drag the background layer until it is dropped on the "**Create a new layer**" button found at the panel's bottom. This will result in the development of a new layer that is an identical clone to the one that was previously there.

Step 3: Edit the picture

Since you now have a duplicate of the picture, you may make the required adjustments to it to design the pattern. To update the picture, you may make use of any of the editing tools that are accessible in Photoshop, such as the Liquify filter, the Healing Brush tool, or the Clone Stamp tool. The purpose is to build a pattern that is continuous and may be used as a background for numerous iter-ations of the picture.

Step 4: Define the pattern

After you've developed the pattern, the following step is to explain it as a pattern that can be applied to a range of different photographs. To accomplish this, go to the Edit menu and then choose "Define Pattern." Simply give your design a name, and then click **"OK."** Your design has been successfully saved to the design Library, where it may be viewed at any time and applied to any photo.

Step 5: Apply the pattern

To apply the pattern to your photo, you will first need to create a new layer and then navigate to the menu marked for Layer Styles. Choose **"Pattern Overlay"** and then choose the pattern you just produced from the available patterns in the drop-down menu. To create the appearance you want, you may modify the pattern's size as well as its degree of transparency.

Tips for generating a pattern for the background

1. Use a high-resolution photograph. Make sure the photo you select to use as the foundation for your pattern has a high resolution so that it may be scaled to a range of different proportions without decreasing in quality.

2. Experiment with different editing tools. Patterns may be made utilizing a broad number of Photoshop tools due to the program's large feature set. Experiment with a number of tools to find which ones offer the greatest effects for the photo you're working with.

3. Make sure the pattern is seamless. If you want to design a seamless pattern, you need to make sure that the edges of the picture match up as you repeat the pattern. You may check for any seams that are obvious by making use of the Offset filter.

4. Use layer styles to improve the pattern. You can give your pattern greater depth and dimension by utilizing different layer styles, including the Pattern Overlay and Bevel and Emboss layer styles.

Refining a mask

Making the right mask can be a tough job, particularly in circumstances when the borders of the topic being masked are convoluted or otherwise unregular. The good news is that Adobe Photoshop offers a number of tools and techniques that may be utilized to increase the accuracy of masks and the outputs they create.

Let's study some efficient techniques to improve a mask, shall we?

1. Select the mask: The first thing you need to do is check to see whether the mask layer is selected in the Layers box. The mask thumbnail must be highlighted.

2. Use the Brush Tool: The Brush Tool is the tool that is utilized for refining masks more often than any other instrument. Choose the Brush Tool, then depending on whether you want to add to or remove the mask, adjust the foreground color to either black or white in the brush's color picker. When painting along the outlines of the mask, use a brush with a low opacity level and a sensitive brush. You may also modify the size of the brush as well as the amount of its hardness.

3. Use the Refine Edge Tool: The Refine Edge Tool in Photoshop is a potent choice that helps to enhance the mask edges so that they are more exact. After choosing the mask layer with the mouse, go to the Options menu and choose the Refine Edge option. Employing the Refine Edge Tool, paint along the outlines of the subject being worked on. The edges are recognized automatically, and the mask is refined in accordance with those results. You may gain more precise results by modifying the edge detection parameters, such as the Feather, Contrast, and Smooth choices.

4. Make Use of the Select and Mask Tool: The Select and Mask Tool is an all-encompassing tool that provides significant options for mask refinement. Navigate to the option labeled Select, and then click Select and Mask. The Select and Mask workspace will display, presenting the photo along with a range of tools and choices for further customizing the image. To fine-tune the mask's edges, you may use either the Refine Edge Brush Tool or the Quick Selection Tool. To fine-tune the mask, utilize the sliders accessible in the Properties section. Examine the appearance of the mask against a range of backdrops by previewing it with a number of varied view choices.

5. Use the Pen Tool: The Pen Tool is another great tool for generating and enhancing masks. With the Pen Tool, you may build precise pathways along the mask boundaries and then turn them into a selection or a mask. Select the Pen Tool and construct a path along the edge of the subject. Once you have constructed the route, right-click and choose Make Se-lection. Set the Feather option to a tiny value and click **OK**. This will make a mask with a polished edge.

6. Make Use of Channels: Channels are an extra powerful tool that may be employed in the process of developing and modifying masks. Navigate to the Channels panel, and in that panel, pick the channel that gives the largest contrast between the subject and the backdrop. Create a clone of the channel and then apply tweaks such as Levels or Curves to it to improve the contrast. To fine-tune the mask edges, you may use either the Brush Tool or the Eraser Tool. After the mask has been made, you should copy it and then paste it into a new layer.

7. Experiment and Practice: To develop the skill of mask-making, it is vital to attempt new things and obtain lots of practice. Because of the chance that each image may ask for a distinct combination of alterations and instruments, you must get familiar with the many various possibilities and techniques that are accessible within Photoshop.

Refining a mask is a key element in the process of making photo edits or composites that are realistic and lifelike. You may boost the overall quality of your images by making use of masks that are polished and exact provided you have the right equipment and know-how.

CHAPTER 7: TYPOGRAPHIC DESIGN

About type

The inclusion of text into your design is referred to as "type" in Adobe Photoshop. You may build new text layers and change existing ones with the aid of the Type tool. To acquire the appearance you desire, you may select from a broad choice of fonts, styles, and sizes. A type layer in Photoshop is made up of vector-based objects that define the letters, numbers, and symbols associated with a typeface. There is a broad range of typefaces that may be purchased in more than one format. The True Type file format is widespread; however, most professionals prefer the Open Type format for their typesetting needs. As you alter, scale, or resize the type layers in a Photoshop project, the vector-based character outlines are maintained by Photoshop, guaranteeing that the type will show at the full resolution of the page. The pixel dimensions of the page, on the other hand, set constraints on how sharp the text may be. When you expand a document, jagged text edges show sooner in a document with less pixel dimensions. For example, low-resolution pictures suitable for websites have fewer pixel dimensions than high-resolution graphics appropriate for print.

Getting started

Creating Text Layers

Select the Type tool from the toolbar, and then click anywhere on your canvas to commence the creation of a new text layer. This will establish a new text layer for you, into which you may imme-diately start inputting. In addition, you may click and drag the mouse to create a text box of a given size. When you have completed creating a text layer, you can navigate to the Options bar at the very top of the screen to pick a font, a style, and a size for the text. The text layer that you're working on can also have other effects added to it, such as a drop shadow or a stroke.

Editing Text Layers

To make modifications to an existing text layer, you need merely to pick the Type tool and then click on the text that needs to be edited. The text, font, size, or style can all be adjusted at this stage. Altering the placement of your text layer may also be performed with the aid of the Move tool. Select the text layer you wish to remove in the Layers panel, and then click the remove key on your keyboard. A text layer will be erased.

Working with Text Styles

You may swiftly give your text a distinct appearance in Photoshop by picking one of the numerous pre-set text styles that are provided in the application. The Text Styles option may be reached by clicking on the Styles panel and making the necessary selection there. From this menu, you may pick a style and then apply it to the text layer you're working on. You may also design your text styles by picking a text layer and then selecting the Layer Style option from the Layer menu. This will allow you to build your own text formatting. From this page, you may apply effects to the style, such as a drop shadow or a stroke, and then save the style for future use.

Warping Text

Photoshop has a number of tools that may be used to warp and distort text, in addition to its usual text editing functions. To warp text, first, choose the text layer you wish to work with, then go to the Type menu and select the Warp Text option. You may pick a warp style such as Arch, Bulge, or Wave from this menu, and then alter the settings to acquire the effect you desire.

Creating a clipping mask from type

A clipping mask is an item or combination of items whose shape covers other artwork such that only areas that are included inside the clipping mask are visible. A clipping mask may be an individ-ual item or a group of objects. You are, in effect, restricting the artwork to only the visible pixels of the layer when you do this.

You can construct a clipping mask in Photoshop out of whatever form you like, including letters. You may construct a design in Adobe Photoshop in which an image or texture is put within the shape of your text by utilizing a helpful approach called **"creating a clipping mask from type**." This may be found in the Help menu of Adobe Photoshop. Here, we will go over the processes necessary to cre-ate a clipping mask in Photoshop based on typography.

Step 1: Create Your Text

The first thing you need to do is utilize the Type tool to generate the text you wish to use. You may pick the font, size, and color of the word or phrase that you wish to use for your design by typing it out and then making the relevant alterations. In the Layers panel, you need to make sure that your text layer is chosen.

Step 2: Create Your Image or Texture Layer

Next, by clicking on the "**Create a New Layer**" button situated at the bottom of the Layers panel, you will be able to add a new layer immediately on top of your text layer. On this layer is where you will place the photo or material that you wish to utilize. Import the photo or texture that you want to use into Photoshop, and then use the drag-and-drop capability to place it on the new layer that you just generated. In the Layers panel, drag the photo or texture layer so that it is immediately above the text layer you wish to alter.

Step 3: Create the Clipping Mask

Go to **Layer > Create Clipping Mask** while you have the layer containing your photo or texture selected. This will generate a mask in the form of your text by clipping the layer to the text layer behind it and making a clipping mask. At this point, you should be able to see your photo or texture inside the outline of your text. You may adjust the position of the image or tex-ture layer by using the Move tool and you can modify the proportions and contours of the mask by using the Transform tool. Both of these tools are featured in the Edit menu.

Step 4: Adjust the Clipping Mask

If you need to make modifications to the clipping mask, you may do so by picking the image or texture layer and then clicking on the Layer Mask button that is situated at the bottom of the Layers panel. This will allow you to make the necessary modifications. This will bring up the mask properties, where you may make adjustments to the opacity, feathering, and any other choices that are avail-able. If you need to adjust the appearance of the mask in any manner, you may do so by altering the text layer as well. To make changes to the text, you need to select the layer that contains the text, then use the Type tool. The clipping mask will be brought up to date instantly after the alterations have been done.

Adding guidelines to position type

The Adobe Photoshop feature known as guides is a valuable tool that may aid you in accurately arranging text in your projects.

Here, we will study the process of adding guidelines to position types in Photoshop.

To utilize guidelines, you'll first need to show the rulers in Photoshop. You may accomplish this by heading to **View > Rulers** or by using the keyboard shortcut **Ctrl + R** (Windows) or **Command + R** (Mac).

To build a guide, click and drag from the ruler on the left or top of the screen, depending on where you want it to appear. As you drag, you'll see a guideline appear on your canvas.

When the guide is at the position you wish, let go of the mouse button so it may move.

You may also make a guide by navigating to the View menu and choosing New Guide. This will bring up a dialogue box in which you may define the precise placement of the guidance in either pixels or percentages.

When you have completed design guidelines, you can next make use of them to appropriately position text in your designs. Simply create a new text layer by picking the Type tool and clicking anywhere on the canvas.

You may align the text layer with other components of your design by dragging it to the area you want it to be in and then employing guidance to do so. In addition to this, you may use the Move tool to nudge the text layer into the correct spot.

Select **View > Snap To > Guides** from the menu bar to make the type align itself with the guidelines. Whenever you move the text layer around, it will automatically align itself with the closest guide.

You may also adjust the snap settings by navigating to **Edit > Preferences > Guides, Grids & Slices**. This will show you a menu with a choice of alternatives. In this area, you may adjust the distance at which the snap happens, as well as any other factors that apply to the snap.

If you decide that the guidelines are no longer essential for your work, you may get rid of them by clicking and dragging them off the canvas, or by selecting **View > Clear** guidelines from the menu bar.

Adding point type

The technique of adding point type in Adobe Photoshop is an easy one. The point type is used for any brief lines of text that do not continue on to the following line automatically. You have the choice of inputting the point type, which is a brief text that is attached to a point, or the paragraph type, which is numerous lines that can recompose themselves based on the size of their text container. You are going to start by making a point type.

Step 1. In the Layers panel, pick the picture layer.

Step 2. Select the Horizontal Type tool, then, in the settings bar, perform the following:

Choose a serif typeface, such as Minion Pro Regular, from the Font Family pop-up

menu.

Type 115 pt for the Size and hit Enter or Return.

Click the Center Text button.

Step 1. In the Character panel, adjust the Tracking value to 50.

The Tracking value determines the total distance between letters, which impacts the density of a line of text.

Step 2. Position the cursor above the center guide you inserted to set an insertion point, about where the guide meets the border of the model's shadow, click, and then write TYPE-CAST in all capital letters. Then click the Commit Any Current Edits button in the options bar.

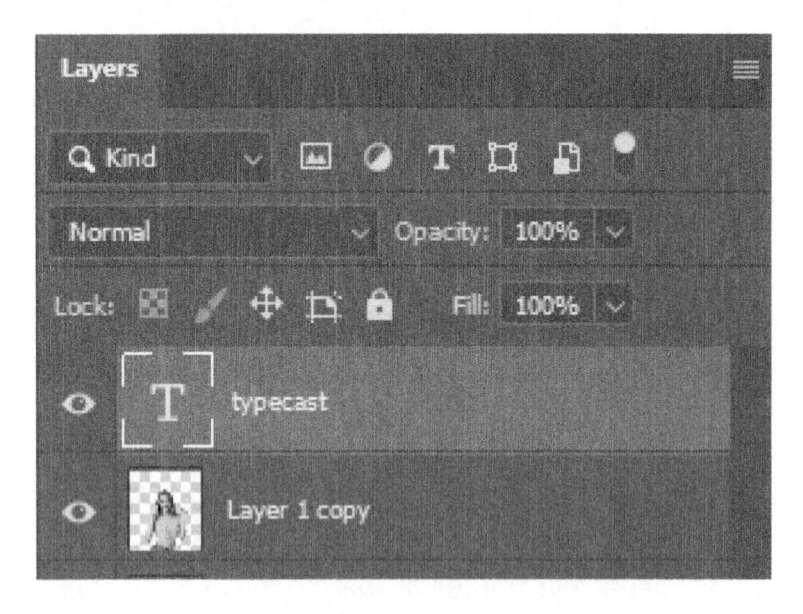

After you enter, you must commit your editing in the layer by selecting the Commit Any Current Edits button, moving to another tool or layer, or clicking away from the text layer. You cannot commit to current modifications by pressing Enter or Return; doing so will produce a new line of type. The term "TYPECAST" is inserted, and it displays in the Layers panel as a new type layer named TYPECAST. You may modify and manage the type layer as you would any other layer. You may add or edit the text, adjust the direction of the type, apply anti-aliasing, apply layer styles and transformations, and create masks. You may move, restack, and copy a type layer, or alter its layer parameters, just as you would for any other layer.

The text is big enough, but not current enough, for this design. Try a different font:

Step 3. Double-click the "TYPECAST" text to modify it.

Step 4. Open the Font Family pop-up menu in the options bar. Hover the pointer over the font list, either with the mouse or with the arrow keys.

TIP: When a type layer is chosen in the Layers panel, the Properties panel provides type settings-another location you may adjust type options such as the font. When you drag the mouse over the name of a font in Photos hop, the computer will briefly apply that typeface to the text you have picked so that you may see how it appears in use.

Step 5. Choose a typeface such as Myriad Pro Semi bold or one that is equivalent, and then in the settings box, click the button labeled "Commit Any Current Edits." That's far more fitting.

Step 6. If required, alter the location of the text that says "TYPECAST" so that it is reasonably near the top of the design by using the Move tool and dragging it.

Step 7. To save your work thus far, go to the File menu and click Save.

Paragraph and character styles

If you deal with type in Photoshop often or if you need to organize a considerable quantity of type inside an image in a consistent fashion, then paragraph and character styles can help you work more efficiently. A collection of type characteristics that may be applied to an entire paragraph with the touch of a single button is referred to as paragraph style. A character style is a preset com-bination of features that may be applied for any specific individual character. You can interact with these styles by visiting the panels that correspond to them: Select Window > Character Styles and Window > Paragraph Styles from the menu bar. The notion of font styles in Photoshop is analogous to that of page layout tools like Adobe InDesign and word processing software like Microsoft Word. The idea of font styles in Photoshop was introduced in version 7.0. On the other hand, the way styles function in Photoshop is a little bit different.

When dealing with font styles in Photoshop, keeping the following in mind will help you produce the best possible results:

The Basic Paragraph style is applied to any new text that you produce in Photos hop. This is the default setting. You may edit the style definition by double-clicking the style name. Your text choices dictate the Basic Paragraph style, but you have the opportunity to adjust the style definition.

• Deselect all layers before you create a new style.

• Even after you apply a new style, any changes made to the chosen text that were made to the existing paragraph style (which is commonly the Basic Paragraph style) will stay as such alterations are judged to be overridden. Applying a paragraph style to text and then selecting the Clear Override button accessible in the Paragraph Styles panel after applying the style will assure that all of the attributes of the paragraph style are applied to the content.

• Do you wish to apply the styles from another Photoshop project? Open the menu for the Character Styles or Paragraph Styles panel, Select Load Styles from the menu, and then select the document that contains the styles you wish to use. Select Type > Save Default Type Styles from the menu bar to make the presently applied styles the defaults for any new documents you create. Select Type> Load Default Type Styles from the menu bar in an existing document to apply your default type styles.

Creating type on a Path

• You will first need to choose the Path Tool before you can construct a type along a path. You can find it in the tool bar that is placed on the left side of the screen. It looks to be a symbol for a pen instrument that also has a curved line beneath it.

• Make the route that you want your text to follow by using the route Tool to construct it. Depending on the needs of your design, you may build a route that is either curved or circular.

• After you have completed sketching your route, go to the toolbar on the left side of the screen and choose the Type Tool from the menu. It resembles a huge letter "T" in its form.

• Move your cursor over the route you just generated while the Type Tool is chosen and leave it there for a bit. After a minute, the Type on a Path Tool will replace your cursor.

• To begin inputting your text, click on the path that you wish to utilize. This will enable a flashing cursor to appear along the path, signaling that you may begin typing once it has been built.

• To enter your text, click on the canvas and a box will open for you to fill in. The text will automatically adapt to any curves or circles that are present along the way.

• Once you have written down your text, you may modify the way it looks by utilizing the various options provided in the Character panel. • You can also move the text along the path by clicking and dragging on the text box that is situated at the beginning of the path.

• After you have altered the location and style of your type on a route to your preference, you can finalize the operation by clicking outside of the text box when you are ready. By doing this, the flickering cursor will be erased, and the type on a path insertion will be done.

Creating a Type in a Circle

Step 1. Using the **Ellipse Tool (U)**, make a circle on the canvas. Hold down the "**Shift**" key while dragging to produce a perfect circle.

Step 2. On the left side of the screen, in the toolbar, click "**Type Tool**" to begin typing. It resembles a huge letter "**T**" in its form.

Step 3. Click within the circle you produced in Step 2 while the Type Tool is active, and it will become active. On the canvas, a text box will be formed as a consequence of this operation.

Step 4. In the area that has been provided for you on the canvas, type your text. Check that your text is not too long to fit within the circle by reading it out loud.

Step 5. From the toolbar that is placed on the left side of the screen, pick the Path Selection Tool. It resembles a black arrow, and a white circle is placed next to it in the image.

Step 6. Click within the text box that you generated in Step 4 while the Path Selection Tool is open on your computer. By doing so, a circle will be generated around the text area.

Step 7. Click and drag the circle to move it around the text box while the Path Selection Tool is still active. This will allow you to modify its placement around the box. You may also modify the size of the circle by clicking and dragging on the anchor points that are situated around the circle.

Step 8. After you have modified the positioning and style of your type inside a circle to your satisfaction, you can finalize the operation by clicking outside of the text box. This will finish the text in a circle insertion while simultaneously deleting the circle.

Warping point type

A warping point is a point on an object that may be used with Photoshop's Warp tool to adjust the shape of the item.

Within Photoshop, there are three main sorts of warping points:

Normal Warp Points: These are the common warping points that are created when you pick an object with the Warp tool. You may generate these points by right-clicking on an object and selecting "Warp Points." They give the power to modify and alter the item in question.

Straighten Points: These points are what are designed to be utilized to straighten the lines in an image. They are produced by utilizing the Warp tool and clicking on a line segment to make them.

Control Points: You may vary the power of a warp effect by adjusting the values of these points. You may make them by clicking on a **Normal Warp** point while holding down the **Alt** (Windows) or **Option** (Mac) key on your keyboard. The warp effect may be fine-tuned with the use of control points, which are depicted as small circles.

Text that follows a meandering route is more aesthetically engaging than text that follows straight lines would be yet, you will need to twist the language to make it look more amusing. You may distort text to correspond to particular forms by utilizing the warping tool. Some examples of these forms include an arc and a wave. The warp style that you pick is a feature of the type layer; you may edit the warp style of a layer at any point to alter the warp's overall shape. You have fine-grained control over the direction and viewpoint of the warp effect with the help of the warping parameters.

Step 1. If needed, zoom in or scroll down to reposition the viewable area of the document window to a place where the phrases are centered on the screen.

Step 2. Right-click (Windows) or **Control-click** (macOS) the picture layer in the Layers panel and pick Warp Text from the context menu. If you don't see the Warp Text command in the context menu, **right-click/Control-click** the layer or layer name, not the layer thumbnail.

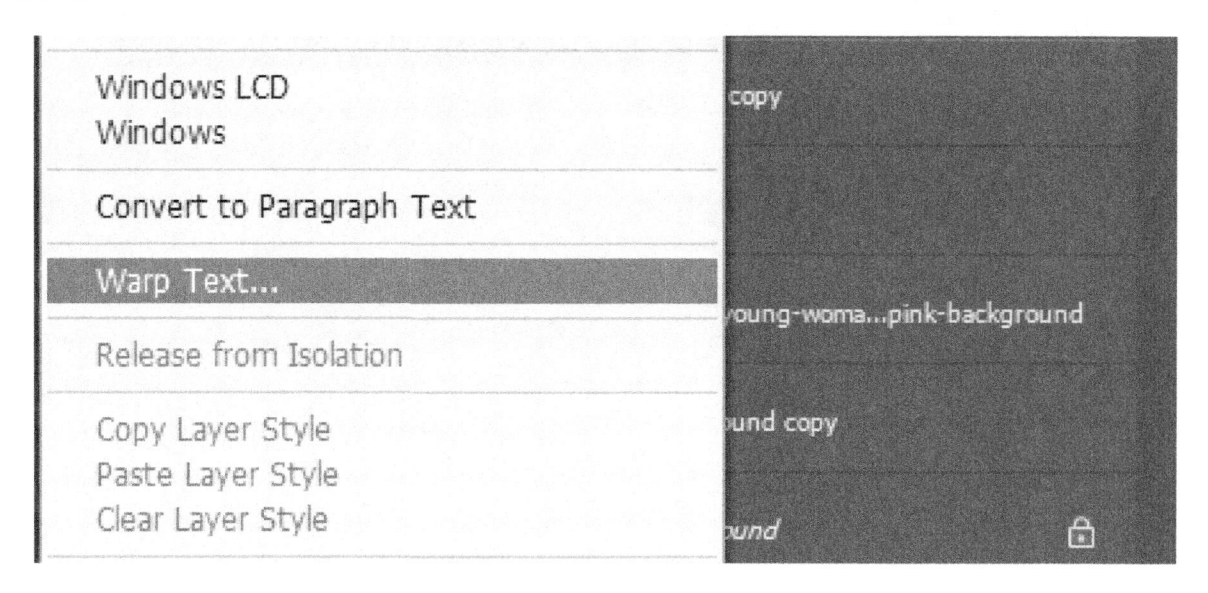

Step 3. In the **Warp Text** dialog box, pick Wave from the Style menu, and then select Horizontal from the list of possible options. Please specify your values as follows: Bend, + 33%; **Horizontal Distortion**, 23%; and **Vertical Distortion**, + 5%. After that, pick the OK button.

Step 4. The amount of warp that is applied may be changed using the Bend slider. The perspective of the warp is formed by the combination of horizontal and vertical distortion.

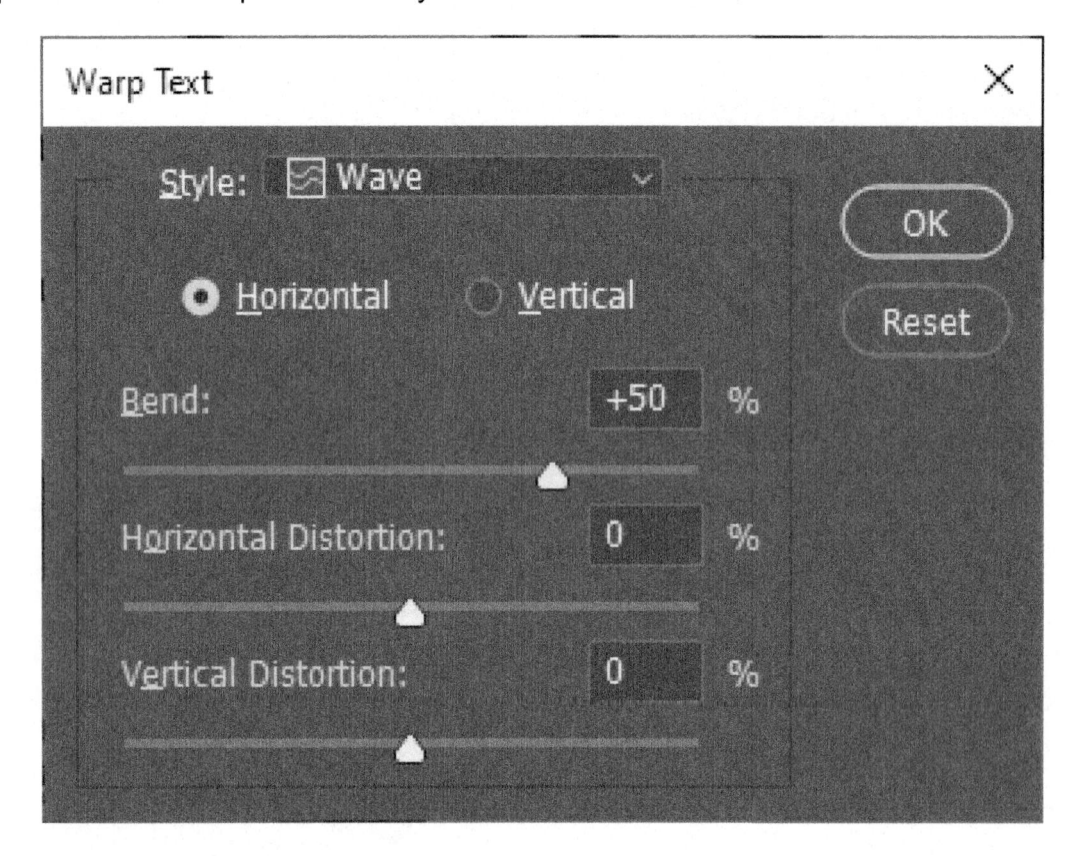

The words "**What's new in 3D type?**" appear to float like a wave on the design.

Step 5. Repeat steps 2 and 3 to distort the other two text layers you typed on a route. Feel free to explore different settings.

Step 6. Save your work.

Designing paragraphs of type

Since each line only has one piece of text, you have been utilizing point type for all of it. However, many designs need complete paragraphs of text to be incorporated. You can add new paragraph kinds and adjust the style of the paragraphs that you are working on. For more extensive adjustments over paragraph type, you won't need to transfer to a tool that's especially developed for page layout.

Using guides for positioning

The design will have additional paragraphs added by you. To begin, you will need to incorporate some guidelines in the working area so that you may order the paragraphs appropriately.

1. If needed, zoom in on the document or scroll so that you can view the full of the top half of the page.

2. Using the left vertical ruler, drag a guide over to the right side of the canvas so that it is about a quarter of an inch from that side.

3. Position the guide so that it is around 2 inches from the top of the canvas by pulling it down from the top horizontal ruler.

Adding paragraph type from a sticky note

You're ready to add the text. In a real-world design setting, the text may be provided to you as a document prepared using a word processor or the body of an email message. In any instance, you would be able to copy and paste the text into Photoshop. You may have to manually write it in instead. The copywriter may also quickly add a piece of text by connecting it to the photo file in the form of a sticky note, which is what we've done for you here.

Place the Move tool so that it is near the boundary of the yellow sticky note that is situated in the lower-right corner of the photo window. Once the Move tool has been reduced to a basic black pointer, double-click it to activate the Notes panel.

TIP: When you are working in the Graphics and Web workspace, the Note tool is unavailable for usage as it is being used to compose notes. You may simply discover the Note tool by selecting **Edit > Search** from the menu bar. On the other hand, if you want to obtain input from multiple folks, it may be simpler to apply the cloud-based Share for Review online remark feature (select **File > Share for Review** from the menu bar).

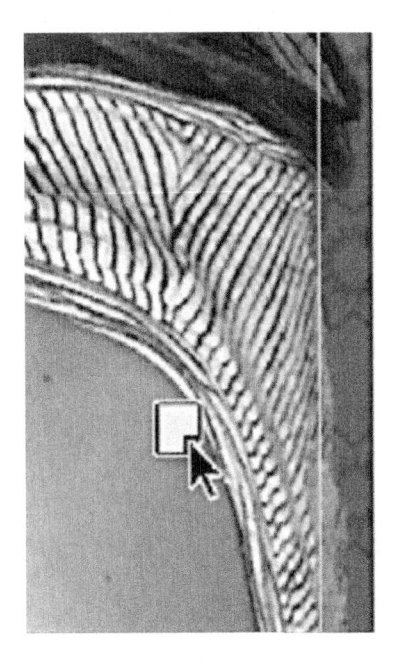

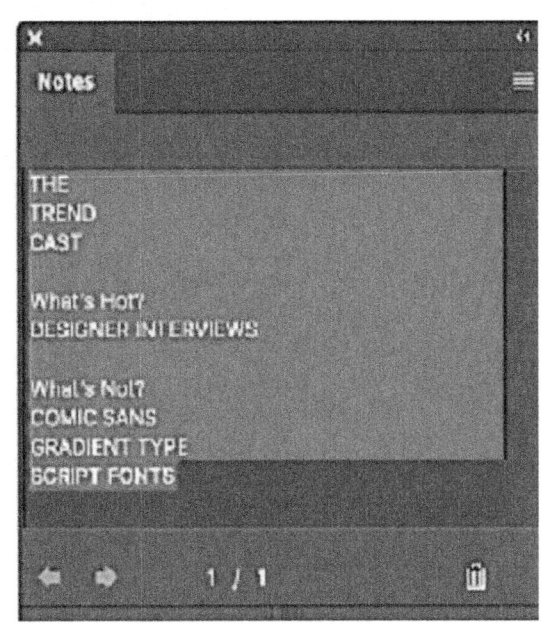

• All nine lines of the text should be chosen; if they aren't, click on the note text and choose **Select > All**. Choose **Edit > Copy** and shut the Notes panel.

• Select the picture layer. Then, pick the Horizontal Type tool (**T**).

• Position the cursor where the guidelines connect at about 1/4" from the right edge and 2" from the top of the canvas. Hold down the Shift key as you start to drag a text box down and to the left. Then release the Shift key and continue dragging until the box is about 4 inches wide by 6 inches high. The new text layer is produced in front of the Model layer that was selected (above the picture layer in the Layers panel).

• Choose **Edit > Paste** to add the text from the note.

• Apply your settings

• With the text still chosen, click the Right Align Text button in the options bar or Paragraph panel.

• Make your required modifications

• Click the Commit Any Current Edits button in the options menu.

• Save your modifications.

CHAPTER 8: VECTOR DRAWING TECHNIQUES

About bitmap pictures and vector graphics

In design and editing applications like Photoshop, bitmap pictures, and vector graphics are two separate kinds of digital images that are widely employed. Raster pictures, generally referred to as bit-map images, are constructed of a grid of discrete pixels. The overall image is made up of individual pixels, each of which is given a specific color. Since bitmap graphics can capture a large variety of colors and tints, they are typically employed for photographs and other images with sophisticated color gradients. On the other hand, the routes and curves of vector graphics are specified by mathemat-ical equations. Vector graphics, as opposed to pixel-based visuals, are constructed of lines and forms that allow for quality scaling. They are thus great for making logos, icons, and other forms of visuals that need continual scaling. Both vector graphics and bitmap pictures may be utilized with Photoshop. Along with features for making and manipulating vector drawings, it provides tools for editing and changing pixel-based pictures. Photoshop's pen tool and shape tools are commonly used to make vector drawings, which may subsequently be exported in various file formats such SVG or EPS.

What is a pixel I hear you ask?

A pixel is merely a block of color. It is the smallest discrete component of a digital picture. Every digital picture is formed of a grid of pixels, and the number of pixels depends on the sort of technology used to produce the image, such as a digital camera or a scanner. The pixels in a typical image produced by a current camera are so tiny and numerous that you cannot distin-guish them individually. However, you'll notice that the image begins to appear blocky when you zoom in and increase your viewpoint on it. Individual pixels are included in the blocks.

You may see an illustration of a photo I captured with my cell phone's camera of one of our dogs, Otto, below. When the image is seen at 100% (or actual size), the individual pixels are invisible and seem to have blended into the backdrop to produce the final image.

But when seen at 800%, each color box or pixel is visible.

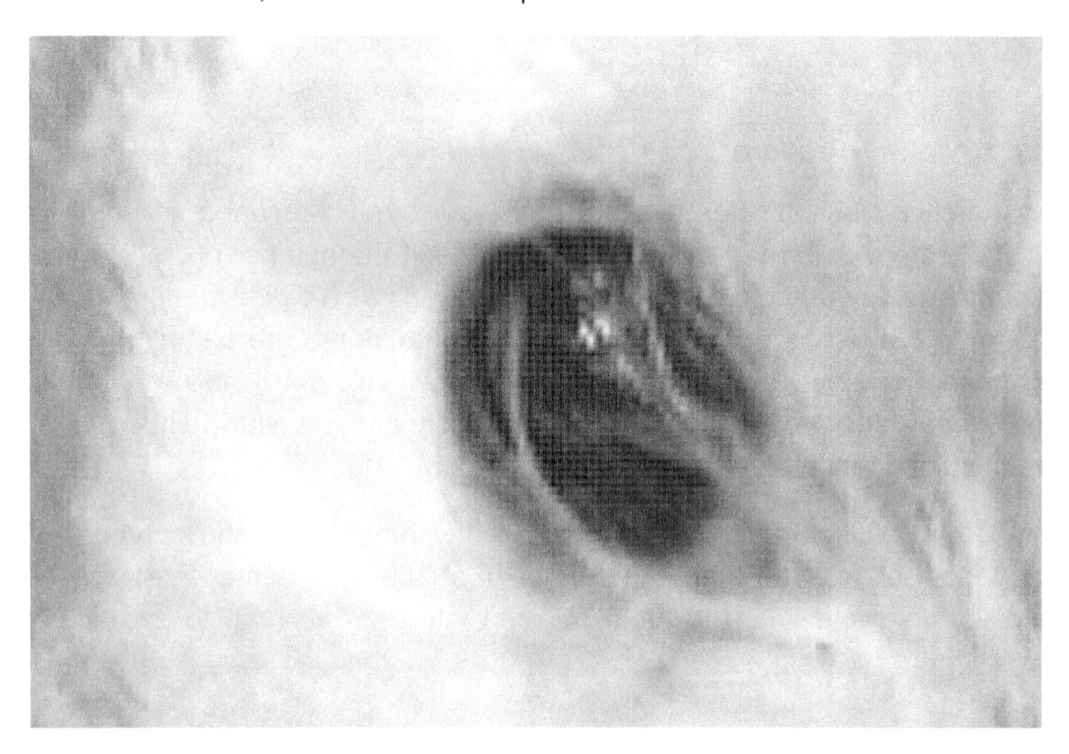

In Photoshop, you may specify the number of pixels a picture will have by entering that information in the New Document dialog box when you're creating a new file. Your file's picture resolu-tion has an influence on the image quality and file size.

Rule of Thumb for picking a resolution

• For images for the web or displays, use 72 pixels per inch (known as low resolution) • For high-quality color printing, use 300 pixels per inch (known as high resolution)

Use High Resolution for Print

Start a new file at a high quality (300 ppi) if you are making graphics or altering pictures that will be used for print use or print AND online. An image's resolution may always be lowered from 300 to 72 ppi. Generally speaking, going from low to high resolution is a terrible idea. Occasionally, shifting from low to high may appear "kind of ok" on the screen, but the qual-ity will be substandard and your design will suffer. It is always advisable to begin with a high-resolution image, lessen its size and quality as necessary, and then proceed.

Use Low Resolution for Web or Screen Graphics

If you know that you are making graphics or altering photographs that will ONLY be used online or on a screen, then you may start your new file with a low resolution of 72 ppi. Here is where you choose the resolution when you pick **File > New** in Photoshop.

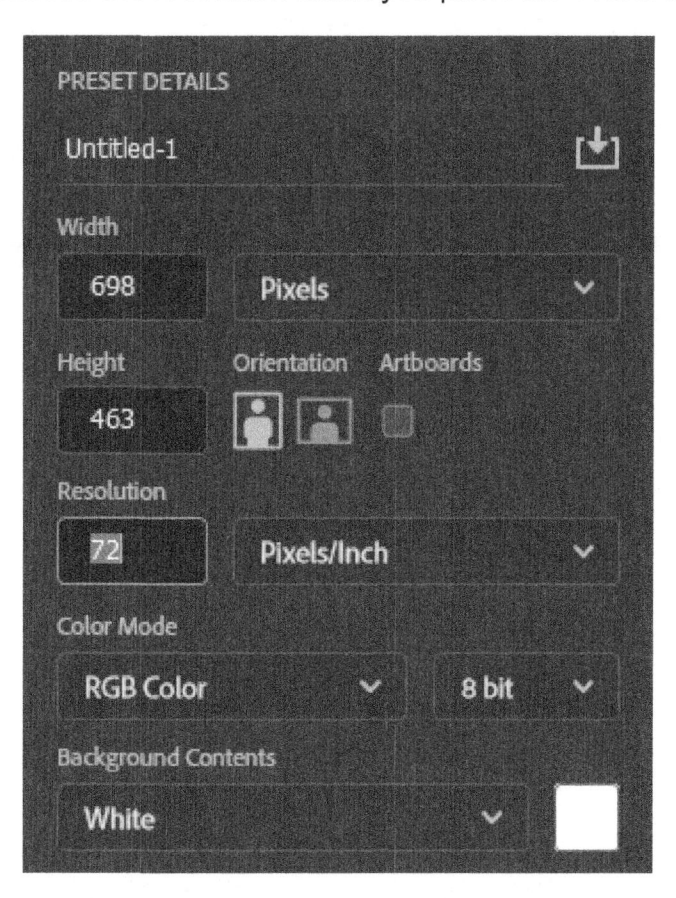

Photoshop Raster Tools

The majority of the Photoshop toolbar's features function via altering pixels. For instance, all of the brush tip-based tools, including painting tools, clone stamp tools, blur tools, and so on, modify or have an effect on the individual pixels in your picture or design.

Pixel-based File Formats

Raster image file formats include JPEG, GIF, PNG, and TIFF for saving your photos. Your camera's raw data is raster pictures as well, and you may manipulate them in Photoshop by employing Camera Raw.

Vector images

Anything you sketch or make using vector pictures may be scaled up without losing any quality, which is a really fantastic feature. Vectors keep their extraordinarily smooth curves and clear lines when scaled up, unlike raster graphics which may become blocky and distorted. Because of this, vectors are often applied in graphic design, notably in logo development.

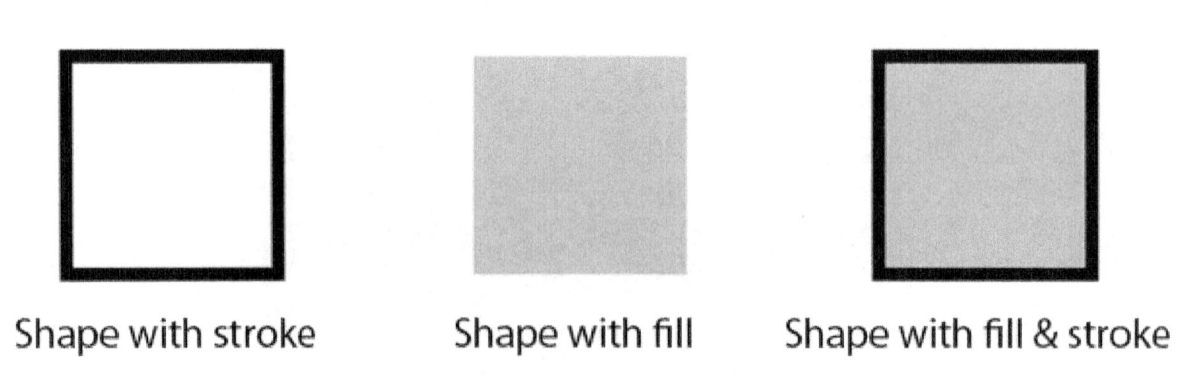

Shape with stroke   Shape with fill   Shape with fill & stroke

Bitmap and Vector Side by Side

Two versions of Puppy are presented in the image below; the one on the right is a raster image built out of pixels, and the one on the left was constructed using vectors. Both appear excellent at 100%.

VECTOR

RASTERISED

The vector version (on the left) retains its gorgeous smooth curves and exact lines as each iteration of the picture is extended, however the raster version appears horrifically blocky and pixelated.

Photoshop Vector Tools

Photoshop includes a restricted number of tools that deal especially with vectors. They are the Pen tools, the Path and Direct Selection tools, the Shape tools, and the Type tools. All of which you may use to build and design visuals that can be extended and lowered in size with no loss of quality.

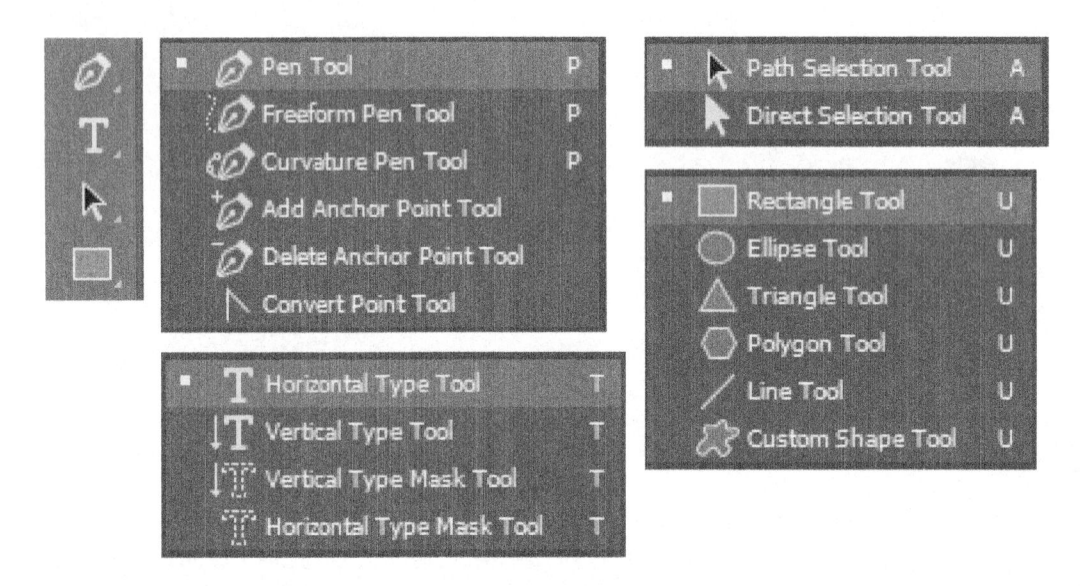

Is Type in Photoshop Raster or Vector based?

In Photoshop, the letters, numerals, and symbols that make up a typeface are represented as vector-based type outlines. These outlines are then employed to produce the characters while constructing type in Photoshop. Operations like text scaling or resizing, file saving as a PDF or EPS, or printing the picture to a Postscript printer have no influence on the vector outlines in any fashion. As a di-rect result, it is now feasible to construct types with attractive, resolution-independent, clean, and sharp edges. The writing will always appear crisp and professional, regardless matter how big you make it.

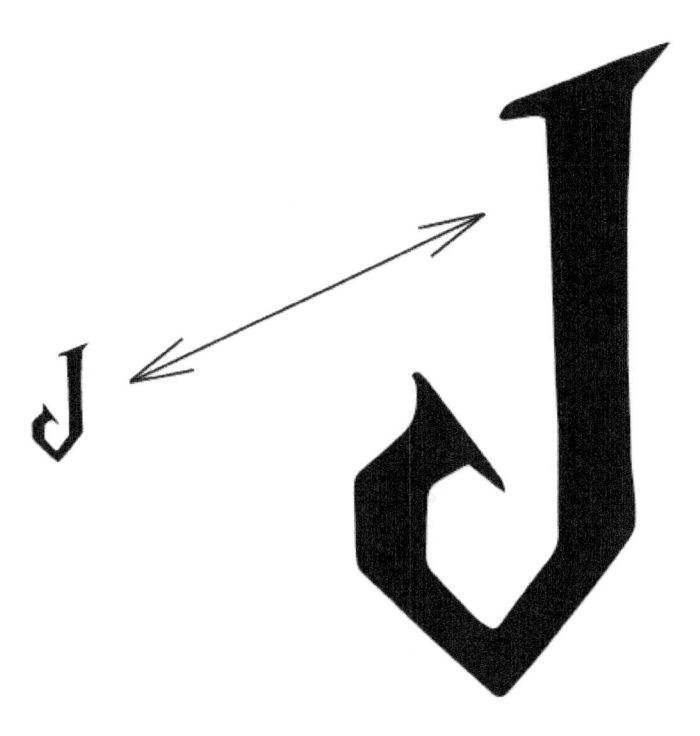

About paths and the Pen tool

Many graphic design and digital art techniques in Photoshop depend on paths and the Pen tool. They allow designers and artists the ability to make specific shapes and lines that may be adjusted in many ways to acquire the desired effects. The outlines of forms or lines that are made in Photoshop using the Pen tool or other shape tools are referred to as pathways. They serve as the basic building blocks of all vector graphics and may be manipulated in a number of ways to form elaborate patterns.

One of Photoshop's most helpful and effective tools for creating routes is the Pen tool. It allows users a substantial degree of control over the development of accurate and intricate pathways. With the Pen tool, you can carefully draw straight lines, curves, and complicated objects. Paths may also be combined with other Photoshop tools to achieve a variety of effects. For instance, pathways may be used to produce individual selections that may subsequently be colored or exploited to provide distinctive effects. Other shape tools that may be used to build routes are featured in Photos hop in addition to the Pen tool. These include the Ellipse tool and the Rectangle tool, both of which make circular and rectangular forms, respectively. Users may pick from a number of predefined forms, such as stars or arrows, then construct pathways from them using the Custom Shape tool. For producing logos, graphics, and other designs that call for precision lines and forms, pathways and the Pen tool are ex-tremely helpful. They give designers and artists a great lot of control over the construction of elaborate designs, and they make it simple to modify and adjust them as necessary.

Working with paths in Photoshop offers various benefits, including the ability to scale them up or down without affecting quality. Paths may be expanded without becoming pixelated or los-ing quality as they are based on mathematical equations rather than pixels. They are therefore great for developing visuals that must be applied in multiple sizes or on several kinds of media.

routes may be used to build bespoke text routes in addition to being used to make shapes and lines. This allows users the ability to generate text that sticks to a specified route or form, which may be particularly beneficial when producing text-based designs like logos. Paths and the Pen tool are crucial aspects of many Photoshop design processes. They give a tremendous amount of accuracy and control, and they are simple to adjust and manipulate to generate a large range of patterns and effects. Learning how to utilize the Pen tool and work with paths, whether you're a hobbyist or a professional designer, can greatly boost your Photoshop creativity.

Getting started

Understanding anchor points, handles, and line segments

The Pen tool in Photoshop depends on anchor points, handles, and line segments to form pathways. To develop exact and accurate forms and designs, knowing these components is vital.

Anchor points: Anchor points are sites where a path's form is established. They are positioned at the start and conclusion of line segments as well as when a line segment changes direction. They are represented by small squares. Anchor points act as the path's anchors and may be modified to modify the direction of the path.

Handles: Small lines that extend from anchor points are referred to as handles. They enable you to adjust a route or a line segment's curvature. Two handles, one on each side, may be connected to each anchor point. The handles' length and angle govern how curved the path will be between the two anchor points.

Line segments: Two anchor points are joined by straight lines called line segments. Depending on where the handles are situated, they might be straight or curved. A path's form and appearance are dictated by its line segments.

You must click on the canvas to establish an anchor point before you can use the Pen tool to draw a route. The Pen tool will add new anchor points and connecting line segments as you click on the canvas. You must click and drag on an anchor point to shape handles that govern the line segment's curvature to build a curve. After you've sketched a route, you may adjust its shape by changing the anchor points or modifying the handles' length and angle. You must click and drag a handle to the right spot after modifying it. You must click and drag an anchor point to a new spot to move it. In general, using the Pen tool in Photoshop to produce precise and accurate forms and patterns needs an understanding of anchor points, handles, and line segments. You can master these components and quickly build elaborate shapes and patterns with practice.

Drawing a shape with the Pen tool

• Open Photoshop and create a new document by navigating to **File > New**. Choose the size and resolution for your document, then click "**OK**."

• From the toolbar on the left side of the screen, pick the Pen tool. A pen tip with a small anchor point appears as the Pen tool's icon.

• To add the initial anchor point for your form, click on the canvas. This will act as the basis for your form.

• For the second anchor point, pick a different region of the canvas by clicking. This will designate the location where your shape's first line segment stops.

• Keep clicking on various parts of the canvas to add more anchor points and line segments. A line segment will link each new anchor point you establish to the one before it as you develop them.

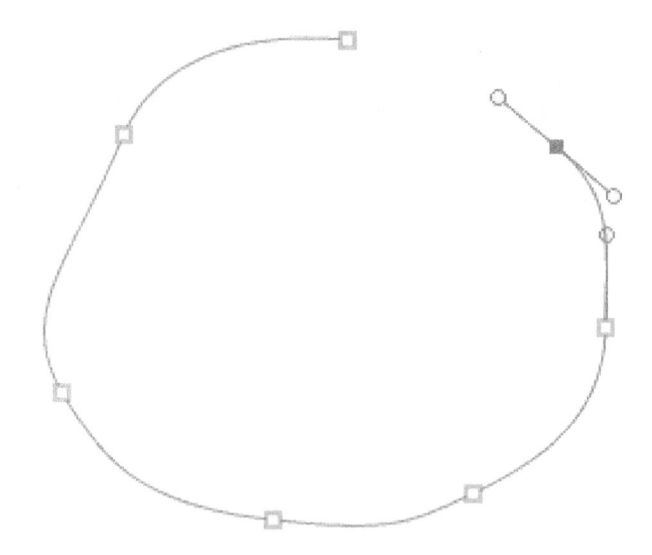

- Click and drag on an anchor point to draw curves in your form. You may use the handle it makes to adjust the curvature. To make the curve seem the way you want it to, adjust the handle.

- After building your form, you must seal it by linking the last anchor point to the starting anchor point. To achieve this, move the Pen tool over the first anchor point until a tiny circle appears next to the icon for the Pen tool. To collapse the form, click on the first anchor point.

- Now that you've constructed your shape, you may add color to it. To do this, click the Fill tool in the toolbar after choosing the form layer in the Layers panel. Click **"OK"** to fill the shape with the appropriate color after picking it from the color picker.

- Choose the Direct Selection tool or the Pen tool from the toolbar to make any required modifications to your form. While the Direct Selection tool lets you to pick and move individual anchor points, the Pen tool allows you to create new anchor points and alter existing ones.

- Save your shape if you are pleased with it by clicking **File > Save As**. After selecting a file type and a name for your shape, click **"Save."**

Creating curves and adjusting curves in shapes

Using the Pen tool in Photoshop entails drawing curves and changing curves in shapes. Learning to generate and edit curves will help you to build more sophisticated and sophisti-cated designs that have a feeling of depth and dimension. You must click and drag on an anchor point to produce handles to utilize the Pen tool to draw a curve. The handles' length and angle govern how curled the line segment between the two anchor points will be. Make sure the handles on each side of an anchor point are the same length and angle if you intend to bend anything gently.

Using the Direct Selection tool, pick the anchor point of the curve that you wish to change. You may pick individual handles, line segments, or anchor points with the Direct Selection tool. Once an anchor point has been chosen, you may adjust its handles to modify the curve's curvature.

In Photoshop, there are numerous approaches to edit curves:

1. Adjusting handle length: The handles' length may be altered to vary the curve's curvature. You must choose the handle and drag it to the desired length to achieve this.

2. Handle angle adjustment: You may tweak the handles' angles to alter the curve's direction. You must choose the handle and move it to the right angle to achieve this.

3. Moving the anchor points: This will allow you to adjust the curve's shape. You must first pick the anchor point and transfer it to the desired position.

4. Anchor point addition or deletion: You can add or delete anchor points to adjust the curve's form. Click on the line segment where you wish to add the point to add an anchor point. Use the Direct Selection tool to pick the anchor point you wish to eliminate, and then press the eliminate key.

Drawing paths with the pen tool

The pen tool is the most common option when starting from scratch to build a route. You are constructing your form with points and handles instead of the pencil tool. To create your forms, you must add points and manipulate them rather than merely sketching on the page. These points are added using the pen tool, and the way you move the tool as you add them impacts how they ap-pear. Keep in mind that the path will be smoother the fewer points there are. Think about creating a smooth curve with a pencil by making a single movement. If you try to draw the same curve with multiple little strokes, the outcome won't be as smooth; the same thing happens if you add too many points to the route.

Advice: You might learn that building routes are comparable to eating spaghetti in that you are unable to control how much of it falls off the plate. Hold the Ctrl or Command key while clicking anywhere within the document window to stop adding to your route. The route is now finished. Here's an overview of various popular line/curve forms you might wish to construct-and how to build them. Once you have mastered these fundamental forms, you will be able to draw practically anything with the pen tool.

Straight line paths

Drawing a straight line is easy; you could use the line tool or the pen tool.

Choose the Pen tool from the toolbox.

Select the drawing option from the options bar to draw either a path, Shape layer or fill pixels.

Click once to mark the initial location, then Ctrl - click Cmd - click) someplace else (without dragging) to indicate the final point. A straight line links the dots.

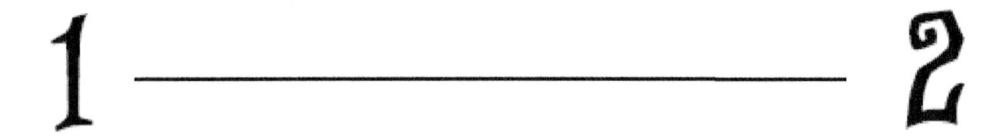

1 ──────────────── 2

You may also keep clicking to keep adding straight-line segments-to build, for example, an irregular straight-line enclosed form. Just remember to Ctrl-click) at the point where you want the line-adding to end.

Curved Paths

You may build trails with ease by selecting the pen tool. You will demonstrate varied behavior if you use a different form of writing utensil. Though more complex than straight lines, curves may be learnt with effort. The trick is to drag after each point is set. To put it another way, when you click to form a point, click and drag in the direction that you want your curve to travel. The arc between the present point and the next one you form will be bigger the farther you drag. These fundamental curves are presented. You can draw nearly any form when you have mastered them.

U-SHAPED CURVES

Create a basic U curve. The further you drag the greater the curve will be. To build a U-shaped curve:

Step 1. Drag downward.

You'll see that two handles are being formed as you drag. These handles govern the curve's sharpness and the direction you desire to draw the curve in.

Step 2. Parallel to the first point you set shift your mouse to the right; then click and drag upward. You can now see a U-shaped curve being generated by clicking and dragging up. As you drag, the curve travels in that direction. If it's not optimal, don't worry; you can alter any curve.

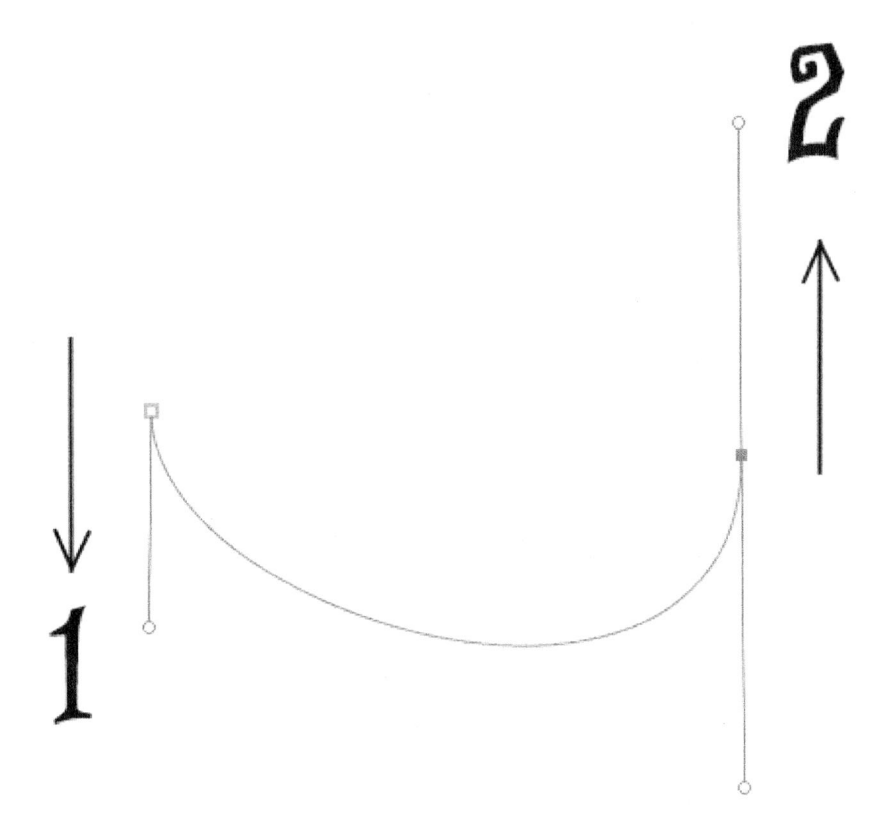

SIMPLE S CURVES

Creating a basic S-curve. Notice that when you adjust the angle of your drag, the form of the curve also changes.

An S-curve is only slightly more complex:

Step 1. Drag to the left.

The direction handles are being produced.

Step 2. Position your pointer beneath the first point. Drag to the left again.

Notice that you have a sloppy S curve. As you alter the angle of your dragging, you modify the form of the curve.

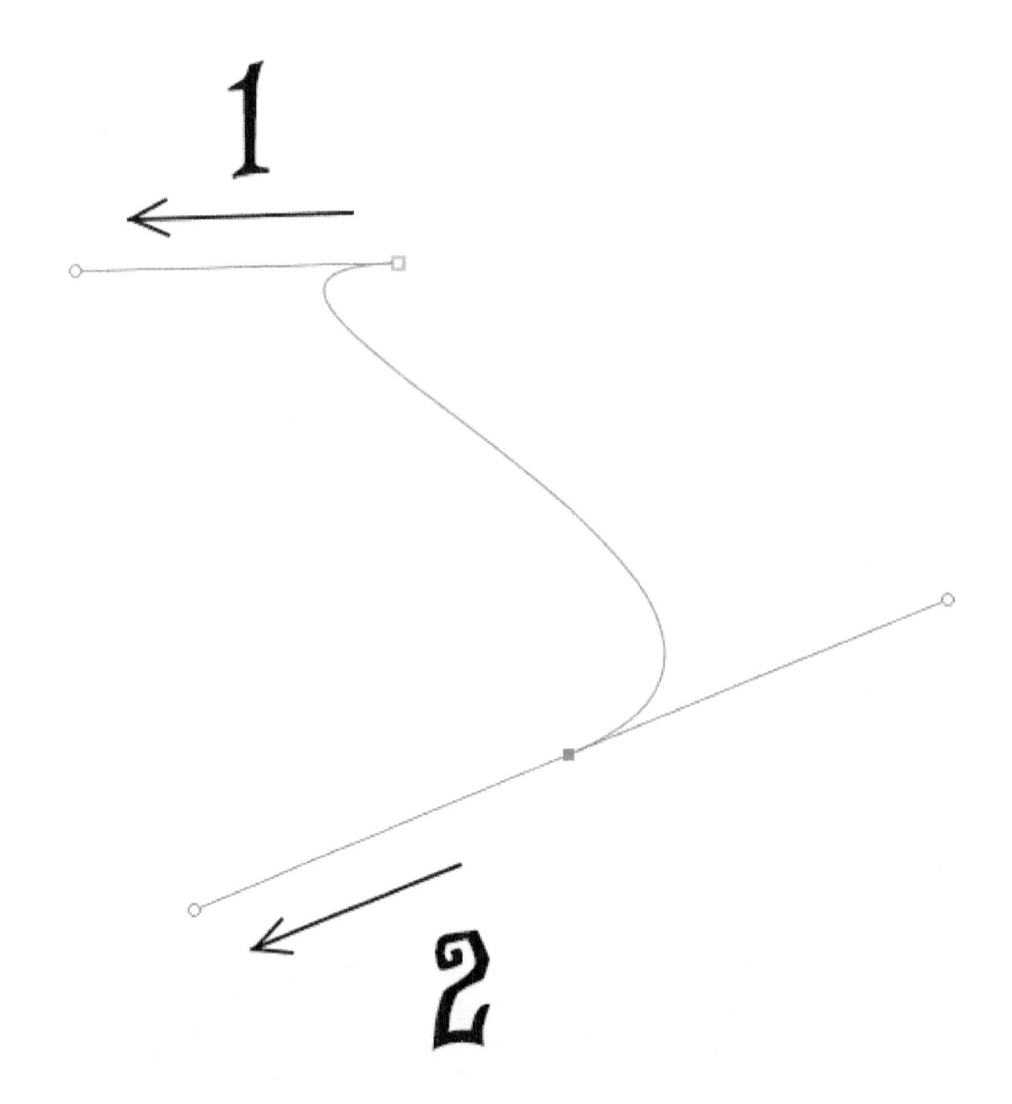

COMPLEX S CURVES

The complicated S-curve. Smooth loose curves are readily made with the pen tool.

Don't be deceived by the title; the sophisticated S curve is straightforward to make. It's considered complicated because it requires three points instead of two. In the previous cases, there were just two points that governed the complete curve.

Greater control is offered with the inclusion of a third point.

Step 1. Choose a starting point; drag to the left.

The direction handles are being produced.

Step 2. Position your pointer beneath the first point and drag it to the right. So far, you are building a U curve, as mentioned above.

Step 3. Move the cursor beneath the second point and drag left once more. You are now constructing the equivalent of two U curves in separate orientations. This is the S-shaped curve.

Step 4. Ctrl-click away from the route to stop drawing.

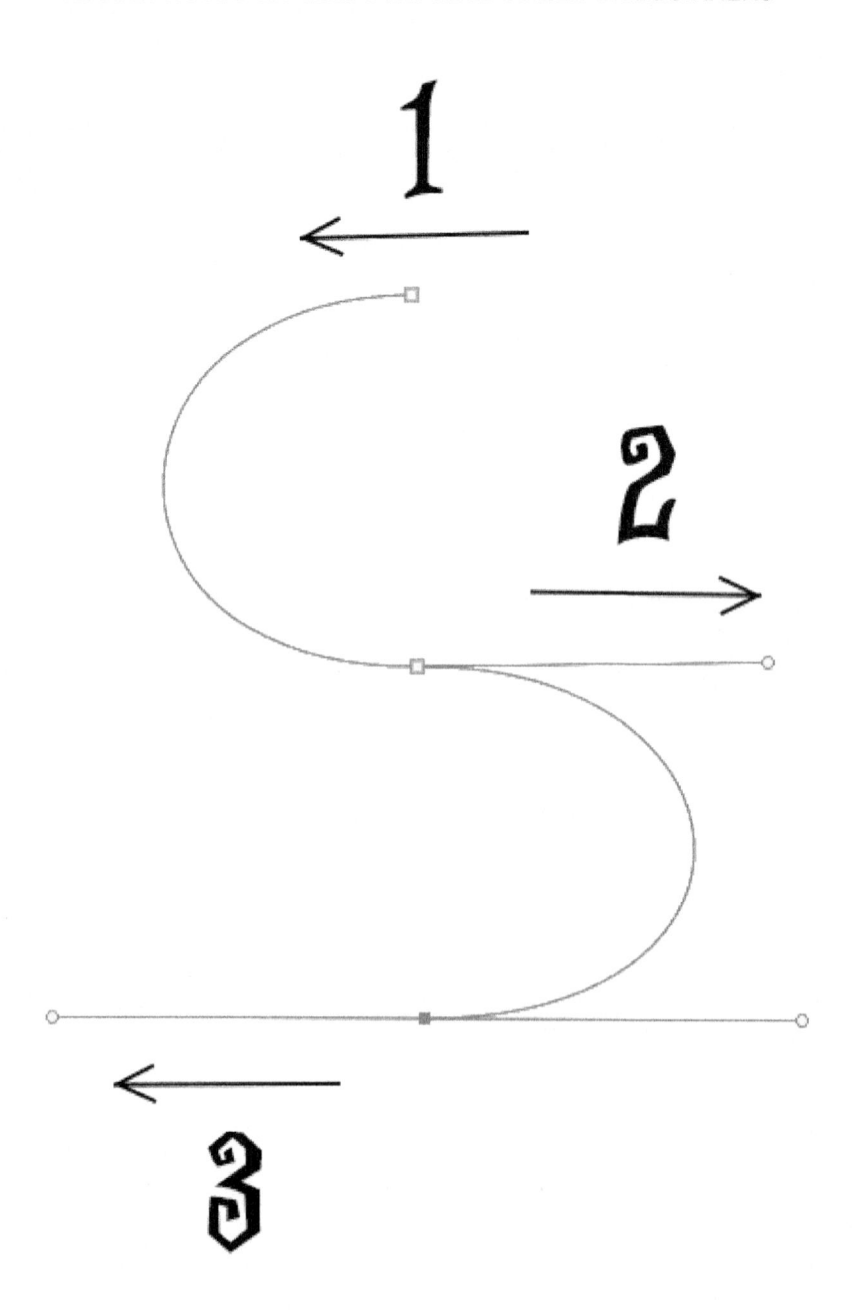

ADOBE PHOTOSHOP 2023 COMPLETE GUIDE FOR BEGINNERS

M CURVES

The M curve is a little difficult since it uses a new tool: the Convert Point tool. The convert point tool is accessible beneath the pen tool in the toolbox.

Step 1. From your starting location, drag upwards.

• You are building the direction handle.

Step 2. Move to the right and parallel, drag downward.

• You are building an inverted U curve right now.

Step 3. Now the tough part: Hold the Alt (Option) Key and drag upward.

Changing the direction handle for the next curve is what you are doing right now instead of drawing a curve. This is how the pen tool works. With a direction handle (the initial drag of the mouse), you first designate a direction. Based on the initial drag and the second's direction, the following click forms the curve. You must first modify the handle's direction without damaging the previously drawn curve if you want a sharp curve or cusp. The tool for this assignment is the Convert Point tool. You may rapidly pick the Convert Point tool for the moment by using the Alt (Option) Key.

Step 4. Drag down while positioning your pointer to the right of the second point.

Just now, you generated a Mcurve.

Step 5. To stop drawing, CTRL-click (ctrl-click) outside of the path.

You may drag any point to a different spot on your screen by hitting and holding the Ctrl key on your keyboard.

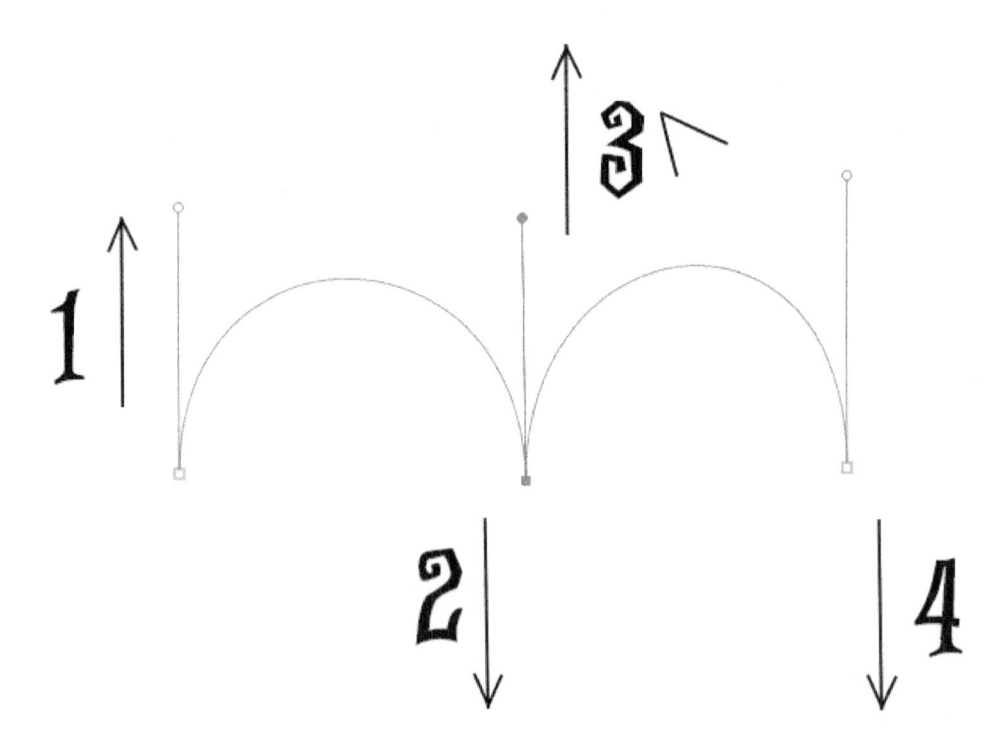

CLOSED PATHS

A blocked route. X represents the start/end point. To aid in constructing your curves, you may choose to reveal the grid under the View>reveal menu. The pathways depicted thus far are open paths-that is, they're not entirely contained forms. They're simply lines, and so you can't use them to pick portions of your image or fill them up with solid colors (Unless you are utilizing the Shape Layer technique of sketching.)

A closed passage, on the other hand, can be filled with color, texture, or patterns. It may be made into a selection to utilize on a picture. Perhaps you want to apply an adjustment or a filter to an isolated portion of your image. You will need a closed path for it. In honor of your new love of curves, here's how to make a closed route.

Step 1. Repeat the procedures for the M curve.

Follow the guidelines in the last example to get to the tip of an M-shaped curve. Don't deselect yet.

Step 2. Click to add a point beneath the other three points.

In the center, the shape of the heart begins developing.

Step 3. Finally, point at the initial point you established, without clicking.

A little circle emerges near the pointer. It notifies you that your mouse is hovering over the original beginning position. Click on the circle to close the route and make a closed loop.

Step 4. Click the spot to close the route and finish your heart.

The pen tool will automatically cease drawing on completion of a closed route. You may now choose the route from the Paths palette and convert it to a selection, export it to Illustrator, or store it for later use.

Tip: Try turning on the grid to aid in creating paths: **View > Show > Grid**.

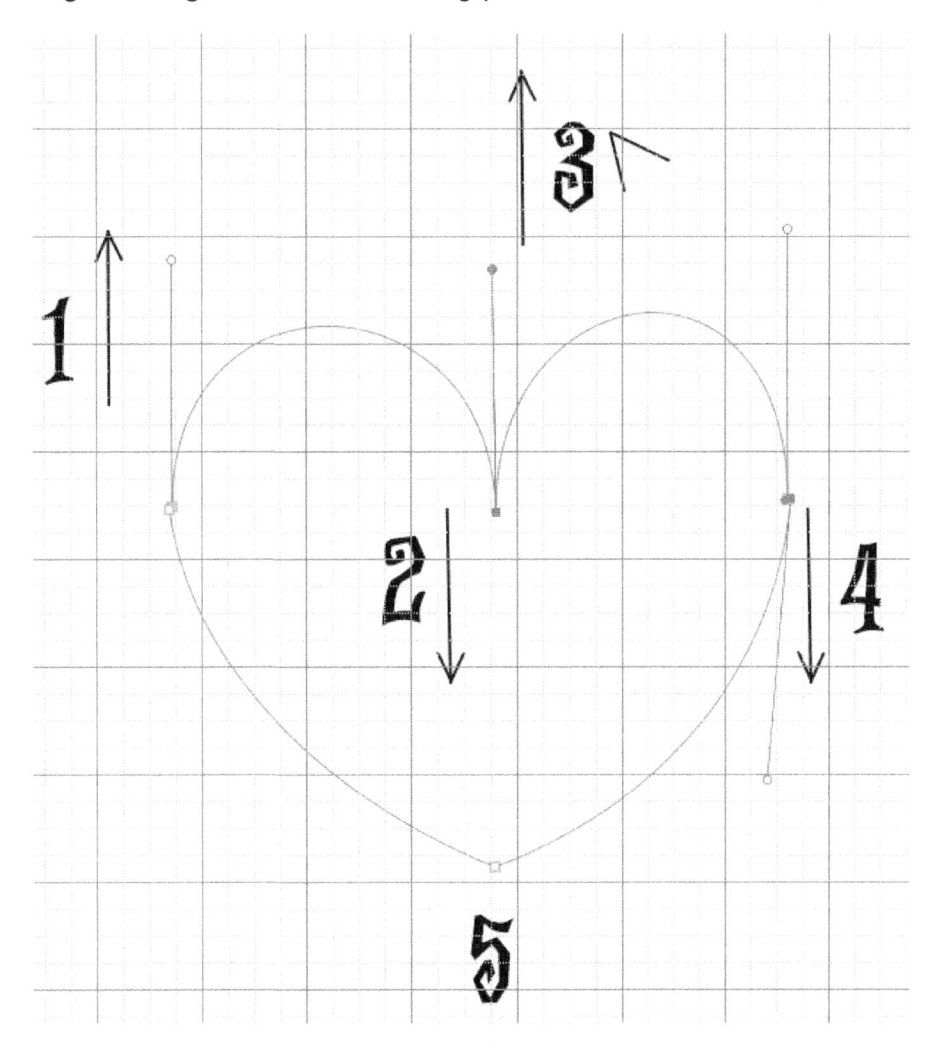

EXTRA TIP

In the settings bar, the Pen tool gives two choices for modifying behavior:

Auto Add/Delete. If this option is enabled, a + sign will display when you point to a route without clicking, suggesting that add a point by clicking there. When you point at an existing point, you will see a - sign, which indicates that if you click here, the existing point will be erased.

Rubber band option. When you enable this option, curves begin to emerge as you move the mouse about the screen, functioning as a type of live preview of the form you'll see after making the next click. It acts as a handy manual for creating routes. This may be found in the options bar's Geometry section.

Advanced approaches for producing complicated forms and patterns

After understanding the fundamentals of employing Photoshop's Pen tool, you may go on to more complicated approaches for constructing intricate form and patterns.

You can use the following strategies to develop your expertise utilizing the Pen Tool:

1. Combine shapes: To construct more sophisticated designs, you may mix different forms. You must first use the Pen tool to construct the component forms before merging them using the Path Operations menu. Shapes can be added to or removed from utilizing operations like Union, Subtract, Intersect, and Exclude.

2. Make advantage of the Convert Point tool: This function enables you to shift between corners and smooth points. When you need to make a sharp corner or adjust the contour of a curve, this might be beneficial. Select the anchor point you desire to convert, and then click the Convert Point tool button in the toolbar to employ it.

3. Create custom shapes: The Pen tool may be used to construct new shapes that are not present in Photoshop's built-in shape collection. You must first construct the form using the Pen tool and then save it as a custom shape to achieve this. The form may then be shared with other designers or utilized in other designs.

4. Make use of grids and guidelines: Grids and guides can aid you in making correct patterns and shapes. You can design personal grids and guidelines or utilize those offered by Photoshop. Go to View > New Guide or View > Show > Grid to design a custom grid or guide.

5. Combine the Pen tool with additional tools: The Pen tool may be used in conjunction with other tools to generate more complicated designs. For instance, you may construct simple forms with the Shape tools and then fine-tune them with the Pen tool. Alternatively, you may use the Pen tool to construct a route using your unique brush strokes after making them with the Brush tool.

6. Make use of keyboard shortcuts: If you wish to utilize the Pen tool more successfully, keyboard shortcuts can aid. For instance, you may momentarily switch to the Hand tool by pressing the Space bar, which will enable you wander around the canvas without deselecting the Pen tool. You may also utilize the Direct Selection tool using the Ctrl / Cmd key, which lets you select specific anchor points, handles, or line segments.

Drawing trail traced from a Photo

An approach that enables you to accurately outline an item or topic in a photograph is sketching a route drawn from the image. This might be handy if you want to isolate a topic from its back-ground or transform a photo into a vector image.

Here are the approaches for designing a route in Photoshop that was obtained from a photo:

Step 1. Open the photo in Photoshop: Open the photo you want to trace in Photoshop by navigating to **File > Open**.

Step 2. Create a new layer: Create a new layer by clicking on the **"New Layer"** button at the bottom of the Layers panel.

Step 3. Select the Pen tool: Select the Pen tool from the toolbar. You may also use the keyboard shortcut **"P"** to pick the Pen tool.

Step 4. Begin tracing the path: Click on a point on the edge of the topic in the shot to establish an anchor point. Continue clicking around the perimeter of the topic to establish addi-tional anchor points. If you need to construct a curve, click and drag to make a handle.

Step 5. Finish the path: To finish the journey, click on the first anchor point when you reach the beginning location.

Step 6. adjust the route: To adjust the path, utilize the Direct Selection tool (keyboard shortcut **"A"**). You can add or delete points, alter anchor points, and modify handles.

Step 7. Add a stroke: After you're comfortable with the route, you may add a stroke to the document to draw the subject's outline. To do this, pick **Layer > Layer Style > Stroke** while the path layer is chosen. As required, adjust the color and stroke width.

Step 8. Save the path: To save the route, pick **"Photoshop Path"** from the list of supported formats under **File > Save As**. By doing this, the path will be preserved as a unique file that you may use in other apps.

Converting a path to a selection and a layer mask

You can make precise selections and masks based on pathways you've drawn with the Pen tool in Photoshop by converting a path to a selection and a layer mask.

The processes to turn a route into a selection and layer mask are as follows:

Step 1. Make a path: To select or mask an area, draw a path around it using the Pen tool.

Step 2. Convert the route to a selection: Go to **Select > Make Selection** after picking the route. Set the feather radius to **0** in the dialog box that opens, then click **OK**. The path will become a selection as a result.

Step 3. Add a new layer: Click the "**New Layer**" button at the bottom of the Layers panel while the selection is chosen and active.

Step 4. build a layer mask: To build a layer mask, choose the new layer and then click the "Add Layer Mask" button in the Layers panel's bottom-right corner. A layer mask based on the selection will be created as a consequence.

Step 5. edit the layer mask: To edit the layer mask, use the Paintbrush tool and the colors black or white. Parts of the layer will be buried when painted black, but they will be made apparent when painted white. The Gradient tool may also be used to produce a seamless transformation from black to white.

Step 6. alter the selection: Select > Refine Edge can be used to alter the selection if desired. You can alter the edge detection parameters in the resulting dialog box to acquire a better view of the subject's characteristics.

Step 7. Save the selection and layer mask: Once the selection and layer mask are to your taste, you may save them. Select > Save Selection should be used to save the selection. Right-click the layer masks in the Layers panel and pick "**Export Mask to File**" to save it.

Converting a path into a selection and layer mask in Photoshop may be a valuable tool for producing perfect selections and masks. When working with intricate forms or when you need to construct a selection or mask that follows a particular route, this method is quite beneficial.

Creating a logo with text and a custom shape

It's a regular difficulty in graphic design to build a logo that blends text with a distinctive form. Using this strategy, you may merge typography and unique graphics to create a distinctive logo that distinguishes your business or organization.

The approaches to build a logo in Photoshop that contains text, and a distinctive form are as follows:

Step 1: Conceptualization and Research

You must study and understand your logo's design before you begin. Consider pulling inspiration from other logos, businesses, and firms in your sector. Make a list of the concepts and design features that best reflect your brand or organization. Think about the colors, typefaces, and forms that most effectively represent your brand.

Step 2: Create a New Document

Go to **File > New** in Photoshop to start a new document. Set the size and resolution of your logo, and make sure RGB is chosen for the color choice. To start a new document, pick Create.

Step 3: Create a Custom Shape

Choose the Custom Shape tool from the toolbar after that. Decide on the form of your logo. If the shape you're searching for isn't there, you may access additional shapes by clicking the arrow next to the Custom Shape tool. To construct the shape in the document, click and drag. The Curative Pen tool is another tool you may utilize.

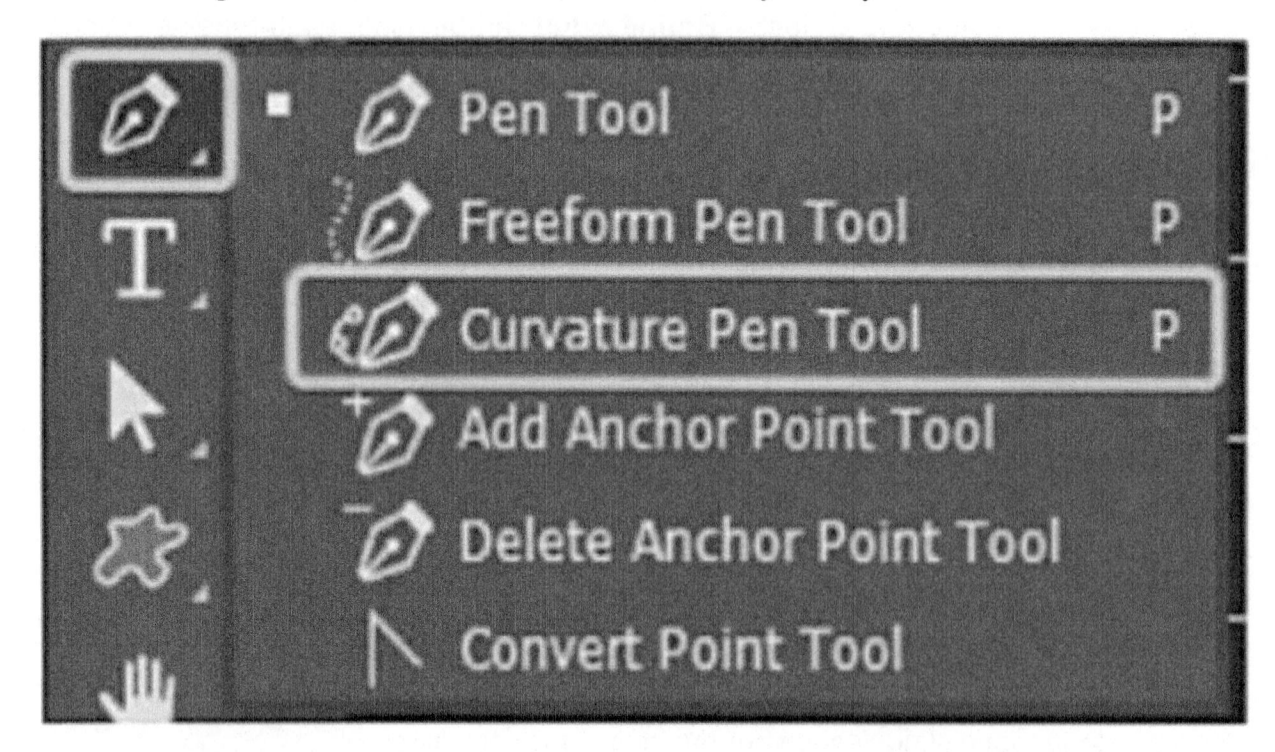

If required, modify the parameters on the parameters tab. Then, after picking a black outline with no fill and a line width of 5px, I set the path type to Shape. Then, begin creating the required form by incorporating anchor points. The form need not be ideal as you may apply the control points to make alterations thereafter.

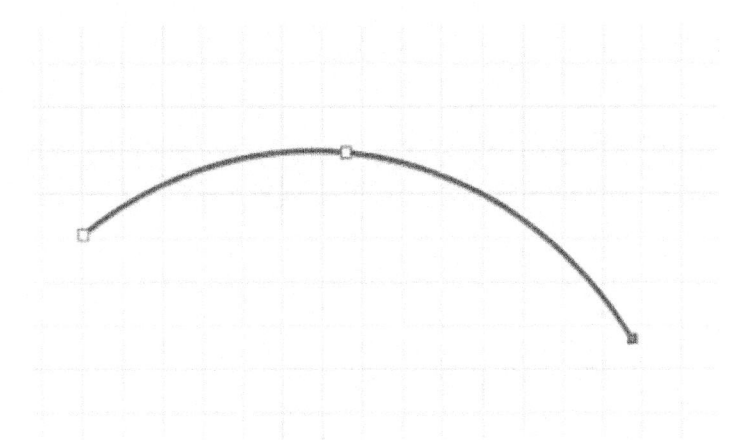

Use the control points to adjust the form when you have the basic one. If required, you may align the form using the grid.

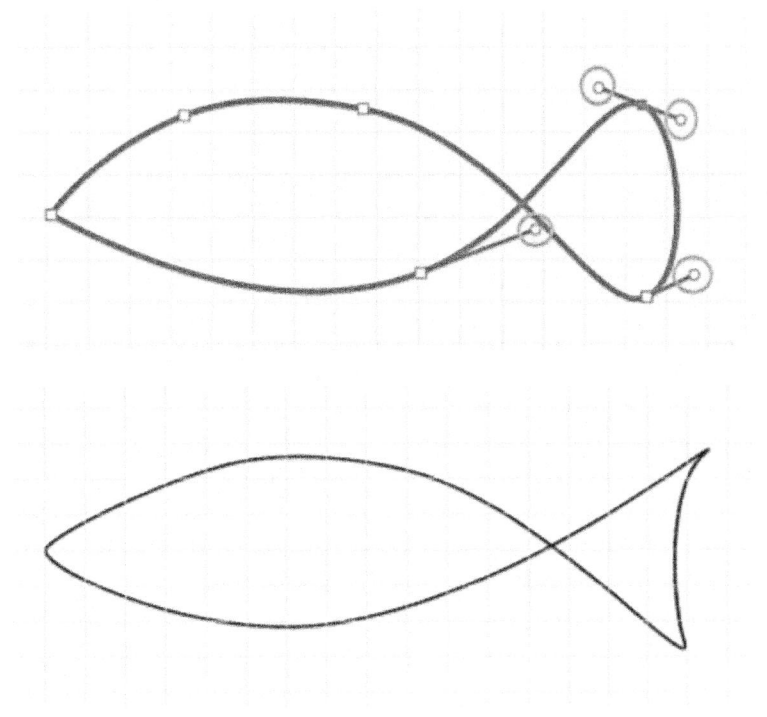

Step 4: Add Text

Always incorporate text when making a logo, particularly if it's for a brand-new firm. Prospective consumers could learn more about a brand by glancing at the name featured in the logo. Once the brand is well-known, the corporation can opt to eliminate the words and solely employ the symbol from the logo, as you can see with well-known companies like Apple, McDonald's, Twitter, and Nike. From the toolbar, pick the Type tool. The document where you desire to add text should be chosen. Enter your text and alter the font's size, color, and any formatting as needed. To acquire the right spacing, you may also alter the tracking and kerning of the text.

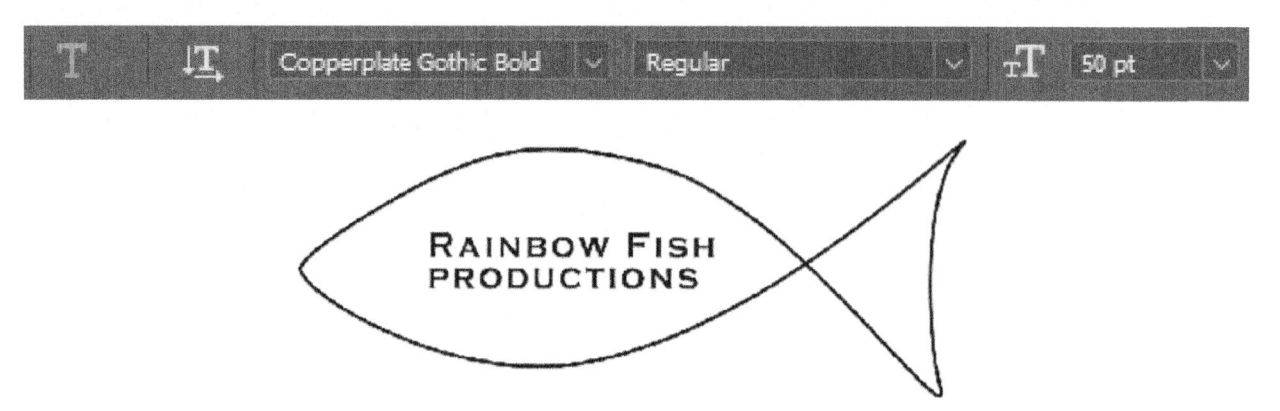

Step 5: Position the Text

To place the text in regard to the custom form as you wish, use the Move tool. By shifting the text box's corners, you may also modify the text's size.

Step 6: Adjust the Shape

To alter the custom shape's handles and points, utilize the Direct Selection tool. The Shape tool may also be used to adjust the shape's size, color, and style. To make the form more obvious, you may also give it color for the stroke and fill.

Step 7: Add Effects

To make your logo more unique and distinctive, you may use effects like shadows, gradients, and textures. Go to **Layer > Layer Style** after selecting the layer to which the effect is to be applied. Effects like drop shadow, inner shadow, gradient overlay, stroke, and more may be placed here.

Step 8: Save Your Logo

When you're delighted with your logo, save it as a high-resolution image file in the suitable format for your requirements. The file can be saved as a PNG, JPEG, or PDF.

Guidelines for Designing a Great Logo

1. Keep things simple: An effective logo is memorable and easy to recognize. In your logo, keep away from utilizing too many colors, typefaces, or forms.

2. Utilize Contrasting Colors: To make your logo more obvious and memorable, utilize contrasting colors.

3. Use Legible Fonts: Choose typefaces that are straightforward to read and readable. Refrain from picking hard-to-read elaborate or decorative typefaces.

4. Harmonize the Elements: Ensure that your logo's text and visuals are both balanced and aesthetically beautiful. Apply the rule of thirds to your logo design to achieve har-mony and balance.

5. Make it Scalable: Make sure your logo is scalable and can be scaled without losing quality. This is especially vital if you want to utilize your logo on numerous platforms and media.

CHAPTER 9: ADVANCED COMPOSITING

Arranging layers

When it comes to the development of sophisticated photographs and composites, one of the most significant parts of Photoshop is the organization of the layers. The layers in a Photoshop project are the essential building blocks of the software, and how those layers are structured may have a huge influence on the final outcome. In this part, we will go over some of the most significant tactics and recommendations for arranging layers in Photoshop.

1. Layer Order

The order in which the layers are exhibited in the picture is dictated by the order in which they are displayed in the Layers panel. The layers that are positioned at the panel's top are exhibited in front of the layers that are located at the panel's bottom. Simply dragging and dropping the layers in the Layers panel will allow you to modify the layer order. Alternatively, you may utilize the Layer menu to swap layers higher or lower in the stack.

2. Layer Grouping

In Photoshop, you may simply arrange your layers by utilizing a process called layer grouping. To group layers, you first need to choose the layers you desire to group, and then use the Command-G (Mac) or Control-G (Windows) key combination on your keyboard. You may also build a new group by clicking the button labeled "Create a new group" which is situated at the very bottom of the Layers panel. When layers are grouped, you may collapse and expand them, which eases difficult project navigation and administration.

3. Layer Blending Modes

Blending modes for layers enable you to exercise control over how one layer interacts with the layers that come before it. Each kind of blending generates a particular affect, such as light-ening or darkening the layer, or combining the colors in a number of diverse ways. Simply choose the layer you wish to alter, and then use the drop-down option at the top of the Layers panel to choose a new blending mode. This is how you adjust the blending mode of a layer.

4. Layer Opacity

The opacity setting of a layer is what sets the layer's level of transparency. A layer's opacity may vary from 0% to 100%; a layer's opacity can also range from 0% to 100%. A layer's trans-parency might range from 0% to 100%. You may modify the opacity of a layer by using the slider called "Opacity" which is situated at the very top of the Layers panel. By reducing the opacity of a layer, you may assist it blend in better with the layers behind it, resulting in a composite that feels more natural.

5. Layer Masks

You have more control over the final composite owing to layer masks, which enable you to cover or reveal particular aspects of a layer. Select the layer you wish to add a mask to, and then click the **"Add layer mask"** button at the bottom of the Layers panel. This will add the mask to the chosen layer. After that, you may use the Brush tool to paint on the layer mask, which will allow you to expose or conceal areas of the layer.

6. Smart Objects

You may apply filters and transformations to Smart Objects, which are layers that comprise one or more additional layers, without incurring any quality loss. Simply right-click on the layer you wish to convert into a Smart Object, and then pick **"Convert to Smart Object"** from the context-sensitive menu that displays. Working with sophisticated projects that demand a broad array of filters and settings calls for the usage of Smart Objects in particular.

Using Smart Filters

Photoshop's Smart Filters are non-destructive filters that may be applied to Smart Objects or layers. You may use Smart Filters in any mode. Smart Filters, in contrast to traditional filters, may have their parameters modified or be eliminated at any point without having any effect on the underlying picture or layer. Because of this, they are an efficient tool for making sophisticated effects and patterns that need a multitude of filters and settings to be modified. In this part, we will go over some of the most critical procedures for using Photoshop's Smart Filters.

1. Converting Layers to Smart Objects

It is important to change your layers into Smart Objects before you utilize Smart Filters. To accomplish this, right-click the layer you would want to convert and pick **"Convert to Smart Object"** from the option that presents. You also have the option of going to the Layer menu, selecting **"Smart Objects,"** and then selecting **"Convert to Smart Object."** Once a layer has been turned to a Smart Object, Smart Filters may be applied to it.

2. Applying Smart Filters

To apply a Smart Filter to a Smart Object, pick the filter you wish to use from the Filter menu, and then click the Apply button. For instance, if you wanted to smooth out the sharp comers of an object, you may apply a filter called Gaussian Blur. Following the application of a filter, a new Smart Filter layer and a filter mask will be added to the Layers panel in Photoshop. Simply dou-ble-clicking on the Smart Filter's layer in the Layers panel will take you to the menu where you can make modifications to the filter's settings.

3. Editing Smart Filters

One of the wonderful advantages of Smart Filters is that you may modify them at any moment. To modify a Smart Filter, just double-click on its layer in the Layers window. This will open the filter settings window, where you may make modifications to the filter parameters. For example, you may increase the radius of a Gaussian Blur filter to make it fuzzier.

4. Adding Multiple Smart Filters

You may apply more Smart Filters to a Smart Object or layer by merely repeating the technique that was just explained. You could, for instance, use a Gaussian Blur filter to make the edges of an item fuzzier, and then use a Curves filter to adjust the brightness and contrast of the same object using the same filter. In the Layers panel, each Smart Filter will show its individual layer, and you may alter its properties as desired.

5. Applying Smart Filters to Selections

In addition, you may utilize Smart Filters to apply effects to selections in your photo. To accomplish this using Photoshop, first, build a selection using any of the various selection tools, and then choose "Convert to Smart Object" from the menu accessible in the Layers panel. After that, you may apply Smart Filters to the region that has been specified, and those filters will be incorporated inside the Smart Object.

Painting a layer

Make a new layer or pick one of the ones that were already there. After that, from the toolbar that is positioned on the left side of the screen, choose the Brush tool. By clicking and holding the icon for the Brush tool, you can have access to other painting tools such as the Pencil, Eraser, or Clone Stamp tools. You may also use these tools to paint. You will need to determine whichever color or colors you will use before commencing the painting procedure. Either the Swatches panel or the Color Picker can be used to pick a color for use. The Swatches panel may be opened by choosing **Window > Swatches** from the main menu. Double-clicking either the Foreground or Background color in the toolbar will bring up the Color Picker for you to utilize.

You may now begin painting on the layer whenever you're ready. To add a new color or texture to the canvas, all you have to do is click and drag the Brush tool. You may adjust the size of the Brush tool, as well as its opacity and other settings, by employing the choices that are found in the tool bar that is situated at the top of the screen. After you have painted on the layer, you may adjust its properties by making use of the choices that are accessible in the Layers panel. Altering the opacity, blend mode, or layer style of a layer, for instance, might result in a range of visually unique effects being generated. You may also apply adjustment layers to perform non-destructive alterations to the layer, as well as layer masks, which enable you to cover or reveal sections of the layer you are working on.

After you have reached the point where you are pleased with the painted layer, you can either save your project as a Photoshop file or export it in a different format. To save the project as a file in Photoshop, go to the File menu and click Save from there. Simply go to the "**File**" menu, then "**Export**," and make your choices there to export the project in a format of your choosing.

Adding a background

Filling a layer with a solid color is one of the quickest and easiest techniques to give it a backdrop in Photoshop. To accomplish this, choose the new layer, and then use either the Color Picker or the Swatches panel to choose a color to apply to the layer. After that, choose "Color" from the selection that displays when you click Edit > Fill from the main menu. When you click the OK button, the layer will be filled with the color you chose. Creating a background with a gradient is still another approach. To achieve this, click the new layer, then go to the toolbar on the left side of the screen and choose the Gradient tool from there. Choose a sort of gradient from the choices bar at the top of the screen, and then set the colors and the points at which the gradient stops. After that, to apply the gradient to the layer, you will need to click and drag the Gradient tool around the canvas.

Add a picture backdrop. To add a photo as a backdrop, choose the new layer, then go to the File menu and select Place Embedded from there. Select the photo file that you desire to utilize and then click "Place." The picture will display on the layer, and you can use the Move tool to modify its size and placement. Altering the layer's opacity as well as the manner in which it is blended can give a range of diverse effects. Last but not least, you may give a layer's backdrop a pattern instead of a plain color. To achieve this, choose the new layer, and then go to the Edit menu and select Fill from there. Select "Pattern" from the list of dropdown menu options, and then use the pattern picker to choose the pattern you wish to use. The size of the design, as well as its alignment, may be changed to fit your demands. After you have added a backdrop to the layer, you may adjust its properties by making use of the choices that are accessible in the Layers panel. Altering the opacity, blend mode, or layer style of a layer, for instance, might result in a range of visually unique effects being generated. You may also apply adjustment layers to make non-de-structive alterations to the layer, as well as layer masks, which enable you to cover or reveal sections of the layer. Lastly, you may build layer masks.

Using the History panel to undo modifications

You may undo and redo any modifications that you have made to your photo due to the History window in Photoshop. If you have made a mistake or would wish to revert to an earlier version of your project, this function might be beneficial.

To undo changes made in Photoshop, follow these procedures in the History panel:

Open the History Panel

You may visit the History panel by selecting **Window > History** from the menu or by hitting the Alt key in conjunction with the **F9** key on your keyboard (Windows) or Option key in com-bination with the **F9** key (Mac). The History panel will come up on the right-hand side of the screen when it loads.

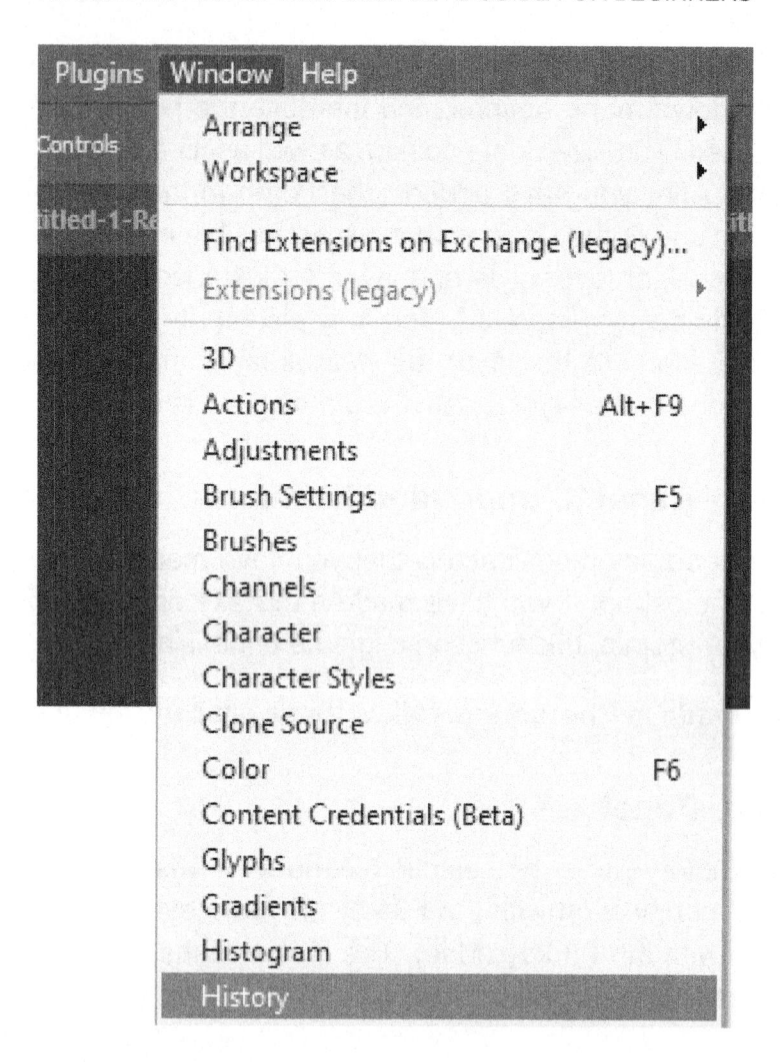

Navigate the History States

The historical panel provides a list of historical states, which are snapshots of your picture at various points in the editing process. These historical states can be accessed by clicking the historical button. Every historical state relates to a particular point in time when you changed the photo in some way. You may browse the History states by clicking on them in the panel or by using the keyboard keys **Ctrl + Alt + Z** (Windows) or **Command + Option + Z** (Mac) to step back through the states, and **Shift + Ctrl + Z** (Windows) or **Shift + Command + Z** (Mac) to go forward through the states. Alternatively, you may use the mouse to move through the historical states.

Undoing Edits

To reverse an edit, you need to pick the prior state in the history from which you desire to revert. For instance, if you wish to erase the most recent brush stroke you generated, pick the historical state immediately before you formed that brush stroke. This will allow you to delete the most recent brush stroke. After you have chosen the history state you wish to use, any modifications you make to the photo after that point will be discarded, and it will be returned to the condition it was in before you made those changes.

Redoing Edits

You may simply redo a modification that you have previously undone by using the keyboard shortcut **Shift + Ctrl + Z** (on Windows) or **Shift + Command + Z** (on Mac) to go forward through the prior states of the document. This will apply any modifications to the photo that you have previously undone, and it will return the image to the condition it was in before you used the undo command.

Setting a Snapshot

If you wish to produce a snapshot of your picture in addition to the historical states, you may do so by clicking the "**Create New Snapshot**" option that is situated at the very bottom of the history panel. This will build a new snapshot, which you may access at any time by picking it from the panel once the snapshot has been created. If you desire to preserve a specific version of your photo before making any additional alterations, you may apply this function to accomplish so.

Clearing History States

If you desire to clear the past states and begin from the beginning, you can click on the "**Clear History**" button that is situated at the bottom of the History panel. This will return everything to its original condition. Your image will be reset to its initial condition when all of the historical states and snapshots are erased as a consequence of this action.

History States

Setting the number of History States.

Click the Preferences drop-down menu and then click the Performance option to modify the number of history states that Photoshop retains track of while an image is open. A bigger number will store more alterations (history states), which will enable you to wander farther back in time. However, selecting a larger number will also need Photoshop to keep track of more information in RAM (or, when the full RAM is being utilized, to the scratch drive). Note that when you make changes to the complete document, such as adding layers or running effects, Photo-shop has to keep track of more information for each historical state. This is in contrast to alterations that are exclusively done to a specific section of the picture, such as small, localized paint strokes. Therefore, if you boost the number of states and discover that performance decreases as a result, you should consider lowering the number of states once again.

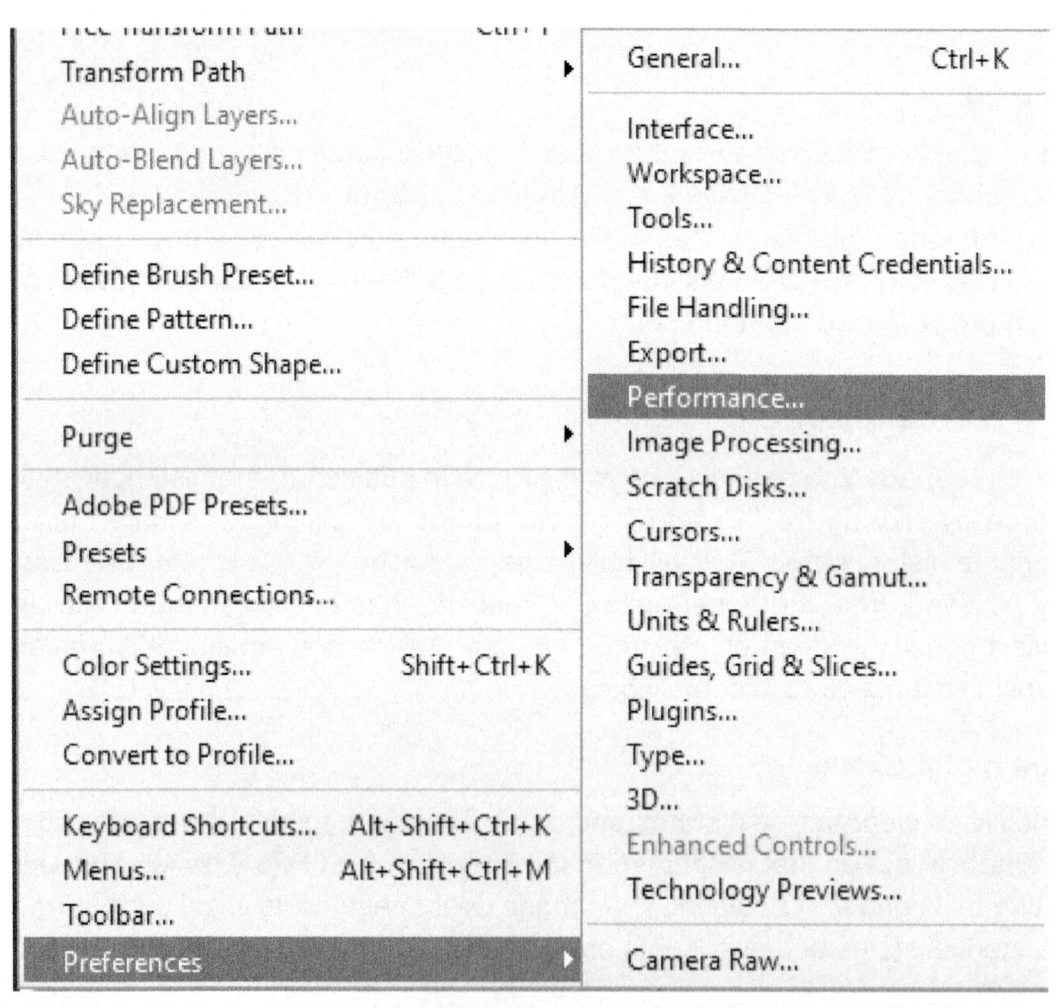

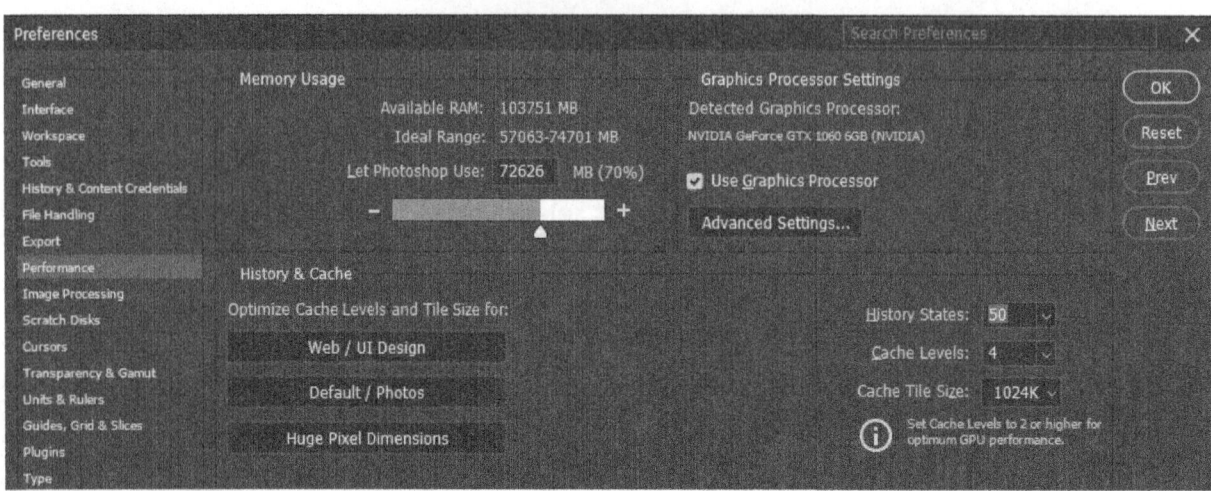

Layer Visibility

If you routinely modify the visibility of layers but do not want these changes to register as a step-in history, use the History panel's fly-out menu to pick History settings and uncheck the box labeled **"Make Layer Visibility Changes Undoable."** This will prevent the visibility changes from being noted in the history log.

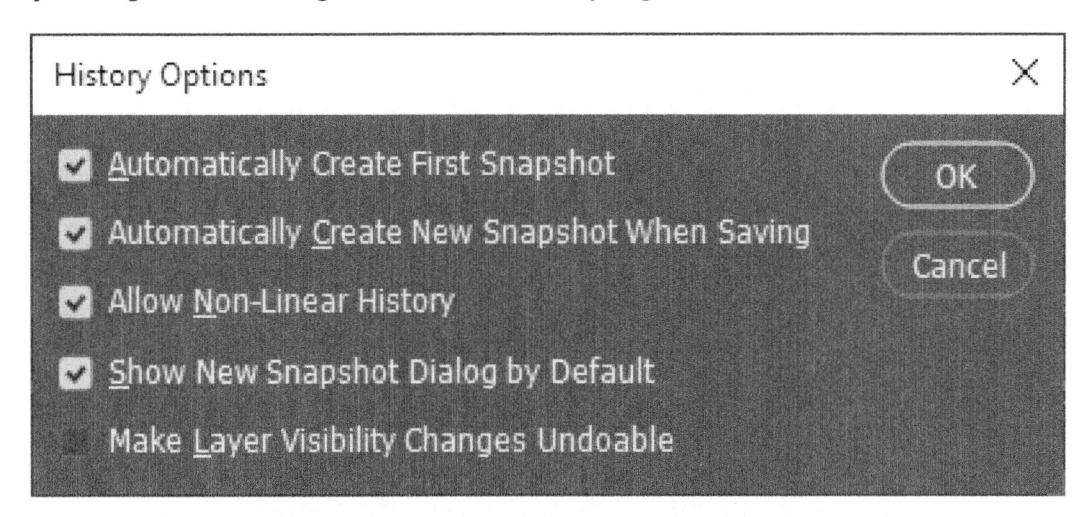

Non-Linear History: History states are introduced in a non-linear fashion, starting at the top of the History panel and working their way down. Therefore, the state that was in existence the longest is at the top of the list, while the state that entered the union the most recently is at the bottom. If you travel back in time and then execute another command, history states that you had from the now targeted state forwards (or towards the bottom of the panel) will be lost. This is due to the default behavior of the program. To maintain the most recent states, open the History panel's fly-out menu, click History Options, and then switch on the Non-linear History option. Now, regardless of whether or not one returns back in time or makes additional modifi-cations after doing so, the previous states in history will continue to exist.

Duplicating History States: To duplicate a history state, you may either control-click (on a Mac) or alt-click (on a Windows computer) on the state you wish to reproduce, except the current state.

Snapshots: Whenever you open a new document in Photoshop, the application automatically produces a "Snapshot" of the file, which is subsequently put at the very top of the History panel. Note that when you paint in Photoshop using the History Brush, Art History Brush, the Eraser, and the Fill Commands, Photoshop will pull from the state of the document that is presently showing.

Creating Additional Snapshots: The history states may "roll off the top" of the panel at some time depending on the number of alterations that have been done to the file and your personal preferences. Simply clicking the camera icon will generate a fresh snapshot of the full document, which you may use to avoid a state from being lost from the History panel. No matter how many changes are made to the document, snapshots will continue to remain at the very top of the History panel right up until the document is saved and closed.

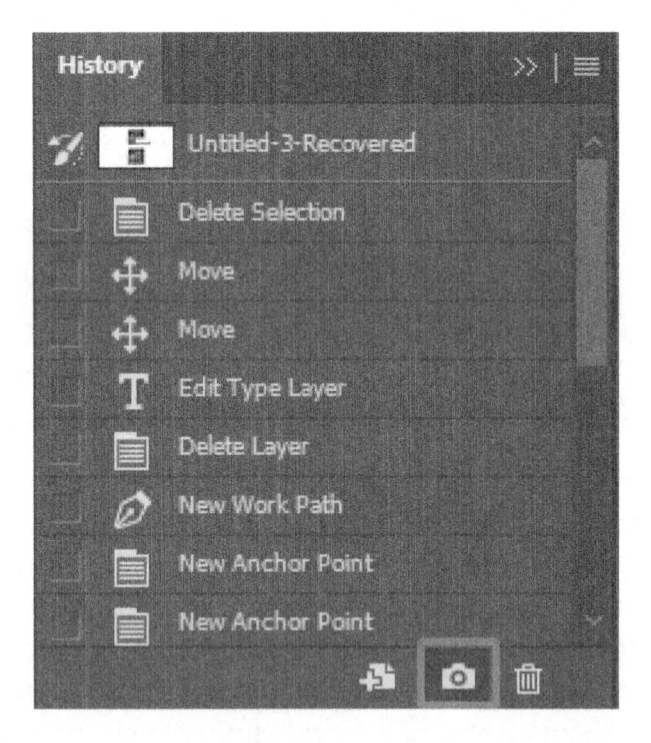

Snapshot choices: To access more Snapshot choices, click the fly-out menu situated on the History panel and make sure the "**Show New Snapshot Dialog by Default**" option is chosen. The next time you produce a snapshot by clicking the camera icon, the New Snapshot window will pop up. From this box, you may pick to make a Snapshot from the Full Document, Merged Lay-ers, or the Current Layer.

Undoing an Accidental Save: Because Photoshop always takes a snapshot when you open a new file, you can "undo" a save that you made inadvertently by clicking on the snapshot in the History panel, saving the file, and then going back to the previous state and selecting "**Save As**" from the drop-down menu.

Automatically Create New Snapshot When Saving: When you save a document (or save it as a new name), the Save command will be added as a state in the History panel. This is done in case you need to recover it after making further modifications to the document.

Having said that, the Save (or Save As) state may finally "toll of the top" of the panel depending on the number of adjustments that have been made to the file as well as your preferences. If you would prefer have access to the **"Saved"** state of the document, regardless of how many modifications are made to the currently open document, click the fly-out menu on the History panel, choose History Options, and enable the **"Automatically Create New Snapshot When Saving"** option. This will allow you to view the **"Saved"** state regardless of how many modifications are made to the document. Until the file is permanently closed, the snapshot will continue to be accessible to everyone who requires it, regardless of the number of times it is updated.

Selecting Different States: Several tools and operations, including the History Brush, the Art History Brush, the Eraser, and the Fill command, will employ the Snapshot as their default configuration. Click the empty well to the left of any Snapshot or state in history to alter the **"History"** state that these tools utilize as their source material. This may be done by picking a different Snap-shot or state in history.

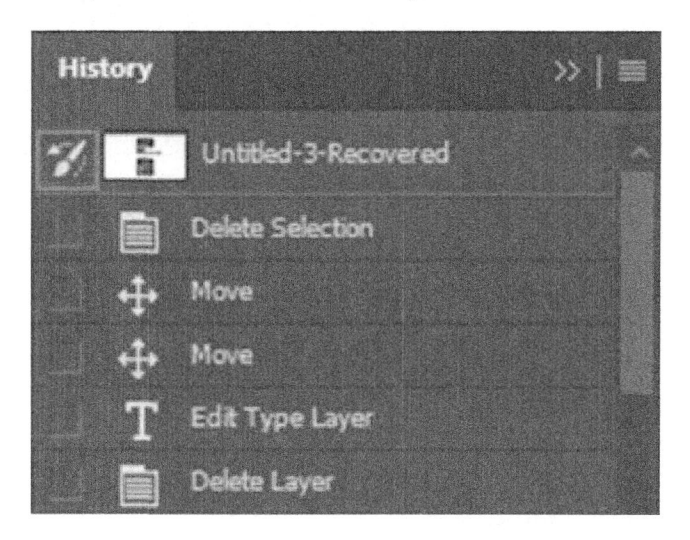

Changing Color Mode, Bit Depth, and Image Size: There are a handful of modifications that may be made to a document (Color Mode, Bit Depth, and Image Size) which will then require new Snap-shots to be taken to be used as the source for the History brush, Art History brush and Fill commands).

Fill using History **Edit > Fill** or, **Option + Command + Delete** (Mac) I **Alt + Control + Backspace** (Win) fills with the presently chosen history state.

Fill Content with History **Option+ Shift + Delete** (Mac) I **Alt+ Shift + Backspace** (Win) + **Shift** will fill with the currently chosen history state and keep transparency (so that only those pixels that contain information in them are filled).

Paint with History -click in the empty well next to any Snapshot or state in history and use the History brush to paint with that state. Note: I prefer utilizing snapshots to paint with as history states may slide over the top of the history panel.

Erase with History-Holding the **Option** (Mac) I **Alt** (Win) with the **Eraser** tool will erase with history.

Duplicating Documents using History: To quickly duplicate a document, click the "**Create New Document from Current State**" icon at the bottom of the History panel.

Clearing History-All Snapshots and History states are destroyed when a document is closed. When a document is open, clicking "**Clear History**" (from the fly-out) will clear the history to free up RAM or scratch disk space; however, you may still pick **Edit > Undo Clear History**. Holding ability (Mac) I **Alt** (Win) + choosing "**Clear History**" will wipe the history without the ability to "undo" (as if you have closed the file and reopened it). This can be handy to free up disk space or to release RAM (or when you just don't want anybody to see what magic you've ap-plied to a picture). Note: you may also pick **Edit > Purge > History** to erase a file's history.

History Log -To retain a record of instructions applied to a file in Photoshop, click **Preferences > History Log**. Choose to store the logged items to the metadata (within of the file), to an exter-nal file, or to both as well as pick a degree of detail to record:

Sessions will only record a basic amount of information such as when files are opened, saved, and closed.

Concise will record the name of the command (such as **Levels** or **Curves**).

Detailed will record the name of the command and the settings used (such as Levels, Input: **0**, **197**, Gamma: **1.48**, etc.).

Program Wide Changes -When modifications are made to Photoshop (instead of the picture), they are not saved as a state in History (for example changes made to panels, color settings, preferences etc.).

The History and Art History Brush Tools -Both the History and Art History Brush Tools sample information from the presently targeted state in the History panel (by default, this is the snapshot made when the file is initially viewed). To keep more detail when using the Art History Brush, consider experimenting with a very small brush. You may also in-crease/decrease the spacing of the brush (located on the Brush Settings panel under Brush Tip Shape) and paint on a different layer to achieve more intriguing effects.

Improving a low-resolution picture

When you are dealing with images that have a poor resolution, it might be tough to achieve high-quality outputs. On the other hand, the quality of a photograph with a low resolution may be increased using Photoshop provided the necessary procedures and tools are employed.

If you wish to enhance a photo that has a bad resolution, you may achieve so by following these steps:

1. Upscale the Image

The first thing that has to be done is to make the picture bigger by scaling it up. In Photoshop, you may accomplish this by choosing Image from the menu bar and then selecting the Size option. If you want the upscaled picture to have a smoother appearance, be sure you pick the "Bicubic Smoother" option from the resampling technique menu.

• Zoom in to at least 300% so that you can see the individual pixels.

• Choose **Image > Image Size**.

• Check that the Resample option is chosen before continuing.

• Convert the measurements for width and height to percentages, and then change their corresponding values to be equal to 400%.

By default, the width and height are linked, which allows photos to enlarge while keeping their proportions. If you need to alter the width and height of a project independently from one another, you may unlink the values by clicking the link icon and deselecting it.

• Drag in the preview window to pan so that you can see the image (or the area of the image).

• In the Resample option, pick Bicubic Smoother (**Enlargement**). The image seems less grainy than it did previously.

On the Resample menu, you'll discover a range of choices that enable you pick how the picture is altered to make it larger or smaller. Automatic is the default setting, and it picks a technique based on whether you're enlarging or decreasing the picture. However, depending on the image, you may realize that a different choice creates a more pleasant outcome.

Ensure that the Resample option is picked, then go to the Resample menu and pick the Preserve Details (**Enlargement**) option.

When opposed to the Bicubic Smoother option, the Preserve Details option generates a more detailed and sharper enlargement; nevertheless, this may also make visual noise more evident.

To smooth out the picture, adjust the slider labeled **"Reduce Noise"** to the 50% position.

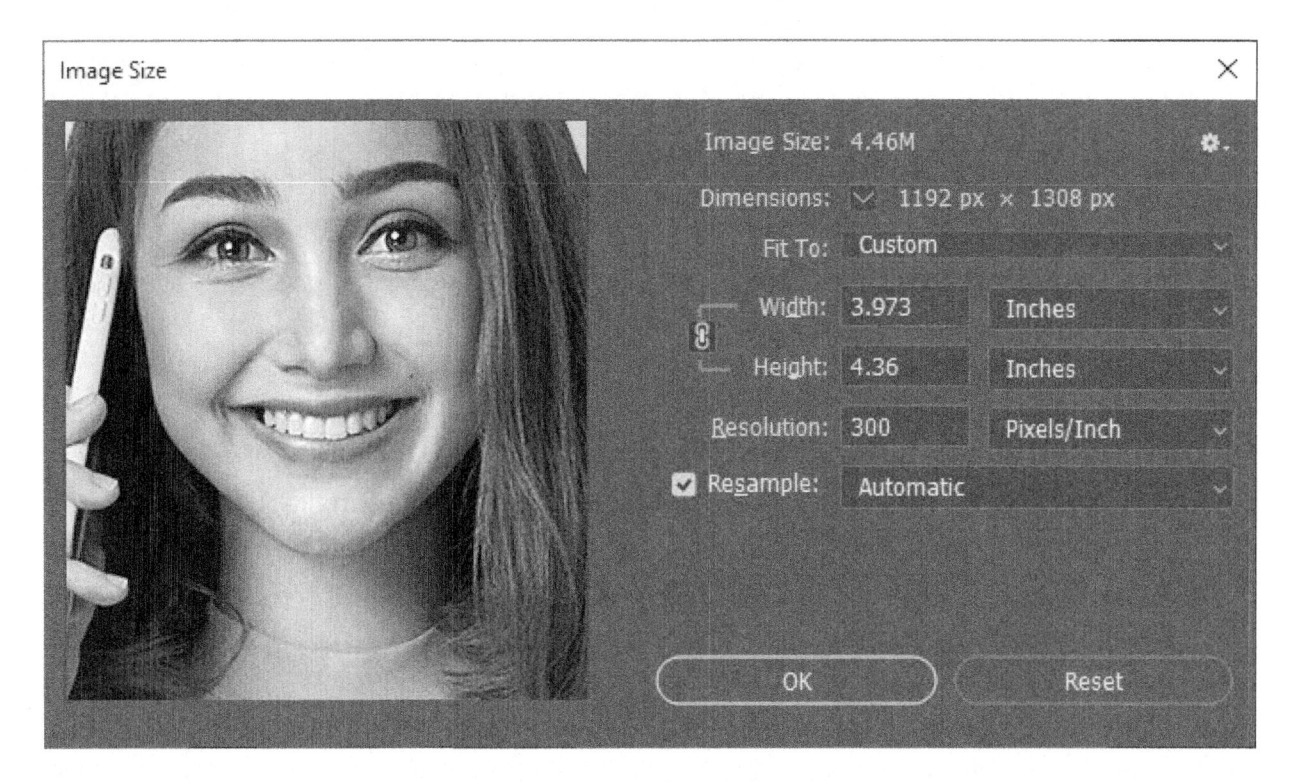

You may inspect the original photo in the picture Size dialog box by clicking and holding it in the preview window. This will allow you to examine the original image alongside the current adjustments. Alternatively, you may utilize the Resample menu to toggle between the current settings and the Bicubic Smoother option, which will allow you to make a comparison between the two.

Choose the Resample approach that strikes the ideal balance between retaining information and smoothing pixel jaggies when upscaling or downscaling a picture, and then use the Reduce Noise method to get rid of any noise that is still present after doing so. Reduce the level of Reduce Noise if you notice that it removes an excessive quantity of information.

2. Apply Smart Sharpen Filter

You might notice that the photo has gone a little hazy once you have scaled it up to a higher size. The photo may be sharpened by going to the Filter menu, selecting Sharpen, and then selecting the Smart Sharpen option. You may modify the degree of sharpness, the radius of the sharpening, as well as the noise reduction with this filter.

3. Apply Noise Reduction Filter

Images with a poor resolution sometimes include perceptible noise, which can be highly distressing to the viewer. You may get rid of the noise by using the Noise Reduction filter, which can be found in the Filter menu. You may alter the amount of noise reduction and the level of detail retention that this filter gives.

4. Use the Clone Stamp Tool

If the photo has any noticeable faults or imperfections, you may get rid of them by utilizing the Clone Stamp tool in your editing software. You can clone an area of the image and then employ that region to paint over elements of the picture that you do not desire.

5. Add Contrast

Increasing the amount of contrast in a low-resolution image can make it look like it has better clarity and sharpness. You may achieve this by employing the Levels or Curves adjustment layers in Photoshop to make modifications to the levels or curves of the photo.

6. Add Texture

You may lessen the impression of blurriness in a low-resolution shot by adding texture to it. This may be performed by employing the Filter Gallery, which gives various alternative choices for the image's texture that can be applied to it.

7. Save the Image in a High-Quality Format

Lastly, before saving the photo, check to verify that it will be stored in a high-quality format such as PNG or JPEG with the highest available quality level. Because of this, the picture will maintain as much of its original information as possible and will appear in its finest possible light.

CHAPTER 10: PAINTING WITH THE MIXER BRUSH

About the Mixer Brush

Users of Photoshop may blend colors immediately on the canvas while they paint owing to a brush tool called the Mixer Brush. It achieves this by replicating the action of a traditional paintbrush and palette, which is how it works. Users may make unique brush strokes with a broad range of colors, textures, and opacities by utilizing the Mixer Brush. It is highly beneficial for making oil and watercolor effects that are realistic in digital artwork.

How does the Mixer Brush work?

The Mixer Brush pulls color samples from the canvas as you paint and blends them into new colors. The colors that were sampled are then blended with the color that was already on the tip of the brush to make a unique color that is utilized to paint on the canvas. The Mixer Brush may be used with a broad range of brush presets, including ones that simulate the behavior of traditional painting materials such oils, watercolors, and acrylics. Users may alter the wetness, load, and mix of the brush when using the Mixer Brush. The amount of paint that is mixed in with the sampled color is determined by the wetness. The load affects how much paint is on the brush at any one moment. The Mix option influences how effectively the brush mixes with the previously applied color on the canvas.

Features of the Mixer Brush

Users may generate distinctive brush strokes and mix colors directly on the canvas with the aid of the Mixer Brush's array of features, which are included in the brush's basic package.

The following is a summary of some of the most essential elements of the Mixer Brush in Photoshop:

Wetness: Wetness control offers users the opportunity to modify the quantity of paint that is blended in with the sampled color. Higher degrees of wetness provide a look that is more fluid and suggestive of watercolor, but lower levels give an image that is thicker and opaquer.

Load: The load control allows users the opportunity to modify the quantity of paint that is on the tip of the brush. Higher load levels generate brush strokes that are thicker and opaquer, and lower load levels produce brush strokes that are thinner and more transparent.

Mix: The mix control allows users the opportunity to modify the degree to which the brush mixes with the color that is already on the canvas. When the mix levels are increased, there is a stronger mixing of colors, but, when the mix levels are dropped, there is less blending, and the brush strokes are more noticeable.

Blending modes: The Mixer Brush can be utilized with a wide variety of blending modes, including Normal, Dissolve, Darken, Multiply, Color Burn, Linear Burn, Lighten, Screen, Color Dodge, Linear Dodge, Overlay, Soft Light, Hard Light, Vivid Light, Linear Light, Pin Light, Hard Mix, Difference, Exclusion, Hue, Saturation, Color, and Luminosity. When you employ the Mixer Brush with a given mixing mode, the impact will be distinct.

Texture: The Mixer Brush may be used with a number of textures, including ones that simulate the behavior of conventional media like oils, watercolors, and acrylics. Among the different textures that may be used with the Mixer Brush are those that replicate the behavior of traditional media. The brush strokes might have specific textures applied to them to offer a more realistic effect.

Brush Setting Panel

The Brush Setting Panel in Adobe Photoshop is a complex tool that enables you to adjust the characteristics of your brushes and produce creative digital artwork.

A large range of brushes and effects may be made by artists by adjusting the numerous variables that are accessible in the panel. These brushes and effects may then be adjusted to match the demands of their creative activities.

In this section, we will analyze the different components of the Brush Setting Panel and illustrate how each of those regions may be leveraged to design personalized brushes.

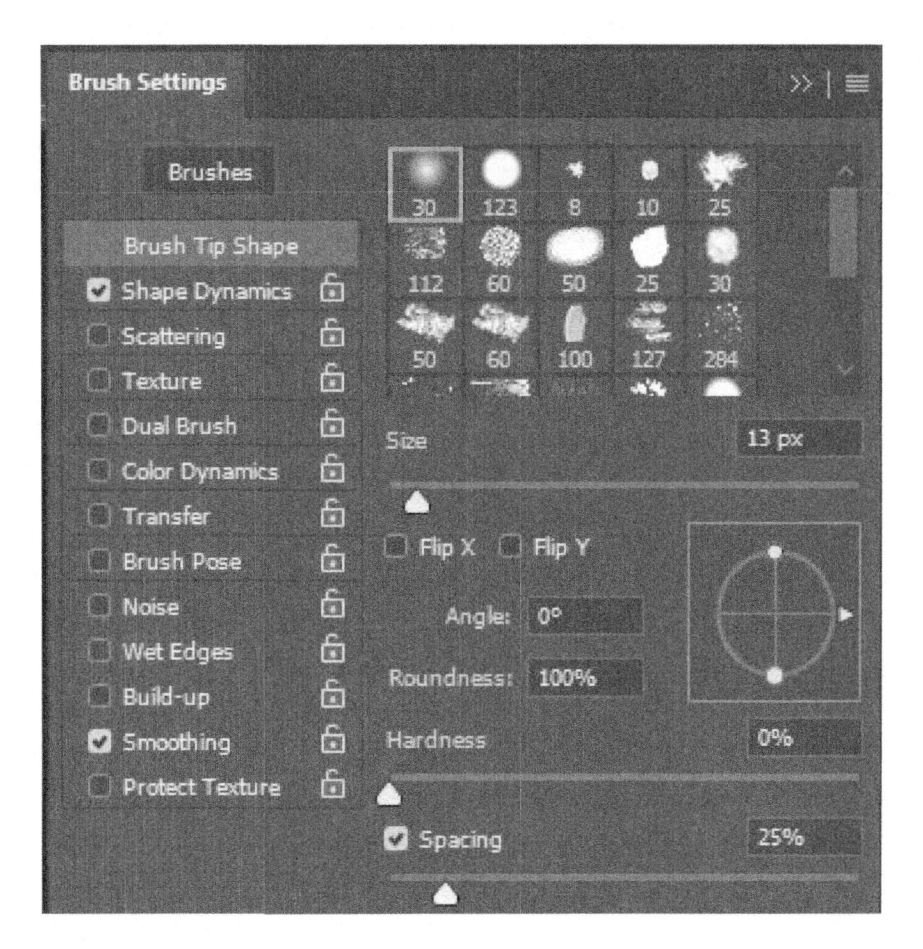

1. Brush Tip Shape

You may adjust the size, shape, angle, and roundness of your brush tip by heading to the Brush Tip Shape section of the Brush Setting Panel. You have the choice of picking one of several predefined brush forms, such as a round or square one, or you may construct your own shape. The Size slider offers you the opportunity to vary the size of your brush tip, while the Angle slider, Roundness slider, and Roundness slider give you the ability to change the angle, roundness, and size, respectively, of your brush tip. To increase space between each mark generated by the brush tip, you may also modify the Spacing slider. You may use this to produce a dotted or dashed effect with your design. You may make a broad variety of one-of-a-kind brushes for usage in a number of applications by adjusting these characteristics, such as for making fine line work, shading, or texture.

2. Shape Dynamics

The part of the Brush Setting Panel known as **"Shape Dynamics"** allows you the flexibility to adjust the brush stroke depending on the amount of pressure, tilt, and rotation applied by your stylus or mouse. This tool is particularly helpful for making brush strokes that seem like they were done spontaneously. You may produce variations in the brush stroke according to the amount of pressure you apply by modifying the sliders for the Size Jitter, Angle Jitter, and Roundness Jitter. You may pick a minimum size for your brush tip by modifying the parameters for Minimum Diameter and Roundness. This helps to guarantee that the brush stroke is still noticeable even when employing a reduced amount of pressure. Additionally, you may make dynamic brush strokes by utilizing the Rotation and Tilt controls. You may produce variations in the brush stroke by utilizing the Tilt X and Tilt Y sliders. These sliders are dependent on the angle that your stylus or mouse is held at. With the Rotation option, you'll be able to create an effect that rotates the picture depending on the angle at which you move your mouse or stylus.

3. Scattering

You may scatter your brush tip in a manner that is fully random by utilizing the Scattering portion of the Brush Setting Panel. You may build a broad range of one-of-a-kind effects by altering the parameters for the Count, Scatter, and Count Jitter. The Count parameter controls the number of brush tips that are employed in each stroke, and the Scatter setting governs the space that occurs between each brush tip. The Count Jitter option causes the number of brush tips to change unexpectedly, while the Scatter Jitter setting causes the space between brush strokes to fluctuate unpredictably. You may make a broad number of effects by altering these variables, such as a starburst effect or a smoke effect, for example.

4. Texture

You may add a texture to your brush stroke by utilizing the Brush Texture section of the Brush Setting Panel. You have the choice of picking one of several established textures, such as canvas or sandpaper, or generating your very own unique texture from start. The scale of the texture is governed by the Scale option, while the depth of the texture is decided by the Depth setting. Adjusting the brightness of the texture as a whole may be done using the Brightness option. Either the brush tip or the paper texture may be altered using the Texture option. It is possible to create a more realistic effect by adding the texture on the paper texture. This provides the idea that the brush is being used on a rough surface.

5. Dual Brush

The Dual Brush section of the Brush Setting Panel allows you the opportunity to combine the functionality of two separate brushes to achieve a one-of-a-kind effect. You may select from certain pre-configured dual brush combinations, such as a solid and splatter brush, or you can construct your unique dual brush. You may tailor each brush in its own right by modifying the available settings, which include the Spacing, Size, and Shape factors. By merging the strokes of two unique brushes, you may make a broad variety of one-of-a-kind effects, such as a brush stroke that has both a solid and a textured component.

6. Color Dynamics

Within the Brush Setting Panel, the Color Dynamics section allows you the flexibility to vary the color of your brush stroke depending on the amount of pressure exerted, the angle at which the brush is held, or randomness. The Hue Jitter, Saturation Jitter, and Brightness Jitter choices allow you to vary the color characteristics based on pressure or tilt, while the Foreground/ Background Jitter settings allow you to add randomness to the color of your brush stroke. To ensure that the color can be seen properly, you may optionally select a minimum and maximum for the level of saturation and brightness. You may build dynamic and changing color effects in your artwork by altering the parameters in the Color Dynamics tab. This component is lo-cated in the Color panel.

7. Transfer

You may alter the quantity of paint that is delivered to the canvas with each stroke by utilizing the Transfer section of the Brush Setting Panel. This is quite beneficial for making a range of brush strokes with varied degrees of opacity and flows in the paint that you apply.

While you may modify the quantity of paint transferred based on pressure or tilt using the Opacity Jitter and Flow Jitter settings, you can also manage the flow and opacity of the brush stroke using the manage settings. You may obtain a more natural and organic feel in your artwork by altering the settings in the Transfer section. This will allow you to make a range of brush strokes with various degrees of opacity and movement in your artwork.

Selecting brush settings

If you want to utilize the Mixer Brush tool in Photoshop to produce digital artwork, it is extremely crucial to set the suitable brush parameters to obtain the desired effect.

The following are some recommendations to consider while choosing brush settings:

1. Brush Presets

Photoshop comes loaded with a range of brush presets that have been built with the Mixer Brush tool in mind specifically. Either the Brush Preset Picker available in the Options bar or the Brushes panel may be used to pick one of these preconfigured brush types. You may customize a broad range of effects by adjusting the size, shape, and texture of each preset feature. These in-clude size, shape, and texture.

2. Brush size

When utilizing the Mixer Brush tool, the size of the brush can have a big effect on the effect that it generates as a whole. When utilizing a greater brush size, you may make strokes that are more blended and broader, while using a smaller brush size can create strokes that are more defined and distinct. You may modify the size of the brush either by moving the Size slider lo-cated in the Options bar or by making use of the keyboard keys [and].

3. Brush shape

The overall impact that the Mixer Brush tool generates may also be considerably altered by the form of the brush that is being utilized. The Brush panel provides certain forms that may be used to achieve a variety of effects. These forms include round, square, and unique shapes that can be utilized. You may modify the form of the brush by using the Brush panel or by using the keyboard shortcut **Shift + [** to increase the roundness of the brush and **Shift + [** to minimize it. These two shortcuts are accessible on the left side of the Brush panel.

4. Opacity

The opacity of the brush affects whether the strokes created by the brush are transparent or opaque. Brush strokes made with a lower opacity will be more transparent, while brush strokes created with a larger opacity will be opaquer. You may modify the opacity by moving the Opacity slider displayed in the Options bar, or you can use the keyboard shortcut Shift + number keys (1-0) to set the opacity to a given percentage. Either way, the opacity may be altered.

5. Flow

The amount of paint that is put onto the canvas with each stroke is governed by the flow of the paint across the brush. When the flow rate is raised, the brush strokes grow thicker, while reducing the flow rate results in narrower brush strokes. You may modify the flow rate by sliding the Flow slider displayed in the Options bar, or you can use the keyboard shortcut **Shift + Alt + number keys (1-0)** to set the flow rate to a given percentage. Either method, the flow rate may be changed.

6. Smoothing

Photoshop's smoothing tool can aid in the creation of brush strokes that are less jagged and more under control. This function may be accessible via the Options bar or the Brushes panel, and its parameters can be tweaked to obtain the effect that is necessary.

Mixing colors

You may need to be patient to accomplish your project, depending on how intricate it is and how quick your computer is. The process of mixing colors may be quite difficult. You may give your digital artwork a more natural and organic appearance by blending colors with the Mixer Brush Tool in Photoshop. This is a great strategy that can help you acquire the look you're going for.

If you want to get started blending colors with this tool, here are a few things you need to take:

1. pick the Mixer Brush Tool To access the Mixer Brush Tool, pick it from the toolbar on the left side of the screen. You may also use the shortcut "B" on your keyboard to access it fast.

2. Select your brush tip After that, navigate to the Brush Presets panel found on the right-hand side of the screen and select the brush tip that you want to use for blending col-ors. You have the choice of utilizing one of the brushes that have been preloaded, or you may design your own brush.

3. Adjust the brush settings Once you have picked the brush tip that you wish to use, you can navigate to the Options bar at the top of the screen to make adjustments to the brush parameters. The brush size, opacity, flow, and wetness are just a few of the factors you may pick.

4. Choose your colors Before you begin to mix colors, choose the colors you intend to use by choosing them from the Swatches or Color panel of the software you're using. You may choose any two or more colors to mix into a new one.

5. Mix your colors To start mixing your colors, click and drag your brush over the canvas. As you paint, the colors will merge, providing a seamless transition between them. To mix the colors more completely, you may use the Alt key (Option on Mac) to pick up the color off the canvas and add it to your brush.

6. Experiment with the many settings of the brush If you want to achieve a range of effects, try playing with the various settings of the brush. You may, for instance, modify the wetness of the brush to regulate how much the colors merge, or you can vary the flow to manage the quantity of paint that is applied. Both of these alterations are under your control.

7. store your own brushes If you have produced a custom brush that you like, you may store it for future use. Simply click on the New Brush Preset icon in the Brush Presets tab and give your brush a name.

Mixing colors with a Photograph

The powerful way of blending colors with an image in Photoshop is one that you may utilize to generate digital artwork that is one-of-a-kind and aesthetically captivating. To develop a customized color palette that may be used to paint or color an image, one approach comprises isolating colors from a photograph and using those separated colors as the basis for the palette.

The following are some processes that might aid you in getting started with color mixing in Photoshop using a photograph:

1. Choose your picture: Before beginning the process of mixing colors using a photograph in Photoshop, the first thing you need to do is choose an image that you want to work with. Whether the photo is of a landscape, a portrait, or an abstract composition, you may employ it. Pick a picture that you enjoy because the colors in it inspire you or draw your attention.

2. Select your color scheme: After you have decided on the image that you want to utilize; the next step is to pick the color scheme that you want to employ. A color scheme is a set of colors that are meant to be used together to express a specific atmosphere or ambiance. There is a broad range of color schemes from which one may pick, including monochromatic, complementary, analogous, and triadic color schemes. Nature, art, fashion, and even design may all serve as sources of inspiration when it comes to color palettes.

3. Extract colors from the image. The colors that you intend to employ in your color palette should be taken from the image. In Photoshop, you may execute this activity by employing the Eyedropper tool. Simply navigate to the toolbar on the left side of the screen, choose the Eyedropper tool, and then click on the colors in the photographs that you would want to employ. This will mimic those colors. You may also use the Color Picker to pick colors manually. This option is available.

4. Create a new document and color swatches. After you have extracted the colors that you wish to utilize, open a new project in Photoshop and navigate to the Swatches panel. Next, create a new document and add color swatches to the document. Simply pick the New Swatch icon found at the bottom of the panel to build a new color swatch. First, give your Swatch a name, and then input the color values that you desire to make use of. Repeat this technique for each color that you desire to add to your custom color palette and save your modifications after each step.

5. Paint with your custom color palette: Once you have built your custom color palette, you can begin painting with it using the Paintbrush tool or any other painting tool that you like. Once you are completed, you will be able to utilize your customized color palette. Try out a range of brush sizes, pressure settings, and opacity levels to come up with one-of-a-kind effects and flawlessly blend the colors.

6. Utilize adjustment layers: You may utilize Photoshop's adjustment layers to further enhance the colors in your photo. Adjustment layers are found in the "Edit" menu. Hue and Saturation, Color Balance, and Curves are three sorts of adjustment layers that could be beneficial. Making modifications to the levels of these layers can aid you in generating a color palette that is more cohesive and well-balanced.

7. Save your work: When you are done altering the colors in your images using Photoshop, be sure to save your work as a high-resolution file so that you do not lose any of your hard work. You may utilize your newly acquired color palette for future projects, or you can continue to play around with color mixing to generate artwork that is even more distinctive and intriguing.

Painting and combining colors using brush defaults

The method of painting and mixing colors in Photoshop using brush presets and the Mixer Brush tool is an effective way to generate artwork that is both appealing and textured. With the aid of the Mixer Brush tool, you'll be able to simply create a natural, painted effect by blending and combining colors.

The following are some approaches that will aid you in getting started with painting and color mixing utilizing brush presets and the Mixer Brush tool:

1. Pick a brush preset that you want to use: The first thing you need to do is pick a brush preset that you want to use. In Photoshop, you may pick from a broad number of brush presets, including natural media brushes, texture brushes, and special effects brushes, among many others. Pick the brush setting that most closely approaches the appearance and feel that you intend to attain.

2. Prepare your canvas: After you have decided on the brush preset you want to use, open Photoshop and create a new canvas. Then, modify the dimensions and resolution of the canvas so that it is the size you want. You may also import a photo to use as your foundation layer, in addition to picking a color to use as the backdrop.

3. Mix your colors: It's crucial to mix your colors before you start painting with your brush preset, so make sure you do that. You may accomplish this by using the Color Picker or the Eyedropper tool to select colors from your canvas. Both of these tools are featured in the Tools palette. To obtain a range of one-of-a-kind appearances, try blending colors in a number of combinations and apply varied degrees of transparency.

4. Begin painting: After you have finished the previous step of mixing your colors, you can now begin painting using the brush preset that you picked. When you want to give your artwork additional depth and texture, consider playing with various brush sizes, opacities, and blending modes. There is also a tool called the Eraser that you may use to erase rid of areas of the image that you don't like.

5. Use the Mixer Brush tool. This tool allows you to blend and combine colors. You may access this tool by using the Shift+ B shortcut, which is situated on the tool bar. You may create a natural, painted effect with the Mixer Brush tool by gathering up colors from the canvas and combining them to form a new color.

6. Experiment with brush settings: The Mixer Brush tool includes numerous brush settings that you can play around with to achieve a range of different effects. For instance, you may alter the settings for Wet, Load, and Mix to govern the quantity of paint that is put onto the brush as well as how it mixes with the colors already existing on the canvas. Experiment with different combinations of these variables to acquire the effect you desire.

7. Use adjustment layers: You may utilize the adjustment layers function in Photoshop to further improve the quality of your artwork. Hue and Saturation, Color Balance, and Levels are three sorts of adjustment layers that could be beneficial. Making modifications to the levels of these layers can aid you in generating a color palette that is more cohesive and well-balanced.

8. Save your work: After you have done painting and mixing colors in Photoshop using brush presets and the Mixer Brush tool, be careful to save your work as a high-resolution file. Your artwork may be utilized in future projects, or you can keep playing with alternative brush settings and color combinations.

Wetness control

The wetness control function of the Mixer Brush tool allows the user to alter the quantity of paint as well as the amount of water that is on the brush. This feature is essential for reproducing the behavior of traditional media such as oil paint or watercolor, in which the quantity of water or solvent on the brush affects the texture, transparency, and blending of the colors. In other words, mimicking the behavior of classic media like oil paint or watercolor requires this functionality.

The Mixer Brush tool's Wetness control may be varied by employing the Wet setting, which governs the quantity of paint and water that is on the brush at any one moment. A lower Wet value will generate a drier brush stroke that will result in less blending, while a higher Wet value will produce a brush stroke that is more fluid and will result in more blending. When working with vast areas or developing gradients, this tool is particularly beneficial for crafting smooth and flowing brush strokes that merge seamlessly. It is also helpful for generating a number of other creative effects.

Load control

The phrase "Load control" refers to the possibility of regulating the quantity of paint that is loaded into the Mixer Brush tool. This is done using the tool. When working with the Mixer Brush tool, this feature is highly crucial as it allows artists the power to adjust the quantity of paint that is blended with the colors that are already on the canvas. Either the Options bar or the Brush Settings panel may be used to make adjustments to the Load setting found in the Mixer Brush tool. When the Load value is increased, more paint will be put onto the brush, produc-ing strokes that are thicker and opaquer. With a lower Load value, less paint will be placed onto the brush, which will result in strokes that are thinner and more transparent.

Because it enables artists to make brush strokes that are more exact and under their control, the Load control function is highly beneficial when working with the Mixer Brush tool. Artists may achieve a broad range of effects by altering the Load setting, which can range from thin and transparent glazes to heavy and opaque strokes. While dealing with wide swathes of color or while attempting to achieve a particular texture or impression, this tool is highly beneficial because of its adaptability.

Mix control

When utilizing the Mixer Brush tool, the term "mix control" refers to the capacity of altering the quantity of paint that is blended with the colors that are already on the canvas at the time that the brush strokes are applied. When artists want to create sophisticated textures that demand several layers of color, or when they want to produce smooth transitions between distinct hues, this function is particularly advantageous as it allows them to combine colors effortlessly. Either the Options bar or the Brush Settings panel may be used to make adjustments to the Mix option available in the Mixer Brush tool. With a larger Mix value, more paint will be combined with the colors that are already on the canvas, resulting in strokes that are smoother and more blended. With a lower Mix value, less paint will be blended with the colors that are already on the canvas, which will result in strokes that are more distinct and textured. Mix control is especially important when work-ing with the Mixer Brush tool as it enables artists to create color effects that are more nuanced and delicate. Artists may make a broad range of effects by adjusting the Mix option, which can range from gradients that are smooth and blended to surfaces that are rough and bumpy.

CHAPTER 11: WORKING WITH CAMERA RAW

About camera raw files

Raw files are a sort of digital picture file that comprises image data that has not been processed since it was captured by the image sensor of a digital camera. Raw files stored from a camera maintain all of the picture data that was taken by the camera, in contrast to JPEG and other compressed image formats. This data contains color information, as well as brightness, contrast, and more.

Raw files acquired by a camera include data that has not been processed, which provides them with a range of benefits over other photo formats. Take, for instance:

1. More control over picture processing: When you utilize a camera raw file, you have full control over the way the image is processed. This includes the ability to make modifica-tions to the exposure, white balance, contrast, and other characteristics of the image.

2. Higher quality images: Camera raw files carry more picture data than compressed image formats such as JPEG, which means that they may make shots of superior quality with more detail and dynamic range.

3. Non-destructive editing: When you edit a camera raw file, the original picture data is not modified in any manner. This is the third and last sort of editing. Instead, what you are doing is constructing a set of instructions that will educate apps such as Adobe Camera Raw or Lightroom on how to evaluate the data and interpret it. As a consequence, you may edit the picture without having an influence on the data that was initially stored.

However, working with camera raw data comes with a few limitations that should be considered. Take, for instance:

1. Large file sizes: camera raw files are sometimes much bigger than other picture formats as they incorporate far more image data than other image kinds. This suggests that they take up more capacity on your hard disk and might be more time-consuming to access and process than other files.

2. Special software required: To work with raw files from a camera, you will need specialist software that can evaluate the data and offer you the opportunity to make modifica-tions. Adobe Camera Raw, Lightroom, and Capture One are three notable examples of accessible software options.

3. More difficult workflow: Working with camera raw files sometimes necessitates a more involved approach than working with other picture formats. This is because the data must first be imported into specialist software, where they must then be altered before the final photos can be stored in a different format.

4. Requires post-processing: post-processing is necessary for raw camera file types to acquire the desired effect. In contrast to JPEG images, which have already been processed by the image processor within the camera, camera raw files must be changed using software such as Adobe Camera Raw or Lightroom to acquire the desired final appearance. To become skilled in this might call for extra time and effort.

5. Limited compatibility: Raw data from cameras are supported by just a few photo editors and programs. This might decrease the number of options open to you when it comes to editing and dealing with files of this sort.

Dealing with camera raw files has various perks that attract a lot of professional photographers, while dealing with them has its problems. Camera raw files are a fantastic alternative for photographers who are interested in getting the best possible level of quality in their images since they allow a greater degree of control over the image processing and result in shots of superior quality. The camera raw file format may be stored by numerous digital cameras. Raw files are files made by digital cameras that comprise unprocessed picture data collected straight from the camera's image sensor. They are equivalent to undeveloped films. The raw sensor data has not been converted into a color image file with a standard set of channels yet. Because it is still one channel of raw sensor data that has not been processed, it cannot yet be perceived as a picture in its current condition.

You may therefore be asking how you may inspect raw files, such as the ones that are included with this session, on the back of the camera as well as on your computer before you open them.

The answer to this query is that a camera will, more often than not, keep a raw file along with an embedded preview picture. This preview image represents the camera's interpretation of the raw data. Raw processing software like Adobe Camera Raw translates the unprocessed raw data into the distinct color channels (such three RGB channels) that photo editing software like Pho-toshop can edit. Raw data is data that has not been further processed. When you edit a JPEG file, which is saved using the camera's interpretation of the data, you have less freedom to make modifications than when you edit a camera raw file, which allows you to interpret the original image data. If the raw data had already been converted to RGB, you would not be able to make as many or as substantial of alterations to the image's white balance, tone range, contrast, color saturation, noise reduction, or sharpness as you would be able to use Adobe Camera Raw. A raw file may be reprocessed forever without causing any degradation to the quality of the original picture data. Setting your digital camera to save data in the raw format rather than the JPEG format will allow you to produce camera raw files. A raw file is identifiable by a filename extension that is peculiar to the camera brand, such as .nef (for Nikon) or.crw (for Canon). You may process camera raw files from a broad variety of compatible digital cameras, including those produced by Canon, Fuji, Leica, Nikon, and other manufacturers, in either Bridge or Photoshop. After that, you may ex-port the proprietary camera raw data to a file format of your choosing, such as ONG, JPEG, TIFF, or PSD.

Should you never capture images in JPEG format but instead utilize the camera's raw format? If you want the maximum freedom possible while editing, then you should click yes. On the other side, camera raw photographs need a greater storage space as well as more processing power to be modified. You can select to capture and edit JPEG shots instead of PNG images if the after-shoot editing requirements for your photos are limited at best.

Processing files in Camera Raw

When you make modifications to a photo in Camera Raw, such as straightening the image or cropping it, Photoshop and Bridge will store these alterations independently from the original file. You are free to adjust the photo in any manner you see fit, save the updated version to a different folder, and save the original copy so that you can make alternative or more refined alterations in the future.

Opening photos in Camera Raw from Photoshop

The first thing you should do is start Photoshop. If you already have a project open and you wish to start a new one, you may easily do so by heading to the File menu and selecting **"New"** from there. In any other instance, you can either create a new project or open an already existing one.

After you have started Photoshop, you will need to open the raw photo file that you wish to alter. To achieve this, go to the menu labeled **"File,"** and then click **"Open."** This will open the Open dialog box, in which you may travel to the directory that holds the raw image file that you wish to access. Inside the Open dialog box, find the folder that contains the raw photo file that you wish to open. After making your decision, click the "Open" button to begin with opening the file. Your raw photo file will open up in Camera Raw when you do this. When you have completed doing so, Camera Raw ought to start up automatically. Your photo will be presented in the Centre of the screen, and a filmstrip will appear to the right of it if you have imported more than one file. You will have the ability to grade your photos and remove it when you scroll down this page. When you are satisfied with an image, you may delete it by pressing the erase button.

Once you have the raw photo file you wish to work with open in Camera Raw, you can begin making adjustments to the image. A preview of your photo, in addition to various additional correction tools and settings, will be provided in the Camera Raw dialog box. When you have done making your initial adjustment, you will discover that Camera Raw has already created the aforemen-tioned XMP sidecar file in addition to the original file it was working with.

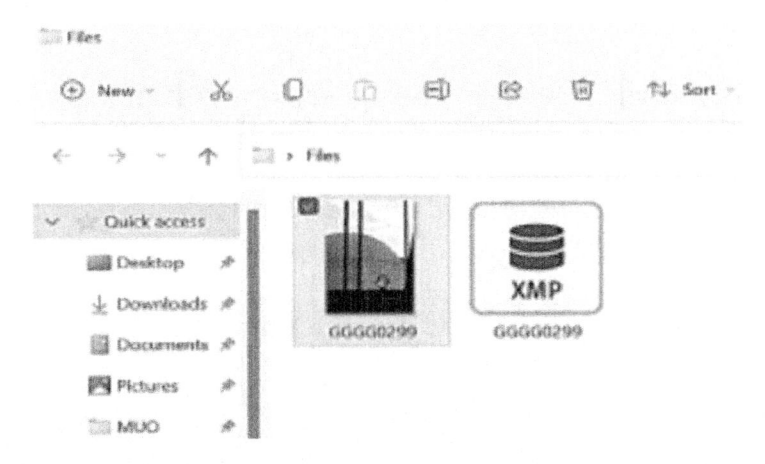

This second file is where all of your edits will be kept, preventing the raw image itself from being ruined by your touch.

Navigating the Camera Raw interface and knowing its tools

The Camera Raw interface

The interface of Camera Raw may be divided down into three basic categories. The tool bar, which gives access to a number of various editing tools, may be located at the very top of the user interface. On the right-hand side of the user interface, you will discover various customization panels. Below the tool bar, you will see a preview image of your photo. The adjustment panels in Camera Raw are broken up into various separate areas, some of which are labelled **"Basic**," "Tone Curve," **"Detail**," **"HSL/Grayscale**," and others.

Each section gives you a number of different editing tools and choices that you can use to change the look of your photo.

• **Basic adjustments:** Within Camera Raw, the editing tools that are utilized the great majority of the time are accessible in the Basic adjustment panel. The following is a summary of some of the most essential tools that can be found in the Basic adjustment panel:

- **White Balance:** Adjusting the color temperature and tint of your photo may be done with the White Balance tool by employing the Temperature and Tint sliders.

- **Exposure:** Make adjustments to the overall brightness of your shot by sliding the Exposure slider.

- **Contrast:** To modify the contrast of your photo, utilize the Contrast slider as mentioned above.

- **Highlights and Shadows:** To alter the brightness of select portions of your photo, use the sliders labeled "**Highlights**" and "**Shadows**" appropriately.

- **Whites and Blacks:** Adjusting the white and black points of your picture may be performed by dragging the **Whites and Blacks** sliders, respectively.

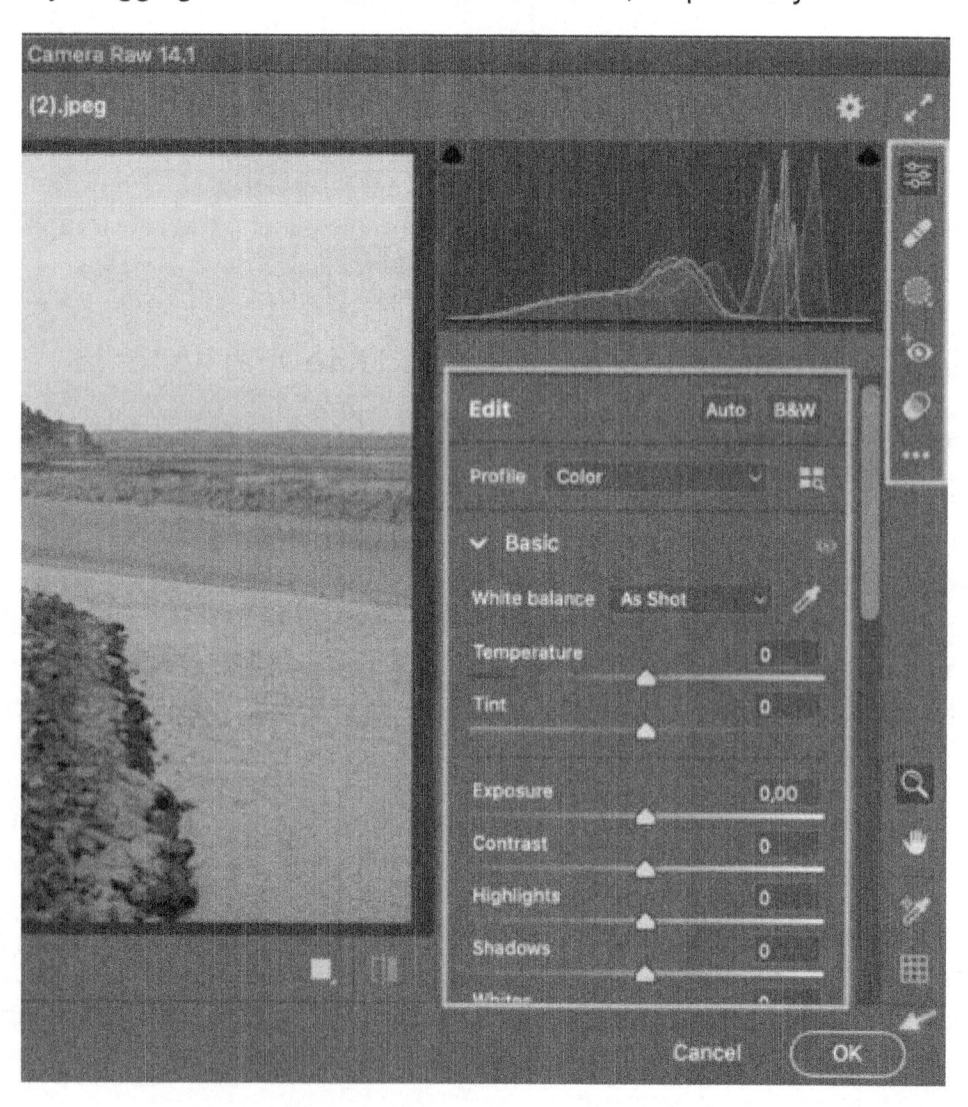

Tone Curve adjustments: The Tone Curve adjustment panel is where you may make more advanced modifications to the tonal range of your picture. You may change the degrees of brightness and contrast of various tonal ranges within your picture by utilizing the tool known as the Tone Curve.

Detail adjustments: The Detail adjustment tab is where you may make changes to the image's sharpness as well as the level of noise reduction. When you use the Sharpening tool, you can make your picture sharper, and when you use the Noise Reduction tool, you can make your image less noisy.

HSL/Grayscale adjustments: The HSL and Grayscale adjustment window provides you the option to tweak the color balance as well as the saturation of your picture. You can edit the color balance of your photo by moving the Hue, Luminance, and Saturation slides, and you can vary the degree of saturation in your image by sliding the Saturation slider.

Lens Corrections: The Lens Corrections tab is where you may make edits to your picture to compensate for lens distortion as well as other optical irregularities. You may use the Lens Profile tool to automatically correct distortion, chromatic aberration, and vignetting in your photo. This may be done by choosing the image and clicking on the **"Edit"** button.

Making simple modifications in Camera Raw, such as exposure, contrast, and white balance

The process of editing images begins with making some fundamental modifications in Camera Raw, which is a vital stage. You may make your images look more well-balanced and artistically beautiful by utilizing the fundamental correction tools in Camera Raw. These tools allow you to make changes to the exposure, contrast, and white balance of your images. The following is a guide that will lead you through the process of making some simple tweaks in Camera Raw:

1. Open the Image in Camera Raw. Go to the File menu in Photoshop, select Open, and then locate the raw photo file you wish to modify. This will allow you to open the image in Camera Raw. You may also open the photo in Camera Raw directly by picking the file in Adobe Bridge, right-clicking, and selecting "Open in Camera Raw" from the context menu that displays.

2. Make Adjustments to the White Balance. The first thing you need to do is make modifications to the white balance. The white balance of the image determines the overall color temperature of the photograph, and you may alter it to make the pictures look either warmer or colder. Utilize the Temperature and Tint sliders contained inside the Basic adjustment panel to make modifications to the white balance. If you want the picture to be warmer, adjust the Temperature slider to the right, and if you want it to be cooler, move it to the left. To modify the relative quantities of green and magenta in the photo, drag the Tint slider to the right or left.

3. Modify the exposure: The exposure setting influences the degree of brightness throughout the complete picture. Utilize the Exposure slider accessible inside the Basic adjustment panel to make changes to the exposure. If you move the slider to the right, the exposure will be raised, making the picture brighter. If you move the slider to the left, the expo-sure will be diminished, making the image darker.

4. Modify the contrast: The contrast setting regulates how much of a difference there is between the areas of your picture that are the darkest and the regions that are the brightest. Utilize the Contrast slider accessible inside the Basic adjustment panel to make modifications to the contrast. If you move the slider to the right, the contrast will be in-creased, which will make the picture livelier. If you drag the slider to the left, the contrast will be lessened, which will make the image flatter.

5. Modify the Highlights and Shadows. Using the settings for the highlights and shadows, you may modify the amount of light that is present in various regions of your picture. Utilize the Highlights slider available inside the Basic adjustment panel to make adjustments to the highlights. The highlights may have their brightness lowered by sliding the slider to the left, and their brightness raised by moving the slider to the right. Use the Shadows slider to make modifications to the shadows. You may brighten the shadows by sliding the slider to the right, or you can darken them by dragging it to the left.

6. Modify the Whites and Blacks: Using the whites and blacks' options, you may make modifications to the portions of your photo that are the lightest and darkest correspondingly. Utilize the Whites slider accessible inside the Basic adjustment panel to make adjustments to the whites. By moving the slider to the right, you can make the whites look brighter, and by moving it to the left, you can make them appear darker. Utilize the Blacks slider to make modifications to the blacks. The blacks may be made darker by sliding the slider to the right, and they may be made lighter by moving it to the left.

7. Preview your Adjustments: The preview that displays in the Camera Raw window will be updated in real-time as you make adjustments to the photo that you are working with. You may also switch the preview on and off by using the P key on your keyboard. This operates in the same way as the previous option. Once you are pleased with the adjustments you have made, you may open the photo in Photoshop by choosing the Open picture option.

Using the graded filter, radial filter, and adjusting brush in Camera Raw

In addition to the core tools for modifying photographs that are available in Camera Raw, there are also more complex tools accessible, such as the adjustment brush, the graded filter, and the radial filter. You may make accurate modifications to select portions of your picture with the aid of these tools.

The following is an instruction manual for utilizing these tools in Camera Raw:

Graduated Filter: With the use of the graded filter tool, you'll be able to adjust a select section of your photo, like the sky, for example.

This is how you should put it to use:

Step 1. In the Camera Raw interface, select the toolbar on the right-hand side of the screen, and choose the Graduated Filter tool from there.

Step 2. Position the graded filter tool where you want it to be and then click and drag it into position. The beginning and finishing points of the graded filter will be represented by a line that looks to have two circular handles attached to it.

Step 3. Make adjustments to the settings in the panel for the graduated filter, which is situated on the right side of the user interface. You may make the needed modifications by modifying the exposure, contrast, saturation, and any other pertinent settings.

Step 4. Conduct a final review of your improvements and, if needed, make more changes.

Radial Filter: The radial filter is an adjustment tool that enables you make adjustments to a circular region of your picture.

This is how you should put it to use:

Step 1. In the Camera Raw interface, locate the toolbar on the right-hand side of the screen, and pick the Radial Filter tool from there.

Step 2. Position the radial filter tool where you want it to be and then click and drag it over the region. You will notice a circle with four handles that appear on the screen. These handles represent the margins of the radial filter.

Step 3. Modify the settings in the radial filter panel, which can be located on the right-hand side of the user interface. You may make the needed modifications by modifying the exposure, contrast, saturation, and any other pertinent settings.

Step 4. Conduct a final review of your revisions and, if appropriate, make more changes.

Adjustment Brush: The adjustment brush tool allows you the power to make fine-tuned modifications to select sections of your photo, such as the face of a person.

This is how you should put it to use:

Step 1. In the Camera Raw interface, locate the toolbar on the right-hand side of the screen, and pick the Adjustment Brush tool from there.

Step 2. Position the adjustment brush where you want it to be and then click and drag it to move it there. A circle with four handles, each of which symbolizes a distinct edge of the brush, will appear before you.

Step 3. Modify the settings in the adjustment brush panel, which is situated on the right side of the user interface. You may make the relevant modifications by modifying the ex-posure, contrast, saturation, and any other pertinent factors.

Step 4. To further fine-tune your adjustments, modify the brush parameters. To create more exact adjustments, the brush's size, feather, and opacity may all be modified individually.

Step 5. Review your edits and make any further changes that are necessary.

About the Camera Raw histogram

The red, green, and blue channels of the selected picture are all presented concurrently in the histogram that is placed in the upper-right corner of the Camera Raw dialog box. This histogram also updates itself in real-time when you make changes to the parameters. The RGB values for the section of the preview picture that is beneath the pointer are presented in the histogram when you move any tool over the image. When you pick the icons positioned at the upper corners of the screen, visual overlays indicate clipping will become accessible. Clipped highlight detail is depicted with a red overlay, whereas clipped shadow detail is shown with a blue overlay.

It's not usually an indication that you've overcorrected a photo if the shadows or highlights appear like they've been clipped. For instance, a clipped specular highlight is good as a specular highlight does not have any information to lose. This is because a reflection of the sun or a studio light on metal is an example of a specular highlight.

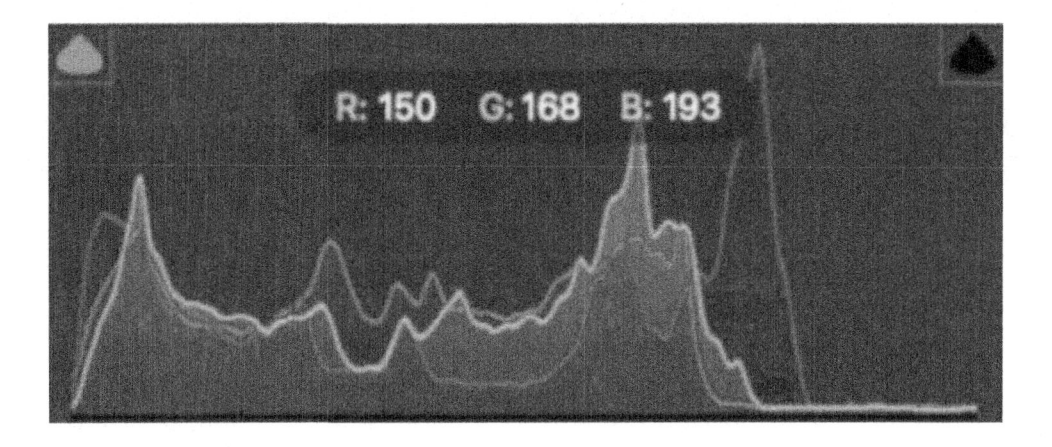

Applying sharpening

The technique of sharpening is a strategy that can aid in bringing out the finer elements and textures in your images, giving the appearance that they are clearer and more distinct. You may apply this effect to any of your images by using one of the various sharpening tools that are available in the Camera Raw application.

The following is an explanation of how to apply sharpening in Camera Raw:

Step 1. Launch Camera Raw and load the photo you desire to sharpen into the software.

Step 2. In the Camera Raw window, navigate to the Detail tab.

Step 3. The sharpening effect may be tweaked by various different settings that may be found on the Detail tab. These are the following:

Sharpening: This option defines how much of a sharpening effect is given to the image. The sharpening effect will be more evident if you pick a greater value.

Radius: The value that you enter here defines the extent to which the details are sharpened. A number that is more than the current one will sharpen bigger features, while a value that is lower than the present one will sharpen smaller details.

Detail: This option dictates how much sharpening is done to the image's finer details to bring them out more clearly. When the value is increased, more fine details will be sharpened, while when the value is dropped, less fine details will be sharpened.

Masking: This is a setting that decides which areas of the picture are sharpened and which parts are not. A larger number will merely sharpen the picture's edges, while a lower amount will sharpen a greater section of the image.

Make the needed modifications to these parameters to acquire the required degree of sharpness. You can get a better sense of what the effect will look like if you zoom in on the photo first, and then switch on and off the Preview button.

Step 4. When you have obtained the appropriate level of sharpness, move to step five and open the photo in Photoshop by choosing the Open picture option.

Step 6. You may further tweak the sharpening effect in Photoshop by making use of additional tools, such as the Unsharp Mask filter and the High Pass filter.

When sharpening a picture in Camera Raw, it is vital to avoid going overboard with the effect and instead apply the effect with a delicate touch. A photograph that has been overly sharpened might have an artificial aspect, complete with artifacts and halos that are obvious to the human eye. When employing any form of editing procedure, the most successful method is to adopt an understated approach and strive toward generating a result that feels natural.

About adjusting color in Adobe Camera Raw

Adobe Camera Raw has expanded over the years to incorporate a range of additional capabilities that give users various options for changing colors and making color repairs. When opposed to making extensive color tweaks in Photoshop, applying these modifications in the raw stage can be more forgiving and result in more preservation of the original picture quality. If you take the effort to accurately capture a raw picture on camera, you usually won't need to do much more than apply the suitable raw profile, tweak the White Balance setting, and make any necessary auto-corrections.

You can employ Camera Raw's more accurate color capabilities when you're trying to solve more tough color difficulties, such as when you desire to:

Masked altering tools. By pressing the Masking button, you may apply an adjustment that is constrained to those portions of an image by masks that you can edit. This allows you to apply various color or tone settings to select sections of an image. Camera Raw contains certain masks that are automatically made, such as Select Subject, Se-lect Sky, Select Background, and Select People, to assist users save time.

Curve panel You may adjust each color channel separately in Camera Raw by utilizing the Curve panel, which is equivalent to the Curves panel in Photoshop. You may modify the amount of a color channel at any level, ranging from black to white. This is one way to compensate for color casts that vary across multiple tonal ranges, such as highlights, mid-tones, and shadows.

Color Mixer panel Using the Color Mixer panel, you may adjust various color ranges by modifying their hue, saturation, or brightness. You may tailor the transition from color to black and white by utilizing the Color Mixer after pressing the B& W button, which is placed at the very top of the Edit mode panel stack.

Color Grading panel Within the Color Grading panel, you will discover color wheels that you can use to make alterations to the hue, saturation, and brightness of the mid-tones, shadows, and highlights in a new manner. Video editors are used to dealing with tools of this nature. Although it may be used for color correction, conventional color grading is frequently a step that is applied after color correction. Its objective is to provide an expressive color palette for a **"look"** or split tone effects, and although it may be used for color correction, this is not its primary function.

Custom raw profiles. It is possible to design bespoke color lookup tables (CLUTs) using Photoshop. These CLUTs may then serve as the foundation for your very own raw profile, which can subsequently be applied in Camera Raw with merely the click of a button.

Calibration panel The Calibration panel is responsible for making modifications to the fundamental color conversion from the camera raw file. These alterations have an influence on the range of modification that is feasible with the other panels. Nowadays, raw profiles are an easier way to alter that conversion, therefore now the Cal-ibration panel tends to be employed as additional creative choice for changing color associations inside an image. This may be done by clicking the Calibration panel's **"Add New Calibration"** button.

In Photoshop, as opposed to Camera Raw, you may reach the Search panel by going to the Edit menu and selecting Search. In addition to interactive lessons and support sites, this panel also gives information about various technologies.

About Camera Raw mask types

Masking changes in Camera Raw might possibly spare you a trip to Photoshop.

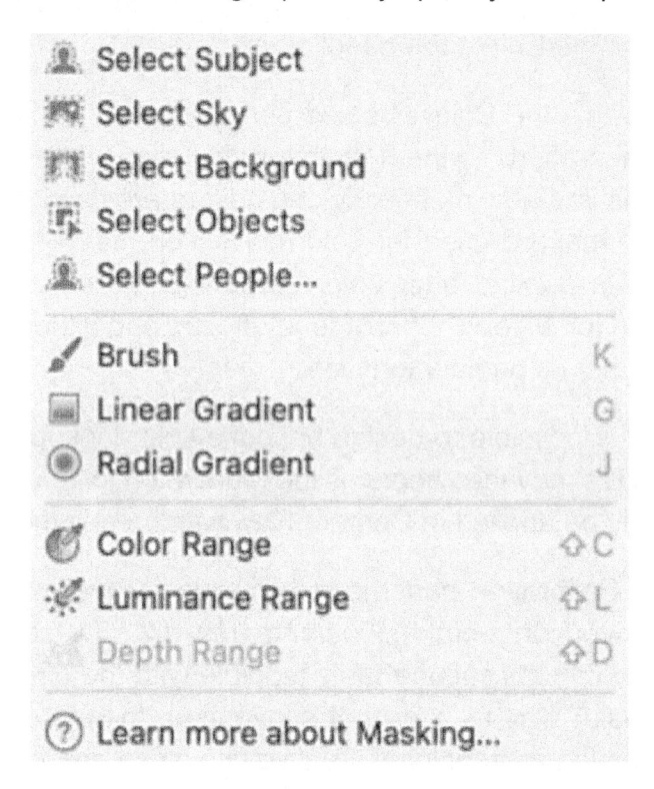

```
  Select Subject
  Select Sky
  Select Background
  Select Objects
  Select People...

  Brush                    K
  Linear Gradient          G
  Radial Gradient          J

  Color Range             ⇧C
  Luminance Range         ⇧L
  Depth Range             ⇧D

? Learn more about Masking...
```

Subject, Sky, Background, and People. Camera Raw employs machine learning to detect various sorts of information and produce a mask for them, akin to the **Select > Sky** and **Select > Subject** commands and Object Selection tool in Photoshop. The distinction between Subject and humans is that Subject can also recognize and disguise items that are not humans.

Objects. When the Select Subject tool does not pick what you want, you may use the Select Objects masking tool to select a specific item more exactly by dragging it around that object. Linear Gradient and Radial Gradient. Both a linear and radial gradient is offered. Make a mask that progressively vanishes from the center of an ellipse outwards (for a Radial Gradient) or from one end to the other (for a Linear Gradient) as indicated by the gradient's direction. The tone or color differences on separate sides of a picture can be brought into visual harmony with the application of a linear gradient. Utilizing a Radial Gradient helps highlight an area of a photograph or create an off-center vignette.

Color Range, Luminance Range, and Depth Range. You may establish the characteristics of a range mask by selecting a range of colors (known as a Color Range), tones (referred to as a Luminance Range), or distances (referred to as a Depth Range).

For instance, if you construct a Luminance Range mask that only impacts the shadow tones in a photo; you can then boost the exposure while simultaneously minimizing the amount of noise that happens over only that range of tones. Alternatively, you may produce a Color Range mask that focuses on the skin tones.

Only cameras that combine depth information into the pictures they capture to make the Depth Range mask available to users. Some smartphone cameras are capable of accomplishing this.

Applying lens corrections and perspective tweaks in Camera Raw

You may fix distortion and other lens-related flaws in your images using the numerous lens correction tools that are accessible to you in the Camera Raw editing application.

The following is a list of some of the most essential lens correction options that are accessible in Camera Raw:

1. Auto Lens Correction: Camera Raw may automatically detect the lens that was used to shoot the image and make any required alterations to compensate for any distortion, chromatic aberration, or vignetting that the lens may have generated.

2. Manual Lens Correction: If you would prefer to make manual changes, you can utilize the panel labeled "Manual Lens Correction" to make tweaks to the image's chromatic aberration, vignetting, and distortion. The panel includes remedies for barrel and pincushion distortion, as well as the eradication of any vignetting or color fringing that may have occurred.

3. Upright Tool: The Upright Tool in Camera Raw helps you to remedy perspective errors in your images. You can locate it under the Edit menu. This tool may be used to straighten both vertical and horizontal lines, as well as remedy errors such as key stoning and lines that converge.

4. Transform Tool: The Transform Tool gives more complicated options for adjusting perspective, letting you modify particular locations on an image to compensate for perspective faults or distortions. This tool may be found in the Edit menu. You may use this tool to rectify any further challenges with the perspective that are present in your picture, such as straightening out buildings that are leaning, altering the perspective of a landscape, etc.

When dealing with lens corrections and perspective modifications in Camera Raw, it is crucial to bear in mind that these tools are designed to be used in a restricted manner to produce the best possi-ble results.

Images might wind up seeming weird or misshapen if too much correction is made to them or if they are over-corrected. Experimenting with these tools to see how they impact your photo-graphs and making revisions depending on what you learn from those tests is a great idea.

Working with settings and profiles in Camera Raw

Presets

Adjustments that are already built up and ready to use may be found in Camera Raw under the category of presets. Camera Raw comes with a range of built-in settings that you may pick from, such as high contrast, vignetting, and black-and-white effects. You may also build your own presets by collecting a series of adjustments that you've made to a photo.

This will allow you to reuse those modifications in the future. To apply a preset to your photo, open the Camera Raw window, click on the Presets tab, and then choose the preset that you want to apply to your image from the drop-down menu that displays. You can also build your unique preset by choosing the make Preset button and utilizing the search bar to filter down the presets depending on the word you wish to use.

Both Photoshop and Camera Raw come packed with a vast choice of distinct creative photo filters. With simply one click, they can make your image appear like it was shot on "existential doomsday" instead of "Sunday at home." To investigate each choice, press Shift + P to see the whole list in all of its overwhelming magnificence. You'll discover monochromatic aesthetics, portrait styles, and antique picture effects for any potential occasion.

You are free to apply any of these prepared settings to your images and make any required alterations to them. You also may import your very own custom LUTs straight into Camera Raw, giving you ultimate creative control over your photographs.

Profiles

Profiles are pretty similar to presets, with the key distinction being that profiles enable you to change the color and saturation of your images. Camera Raw comes with a range of preset profiles already installed, such as Camera Landscape, Adobe Color, and Adobe Monochrome, among others. Your picture may have its appearance and feel adjusted in a hurry by employing profiles, which reduces the necessity for making modifications manually. To apply a profile to your photo, open the Camera Raw window, go to the Profiles tab, and then pick the profile you wish to apply to your image from the drop-down menu that displays. You can also construct your unique profile by clicking the construct Profile button and utilizing the search bar to limit profiles based on the terms they use.

Combining Presets and Profiles

You have a lot of versatility with Camera Raw owing to the fact that you can mix and match different presets and profiles to give your photographs a distinctive look. For instance, you may apply a preset that transforms the photo to black and white, and then you can apply a custom profile to fine-tune the image's tone and color. To apply a preset and profile together, first, apply the pre-set to your image, and then click the Profiles option in the Camera Raw window to apply the profile. You may then modify the power of the preset and profile using the Amount slider.

Syncing modifications across many pictures in Camera Raw

You may wish to make enhancements to one image and then apply those adjustments to the others when you have a set of photos that were shot under comparable circumstances or have similar subjects. The ability to sync edits across several images is one of the many ways that Camera Raw streamlines this operation.

This is the method to follow:

Step 1. Launch Camera Raw and pick the photo that will serve as the starting point for your changes.

Step 2. Make the alterations that you desire to utilize for the other photographs in the collection. You may, for instance, play about with the exposure, contrast, white balance, and any number of other parameters.

Step 3. When you are pleased with the alterations, pick the picture that you just updated, and then, while holding down the Shift key, click on the other photographs to which you want to make the edits and sync them.

Step 4. Within the Camera Raw box, pick the Sync Settings button and click it. This will launch the Synchronize Settings dialog box.

Step 5. In the Synchronize Settings dialog box, pick the alterations that you wish to apply to all of the other images. You have the option to sync any or all of the modifications. You may also decide which ones to sync.

Step 6. To apply the modifications to the other photographs, pick the OK option from the drop-down menu.

Step 7. Look over the adjustments you've made to each photo and make any more tweaks that are needed to attain the results you desire.

It is crucial to bear in mind that each picture may ask for somewhat distinct alterations to produce the best potential results when synchronizing adjustments across several pictures in Camera Raw. For instance, if you are working with a group of images shot outside, you may discover that one picture requires more revisions to be made to the sky, while another image may need more edits to be made to the foreground. You may verify that each photo appears at its very best by assessing it after making the synchronized modifications and then comparing it to the others.

Using Camera Raw as a filter in Photoshop

Utilizing Photoshop's Camera Raw capability as a filter may be a highly efficient approach for increasing the quality of your images. Camera Raw may give an additional layer of control to your photo editing process when it is utilized as a filter in Photoshop. This allows you the flexibility to fine-tune your images and get a completed output that is more professionally presented.

The following is a guidance on how to apply the Camera Raw filter in Photoshop:

Step 1. Launch Photoshop and open your photo.

Step 2. Choose the layer or group of layers that you desire to alter using the Camera Raw settings, and then click the Edit button.

Step 3. Go to the option labeled Filter, and then pick Camera Raw Filter from the list.

Step 4. The Camera Raw window will open, and any layers that you have chosen will display in the preview part of the window. To enhance the picture, you may make use of the tools and changes offered in Camera Raw.

Step 5. Once you are pleased with the way the image looks, click the OK button to save your adjustments and then exit the Camera Raw window.

Applying Camera Raw as a filter provides you the ability to work on your photo in a non-destructive manner, which is one of the numerous benefits of applying this filter. This signifies that the origi-nal picture is not modified in any way, and you can always go back to it at any point to make further alterations. You have access to all of the same tools and modifications that are accessible in the standalone version of Camera Raw when you use it as a filter in Photoshop. These tools and changes include exposure, contrast, clarity, saturation, and many more. This suggests that you have total control over the appearance of your photograph and that you may construct a personalized design that is ideally suited to match your requirements.

Using Camera Raw as a filter in Photoshop is advantageous for various reasons, one of which is that it enables you to make modifications to select portions of a picture by use of the adjustment brush tool. This tool lets you brush on improvements to select sections of your photo, which may be quite handy when you need to make small adjustments such as erasing red eyes, whitening teeth, or deepening shadows. The tool may be found under the "**Image**" tab of the "**Edit**" menu in Adobe Photoshop. In addition, the graduated filter and radial filter tools may be used to produce selected adjustments that have an influence on particular sections of your picture, such as the sky or the foreground, respectively. When utilizing the Camera Raw filter in Photo-shop, it is necessary to keep in mind that certain adjustments will have a more obvious influence than others. For instance, making considerable adjustments to the exposure or contrast of an image might make it look unnatural, yet making very minor tweaks to the white balance or saturation of an image can offer a more understated impression. In addition, it is strongly recommended that you always preview your alterations before applying them to your photo to assure that you will be delighted with the ultimate effect.

Batch processing photographs in Camera Raw

Photographers who need to make the same modifications to multiple shots can save a substantial amount of time by altering images in Camera Raw utilizing the batch processing tool. You can apply the same modifications to an entire set of photographs with simply a few clicks, as opposed to individually changing each image in the collection.

Here is how to process numerous images at once using Camera Raw:

Step 1. Open Adobe Bridge.

Step 2. Find the folder that contains the images you desire to process, then go to that folder.

Step 3. Choose the photographs that you wish to have processed.

Step 4. pick Photoshop from the Tools menu, then after that, pick Image Processor from that menu.

Step 5. Choose the folder where you wish to save the processed photographs from the drop-down option in the Image Processor box.

Step 6. Select the sort of file that you would want to use to save the processed photographs.

Step 7. If you desire to adjust the size of the images, select the option that reads "**Resize to fit.**"

Step 8. Make the suitable pick for the JPEG Quality choice that you intend to employ.

Step 9. If you intend to apply an action on the photographs, make sure that the box next to Run Action is ticked.

Step 10. To begin the batch processing, pick the Run option from the menu.

When you click the Run button, Camera Raw will open for each photo in the batch, and it will perform the alterations that you asked for each one separately. After it is done, the images that have been processed will be stored in the spot that you choose.

When conducting batch processing with Camera Raw, there are a few aspects that should be kept in mind:

Step 1. Check to check that all of the images in the batch were shot using a lighting setting that was constant throughout. You may need to make individual modifications to the settings for each photo if there are considerable differences in the illumination.

Step 2. You may want to consider building an action to automate the changes you intend to make. If you discover that you routinely need to make identical adjustments to multiple images, this might save you a substantial amount of time.

Step 3. Be sure to inspect the final processed images to determine whether the alterations were successful in achieving the intended outcomes. If the photographs do not have the intended impact, you will probably need to alter the parameters and then reprocess the pictures.

Step 4. It is vital to keep in mind that batch processing might require a lot of resources. When you have a significant number of images to edit with Camera Raw, it may take some time for the application to finish processing all of them.

Photographers who need to make the same modifications to multiple shots can save a substantial amount of time by altering images in Camera Raw utilizing the batch processing tool. You can simply perform the same modifications to a group of images by employing Adobe Bridge and the Image Processor tool. All it takes is a few clicks to perform this operation.

However, it is vital to bear in mind that batch processing is not a generally applicable solution, and you may need to make tweaks to the settings for each photo to achieve the best results. Through trial and error with a number of techniques and settings, you can develop a workflow that is personalized to your individual requirements and helps you to get the most out of your images.

Creating custom presets in Camera Raw

Step 1. Open an image in Camera Raw.

Step 2. Carry out the adjustments that you wish to incorporate in the preset. This can involve making adjustments to the exposure, contrast, color temperature, sharpness, and other aspects of the image.

Step 3. Click the Presets option at the very top of the Camera Raw user interface as soon as you have completed making all of the adjustments that you desire to include in the preset.

Step 4. At the very bottom of the Presets window is a button titled "**Create New Preset**." Click this button.

Step 5. Within the New Preset dialog box, supply your preset with a name that is instructive and will aid you in remembering what it is that it accomplishes.

Step 6. By choosing the boxes connected with the settings you desire to include in the preset, you may make your selections. You have the choice of incorporating all of the op-tions that you've personalized, or you may choose to include only some of them.

Step 7. To save the preset, you must first click the Create button.

After a preset has been developed, it may be used in Camera Raw on any photo by picking it from the Presets panel and pressing the Apply button. You can also alter presets or remove them by right-clicking on the presets in the Presets panel and selecting the relevant option from the context menu that displays. Creating your custom presets may help you save a lot of time while editing your pictures, particularly if you edit numerous images using the same settings routinely. You may also use presets to establish a uniform aesthetic throughout a series of pho-tographs, which can be advantageous if you are working on a project such as a photo book or a gallery exhibit. This may be performed by applying identical parameters to all of the photos in the scenes.

You may choose to make your own presets, acquire presets that were made by other photographers, or buy presets from online markets in addition to having the ability to create your own. Your workflow for editing can be starting off in a fruitful direction or new editing abilities can be mastered with the aid of these presets. However, it is necessary to bear in mind that pre-sets are not a solution that is universally applicable to all circumstances. Every photo is unique, and approaches that work well for one image may not apply to another. It is typically a good idea, to begin with, a preset, and then makes further alterations as necessary, to achieve the finest results possible for each given picture.

Retouching a portrait in Camera Raw

1. Open your portrait in Camera Raw. You may accomplish this by picking the photo, and then opening it in Camera Raw from either Photoshop or Adobe Bridge, depending on which application you use.

2. Make basic tweaks. Before beginning the process of editing, make any essential basic modifications to your shot using Camera Raw. These may involve altering the exposure, contrast, and white balance of the image.

3. Apply a local correction for skin retouching. Choose the correction brush tool in Camera Raw, and then make a minute but visible increase to the image's clarity, sharpness, and texture. Select the right brush size, and then paint over the damaged part of the skin. This will make the skin look smoother and will elim-inate any blemishes that may have been present. You may alter the characteristics of the brush to make it more fit for your purposes.

4. Whiten eyes and teeth. Repeatedly pick the adjustment brush tool, and then make changes to the exposure and saturation sliders. Applying paint to the eyes and teeth will make them look brighter and whiter.

5. Adjust the color balance. Adjusting the colors of your portrait may be done with the aid of the color balance tool. Depending on how you prefer your skin, you can either make it warmer or make it colder by altering the temperature of the skin.

6. Reduce noise. If there is any noise or grain in your photo, you may get rid of it by utilizing a tool that lowers noise. The picture will look cleaner and clearer as a consequence of this modification.

7. Sharpen the picture. Increase the sharpness of your portrait by making use of the tool created exclusively for that purpose. This will create the sense of increased clarity and detail.

8. Save your modified portrait. After you have completed the retouching to your satisfaction, save the photo in a file format of your choosing.

Saving Camera Raw modifications as new files

After making alterations to your image in Camera Raw, you may wish to save the changes as a new file. There is a various method to achieve this:

1. Save the image as a new file: Click the Save picture button at the bottom of the Camera Raw window to save the photo as a new file. This is essential to save the adjustments made to the picture as a new file. Select a location on your computer as well as a file type for the new file, and then click the Save button.

2. Use the Save Image option in Photoshop: If you opened the photo in Photoshop, you could also use the Save Image option available in the File menu to save the adjustments as a new file. This is important if you want to share the altered image with others.

3. Use the preserve Settings option: You may preserve the Camera Raw settings without generating a new file if you utilize the Save Settings option, which is accessible to you if you desire to do so. Simply pick a spot to save the .xmp file after clicking the Save Settings button found at the very bottom of the Camera Raw box. After that, you'll want to pick the Load Settings option in Camera Raw so that the modifications you made may be applied to further photographs.

4. Use the Export option: You may also use the Export option to save the adjustments as a new file with precise parameters. This can be done in many ways. Simply pick a location, or a file type, and make any required tweaks to the settings before hitting the Export button at the very bottom of the Camera Raw window. To save the new file, click the Export option.

It is crucial to choose the right file format and specifications when storing the adjustments as a new file, and you should base your decision on your requirements. If you desire to share the photo-graph on social media or the web, for instance, you should definitely save it as a JPEG with a decreased quality. If you wish to print the photo, you should definitely save it as a TIFF with a better resolution before you do so. You will be able to keep the original photo while also making improvements that increase its overall quality and visual appeal if you utilize the Camera Raw editing mode and save the changes as new files. You may rapidly save your edits as new files and share them with others if you follow these guidelines.

About saving files from Camera Raw to other formats

The great majority of websites, software, and social media applications are unable to read camera raw files or the metadata files that link to them. These metadata files include photo edits, keywords, and other information that you may have supplied. Clicking the Open button in Adobe Camera Raw will allow the photo to open in Photoshop, where you can then use the in-structions in Photoshop to save or export the file in preparation for usage in other apps. This is one approach for preparing a camera raw file for usage in other applications.

NOTE: The Camera Raw dialog box does not have a Save command in the normal sense (remember that pressing the Save button exports a copy of each photo that is chosen). When you click Done or Open, your edits will be saved, but Camera Raw will be closed as a result. Because hitting the Cancel option causes all of the alterations that have been done during the Camera Raw session to be lost, you should be careful not to click the Cancel button unless you are confident that you want to start the session again. It is crucial to prevent from using the Esc key as it is a shortcut for the Cancel button. You can skip the stage that entails continuing to Photoshop if you do not feel the need to make any more modifications to the photo employing the choices that are accessible in Photoshop. You may pick numerous shots in Camera Raw, and then click the option labeled "Convert and Save Image" to convert those images to either Adobe DNG, JPEG, TIFF, or PSD format. The converted photographs will then be stored as new files in the appropriate format.

The Adobe Digital Negative (DNG) format contains raw picture data from a digital camera with metadata that determines how the image data should appear. This format is also known as "Adobe Digital Negative." DNG was created to become an industry-wide standard format for raw image data. This will aid photographers in better managing the diversity of proprietary raw formats presently accessible, as well as providing a comparable archive format. (The Camera Raw dialog box is the only place from which you may save this format.)

The JPEG (Joint Photographic Experts Group) file format is extensively used to show pictures and other continuous-tone RGB images on the web. JPEG minimizes the size of the file by deleting data in a predetermined manner, beginning with the visual information that is less likely to be perceived by human eyes. The quality of the picture declines proportionally with the quantity of compression utilized.

TIFF, which stands for "Tagged Image File Format," is a flexible file format that practically all painting, image editing, and page layout tools can read and write. It can save the layers from Photoshop. The great majority of programs that control image capturing hardware such as scanners are also able to create TIFF photos on demand.

PSD format is the Photoshop native file format. Because of the strong connectivity between Adobe products, other Adobe apps such as Adobe Illustrator, Adobe InDesign, and Adobe After Effects may easily import PSD files and keep many Photoshop capabilities.

If you choose to convert and open a raw file in Photoshop by selecting the Open button in Camera Raw, you will have the choice to save a copy of the raw file in one of the several formats that Photoshop supports, such as Large Document Format (PSB), Photoshop PDF, GIF, or PNG. You may also export the raw file. Do not combine the Photoshop Raw format with the raw data supplied by your camera. The Photoshop Raw format is a specialist technical file format that is not typically utilized by photographers and designers. If you come across the Photoshop Raw format (RAW), do not mistake it with camera raw files.

Tips and strategies for working successfully with Camera Raw in Photoshop.

1. Use shortcuts: You may save a substantial amount of time by becoming familiar with and making use of the shortcuts on your keyboard.

The following is a list of some of the most beneficial shortcuts that may be utilized in Camera Raw:

• **Ctrl+ Shift+ A** (Windows) or **Command+ Shift+ A** (Mac) to reset all settings.

• **Ctrl + Alt + Z** (Windows) or **Command + Option + Z** (Mac) to reverse the last modification.

• **Ctrl + Shift + S** (Windows) or **Command + Shift + S** (Mac) to save the changes.

• **Ctrl + Shift + O** (Windows) or **Command + Shift + O** (Mac) to open a picture in Camera Raw.

2. Make use of presets: If you want to fast apply a specific adjustment set to a photo, applying presets might aid you. In Camera Raw, you have the choice of either making your own presets or using the ones that are pre-installed. After making the necessary alterations, click the **"Presets"** tab, and then select the **"New Preset"** option. This will result in the establishment of a new preset.

3. Utilize batch processing: If you need to apply the identical alterations to several other images, the batch processing function in Camera Raw is a wonderful tool to utilize. To accomplish this, pick the photographs you wish to edit, open them in Camera Raw, make the adjustments you desire, and then click the **"Save Images"** button at the bottom of the window.

4. Utilize the before and after view: The before and after view in Camera Raw is a valuable tool that may aid you in viewing the alterations that you've made to an image. You may flip between the before view and the after view by pressing the P key on your keyboard.

5. Use the spot removal tool: Use this to remove blemishes, dust, and other imperfections from your images. You may utilize the spot removal tool in Adobe Photoshop and Adobe Lightroom. To use So, first, pick the tool, then alter the brush's size and feathering, and finally click on the section of the image that you desire to erase.

6. Utilize the adjustment brush: Use this to make local modifications to your images. You may employ the adjusting brush in many ways. You may use it to brighten or darken select parts, add saturation or vibrance, and a number of other effects. To use it, first, choose the tool, then make the required modifications to the settings, and finally, paint over the region that has to be altered.

7. Utilize the "auto" button: Use this to gain a suitable launching point for your customizations. Utilizing the "auto" option might be a speedy technique to gaining a great beginning point for your improvements. When you click the auto button, your picture will have automated alterations performed to it depending on the subject matter of the photo you are altering.

8. Utilize the histogram: The histogram in Camera Raw can aid you in seeing the tonal range of your photo so that you can make alterations that are acceptable for the scenario. Additionally, it might aid you in keeping the highlights and shadows from getting clipped. Observe how the histogram responds as you make modifications to the exposure, highlights, shadows, and black slides.

9. Utilize the HSL/Grayscale panel: The hue, saturation, and brightness of particular colors in your photo may be adjusted by utilizing the HSL/Grayscale panel in Camera Raw. When you want particular colors to stand out more from the rest of the picture or integrate in more smoothly with it, you may utilize this to your advantage.

10. Utilize the crop tool: The crop tool in Camera Raw may be used to straighten and crop your images, among other things. Altering the picture's dimensions by cropping it may also be performed with its aid. To make use of it, you must first choose the tool and then move the corners of the crop box.

11. Use the adjustment sliders: The adjustment sliders in Camera Raw may be used to make simple modifications to your image, such as exposure, contrast, highlights, shadows, whites, and blacks. They can also be used to modify color temperature and tint.

12. Utilize the white balance tool: The white balance tool in Camera Raw is a valuable tool that can be used to modify the color temperature as well as the tint of your photo. To modify the white balance, click on the tool, and then click on an area of the photo that is relatively undisturbed.

13. Utilize the radial filter: The radial filter in Camera Raw may be used to make alterations to a portion of your photo that has the shape of a circle or an oval. You may use it to make a vignette effect or call attention to a particular portion of the photo. Both of these purposes are conceivable with this tool.

14. Use the graduated filter: The graduated filter in Camera Raw is a tool that may be used to make modifications to a linear part of your photo. You may use it to, for example, brighten the foreground or darken the sky. You may also use it to make the sky darker.

15. apply the adjustment brush presets: If you want to make exact modifications to your photo in a hurry, you may apply the adjustment brush presets that are provided in Camera Raw. You may employ the presets that are preinstalled, or you can design your own.

CHAPTER 12: EDITING VIDEO

About the Timeline Panel

Users of Adobe Photoshop have access to a valuable tool inside the application known as the Timeline panel. This panel enables users to make animations and manipulate video material. Users may cre-ate and manage numerous layers of animation and video, as well as add effects and other features to their work using the Timeline panel, which is an interface based on a timeline. Digital artists, graphic designers, and video editors that need to develop and change multimedia material should use the Timeline panel as it is an essential feature for their job. The production of animations is one of the major things that the Timeline panel in Photoshop is utilized for. Users may compose animations frame-by-frame with the aid of the Timeline panel by layering individual pictures or layers on top of one another. After that, users may modify the amount of time that each frame is presented, in addition to the inclusion of effects, transitions, and other components that can be utilized to build a more sophisticated animation. The Timeline panel now supports keyframe animation, which helps users to design more complicated animations with movement and changes over time. These animations may be produced on the Timeline panel.

Video editing is one additional essential application that makes full use of the Timeline panel. Users of Photoshop may import and edit video files, which includes the ability to cut and chop clips, adjust colors and effects, as well as add text and other components to the video content. Users may organize and alter the various layers of video and effects that are included in their project using the Timeline panel. Users may also preview and export their video output using this interface. The Timeline panel in Photoshop is packed with several additional sophisticated functionalities, which enable digital artists and video editors to use it in a number of settings. For instance, users may build and alter their 3D animations, add audio tracks to their projects, and work with intricate effects like camera motion and lighting. Users may import and export their projects across a range of platforms and applications owing to the Timeline panel's support for connectivity with other Adobe Creative Cloud products including Adobe After Effects, Premiere Pro, and Audition.

To utilize the Timeline panel in Photoshop, you will need to have a rudimentary grasp of animation and video editing techniques, in addition to being acquainted with the interface and the tools that are accessible in Photoshop. On the other hand, the panel gives a huge variety of tools and features that may make it extremely simple for users to develop animations and video content of a professional grade. Users of Photoshop may create and alter animations and video content immediately inside Photoshop owing to the Timeline panel, which removes the need for any other program or plugins. This is one of the most major benefits of employing the Timeline panel. For digital artists and graphic designers that need to develop multime-dia content for web or print projects, this may be an immensely valuable tool.

When employing the Timeline panel, you have the capacity to create animations and video content with higher accuracy and control, which is another benefit of using this panel. The panel allows users the opportunity to make edits to individual frames, add keyframes for more advanced animations, and work with a large array of effects and tools to build personalized animations and video content. However, there are significant constraints when it comes to utilizing the Timeline panel in Photoshop, and these restrictions are especially obvious for more sophisticated animations and video projects. Because the Timeline panel is not meant to serve as a full-featured video editing or animation tool, several of its features may be re-stricted or necessitate the usage of additional plugins or apps to acquire the desired results.

Creating a new video

The Timeline panel in Photoshop may be utilized to build a new film, which is a superb technique to develop videos that appear professional employing the resources that you presently have available to you.

To aid you in getting started, we will lead you through the procedure step-by-step.

Import Your Footage: Importing your footage is the first thing you'll do when you start a new video project in Photoshop. To achieve this, click the "File" menu, then "Import," and finally "Video Frames to Layers." Click the Open option once you have picked the video file that you intend to employ. Using this procedure, each frame of the movie will be imported into Photoshop as a different layer.

Developing an Alternative chronology: After you have done importing your film, you should proceed to construct a new chronology. To reach the Timeline panel, choose Window > Timeline from the menu bar. Click the Create Video Timeline button situated in the panel. Your video will gain a completely new chronology as a result of your action.

Organizing Your Layers: In the section labeled **"Layers,"** organize your video frames so that they will display in the order that you chose in your finished film. Additional layers, such as text or graphics, can also be added to your video if you choose.

Changing the Length of Each of Your Frames: You may modify the duration of each frame in the Timeline panel by dragging the borders of the frames. This will adjust the length of each frame. The amount of time that each frame is presented in your video will be decided by this parameter. You may also alter the length of time that several frames are shown by picking them and sliding the borders of the selected frames.

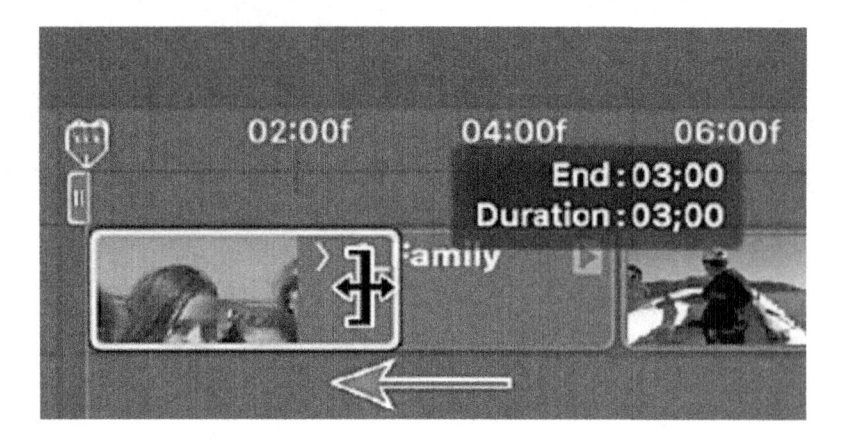

Adding Transitions and Effects: You can add transitions and effects to your movie by going to the Timeline panel and clicking on the Effects option at the bottom of the panel. This will allow you to apply transitions and effects to your video. This will open the Effects panel, inside which you will discover a variety of various effects and transitions that may be applied to your video. You may also adjust the settings of each effect to tailor the way it appears in your film.

Previewing Your Video: To get a preview of your video, click the Play button that is available in the Timeline panel. Using the options on the panel, you may also modify the playback speed, loop your video, and scrub through your movie. Other choices include. Before you export your video, you may use this to ensure that everything appears and sounds the way it should.

Exporting Your Video: When you've completed editing your video and are pleased with how it came out, it's time to export it. To achieve this, go to File > Export > Render Video. Click the Render button after making the proper options for the video's output file format and settings. After you've made your edits, Photoshop will export your movie using the settings you've specified.

Additional Tips & Tricks

If you want to add audio to your video, all you have to do is import the audio file as a layer into Photoshop and position it in the timeline so that it is below the frames of your movie. The Timeline tab allows you to additionally add keyframes, which you may use to create animations and other special effects.

If you need to make improvements to your movie after you've already exported it, you may simply do so by importing the video back into Photoshop, where you can then make the required alterations.

Let's go a bit more in-depth with the process of generating a new video in Photoshop by utilizing the Timeline panel. When you make films using Photoshop, you have the chance to work with individual frames as layers, which is one of the program's numerous advantages. You will have a great lot of discretion and control over the video as a result of this. For instance, you may simply improve the appearance of individual frames by applying filters to them or modifying the brightness and contrast of such photographs. To produce your film with Photoshop, you may make use of the same tools and procedures that you are already accustomed with, which is even another benefit of the application. This indicates that you do not need to get comfortable with a new piece of software or spend a substantial amount of time getting up to speed with a different method. You may alternatively produce videos that have a more polished and professional image by utilizing the tools that you is already familiar with and like using.

It is crucial to have in mind that video files might be fairly enormous if you are dealing with the Timeline panel in Photoshop. This suggests that you will demand a substantial quantity of memory as well as computer power to adequately deal with them. It is also advised that you save your work often to prevent losing any changes made to your project if Photoshop unex-pectedly shuts or your machine abruptly stops. In addition to the core steps that I discussed earlier, the Timeline panel offers several other features and tools that can aid you in the process of generating movies that are more sophisticated and fascinating. You may utilize the Animation panel, for instance, to develop keyframe animations, which let you generate movement and motion in your film. This provides you with greater control over how your movie appears. You may also add and alter audio tracks by utilizing the Audio panel, which contains the power to edit music, voiceovers, and sound effects.

Having the potential to build many layers for your video frames is yet another helpful function given by the Timeline panel. Because of this, you'll be able to build animations and effects that are more complicated than ever before, as well as interact with several components of your movie all at once. You may build a film, for instance, in which the text and vi-suals flow across the screen as the video frames play in the backdrop. Using the Timeline panel in Photoshop to make a new film may be an effective and versatile approach for making videos that have a professional appearance. You may import your footage, arrange your layers, apply transitions and effects, preview your video, and export it in the format of your choosing all by following these steps in the right order. You can build lovely videos that express your message in a manner that is both original and entertaining with a little bit of expertise and some testing.

Animating text with keyframes

In video production, one typical approach for adding motion and interest to text components is to animate them, using keyframes. This gives the writing a more human quality. Whether you're preparing a promotional video, a lesson, or a post for social media, animating text with keyframes may help you grab the attention of your audience and communicate your message in a visually in-teresting manner. This is especially important if you're trying to deliver complex information. In this part, we'll take a more in-depth look at how to animate text in Adobe Photoshop by mak-ing use of keyframes. First, let's define what keyframes are. Keyframes are markers that show the beginning and ending points of a change in a video element, such as a text layer. Keyframes are utilized in the making of videos. You may construct an animation that alters and evolves gradually over time by placing keyframes at various points in time during the animation. Depending on the quantity of keyframes and the sort of keyframes that you use, the animation may be as easy or as sophisticated as you desire.

To animate text in Photos hop utilizing keyframes, you are going to need to follow a few essential processes. First, a new document should be created, and a text layer should be added to it. You may accomplish this by choosing Layer > New > Text Layer from the menu. You may enter in the text that you want to animate, and then use the Options bar at the top of the screen to alter the font, size, and color of the text. Next, activate the Timeline panel by choosing Window> Timeline from the main menu. To produce a fresh new video timeline, navigate to the Timeline panel and click the option labeled "Create Video Timeline." The Timeline panel displays you with a succession of still pictures that collectively indicate the length of your video production. You may uti-lize the timeline to create keyframes for different components of your project, including text layers, as well as update those keyframes as appropriate.

To add a keyframe to your text layer, expand the characteristics of the layer by clicking on the small arrow that is positioned next to the name of the layer in the Timeline panel. To set a keyframe at the current time, create a keyframe by clicking on the stopwatch symbol that is positioned next to the property that you wish to animate, which in this instance is the Opacity property. This keyframe signifies the beginning of the animation that is being presented. Next, advance the play head to a new point in time, say one or two seconds later than where it was previously. To construct a second keyframe at this step, you will need to click the Opacity attribute once again. The animation has finally reached its finish, which is indicated by this keyframe.

Adjusting the opacity of the text layer between the two keyframes is all that has to be done to animate the text. You may accomplish this by sliding the Opacity slider placed in the Layers panel or by clicking on the Opacity property located in the Timeline panel and altering the value. Both of these choices are found in the Timeline panel. Photoshop will automatically produce a smooth animation between the two keyframes, which will consist of the text softly fading in or out over time. When you wish to make your animations more intricate, you can also use other sorts of keyframes. You may, for instance, add a Position keyframe to move the text layer across the screen, or you can add a Scale keyframe to adjust the size of the text. Both of these keyframes may be seen in the Keyframes panel. Create a keyframe for the Position property by clicking on the little arrow that is displayed next to the layer name in the Timeline panel. This will allow you to add a keyframe for the Position attribute. The play head should then be relocated to a different instant in time, and the text layer should be dragged to a new place. The text will be moved across the screen in a smooth animation that will be made by Photoshop in the period between the two keyframes. You may make tweaks to the timing and softness of the keyframes to optimize the animation. You may accomplish this by clicking on the keyframes in the Timeline window and modifying the curve using the Bezier handles. This is an option. You may even add more keyframes to create more intricate animations, such as a series of text items that fly onto the screen one at a time. This is one example of what you can achieve with animation.

Creating effects

Even if the Timeline panel in Photoshop is most typically used for the development of animations and films, it is also a great tool that can be applied for the creation of effects. You may impart the impression of motion to a picture or make dynamic changes to it by adding keyframes to the properties of the layers in the image. Animating the amount of transparency of a layer is one of the easiest approaches for achieving an effect by making use of the Timeline panel. For instance, you may make a fade-in effect by initializing the opacity of a layer at 0% at the beginning of the timeline, and then gradually boosting it to 100% during a set length of time. This will deliver the required outcome. To achieve this, you will first need to establish a new video timeline by heading to the File menu and choosing New > Video Timeline from the drop-down menu. After that, you would simply drag the layer onto the timeline that you want to animate, and then you would use the keyframe timeline to define the opacity values at each point in time. A motion blur effect is yet another well-known effect that may be achieved with the aid of the Timeline panel. You may generate the appearance that anything is moving or traveling rapidly by animating the motion blur filter that is applied to a layer. To accomplish this purpose, you will first need to construct a new video timeline in the same manner as previously. After that, you will need to apply the Motion Blur filter to the layer that you wish to animate.

Following this step, you will need to construct keyframes for the blur angle and distance, and then you will need to alter them over time to obtain the effect you desire.

You may also leverage the Timeline panel to create more intricate effects, such as a glowing or pulsating effect. This may be done by following the directions in the Help file. To accomplish this purpose, you will first need to build a completely new movie timeline and then add the layer that you wish to animate. After that, you would go to the Layer Style panel and give the layer either a Glow or an Outer Glow effect. At this stage, you would employ the keyframe timeline to adjust the glow's settings over time. For example, you may adjust the glow's size, intensity, or color using this approach. The Adjustment layer in Photoshop is yet another helpful tool for the production of effects in the application. You may make non-destructive modifications to an image's color, contrast, or brightness using this layer and the Timeline panel can be used to animate the changes you make to the layer. For instance, you may create a color wash effect by creating a Color Fill layer and then animating the opacity value throughout the project.

The Timeline panel in Photoshop provides users with a varied variety of choices, which may be utilized while producing effects and animations. You may bring your images to life by generating dynamic effects that are visually beautiful and that you develop by employing keyframes and the properties of layers. You can unlock the full potential of the Timeline panel and move your ideas to the next level with just a little bit of imagination and experimenting on your side.

Adding adjustment layers to video clips

Adding adjustment layers to video clips in Photoshop is a powerful tool that enables you to make non-destructive alterations to the color, tone, and general aesthetic of your videos. These adjustments may be made in any way you wish, from subtle to extreme. Adjustment layers give flexibility and control over the editing process, enabling you to experiment with a va-riety of effects without permanently changing the original video content. This is made feasible by the fact that adjustment layers are situated above the footage being edited.

Launch Photoshop and add your video clip to the project by selecting **File > Import > Video Frames** to Layers from the menu bar. Choose the file you wish to import, and then click Import. Photoshop will break the frames of the movie into layers, and then it will generate a new document that contains the video clip. Next, navigate to the Layers panel in Photoshop by selecting the Window menu. If it is not currently accessible, you may access it by selecting **Window > Layers** from the menu bar. In the Layers panel, each frame of the video clip will display as its layer, and these layers will be grouped like a timeline. To create an adjustment layer, pick the Layers panel and then click the New Adjustment Layer button that is situated at the bottom of the panel. This button resembles a circle that is barely partly filled up. The Levels, Curves, Hue/Saturation, and other altering choices will be provided to you in a drop-down menu that will now appear on the screen. Choose the adjustment layer that is linked with the alterations you intend to make to your movie and click on the Edit button.

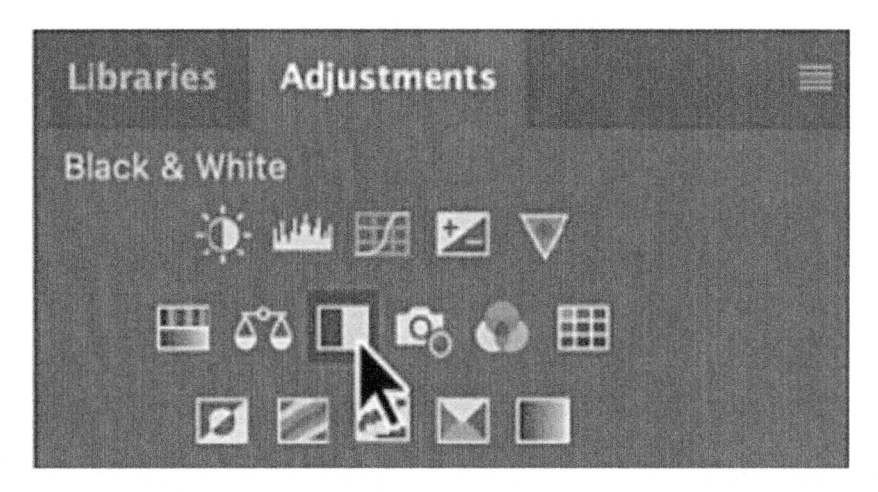

As soon as you create the adjustment layer, it will travel to the top of the Layers panel, where it will be visible above the video clip layers. All of the layers that are impacted by the adjustment layer include the video clip layers. Controlling how the adjustment layer modifies the appearance of the video may be performed by adjusting the settings of the adjustment layer. You may, for instance, vary the tonal range of the video clip by modifying the black, gray, and white sliders if you pick a Levels adjustment layer as the adjustment layer you wish to utilize. Moving the sliders can result in changes to the video's shadows, mid-tones, and highlights, which in turn results in changes to the video overall contrast and brightness.

Similarly, you may tweak the tonal values throughout the video clip by using a Curves adjustment layer and modifying the curve in such a manner that it matches your demands. You may create the desired effect by altering the highlights, shadows, and mid-tones to a finer degree by dragging points on the curve. You may modify the video clip's color properties by selecting a Hue/Saturation adjustment layer. You may adjust the video's color balance, intensity, and general aesthetic by altering the sliders for hue, saturation, and brightness. This will also affect the video to seem differently.

The fact that adjustment layers are non-destructive is one of the most significant benefits of adopting them. They make it feasible for you to experiment around with a range of parameters without making any irrevocable adjustments to the real video clip. If you discover that the alterations do not fit your needs, you may always reverse them, modify the settings, or eliminate the adjustment layer completely. You may add a layer mask to the video clip if you wish to restrict the influence of the adjustment layer to just particular areas of the clip. Click the Layer Mask button at the bottom of the Layers panel once the adjustment layer has been chosen to create a layer mask. By doing so, a layer mask that is associated to the adjustment layer will be produced.

You can paint over the areas of the layer mask that you desire to keep hidden or protect from alteration by using the Brush tool and setting black as the foreground color. This will allow you to do so. Using this strategy, you may make selective adjustments, which offers you the option to concentrate the influence on selected items or locations featured inside the video clip. Playing the movie in Photoshop's Timeline panel will allow you to see how the edits will look once you have done making the proper adjustments and, if necessary, adding the layer mask. You may control playback using the tools offered in the Timeline panel, and you can also browse through the frames to examine the results of your adjustments.

Adding transitions

The process of video editing begins and concludes with the inclusion of transitions. Transitions are utilized to aid produce a seamless flow from one clip to the next and can also be used to help com-municate a specific feeling or mood. They can be employed to generate a stylistic impression, to transition from one scene to the next, to symbolize the passage of time or any combination of the three. In this part, we will go through the numerous sorts of transitions that may be used in video editing, as well as illustrate how to apply such transitions to your video clips by making use of the timeline panel in Photoshop.

Types of Transitions

Video editing makes use of a broad number of transition styles, each of which has its purpose and impact. Each transition type performs a somewhat distinct role.

The following is a list of some of the most often-seen kinds of transitions:

1. Cut: The cut is the simplest form of transition, and it comprises the quick ending of one clip and the starting of the following one. When there is a need to portray a feeling of urgency or underline a big shift in the action, cuts are employed.

2. Fade: The term **"fade"** refers to the gradual transition that happens between two clips, in which the prior clip fades out as the new one fades in. The passage of time may be conveyed by utilizing fades, which are employed to make a transition that is both soft and smooth between portions.

3. Dissolve: A dissolve is a transition effect that is quite similar to a fade. However, rather of fading out one clip while fading in the next, a dissolve makes both clips partly visi-ble at the same time, generating an effect that is comparable to a cross-fade.

4. Wipe: A wipe is a form of transition in which one clip pushes another clip off the screen, exposing the next clip that was hiding behind the preceding one. Wipes are commonly employed to portray the sensation of movement, as well as to introduce a new environment or character.

5. Zoom: The transition from one clip to the next is called a zoom, and it consists of the camera zooming in or out as it transitions from one clip to the next. Zooms are commonly utilized to produce a dramatic effect or to concentrate the audience's attention on a single object or figure.

Adding Transitions: To create a transition to your video clip in Photoshop, follow these steps:

Step 1. You may watch your video by dragging and dropping it into the timeline, which is found in the panel on the left.

Step 2. Find the folder titled **"Transitions"** in the **"Effects"** panel, which may be found in the bottom-left area of the display screen.

Step 3. Choose the transition you want to use, and then use the drag-and-drop method to arrange it on the timeline between the two clips in that you want the transition to occur.

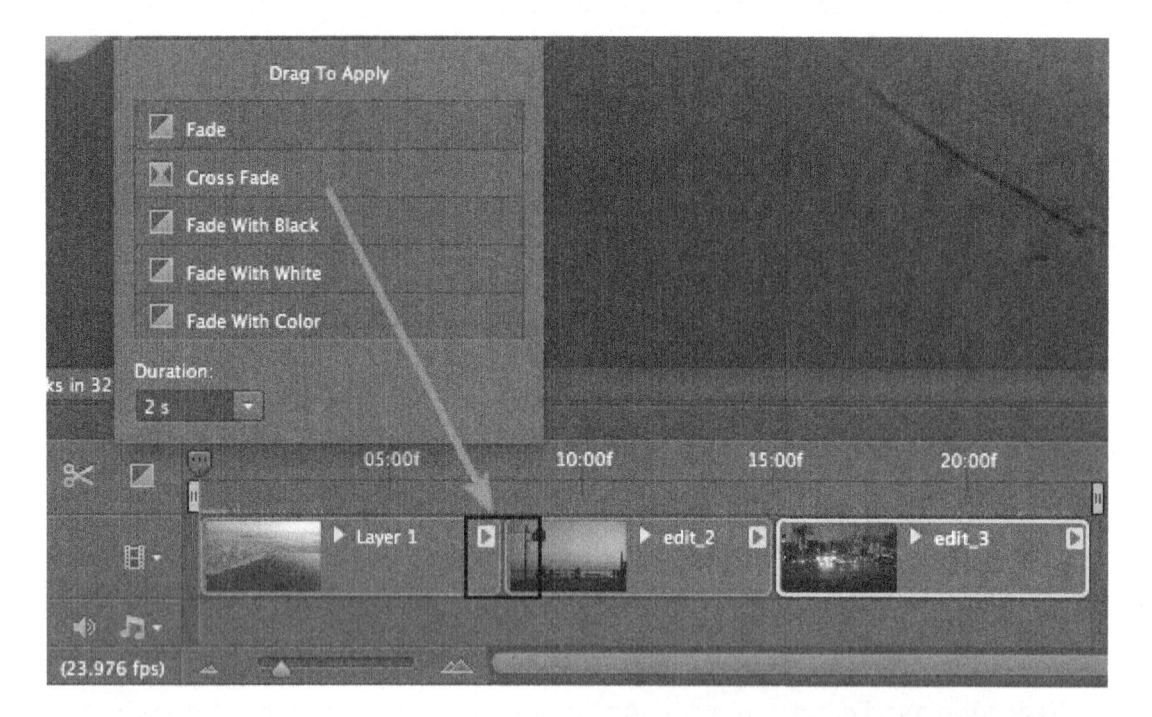

Step 4. Wipe: A wipe is a form of transition in which one clip pushes another clip off the screen, exposing the next clip that was hiding behind the preceding one. Wipes are commonly employed to portray the sensation of movement, as well as to introduce a new environment or character.

Step 5. Zoom: The transition from one clip to the next is called a zoom, and it consists of the camera zooming in or out as it transitions from one clip to the next. Zooms are commonly utilized to produce a dramatic effect or to concentrate the audience's attention on a single object or figure.

Adding Transitions: To create a transition to your video clip in Photoshop, follow these steps:

Step 1. You may watch your video by dragging and dropping it into the timeline, which is found in the panel on the left.

Step 2. Find the folder titled **"Transitions"** in the **"Effects"** panel, which may be found in the bottom-left area of the display screen.

Step 3. Choose the transition you want to use, and then use the drag-and-drop method to position it on the timeline between the two clips in that you want the transition to occur.

Step 4. Clicking and dragging the border of the transition in the timeline will allow you to vary the length of the transition by adjusting its duration. You may also adjust where the transition is positioned in the timeline by dragging it to a different point there. This is another alternative.

Step 5. You can witness the transition in action by choosing the "**Play**" button situated in the timeline panel.

Adding many Transitions: You may also apply many transitions to your video clip to create a more sophisticated effect. To achieve this, simply add a transition to the end of each clip and alter the time and position of each transition as needed. You may also apply multiple sorts of transitions to different areas of your video clip to create a distinct impression.

Adding Sound Effects: Adding sound effects to your transitions may help enhance the overall impression of your movie.

To add a sound effect to your transition, follow these steps:

Step 1. Import your sound effect into the project by clicking on "**File**" > "**Import**" > "**Import to Library**" in the menu bar.

Step 2. Drag and drop the sound effect onto the timeline, beneath the transition.

Step 3. Adjust the duration of the sound effect to fit the duration of the transition.

Step 4. Preview the transition with sound by clicking on the "**Play**" button in the timeline panel.

Customizing Transitions: Photoshop also allows you to edit transitions to create a distinctive look. To achieve this, take these steps:

Step 1. Choose the transition in the timeline window that you wish to edit and click the Edit button.

Step 2. Simply go to the upper-left-hand corner of the screen and pick the "**Effect Controls**" option.

Step 3. Make modifications to the "**Effect Controls**" panel's sliders and other settings.

Adding transitions in a video is an effective approach to create the impression that it was prepared with greater care and attention to detail. Your video may be given a more professional look by adding transitions, which also help to make the cuts between the various materials smoother. Your video projects may have smooth transitions added to them with the aid of Photoshop's Timeline panel. To make a transition in Photoshop between two clips, you must first confirm that the Timeline panel is enabled and that there are two clips on the timeline that you want to transition between. Once these two prerequisites are satisfied, you may add the transition. Next, pick the transition by clicking on the icon placed at the very bottom of the window. This will open the Transitions panel, in which you can pick an effect to utilize as a transition between two slides.

There are many distinct transition effects accessible, such as fades, wipes, and dissolves and you may chose whichever one you prefer best. You may receive a preview of each effect by moving your mouse over it while it is chosen. When you discover a transition that you like, all you have to do to utilize it is click on it and it will be applied to the edit point that you have specified between the two clips. You may modify the length of the transition by dragging the edge of the transition symbol on the timeline. This is positioned on the left side of the screen. You may also adjust the timing of the transition by shifting the edit point to the left or right on the timeline. This will allow you to customize. Photoshop provides you the opportunity to employ ordinary transitions as well as more sophisticated transi-tions, in addition to typical ones. For instance, you may create a more dynamic and dramatic appearance by utilizing the Motion Blur transition to add a blur effect to your transition. This may be done by utilizing the Motion Blur transition. Create a transition that will progressively expose the following clip by applying a gradient by making utilization of the Gradient Wipe transition. This transi-tion may also be generated with the Wipe transition.

To apply any of these more sophisticated transitions, you must first pick the edit point that is between the two clips that you wish to join on the timeline. After that, choose the transition effect you desire to apply by clicking on the Transitions menu and making your decision there. After that, navigate to the panel labeled "**Effect Controls**." This is the part where you may make adjustments to the parameters of the transition effect.

You may, for instance, alter the quantity of blur as well as the direction in which the blur is applied when you utilize the Motion Blur transition. You may modify the gradient's direction and angle by utilizing the Gradient Wipe transition. Adjustment layers can also be used to create transitions that are put between individual clips. Create an adjustment layer and position it on the timeline so that it is above the two clips that you want to transition between after you have completed doing so. Applying a transition effect to the adjustment layer should subsequently be done in the same manner as was explained previously. When you add a transition to an adjustment layer, it will affect all of the clips that came before it in the timeline. Applying a transition effect that is continuous over numerous clips may be performed with the aid of this approach, which can be useful.

It is vital to bear in mind that transitions, although they may be a wonderful way to add polish to your movies, can also be overdone. Make an attempt to utilize transitions only when essential and only when there is an evident necessity for them in the video. In addition to utilizing the Timeline panel to give normal transitions between clips, you may also use it to create more intricate effects, such as picture-in-picture and split-screen effects. These effects may be applied by utilizing the panel. For instance, to create a picture-in-picture effect, merely place one clip in the timeline, and then drag a second clip onto the timeline above the first clip, placing it such that it overlaps the first clip. Next, alter the proportions of the second clip as well as its loca-tion by utilizing the Scale and Position options accessible in the panel under Effect settings. Adjusting the second clip's degree of transparency may also be done with the aid of the Opacity control. The picture-in-picture window's dimensions and form may be customized by utilizing the Crop settings, which are the last set of choices accessible. An approach similar to this one is used to achieve a split-screen effect. To begin, arrange two clips on the timeline so that they are next to one another. The next step is to adjust the size and form of each clip by utilizing the Crop settings, which are found in the Effect settings panel. You may also alter the placement of each clip as well as its opacity to acquire the effect you desire.

Animating a zoom effect

Your video projects will profit immensely from the addition of depth and dimension when you create a zoom effect. You may quickly and successfully create a zoom effect in Photoshop with the aid of the timeline panel, which will bring your audience members closer to the action and deliver a more immersive experience.

To get started, open Photoshop and import your video clip into the software by selecting **File > Import > Video Frames** to Layers from the menu bar. This will cause a new window to open, in which you may choose the video file you want to import and define the range of frames that you want to bring in. After you have made your selections, go ahead and push the **"OK"** button to import the frames into Photoshop. After that, choose the layer that already has your video clip on it, and then click the **"New Layer"** option at the bottom of the layers panel to create a new layer right above the one you just chose. The zoom effect will be achieved with this new layer that we have introduced.

Choose the **"Rectangular Marquee Tool"** from the tool bar, and while your new layer is chosen, build a rectangle around the area of the movie that you desire to zoom in on. Ensure that the rectangle is positioned in the center of the video and that it has the proportions and form that you need for the zoom effect that you are striving for. After you have constructed your rectangle, go to the **"Edit"** menu, and then click **"Fill"** from the list of alternatives. Select **"Content-Aware"** in the fill dialog box, and then click **"OK"** to fill the rectangle with the video material that is surrounding it.

It is now time to concentrate on the animation that will accompany the zoom effect. Click on the freshly formed rectangle after selecting the **"Zoom Tool"** from the toolbar. The level of zooming will be set to 100% when you do this. Place the play head, which is situated in the timeline panel, at the spot where you would want the zoom effect to commence. Click the **"Create a new keyframe"** button at the bottom of the timeline panel while your new layer is selected. By doing this, a new keyframe will be added to the layer. Place the play head in the timeline panel at the point where you want the zoom effect to complete after it has been applied. Click the **"Zoom Tool"** icon while your newly created layer is still selected, and then raise the zoom level until it reaches the desired level. At this point in the timeline, a new keyframe will be produced as a result of this action. Scrubbing the play head back and forth in the timeline panel will let you get a preview of your zoom effect, which you can see now that both keyframes have been set. If you need to make adjustments to the time or the zoom level, all you have to do is move the keyframes to the regions you want them to be in.

You may add a motion blur to the layer if you want to make the zoom effect even more spectacular. Ensure that the layer is picked before going to the **"Filter"** menu and selecting the **"Blur > Motion Blur"** decision. You may acquire the needed effect by tweaking the angle and distance settings in the motion blur dialog box until you get the result you want. In conclusion, if you want your zoom effect to have a smoother transition, you may give it a fade-in and a fade-out effect. To achieve this, create a new layer above the one holding your movie and paint that layer black. After that, make use of the **"Rectangular Marquee Tool"** to design a rectangle that surrounds the whole of the frame. With your new layer chosen, go to the **"Edit"** menu and pick **"Fade"** from the drop-down menu. Click the **"OK"** button once you have entered the proper timings into the **"Fade In"** and **"Fade Out"** sections of the fade dialog box. The zoom effect you were working on is done and is now ready to be saved as a video file. You may effortlessly create dynamic and fascinating video effects in Photoshop by using the timeline panel in the pro-gram. These effects will take your work to the next level.

Animating a picture to generate a motion effect

To convey the idea that something is moving, you will initiate another change. The photo should start with the diver's legs and continue with his hands.

This is the desired effect.

Step 1. Bring the play head to the very end of the clip, and then pick the clip from the menu. While dragging the photo down in the document window using the Move tool, make careful to hold down the Shift key and move it closer to the top of the canvas.

Step 2. To see the clip's properties, click the triangle to the left of the clip title, and then click the stopwatch icon next to the Position property. This will add a keyframe (indi-cated by a yellow diamond symbol) underneath the clip.

Step 3. Position the play head so that it is at the beginning of the video. While using the Move tool, with the picture still chosen, hold down the Shift key and move it up so that the feet are now situated at the bottom of the canvas.

To finish off the animation, Photoshop will add a second keyframe underneath the clip.

Step 4. To obtain a preview of the animation, drag the play head over the time ruler.

As can be seen, the sequence in which you generate animation keyframes is not significant. It is sometimes simpler, like in this picture, to begin with, the final look and then work your way backward.

Step 5. Exit the clip's attributes and settings. Then, to save what you've done thus far, pick the **File > Save** menu option.

Adding the Pan & Zoom effect

You may easily add features that are equivalent to the pan and zoom effects that are used in documentaries. You are going to add them to the scene of the sunset so that the film has a dra-matic finale.

Step 1. Move the playing head to the beginning of the clip.

Step 2. Click the triangle at the top-right corner of the clip to see its Motion panel. pick Pan & Zoom from the pop-up menu, pick Zoom Out from the Zoom option, and make sure Resize to Fill Canvas is chosen. Then select an empty spot on the Timeline panel to collapse the Motion panel.

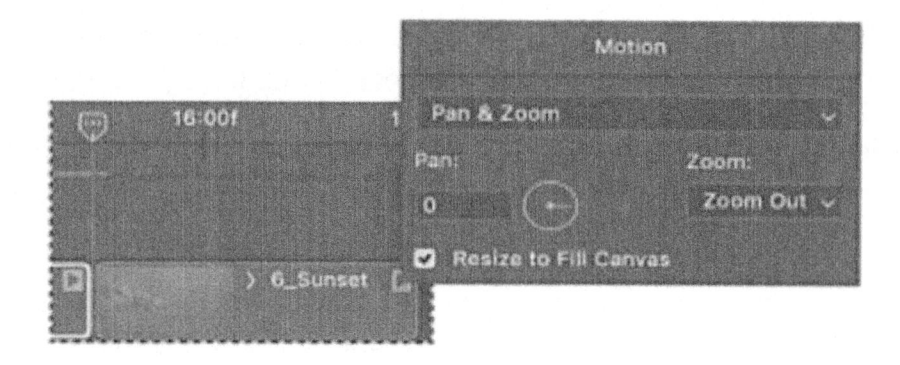

Step 3. Move the play head across the final clip to examine the effects.

Adding audio

In Photoshop, a video file may have an extra audio track added to it so that it can be played separately. The Timeline panel always has a blank audio track included in it by default. You will provide the video with a soundtrack by uploading an MP3 file to play in the background.

Step 1. Click the musical-note icon in the Audio Track at the bottom of the Timeline panel and pick Add Audio from the pop-up menu. You may also add an audio track by clicking the plus symbol at the far-right end of the track in the Timeline panel.

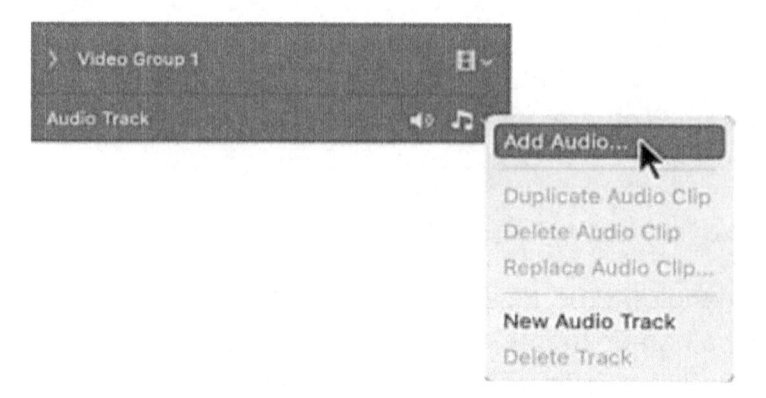

Step 2. Select the song file from its folder and click Open.

The audio file is added to the timeline, but if it's considerably longer than the video, you'll utilize the Split at Play head tool to reduce it.

Step 3. Move the playing head to the conclusion of the video. With the audio file still chosen, click the Split at Play head tool in the Timeline panel. The audio file is truncated at that time, becoming two audio snippets.

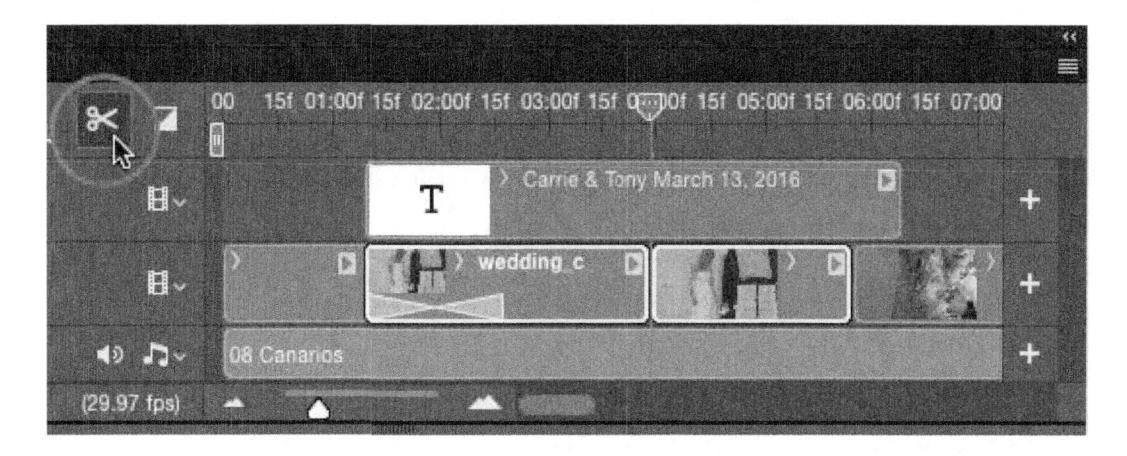

Step 4. Select the second audio file section, the one that begins after the finish of the video. Press the Delete key on your keyboard to erase the chosen clip. Now the audio file is the same length as the video. You'll add a fade so that it ends gracefully.

Step 5. Click the little triangle at the right border of the audio clip to access the Audio panel. Then input 3 seconds for Fade In and 5 seconds for Fade Out.

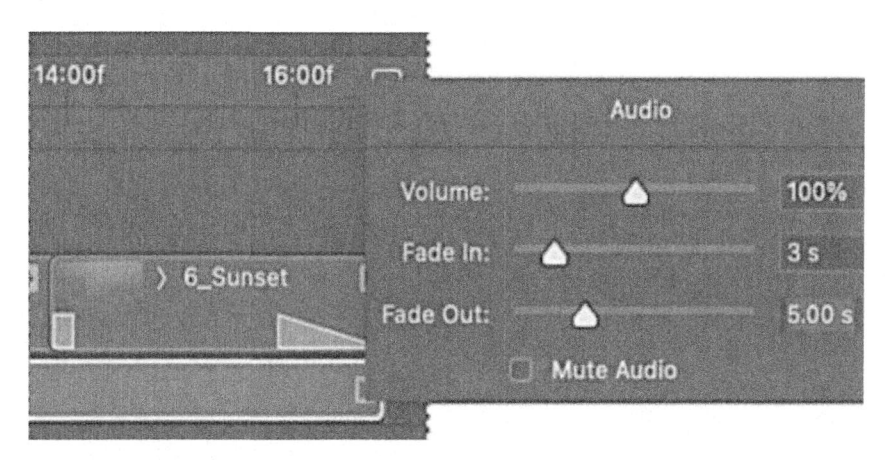

Step 6. Click an empty spot of the Timeline panel to shut the Audio panel and preserve your work thus far.

Muting undesired audio

• Click the Play button in the upper-left corner of the Timeline window to preview the video.

• Click the tiny triangle at the right end of the clip.

• Click the Audio tab to display audio choices, and then pick Mute Audio. Click an empty space in the Timeline panel to shut the Audio/Video panel.

Rendering video

Now that you've completed making edits to the timeline, you may export it as a single video file. Photoshop provides customers with various distinct rendering choices. You will pick settings that are ideal for streaming videos to post to the YouTube website. Check out the Photoshop Help file for extra information on the various rendering choices.

Step 1. When you have completed editing your video, go to the "File" menu and click **"Export"** > **"Render Video"**.

Step 2. In the Render Video dialog box, pick the output format along with any extra settings (such as the resolution and frame rate) that you wish.

Step 3. To begin the process of rendering, you must first pick the **"Render"** button. This can take some time depending on the length of the video you want to convert as well as the settings you specify.

Step 4. When the rendering is done, your video file will be in the directory that you chose during the export method. You can locate it there soon as the rendering is completed.

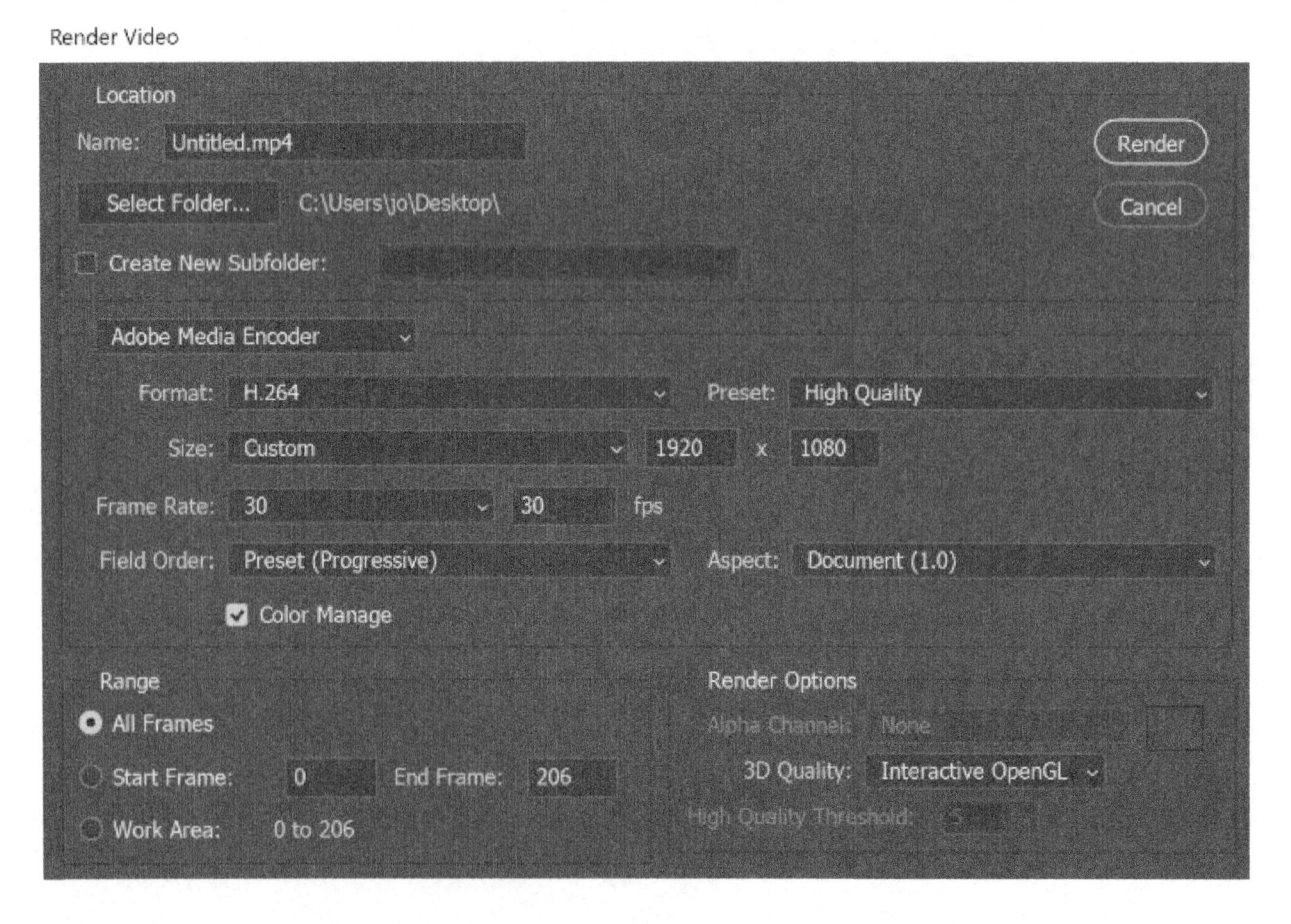

CHAPTER 13: PREPARING FILES FOR THE WEB

Creating placeholders with the Frame tool

Users of Photoshop may create placeholders for pictures or other graphic components with the aid of the Frame tool, which is a feature that is both flexible and straightforward to use. Because it offers a rapid and effective technique to produce and alter placeholders, this tool may be of great value to designers who are entrusted with the construction of layouts that feature diverse photographs or graphics. The ease of use of the Frame tool is among the most notable benefits of its use. Simply choose the Frame tool from the toolbar, click and drag to create a form that is either rectangular or square, and then alter the size and rotation of the shape as desired. This will produce a placeholder for you.

Because this approach is both fast and simple to grasp, it is incredibly useful to be able to produce placeholders on the fly while you are writing.

• Launch Adobe Photoshop and start a fresh document creation. Make your pick using the tool bar on the left side of the screen, then choose the Frame tool.

• By clicking and dragging with the Frame tool, you may build a form that is either rectangular or square. As your replacement, this form will be utilized.

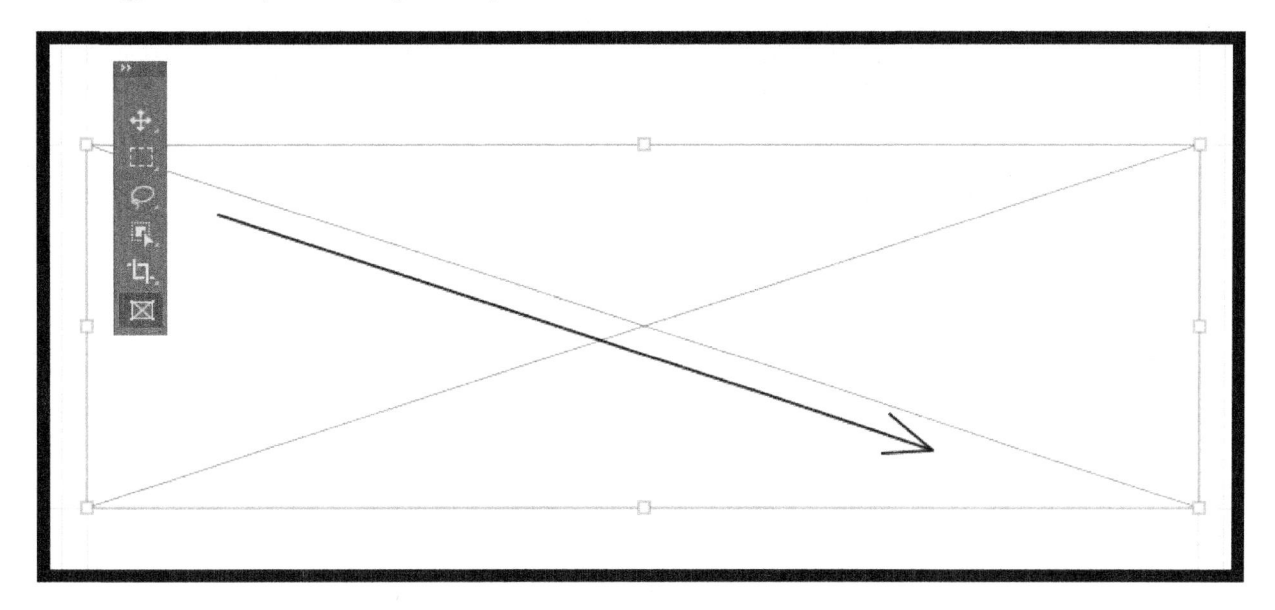

You may modify the size of the frame by clicking and dragging on the frame's borders or comers. This will bring up a menu where you can make your pick. You may also rotate the frame by putting your mouse over one of the corners until a curving arrow appears, then clicking and dragging in the desired direction. This may be done simply by mov-ing your cursor over the frame.

Select the frame layer in the Layers panel so that a picture may be added into the space. Choose the picture you like to use, then go to the File menu and pick the embedded option.

The picture will be altered accordingly so that it may be presented inside the placeholder.

• If you decide at a later time that you want to alter the picture, all you have to do is double-click on the frame layer in the Layers panel, then pick a new image to set in its place.

• You can also add a stroke or other effects to the frame by picking the frame layer and altering the layer styles in the Layers panel. This allows you to add or delete effects from the frame.

Adding graphics to a frame

In Photoshop, putting a graphic to a frame is an easy method that comprises applying the Place Embedded command to import the visual into the frame.

This command imports the graphic into the frame.

• Launch the file in which you intend to place the graphic into a frame and pick it.

• Make your selection using the toolbar on the left side of the screen, then choose the Frame tool.

• By clicking and dragging the Frame tool, you will give the frame a form that is either rectangular or square.

• In the Layers panel, pick the layer that is called "**frame**."

• To open the Place dialog box, go to the File menu and pick the Embedded Place option.

• Click the Place button once you have browsed to the location of the graphic file that you desire to import into the frame.

• The size of the graphic will be modified mechanically so that it may be seen inside the frame.

• If needed, use the Move tool or the Free Transform command (Ctrl / Cmd +T) to adjust the placement of the graphic inside the frame, as well as the size of the graphic.

• After putting the picture inside the frame so that it is the right size and placement, you may next make any required alterations to extra effects or settings.

• Simply double-click on the frame layer in the Layers panel, choose the graphic layer, and then use the Place Embedded command to import a new graphic to replace the one that is already there. This will replace the graphic that is already present inside the frame.

Using layer groups to generate button graphics

1. By pressing the **"New Group"** button found at the very bottom of the Layers panel, you will create a new layer group.

2. You may call the layer group **"Button"** or anything else that makes sense to you.

3. By clicking the New Layer icon situated at the bottom of the Layers panel, a new layer can be created for the button background and added to the layer group it is part of.

4. On the new layer, you may design the shape of the button backdrop by using the Shape tool or one of the other available alternatives.

5. You can build a new layer inside the layer group for the button text or icon by choosing the New Layer icon at the bottom of the Layers panel. This will create a new layer within the layer group.

6. To add the button text or icon to the new layer, you may either make use of the Type tool or another technique.

7. If required, make the appropriate modifications to the button background and text layers' locations, sizes, and any other attributes.

8. To further improve the overall look of the button, you may apply layer styles or effects to the text or background layers, if you choose.

9. Make your pick using the toolbar on the left side of the screen, then choose the Frame tool.

10. By clicking and dragging the Frame tool, you may create the button frame into a shape that is either rectangular or square.

11. Drag the layer that contains the frame into the "Button" layer group after selecting it in the Layers panel.

12. Within the "Button" layer group, place the frame layer such that it is exactly above the button background layer.

13. You can rapidly generate a clipping mask using the frame layer by choosing the button background layer and using the keyboard shortcut **Cmd / Ctrl / Opt + Alt / Option + G**.

14. Make any required modifications to the placement and dimensions of the button background layer so that it may be contained inside the frame.

15. To produce extra button graphics, clone both the **"Button"** layer group as well as the frame layer.

You can develop button visuals that are exact and consistent if you use the frame tool in combination with the layer grouping capability. The frame tool provides you with the power to give your buttons an exact size and form, and the layer group tool gives you the opportunity to keep your design components organized in a way that makes them easy to edit.

By adding a clipping mask to the layer that includes the button background and the layer that contains the frame, you will be able to produce a perfect match between the two components. This assures that the graphics on your buttons have a clean and skilled appearance.

Automating a multistep task

When you work in creative professions like design or photography, you often confront obstacles that demand you to complete multiple phases and occupy a big amount of your time. These activities, whether they entail reducing and optimizing images for usage on the web or employing certain filters to improve the aesthetic of your photos, may be laborious and time-consuming. Nevertheless, there is a technique to increase the effectiveness of your procedure and save time: you may automate these activities by applying Photoshop Actions.

What are Photoshop Actions?

You may automate a sequence of activities or operations that you do often in Adobe Photoshop by utilizing Photoshop activities. This feature is available in Adobe Photoshop. You may automate a process for later use by documenting the steps you take to finish a project and saving them as an Action.

This allows you to reuse the recorded steps in the future. Actions may be applied to a single image or a batch of images, making them a handy tool for improving your process and saving time. Actions can be applied to a single image or a group of photos.

The steps to generating your own Photoshop Action

Step 1. Launch Adobe Photoshop and start a fresh document creation.

Step 2. In the top menu bar, go to the "**Window**" option, and then pick "**Actions**."

Step 3. To create a new action, utilize the "**New Action**" button accessible on the Actions panel.

Step 4. Give your new action a name, and if you wish, you can even place it in a set.

Step 5. To begin recording your actions, click the "**Record**" button. When recording is in process, the Begin Recording button that is situated at the bottom of the Actions panel will become red to signal this fact to you.

There is no need to be in a hurry, even if you are recording this. Take as much time as you need to ensure that the procedure is carried out appropriately. Actions do not record in real time; rather, they catch steps as you finish them and then play them back as fast as feasible.

This is because actions are not recorded in real-time.

Step 6. Carry out the task that you wish to automate subsequently. This can consist of resizing an image, applying filters to the image, and saving the image. You should begin by altering the proportions of the image and then sharpening it.

Select Image > Image Size, and then carry out the actions that follow:

Ensure that the Resample option is chosen.

In the "Width" field, pick Pixels from the "**Units**" drop-down box. Next, set the "**Width**" value to 180.

Verify that the Height was set to 180 pixels when you initially entered it. It should, considering that the image's basic proportions are kept by the Constrain Aspect Ratio link icon that is positioned to the left of the Width and Height values and that has its default setting chosen.

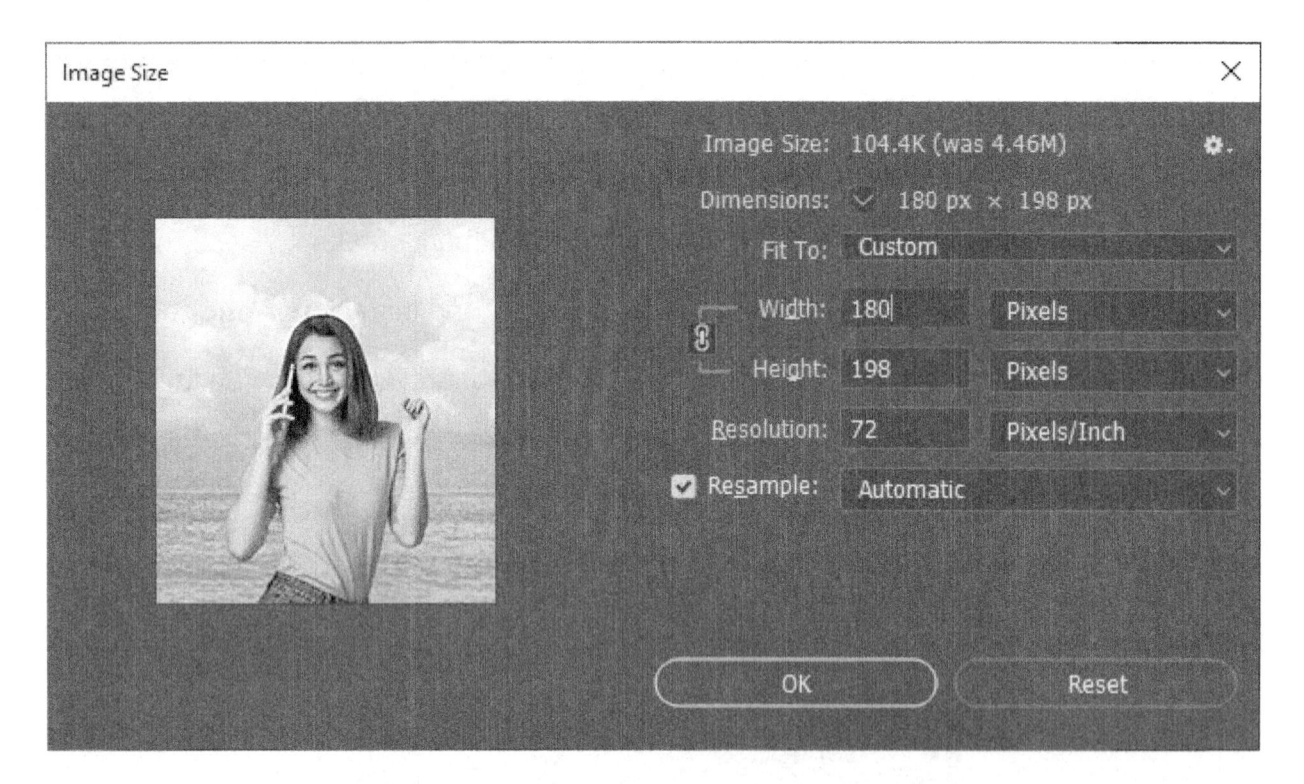

• Click OK.

Select "**Filter**" > "**Sharpen**" > "**Smart Sharpen**," make the appropriate modifications, and then click the "**OK**" button:

• Amount: 100%

• Radius: 1.0 px

Step 7. If you wish to halt recording once you've done the work, click the "**Stop**" button in the Actions window. This will bring the recording to an end.

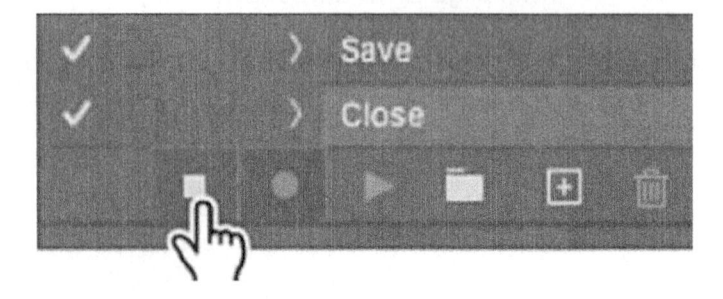

Step 8. To put the action through its paces, pick a fresh image to work with and then click the "**Play**" button available in the Actions panel.

Step 9. If the process succeeds as expected, you may apply it to some images at once by heading to the "**File**" menu in the top-right corner of the screen, choosing "**Automate**," and then selecting "**Batch**."

Step 10. Pick the action that you just produced in the Batch dialog box, then pick the source files and the destination folder.

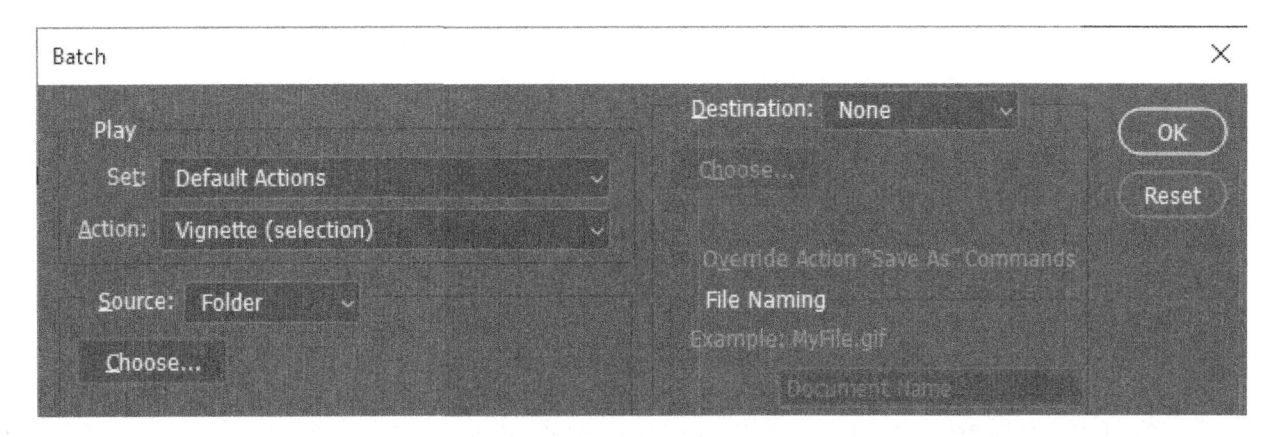

Step 11. Click "**OK**" to conduct the operation on the collection of photographs.

Benefits of automating chores with Actions

1. Saves time: When you automate repetitive tasks, you may save a large amount of time for yourself. You may spare yourself the hassle of manually carrying out each step by merely executing the Action and letting Photoshop carry out the necessary activities for you.

2. Consistency: Automating repeated tasks with Actions can help you maintain a high degree of consistency in your profession. You can be confident that each image is processed in the same manner if you keep a record of the particular steps you take to accomplish a job and follow them exactly.

3. Productivity boost: Automating repetitive jobs with Actions will help you attain better levels of productivity. You will be able to dedicate more of your focus to more vital elements of your business, such as innovative design or photo editing if you get rid of monotonous jobs.

4. Error Reduction: Automating repetitive procedures with Actions can help cut down on the number of mistakes that are made. You may decrease the probability of making errors by doing away with the necessity for each step to be carried out manually.

Examples of jobs that may be automated with Actions

Many processes may be automated with Actions in Photoshop. Here are a few examples:

1. Resizing and optimizing photos for web use: When producing photographs for websites, graphic designers often find themselves faced with the difficulty of resizing and optimizing images for usage on the web. You may simply and quickly process multiple pictures if you design an Action that lowers the size of the images to a specified size and optimizes them for consumption on the web.

2. Adding filters: Adding various sorts of filters to a photograph may improve both its look and its overall feel. You may quickly and simply enhance multiple pictures with the same impression by building an Action that applies specific filters to images. This Action may be found in the Filters panel of the Actions panel.

3. Batch processing: This is a technique that performs the same procedure to a large number of photos all at once. This might entail operations such as resizing photographs, updating the categories of data, and renaming and reorganizing file directories. You may process a huge number of images in a short amount of time and with little effort if you develop an Action that is responsible for carrying out the needed operations.

4. Color correction: The act of altering an image's colors and tones to enhance the image's overall appeal is known as color correction. You may quickly and simply adjust the color and tone of many pictures by building an Action that applies specified color correction settings to images. This allows you to accomplish this swiftly and simply.

Tips for generating successful Actions

The following are some aspects to take in mind while building effective Actions in Photoshop:

Step 1. Before you begin to record an Action, you should first plan out the activities that you will need to take to finish the assignment. By doing so, you will decrease the potential of making mistakes and assure that all of the needed tasks are recorded.

Step 2. When building an Action, make careful to keep it as plain and uncomplicated as possible. This will make it much simpler to address any difficulties that may occur and will also assist in guaranteeing that the Action operates without any glitches.

Step 3. Use terms that explain what the activity does and are descriptive. When naming your Actions, choose names that are descriptive and that reflect what the action accomplishes. Because of this, it will be much simpler to identify and employ Action in the future.

Step 4. Test your Actions: Before you apply an Action to a set of images, make sure it works properly by trying it on a single image first. You may accomplish this by navigating to **Edit > Test Action**. Before processing a large number of images, doing this will aid you in discovering and fixing any difficulties that may develop.

Step 5. Save your Actions: When you have completed developing an Action, you should immediately go to a secure area and store it so that you may use it again in the future. In addition, you may exchange Actions with other individuals who use Photoshop or download Actions that were produced by other people.

By employing Photoshop Actions to automate multistep operations, you may save a large amount of time and enhance the amount of work that you get done. You may ensure consistency in your job, decrease the number of mistakes, and concentrate on more crucial elements of your career if you build Actions that automate repeated procedures. Whether you are resizing and optimizing photographs for use on the web, adding effects to your photos to improve them, or processing a large number of images in batch, Photoshop Actions may help you save time and streamline your workflow.

Designing with artboards

You may require separate image files for the buttons and other information if you're designing user interfaces for mobile devices or websites to be utilized on such devices. Using the Export As option in Photoshop, you can export either the full project or select layers to formats that are compatible with the web and mobile devices. These formats include PNG, JPEG, and GIF. Export As not only allows you to export several layers to distinct files at the same time, but it also allows you to export several sizes at the same time. This is handy if you need to create sets of photographs for low-and high-resolution screens concurrently. You may wish to look out Adobe Generator if you're interested in the automatic output of layers for online and mobile user interfaces. When Adobe Generator is turned on, Photoshop automatically produces the layers you are working on into picture assets. The properties of the exported assets are controlled by a layer naming standard.

You may need to coordinate multiple concepts for a single design or come up with numerous design variants for various display sizes. When you employ artboards, which are effectively numerous canvases packed inside a single Photoshop document, this work becomes much simpler. You may even export full art boards by utilizing the Export As feature. Selecting artboards or layers in the Layers panel allows you to tailor what is exported when using the Export As feature. The ability to create in Photoshop utilizing art boards might be a game-changer for your design process as it enables you to build multiple versions of a design inside a single document.

The following is an in-depth lesson that will lead you through the process of designing in Photoshop using Artboards:

You'll need to start a fresh Photoshop document before you can begin the design process with art boards. To alter the size and resolution of your document, click **File > New** from the menu bar. You have the choice of starting with a blank canvas or picking a size from the drop-down box to employ as your starting point.

To add an artboard, go to the Layers panel and then click on the icon labeled "**Artboard**" which is positioned at the very bottom of the panel. This will add a new artboard to your project when you click this button.

After you have made your art board, you may further customize it by adjusting its dimensions and orientation. To achieve this, first, pick the artboard you wish to work with and then enter the Properties panel. The width, height, and orientation of your artboard may all be modified here.

Now that you've prepped your artboard, it's time to start thinking about what you want to create. You may add things to your art board by making use of the tools and features that are offered in Photos hop. Some examples of these elements are text, images, and shapes. Your design components can also be grouped inside the artboard by utilizing layers.

If you want to build multiple artboards, all you have to do is click the Artboard icon in the Layers panel a second time. This will produce a new artboard inside the same document, enabling you to develop several revisions of your artwork without having to start again.

When you have completed design, you may quickly export your artboards. To accomplish this, go to the File menu and pick Export> Artboards to Files. This will launch the Art boards to Files dialog box, in which you can specify the format and location for the files that are exported from the Art boards.

Tips for Designing using Artboards

Use a Template: You might consider adopting a template with guidelines or a grid to save effort and ensure uniformity across all of your artboards. You will be able to build a layout that is uniform across all art boards with the assistance of this.

Always remember to keep things basic and avoid putting too many design elements onto your art boards. Ensure that your message is understood by keeping the designs you employ uncomplicated and focused.

• **Utilize Keyboard Shortcuts:** Utilize keyboard shortcuts to create new artboards, duplicate layers, and conduct a range of other operations to speed up your production.

• **Group Your Layers:** To keep order among all of the design components contained inside each artboard, create layer groups.

• **Give Each Art board a Descriptive Name**: Naming your art boards will aid you in keeping track of the designs you have made.

CHAPTER 14: PRODUCING AND PRINTING CONSISTENT COLOR

Preparing files for printing

After modifying a picture, you will most certainly want to share it with others or publish it in some form. In an ideal case, you have been editing with the goal in mind the whole time, and you have managed the file quality, colors, file size, and other properties of the image appropriately. However, when you are ready to export the photo, you have still another option to en-sure that your image will come out looking its absolute finest. The process of preparing files for printing in Photoshop can be a hard one, but there are a few key steps that need to be performed to maximize the possibility that the completed output will be just as you had envisioned it.

When preparing files in Photoshop for printing, the following are some of the most crucial factors to take in mind, as detailed in greater detail below.

Color Mode: When it comes to preparing files for printing in Photoshop, choosing the suitable color mode is one of the most crucial tasks you can perform. When your design is printed, the printer will utilize cyan, magenta, yellow, and black ink to produce all of the varied tones that are present in your design. This color choice is referred to as the CMYK color mode. Before you begin working on your design, you need to make sure that your color mode is set to CMYK. This will ensure that your colors are recreated as accurately as possible.

Photoshop's color mode may be changed by choosing **Image > Mode > CMYK** Color from the menu bar.

Resolution: Making sure that your image has a resolution that is high enough for printing is another key step in the process of preparing files for printing in Photoshop. When printing, the printer requires a high-resolution picture to generate a result that is clear and crisp in appearance. It is advised that a resolution of at least 300 dots per inch (dpi) be utilized for printing.

In Photoshop, you may inspect your resolution by choosing **Image > Image Size** from the menu bar. If the resolution of your image is too low, the resulting prints might be pixelated or unclear.

Bleed: The bleed option in Photoshop is an important component of the process of preparing files for printing. When you send anything to be printed, the printer demands a tiny amount of additional space around the borders of your design. This is done to ensure that nothing significant is lost in the cutting process. This occurrence is referred described as "bleed." When you add bleed in your design, you are assuring that there will be a margin of error when the final output is cut. This can assist stop ugly white borders from developing around your design.

Extending the backdrop color or design 1/8 inch (0.125 inches) over the border of your document is what you need to do in Photoshop to generate bleed.

Save Your Document in the Appropriate Format: It is vital to ensure that your document is saved in the appropriate format before you prepare it for printing in Photoshop. You may need to save your work in a specified format, such as PDF or TIFF, but this will be determined by the printer that you pick. Inquire with your printer about the for-mat parameters they need.

To save your file in Photoshop, go to the **File** menu, then **Save As**, and pick the sort of file you wish to save it as.

Flatten Layers Before Saving Your Project: It is crucial to make sure that your layers are flattened before you save your project. When you flatten your layers, all of your photos are merged into a single, simpler image that can be more simply handled by the printer. When the file is opened on a separate computer, this not only prevents anything from being copied or deleted by accident but also ensures that nothing is moved.

In Photoshop, you may flatten your layers by using the **Layer > Flatten Image** menu option.

Color Profile: Check to check that the color profile you are using is adjusted adequately for the printer you are using. The CMYK color profile is utilized by the great majority of printers.

Check with your printer or the print firm you wish to use if you are uncertain about the color profile to utilize.

In Photoshop, go to the Edit menu and click Color Settings to test your color profile.

Make Sure you check for issues: Before you send your file to the printer, make sure to verify it for errors such as missing photographs or typos. Before printing the final edition, it is advised that a test copy be produced prior to guarantee that the final product will have a good appearance. Error checking can wind up saving you both time and money in the long run, not to mention ensuring that the final product is as good as it can be.

Zoom test

Before sharing or publishing a digital photo or video, completing what's known as a "**zoom test**" is an easy and reliable approach to verify the visual quality of the file in issue. The proce-dure requires zooming close on a picture to check for any pixelation or blurriness that may not be obvious at first sight. Here, we are going to speak about the necessity of performing a Zoom test, how to run a Zoom test, and how to interpret the results of a Zoom test.

Importance of Performing a Zoom Test

It is crucial to run a zoom test as doing so helps you to notice any issues with the image quality that may not be immediately evident. This is of the highest necessity whether you wish to print the image, utilize it in a presentation, or include it in marketing materials.

A presentation that has low image quality might be distracting and create the impression that the whole thing is unprofessional. Before you publish or print the image, it is vital to run a zoom test so that you can discover any faults and make any modifications.

Performing a Zoom Test

It is fairly simple to carry out a zoom test, and you can do it with any digital image or video.

To conduct out a zoom test, you will need to follow these steps:

Step 1. Launch Photoshop. Load your picture.

Step 2. Choose **Image > Image Size**.

Step 3. Ensure that the width and height values correspond to the final output size in inches and that the resolution is adequate. The resolution of 300 ppi is suitable for the majority of printing applications.

Step 4. The completed size of the poster will be 11 inches wide and 1 7 inches tall, which matches the specifications of this image. It has a resolution of 300 pixels per inch. The proportions as well as the resolution are good.

Step 5. To exit the dialog box, click the **OK** button.

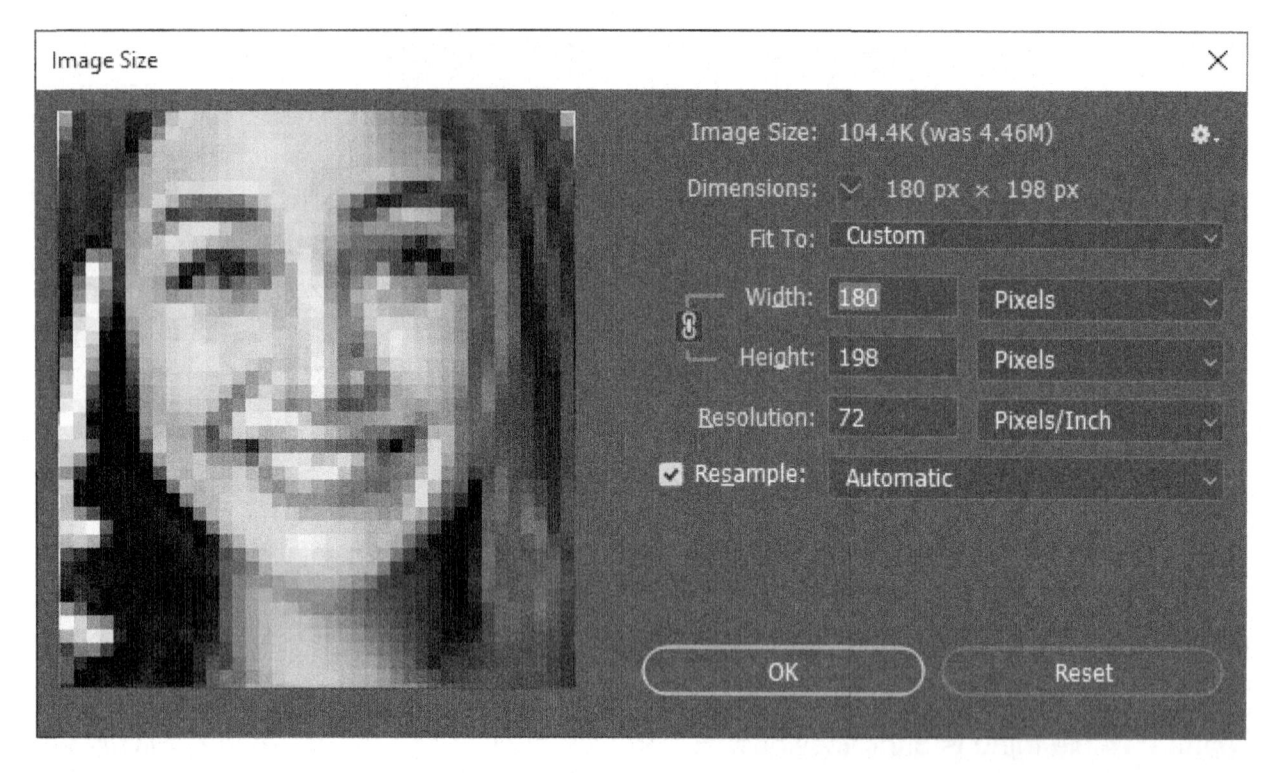

Step 6. Using the zoom tool or by tapping "**Ctrl**" and the "+" key on a PC or "**Command**" and the "+" key on a Mac, zoom in on the picture.

Step 7. Make sure the image quality is still decent when you zoom in. Examine the image to determine whether it has any pixelation or blurriness.

Step 8. Begin by zooming out and then repeat the technique at a range of zoom levels to check that the image quality is constant throughout.

Interpreting the Results

It is not difficult to grasp how to interpret the outcomes of a Zoom test. If the image quality does not change and it does not grow pixelated or fuzzy as the zoom level increases, then the image quality is of a high enough grade. At increased zoom settings, however, if the image quality deteriorates and becomes pixelated or fuzzy, this indicates that the image quality is low and that alterations need to be done to enhance it.

Causes of Poor Image Quality

When you zoom closer onto a picture, the quality of the image may degrade for several reasons.

Low resolution and compression are the most commonly encountered reasons.

Low resolution: Images are deemed to have a low resolution if they do not have enough pixels to generate an image that is both clear and detailed. If you zoom closer on a picture with a poor quality, the image will become more fragmented and confusing since the absence of pixels will become more obvious.

Compression: Compression is the process of shrinking the size of an image's file by deleting data that is not essential for seeing the image. This is done via the process of compression. However, although compression might lower the total file size and make it easier to work with, it generally comes at the sacrifice of image quality. If you zoom close on a picture that has been compressed, you will find that there is a lack of data, which will result in an image that is jagged and blurry.

Tips for Improving Image Quality

If you have carried out a zoom test and noticed that the image quality is poor, there are various things that you may do to increase it, including the following:

1. Raise the image's resolution: If the image has a poor resolution to begin with, raising the image's resolution can help enhance the image quality. However, raising the reso-lution can also result in greater file size, therefore it is important to pick a resolution that strikes a good balance between image qualities and file size.

2. Reduce compression: If the image is compressed, decreasing the amount of compression used to save the image can increase its quality. However, decreasing the compres-sion level can also result in a higher file size, therefore it is important to strike a balance between the image quality and the file size.

3. Use a better camera: If you are currently shooting images using a camera that is of poor quality, shifting to a camera that is of higher quality might greatly boost the image quality.

4. Use suitable lighting: the lighting has a great influence on the overall quality of the image. When shooting images, be sure to make advantage of the right lighting to boost the overall image quality.

About color management

Monitors, printers, and scanners are all examples of various devices that are part of the "devices" that are managed by Photoshop's "color management" process. This process ensures that colors are shown reliably and consistently across all of these varied devices. Here, we are going to talk about the significance of using color management in Photoshop, as well as how it works and how to configure it.

The Importance of Color Management in Photoshop and Why You Need It

Because various devices can cause colors to appear differently, color management is a crucial part of using Photoshop. For instance, a photograph that, when seen on the screen of your computer, seems brilliant and colorful may, when printed, appear muted and washed out. The process of color management guarantees that the colors you see on your screen are as accurate a representation as possible of the colors that will be printed or shown on other devices. This guarantees that the finished result appears exactly like you envisioned it would when you were finished.

How Color Management Works in Photoshop

The usage of color profiles is the foundation of Photoshop's approach to color management. A color profile is a collection of data that explains the color properties of a device like a monitor or a printer. A color profile may be downloaded from the manufacturer's website. Photoshop makes use of these profiles to ensure that colors are appropriately translated across different devices.

When you open an image in Photoshop, the image's color profile is analyzed and applied to the new document automatically. Photoshop will apply a default color profile to the image if it does not already have a color profile linked to it. You have the option to integrate the color profile into the saved image, or you can change the colors to a different profile before saving the image.

Setting Up Color Management in Photoshop

Make sure you are using the suitable color profile for your equipment. This refers to your display as well as your printer and scanner. The correct color profiles have to be given by the producer of your device.

Configure Photoshop's color management settings. Navigate to the **Edit > Color Settings** menu option. You can choose your working area from the Color Settings dialog box, which allows you to control the color range of the photos you create. The color gamut of your photographs can be determined by the RGB, CMYK, and gray working spaces that you choose.

Calibrate your monitor. The accuracy of the colors that are exhibited on your screen may be enhanced by calibrating your monitor. Either a hardware calibrator or manual modifications to the settings of your display can be done by you.

When storing your files, be sure you select the right color settings. You have the choice to include the color profile into the file when you save it, or you may convert the colors to a different profile.

The color management system in Photoshop makes use of color profiles that are consistent with the International Color Consortium (ICC). These color profiles act as translators and assist in maintaining the look of colors throughout the process of converting colors from one color space to another. An ICC color profile is a description of a device's color space, such as the CMYK color space of a specific printer. An ICC color profile may be downloaded from the ICC website. To correctly proof and print your photographs, you must indicate which profiles should be used. After you have made your selection, Photoshop will be able to integrate the profiles into your image files so that it and other apps can accurately reproduce the colors in your photographs.

About calibration and profiling

Calibration

The process of altering the parameters of a gadget to guarantee that it generates proper colors is referred to as calibration. In most cases, this is carried out with the assistance of a piece of hardware known as a colorimeter or spectrophotometer. This tool takes readings of the colors that are generated by the device and then generates a profile that maps those colors to a conven-tional color space.

Calibration of a monitor, for instance, entails making adjustments to the brightness, contrast, and color temperature of the monitor to verify that the colors it shows are correct. Calibration of a printer entails making adjustments to the ink levels and color output of the printer to guarantee that the colors that are printed are correct. It is essential to calibrate devices since their settings can wander over time, resulting in colors that are not true. You can make sure that the colors that your gadgets output are correct and consistent if you calibrate them regularly.

Profiling

The process of developing a profile that identifies and specifies the color features of a device is referred to as profiling. The color management software makes use of this profile to correctly convert colors across different devices. For instance, if you have a monitor that displays colors in a broader color gamut than your printer, the profile program will change the colors in your image so that they are inside the color gamut of the printer. This is done to guarantee that the image prints correctly. Profiling is essential since various gadgets create colors in a variety of unique ways. You can guarantee that the colors you see on your screen are as similar as possible to the colors that will be printed or shown on other devices if you use profiles to translate colors across devices. This can be done by ensuring that the colors you see on your screen are as near as possible to the colors that are displayed on other devices. Calibration and profiling are necessary phases in the color management process in Photoshop. These procedures are used to guarantee that colors are represented accurately and consistently across a variety of devices. We'll be covering how to calibrate and profile your display in Photoshop here.

Calibrating Your Monitor

To calibrate your monitor in Photoshop, you'll need a hardware device called a colorimeter or spectrophotometer. This equipment can be costly, but it's crucial for producing correct color.

Here are the general procedures for calibrating your display in Photoshop:

Step 1. Install the calibration software that comes with your colorimeter or spectrophotometer.

Step 2. Connect the gadget to your computer and follow the software's instructions for calibration.

Step 3. The program will assist you through setting the monitor's brightness, contrast, and color temperature.

Step 4. Save the generated profile to your PC.

Profiling Your Monitor

After you have properly calibrated your monitor, the next step is to develop a profile that describes the color characteristics of your display. The color management software makes use of this profile to appropriately convert colors across multiple devices.

Creating a profile for your display in Photoshop frequently requires the following steps:

- Launch Photoshop and go to the Edit menu, then go to Color Settings.

- In the Color Settings dialog box, navigate to the Working Spaces section and choose the working environment that best meets your needs.

- In the Color Management Policies section, pick "**Preserve Embedded Profiles**" as the choice for both the RGB and CMYK policies.

- Select "**Use my settings for this device**" from the drop-down menu that appears after selecting the "**More Options**" button.

- Select the profile you just established during the process of calibration from the drop-down menu in the Device Profile section.

- To save your change, click the "**OK**" button at the bottom of the window.

You can verify that the colors you see on your screen are true and constant by calibrating and profiling your monitor in Photoshop. This will allow you to see the colors as they are. When working on color-sensitive tasks, such as picture editing or graphic design, this is of the utmost importance for you to keep in mind.

The RGB color mode

The red, green, and blue color models are the foundation of the RGB color model, which is a method for describing colors that are based on the three basic hues of light. According to this representation, each color is made up of a different mix of these three main hues. The RGB color model is used in a vast array of applications, ranging from computer graphics and digital photography to television and video production.

Photoshop RGB Color mode employs the RGB model, assigning an intensity value to each pixel. of 8-bits-per-channel pictures, the intensity values vary from 0 (black) to 255 (white) for each of the RGB (red, green, blue) components of a color image. For example, a strong red hue has an R value of 246, a G value of 20, and a B value of 50. When the values of all three components are identical, the outcome is a shade of neutral gray. When the values of all components are 255, the outcome is pure white; when the values are 0, pure black.

RGB pictures employ three colors, or channels, to replicate colors on screen. In 8-bits-per-channel pictures, the three channels convert to 24 (8 bits x 3 channels) bits of color information per pixel. With 24-bit pictures, the three channels can generate up to 16.7 million colors per pixel. With 48-bit (16-bits-per-channel) and 96-bit (32-bits-per-channel) pictures, even more colors may be represented per pixel. In addition to being the default mode for new Photoshop pictures, the RGB model is utilized by computer displays to show colors. This implies that while working with color modes other than RGB, such as CMYK, Photoshop transforms the CMYK picture to RGB for display on screen.

Although RGB is a common color model, the specific range of colors depicted might vary, depending on the application or display device. The RGB Color mode in Photoshop changes depending on the working space setting that you pick in the Color Settings dialog box.

CMYK Color mode

In the CMYK mode, each pixel is allocated a percentage value for each of the process inks. The lightest (highlight) colors are allocated small percentages of process ink colors; the darkest (shadow) colors bigger percentages. For example, a brilliant red may comprise 2% cyan, 93% magenta, 90% yellow, and 0% black. In CMYK pictures, pure white is formed when all four components have values of 0%.

Use the CMYK mode when creating an image to be printed using process colors. Converting an RGB picture into CMYK provides a color separation. If you start with an RGB image, it's better to edit first in RGB and then convert to CMYK at the conclusion of the editing process. In RGB mode, you may use the Proof Setup instructions to simulate the effects of a CMYK conversion without affecting the real picture data. You may also utilize CMYK mode to work directly with CMYK pictures scanned or imported from high-end computers.

Although CMYK is a standard color model, the specific range of colors displayed might vary, depending on the press and printing conditions. The CMYK Color mode in Photoshop changes according to the working space setting that you pick in the Color Settings dialog box.

Specifying color management defaults

Color management is an essential part of digital photography because it guarantees that colors are shown correctly in photos regardless of the device being used to view them or the printing method that is being used. In Photoshop, one of the most critical steps you can do to ensure that your photos have a consistent and correct appearance is to select the color management defaults. Here, we will take a more in-depth look at the color management options that are available in Photoshop, as well as how to establish color management defaults depending on the particular workflow and output requirements that you need.

Understanding Color Spaces

We must have a firm grasp of the idea of color spaces before delving into the color management options that are available in Photoshop. A digital image can include only a certain range of colors, and this range is referred to as the "color space." A gamut is a range of colors that can be represented by a color space. Varying color spaces have varying gamut's. The sRGB color space, which is used extensively for the creation of online graphics, and the Adobe RGB color space, which is utilized in professional photography and printing, is two examples of color spaces that were developed to serve particular objectives. Adobe RGB is the color space that is set as the default in Photoshop. Because it offers a broader range than sRGB, Adobe RGB is well-suited for use in professional printing and photography. Nevertheless, it is essential to choose the correct color space for the workflow and output needs that are unique to your organization. For instance, if you're working on graphics for the web, you may want to use the sRGB color space since it's designed to look well when shown on computer displays as well as mobile devices.

Choosing Working Spaces

For RGB, CMYK, and Grayscale picture formats, you may select the default working space in Photoshop. When working with photographs in Photoshop, the color gamut that is utilized is decided by the

working space. Color Settings may be found in the Edit menu, which can be accessed by going to the menu's top-right corner. You will see options in the Color Settings dialog box for working in RGB, CMYK, and gray working spaces respectively. The default working space for RGB pictures is Adobe RGB (1998), which is a color space, designed for use in printing and photography in a professional setting. On the other hand, depending on the specifics of your workflow and the output you demand, you could wish to choose a different kind of working environment. If you're working on anything like online graphics or video, for instance, you may wish to choose the sRGB or Rec. 709 working areas, respectively.

The U.S. Web Coated (SWOP) v2 color space is a standard CMYK color space that is used in commercial printing. This color space is used as the default working space for CMYK pictures. However, depending on the printing technique that you use and the criteria that you have for the output, you may wish to choose a different working environment. For instance, if you are going to be printing on a certain kind of paper, you may want to choose a working environment that is tailored specifically to accommodate printing on that kind of paper. Gray Gamma 2.2, often known as the standard gray working space, is typically used as the default working space when dealing with grayscale photographs. On the other hand, depending on the specifics of your workflow and the output you demand, you could wish to choose a different kind of working environment. For instance, if you are working on a black-and-white photography project, you may want to choose a distinct gray working area that is tailored specifically to the task at hand.

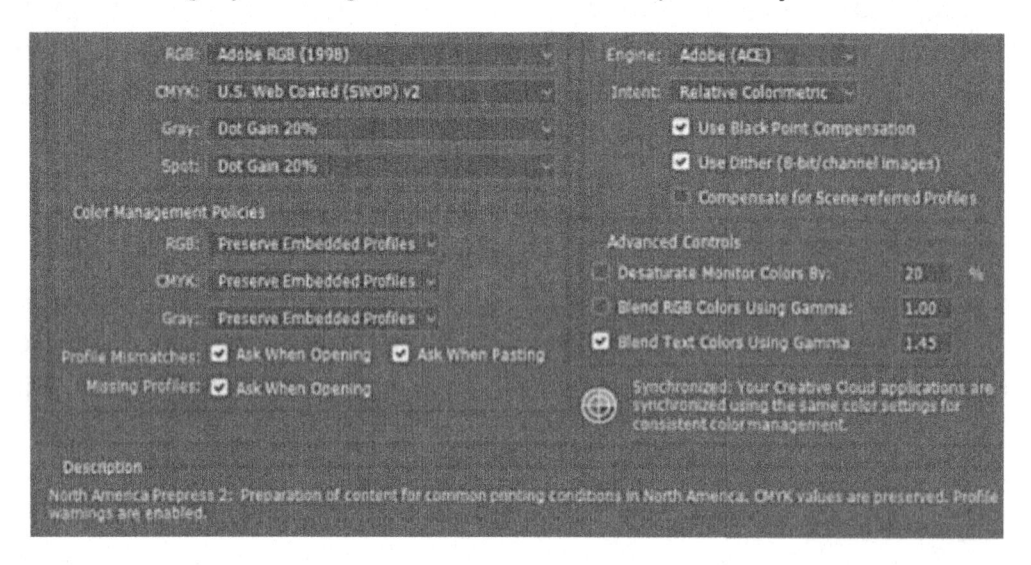

Choosing Color Management Policies

In the Color Settings dialog box, in addition to selecting the working areas you desire, you can also specify the color management rules that work best for you. Photoshop's response when dealing with embedded color profiles and mismatched color spaces is dictated by its color management standards. Photoshop will respect the color space information that is present in each picture file as the normal color management method for RGB photographs is to retain embedded profiles. This guideline guarantees that photos preserve their original color spaces. This is frequently the greatest option to go with as it guarantees that the colors in your images will be displayed accurately. The conversion to the working space is the color management approach that is utilized by default for CMYK photographs. If the picture is previously stored in a different CMYK color space, Photoshop will automatically convert it to the CMYK working space that is specified as the default. This is frequently the best option to go with as it guarantees that the colors will be reproduced accurately in the output that is printed. Preserving embedded profiles is the default step done by the color management policy when dealing with grayscale photographs. The gray working area information that is embedded in each picture file will be honored by Photoshop as a result of this update.

However, depending on the details of your workflow and the output demands, there may be occasions when you will need to make modifications to the color management principles you have in place. For instance, if you are working on a legacy picture that does not have an embedded profile; you may wish to pick the "Ask When Opening" option for RGB photos to assure that Photoshop offers you the chance to select a working area when you open the image. This option is accessible for both RGB and CMYK files. Alternatively, if you are dealing with photographs that have color spaces that do not correlate with one another; you may decide to select the "Convert to Working Space" option from the drop-down menu to assure that colors are presented accurately in the final output.

Specifying Other Color Settings

In addition to selecting working regions and color management rules, you can also configure numerous color settings in Photoshop to assure that your images are exhibited accurately.

The following are examples of these environments:

Rendering Intent: This parameter determines how colors are mapped when they are converted from one color space to another. It is utilized for converting colors from one color space to another. The rendering intent that is used by default is called Relative Colorimetric, and it is frequently the one that delivers the most realistic portrayal of colors. However, depending on the nature of your workflow and the output demands, there may be scenarios in which you will need to pick a different rendering purpose.

Proof Setup: This option offers you the chance to check a preview of how your image will appear when it is printed or viewed on a range of devices. CMYK, RGB, and Grayscale are just a handful of the proof settings that you may pick from. This is a great tool for ensuring that the appearance of your images stays the same across a range of platforms, including printing techniques.

Black Point Compensation: This adjustment makes sure that the darkest tones in your image are seen accurately by providing them the necessary level of contrast. It is advised that you keep this option activated so that your images have a comprehensive spectrum of tones.

Use Black Point Compensation: Make sure the darkest tones in your image are portrayed accurately by utilizing the Black Point Compensation option. This may be found in the Advanced Settings menu. It is advised that you keep this option activated so that your images have a comprehensive spectrum of tones.

Identifying out-of-gamut colors

When working with Photoshop, one of the most critical tasks in color management is finding colors that are outside of the program's range. Out-of-gamut colors are colors that are not within the range of hues that may be reproduced by a specific output device, such as a printer or monitor. These colors cannot be seen on the device. When these colors are present in an image, they can generate color shifting, banding, and other anomalies when the image is printed or seen on a screen.

Understanding Gamut

The term **"gamut"** refers to the range of colors that a certain output device, such as a printer or monitor, can reproduce. It is crucial to grasp what we mean when we say "gamut" before we begin distinguishing out-of-gamut colors. Various electrical instruments each have their specific gamut, which represents the color space that may be reproduced by that particular tool. A conventional CMYK printer, for instance, has a gamut that is smaller than that of a current RGB display. When working in Photoshop, it is crucial to be aware of the gamut of the output device you are using so that you can take photographs that are suited precisely for that device. If you produce a picture using colors that are not inside the gamut of your output device, it is possi-ble that those colors may not be represented properly when the image is printed or viewed. Identifying colors that are outside of the gamut is crucial at this time.

Identifying Out-of-Gamut Colors

In Photoshop, identifying colors that are outside of the program's color space may be performed in a few various approaches. The "Gamut Warning" function, which indicates any colors in your image that fall outside of the gamut of your working area or output device, is one of the simplest techniques. This feature is also one of the easiest.

To make benefit of the Gamut Warning feature, please proceed as follows:

• Launch Photoshop and open your image there.

• Select "**View**" from the primary menu, and after that, pick "**Gamut Warning**."

• Gray will be used to accentuate any colors in your image that are outside of the gamut of your working space or output device if those colors are determined to be present.

• To disable the Gamut Warning feature, select "**View**" from the main menu, and then pick "**Gamut Warning**" once again from the drop-down menu that displays.

Utilizing Photoshop's "**Color Picker**" tool is yet another approach for discovering colors that are outside of the gamut's range. If you use the Color Picker tool in Photoshop to sample a color from your image, the application will show you the RGB or CMYK values associated with that color. These colors are deemed to be out-of-gamut if any of those values fall outside of the range of values that can be reproduced by the output device you are using.

Follow these steps to identify colors that are outside of the color spectrum using the Color Picker:

- Make a selection using the "**Color Picker**" tool, which can be located in the toolbar on the left side of the Photoshop interface.

- To pick a color from your image, just click on the one you want.

- The Color Picker window will update to reflect the RGB or CMYK values that match the color that was just picked.

- The colors in question are regarded to be "out-of-gamut" if any of the RGB or CMYK values are greater than the range of values that can be reproduced by your output device.
- Simply make a pick of a different tool from the toolbar to disable the Color Picker tool.

The use of a third-party plugin or software is yet another approach for assessing whether colors are outside of the gamut. You may identify colors that are outside of Photoshop's gamut with the aid of several plugins and programs that are available for download. The Color Think plugin and the Adobe Color Management Module are two outstanding examples of well-liked alterna-tives.

Managing Out-of-Gamut Colors

After you have discovered which colors in your image are outside of the gamut, there are a few various activities you can take to regulate those colors and assure that your images seem their best when they are printed or presented. These approaches may be found in the next section. You have numerous options here, one of which is to adjust the colors in your image so that they fit inside the gamut of the output device you're using. Several alternative ways, such as altering the image's color balance, saturation, and brightness settings, can be utilized to ac-complish this purpose. You may also target particular sections of your image that have colors that are outside of the gamut by applying selective adjustments to the colors in those spots.

Converting your image to a different color space that has a broader gamut is an extra choice that you have. For instance, if you are working in the sRGB color space but your printer has a broader gamut, you may convert your image to the Adobe RGB color space to make use of the larger gamut. This would allow you to get the most out of your printer's capabilities. However, it is vital to bear in mind that converting your image to a new color space might also result in the development of color shifts and other artifacts. Because of this, it is necessary to thor-oughly examine the effects of any conversions that you conduct. You might also consider employing a different output device that gives a broader gamut, which is the last choice. For instance, if you are presently working with a printer that has a restricted gamut, you may want to consider switching to a different printer that can reproduce a greater variety of colors. In a similar vein, if you are working with a monitor that has a narrow gamut, you may want to think about moving to a more current display that can show a broader variety of colors.

Proofing document colors on a monitor

You are going to pick a proof profile so that you may view a simulation of what the colors of the document will look like when it is printed on the screen. Having a precise proof profile enables you to prove the printed output on the screen, sometimes known as soft proof. This on-screen simulation was constructed using a proof setup, which describes the circumstances under which printing should take place. Photoshop offers you access to a wide number of features that might aid you in proofing images for various activities, including printing on a variety of devices and printers.

In this activity, you will focus on developing a personalized proof setting. After that, you have the option to retain the settings so that you may apply them to subsequent photographs that will be reproduced in the same manner.

Select **View > Proof Setup > Custom** from the navigation bar. The dialog window for setting the proof condition displays. Check that the **Preview** option is selected.

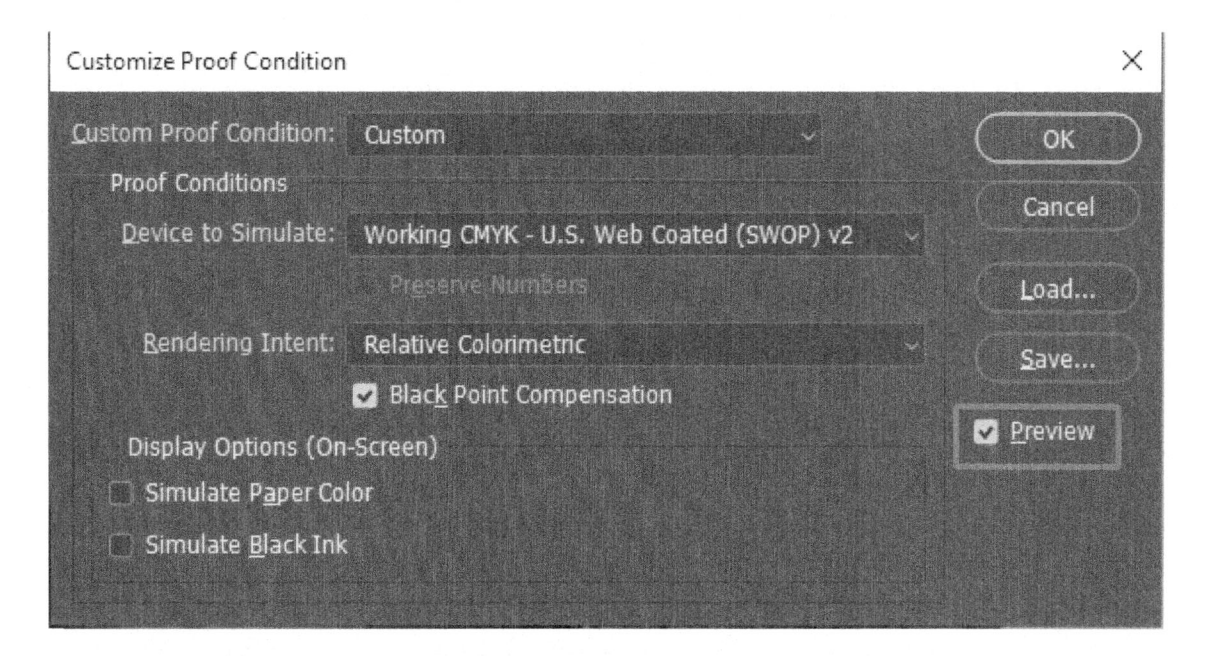

Select a profile that represents the final output device from the Device to Simulate option. For example, pick the profile that corresponds to the printer that you will use to print the image. If you do not have a specific printer, the profile Working CMYK-U.S. Web Coated (SWOP v2) should be utilized. This is the one that is presently defaulted.

A printer profile not only specifies the output device, but also the precise settings, ink, and paper that were utilized to construct the profile. Changing even one of these elements might result in a shift in the color gamut that is replicated by the onscreen proof; consequently, it is crucial to pick a profile that is as faithful as possible to the final printing circumstances.

If you have selected a different profile, you need to ensure that the option to Preserve Numbers is deselected.

The Preserve Numbers option generates a virtual depiction of how colors will look if they are not converted to the color space of the output device. Depending on the CMYK output profile that you pick, this option might be designated as Preserve CMYK Numbers.

Check the Rendering Intent option and make sure Relative Colorimetric is picked there.

The manner by which color is changed from one color space to another is governed by the rendering intent. The Relative Colorimetric approach preserves the links between colors without losing color integrity.

Choose the option to Simulate Black Ink if it is shown to you for the profile that you have selected. Then uncheck that option and choose the one that reads Simulate Paper Color; you'll notice that doing so also chooses the one that says Simulate Black Ink automatically.

Take notice that the image looks to have lost part of its contrast. The bulk of paper is not a completely bright white hue; Paper hue imitates that look. Because most black ink is not totally uniform or neutral black, Black Ink is meant to replicate the look of black ink. Each one takes this information from the output profile if it is available. When the Customize Proof Condition dialog box isn't active, you may see the document with or without the current proof settings by choosing or deselecting the see > Proof Colors command.

When you switch on the Display Options, you may see that the contrast and saturation have diminished, but you shouldn't be worried by this. Even if the image may seem to be worse, the soft-proofing simulation is only being honest about how the image will print; paper and ink simply cannot recreate the same range of tones and colors that a monitor can. If you pick a paper substance and inks of greater quality, you may aid the printed picture to more nearly resemble the image on the screen.

To compare the image as it looks on the computer with how it will print based on the profile you picked, you may toggle the Preview option. This will allow you to observe the difference between the two. After that, pick the OK button.

You may swiftly toggle Proof Colors on or off by using the keyboard shortcut for View > Proof Colors: Press Ctrl-Y (Windows) or Command-Y (macOS). This will allow you to check the print color simulation while you work.

To turn off Proof Colors, go to the View menu and then pick Proof Colors if the function is already set on. This command allows you to activate or disable the soft-proof settings that you defined in the Customize Proof Condition dialog box. These choices may be accessed in the Customize Proof Condition dialog box.

Bringing colors into the output gamut

A key aspect of the picture editing process in Photoshop is bringing colors into the output gamut of the application. It is the process of changing and mapping the colors of an image so that it may be shown appropriately on various output devices such as printers, monitors, and projectors. The purpose of this method is to assure that the colors can be presented precisely. A specified color space, also known as a gamut, is employed during the generation of a picture in Photoshop. However, not every output device can exhibit the full-color spectrum. Because of this, it is highly vital to include colors in the output gamut to guarantee that the final image will appear the same on all devices.

The first thing you need to do to bring colors within the output gamut in Photoshop is to establish the color space, also known as the gamut, of the output device. This information can be collected from the device's specifications, or more accurately measuring the colors can be done with a colorimeter or spectrophotometer. After finding the color space of the output device, the following step is to change the colors of the picture such that they are contained inside the gamut. In Photoshop, bringing colors within the output gamut may be performed by the use of a variety of various approaches. Utilizing the Gamut Warning feature is one of the most frequent methods to solve this problem. This function reveals the portions of the picture that are out of gamut, which means that they cannot be shown properly on the output device. This may be done by comparing the produced image to the original. You may access the Gamut Warning feature by choosing **View > Gamut Warning** or by using the keyboard shortcut **Ctrl + Shift + Y** (Windows) or **Command + Shift + Y** (Mac).

Utilizing the Soft Proofing tool that's accessible in Photoshop is yet another approach for getting colors inside the output range that you're dealing with. Before you print the image or send it out to be exported, you may use soft proofing to simulate how it will appear on the output device. You may access this feature by choosing **View > Proof Setup > Custom** or by using the keyboard shortcut **Ctrl + Y** (Windows) or **Command+ Y** (Mac). Alternatively, you may use the **Y** key on your keyboard. Select the color space or gamut that corresponds to the output device in the Proof Setup dialog box, and then click the **OK** button. After that, Photoshop will simulate how the picture will appear on the output device and indicate any sections that are not inside the gamut of permitted colors. After you have discovered the areas of the image that do not fall within the gamut, you may make use of the various correction tools that are available in Photoshop to bring the colors back into the output gamut. The **Hue/Saturation** adjustment layer is one of the most widely used tools for changing colors in digital photographs.

With the aid of this tool, you'll be able to adjust the hue, saturation, and brightness of particular colors inside the image. You may change the hue of colors that are outside of the output gamut by using this tool, or you can lower the saturation of colors that are out of the gamut by using this tool. The Selective Color adjustment layer is yet another approach that may be used to bring colors into the output range. Using the multiple color channels of the image as a reference, this tool enables you to adjust the colors within the image.

If the blues in a picture are, for instance, outside of the output gamut, you may use the Selective Color adjustment layer to make modifications to the cyan and magenta channels to bring the blues within the gamut for output. In addition to adjustment layers, Photoshop contains various color correction tools that may be used to bring colors inside the output range. These tools may be found in the Edit menu of the software. Adjustment tools such as Color Balance, Curves, and Levels are covered in this category. The colors may be tweaked in a variety of ways, depending on which of these tools is employed, and each of these tools has its own set of specific capabilities. For instance, you may vary the tone range of the image by using the Curves tool, and you can edit the color balance of the image by using the Color Balance tool. Both of these tools are featured in the Edit menu.

Converting a picture to CMYK

In general, it is a good idea to operate in RGB mode for as long as possible so that your alterations can take place inside the broader color range that RGB gives. Converting between modes can also generate color value rounding issues, which can result in unwanted color alterations, particularly when conducted numerous times. These alterations may become more pro-nounced as the number of conversions grows.

TIP: Ask the print service provider who will be responsible for the output of your work if you are confused as to whether or when it is essential to convert photographs to CMYK. They can advise you on the image preparation processes that will produce optimum results when utilized with their prepress equipment. Save CMYK copies of your final pictures after making any required modifications if the printing technique you employ needs images to be stored in that color mode. You should preserve the original document in RGB mode if you also intend to print the image using an inkjet printer or distribute it digitally at a later time.

1. Click the Channels tab to bring up the Channels panel.

Because the image is now being presented in RGB format, there are three channels available for selection: red, green, and blue. In actuality, the RGB channel is not independent but rather a synthesis of the other two. You will also notice a channel with the label Hue/Saturation 1 Mask; this channel keeps the mask information for the layer that is chosen in the Layers panel at now.

2. Select CMYK Color from the Color Mode selection under Image.

3. When you see the message that informs you that you may lose some adjustment layers, click the Merge option. When the layers are blended, it is simpler to retain the appearance of the colors.

A new message comes on the screen, which reads as follows: "You are about to convert to CMYK using the "U.S. The profile is named "Web Coated (SWOP) v2." It's conceivable that this is not what you had in mind. To choose a different profile, go to the Edit menu and click "Convert to Profile." This message notifies you that the presently selected CMYK profile is in the United States. Web Coated (SWOP) v2 is the CMYK color profile that is set as the default in Photoshop. It is likely that the actual prepress specification or proofing standard that will be employed will not be reflected by that profile. In a project that takes place in the real world, you would ask the print service provider which CMYK profile to employ for color conversions. The print service provider may be able to give a customized profile that closely represents the tone and color range of their equipment. You would then load that custom CMYK profile into the standard location for ICC profiles on your operating system so that you can choose it as the CMYK Working Space in the **Edit > Color Settings** dialog box, or so that you can choose it when converting the image to CMYK using the more advanced and precise **Edit > Convert to Profile** command.

4. When you see the message regarding the color profile that was used during the conversion, click the OK button.

Cyan, magenta, yellow, and black are the channels that are currently presented on the Channels pane. In addition to that, the CMYK composite is presented. During the converting process, the layers were consolidated into a single layer, hence now there is just one layer displayed in the Layers panel. When converting a picture to CMYK, it is vital to take into consideration how the image will ultimately be utilized. The color profiles of various printing equipment vary, and these variances might alter the picture that is finally created. It is strongly advised that you establish a suit-able color profile by first receiving some advice from the device maker or the printing business. In addition to converting the color mode of the complete picture to CMYK, you can also change the color mode of individual layers. This is beneficial if you have an image that comprises of numerous layers, and you merely want to convert parts of those layers to CMYK. click the layer you wish to con-vert to CMYK, and then from the main menu, click **Layer > New Adjustment Layer > Hue/Saturation**.

This will transform the layer to CMYK. Within the **Hue/Saturation** dialog box, pick the Colorize option. Then, under the **Hue/Saturation** dialog box, change the sliders for Hue, Saturation, and Lightness to obtain the desired color. Then, from the main menu, click **Image > Mode > CMYK** Color to change the color mode of the layer to CMYK.

Saving the picture as Photoshop PDF

• Go to the main menu and click **File > Save As** from there.

- Make your selection in the Save As dialog box to designate the file's destination before clicking Save.

- In the "**File Name**" section, input the name you want to assign the file.

- Make your pick using the Format (or Save As Type) drop-down menu and Select Photoshop PDF.

- To continue, you must first choose the Save option.

You will see that a new dialog box entitled Adobe PDF Options has emerged. This dialog box will offer you a choice of settings that you may use to adjust the PDF output.

The following is a list of major alternatives that you may wish to take into consideration:

Adobe PDF Preset: You may pick from numerous different settings, including High-Quality Print, PDF/X-la, and the Smallest File Size. Choose the one that caters most closely to your requirements.

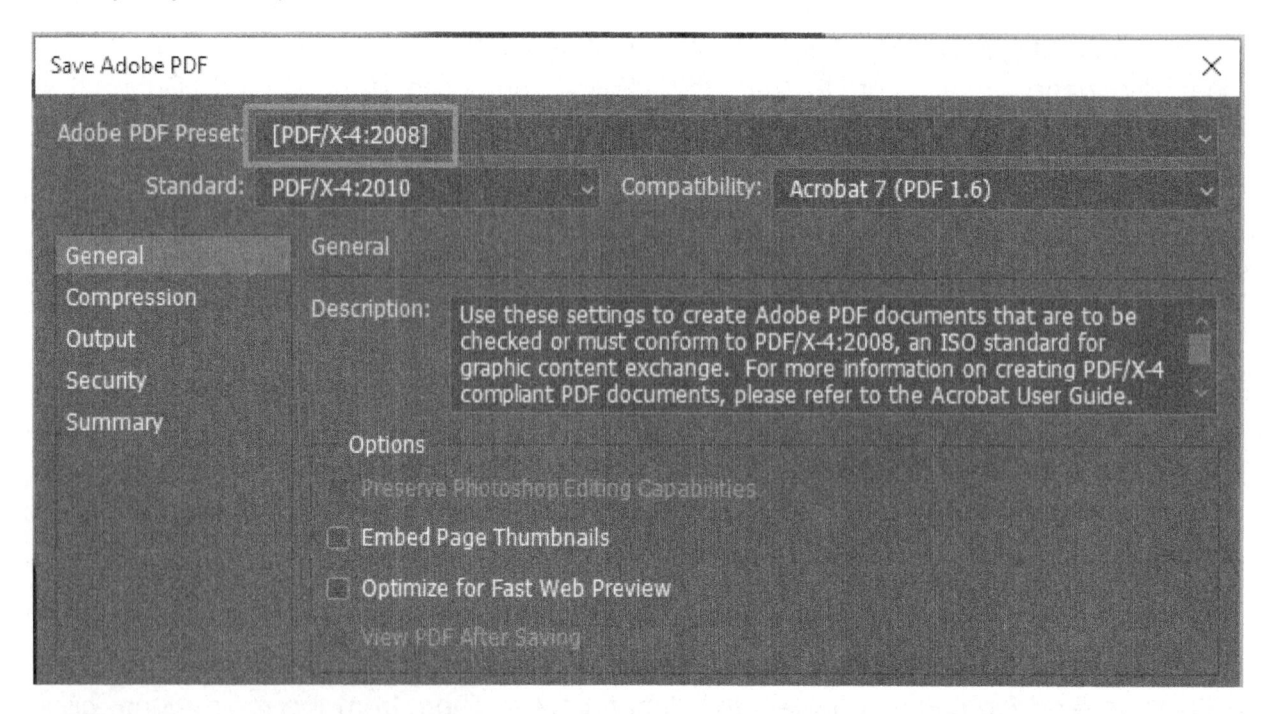

Compression: This section allows you the opportunity to alter the compression settings for color pictures, grayscale photos, and black-and-white images correspondingly. You have the option of picking the amount of compression, or you may choose to have none at all.

Output: This is where you may pick the profile, color space, and resolution settings for the output. You should be able to get by with the default settings in the great majority of circumstances, but you may always adjust them to better suit your needs.

Layers: If you desire to maintain the ability to utilize Photoshop to change layers, text, and other objects included inside the PDF, you will need to make sure that the Preserve Photoshop Editing Capabilities option is switched on.

Security: If you feel it is critical, you can impose password protection and limitations on the PDF file. This will allow you to regulate who may access the file and prevent illicit adjustments. After you have changed the parameters to your desire, go to the File menu and pick Save PDF to save the picture as a Photoshop PDF.

Printing a CMYK picture from Photoshop

You may examine the quality of your image by making a color composite, which is commonly referred to as a color comp. The red, green, and blue channels of an RGB picture, or the cyan, ma-genta, yellow, and black channels of a CMYK image, may be merged into a single print to make a color composite. This represents how the printed picture will appear in its final form.

TIP: Your desktop printer is a wonderful tool for creating color separations, which may aid guarantee that colors will be printed on the right plate. However, the precision of a true plate setter can't be equaled by the separations created by a desktop printer. Printing proofs for tasks that are going to be executed on a press utilizing a desktop printer equipped with an Adobe Postscript RIP (raster image processor) will result in more accurate proofs. When you pick the option to print color separations in Photoshop, the computer generates a separate sheet, also known as a plate, for each ink. Printing a CMYK image requires four separate plates, one for each color utilized in the process. You'll be printing color separations as part of this practice.

In most circumstances, the following procedure will be used for printing color separations straight from Photoshop:

You will need to alter the settings for the halftone screen. Your print service provider should be checked for the required settings. You should print some test separations to ensure that the items are shown on the right separation.

Print the final separations onto the film or the plate. Your print service provider will generally take care of this task for you.

Step 1. Select "**File**" > "**Print**" from inside the image.

Any document you print in Photoshop will appear as a composite picture by default. To print this file with separations, you will need to edit the parameters in the Photoshop Print parameters dialog box to match the desired results.

Step 2. In the dialog box called "**Print Settings**," make the following adjustments in Photoshop:

TIP: If the Separations option is not available in the Color Handling menu of the Photoshop Print Settings dialog box, click the Done button, make sure the project is in CMYK mode (**Image > Mode> CMYK Color**), and then try again.

In the section marked "**Printer Setup**," check to confirm that the Printer that is currently chosen is accurate.

Select Separations from the Color Handling option inside the Color Management section of the software.

In the Position and Size section, validate the adjustments. This **11" x 7"** document may be too big for many desktop printers to print at its real size. You may pick Scale to Fit Media to fit the document to the current print size; to view this option you may need to scroll down or enlarge the dialog box.

You will need to scroll down and alter the Postscript parameters, such as the halftone choices if you are using a printer that is compatible with Adobe Postscript. Be aware that the outcomes of printing on a desktop printer might not be the same as those generated by a prepress output device.

Choose Print from the menu. (If you are confident that you do not want to print color separations, you may either click the Cancel button or the Done button; the only difference is that picking Done will keep the existing print settings.)

TIP: If you cannot see the area named "**Position and Size**" in the Photoshop Print Settings dialog box, you will need to scroll down the right-side panel until you do. This section is situated two sections below the one labeled "Color Management." You may also make the Photoshop Print Settings dialog box bigger by dragging one of its corners or borders, which will allow you to examine more settings at the same time.

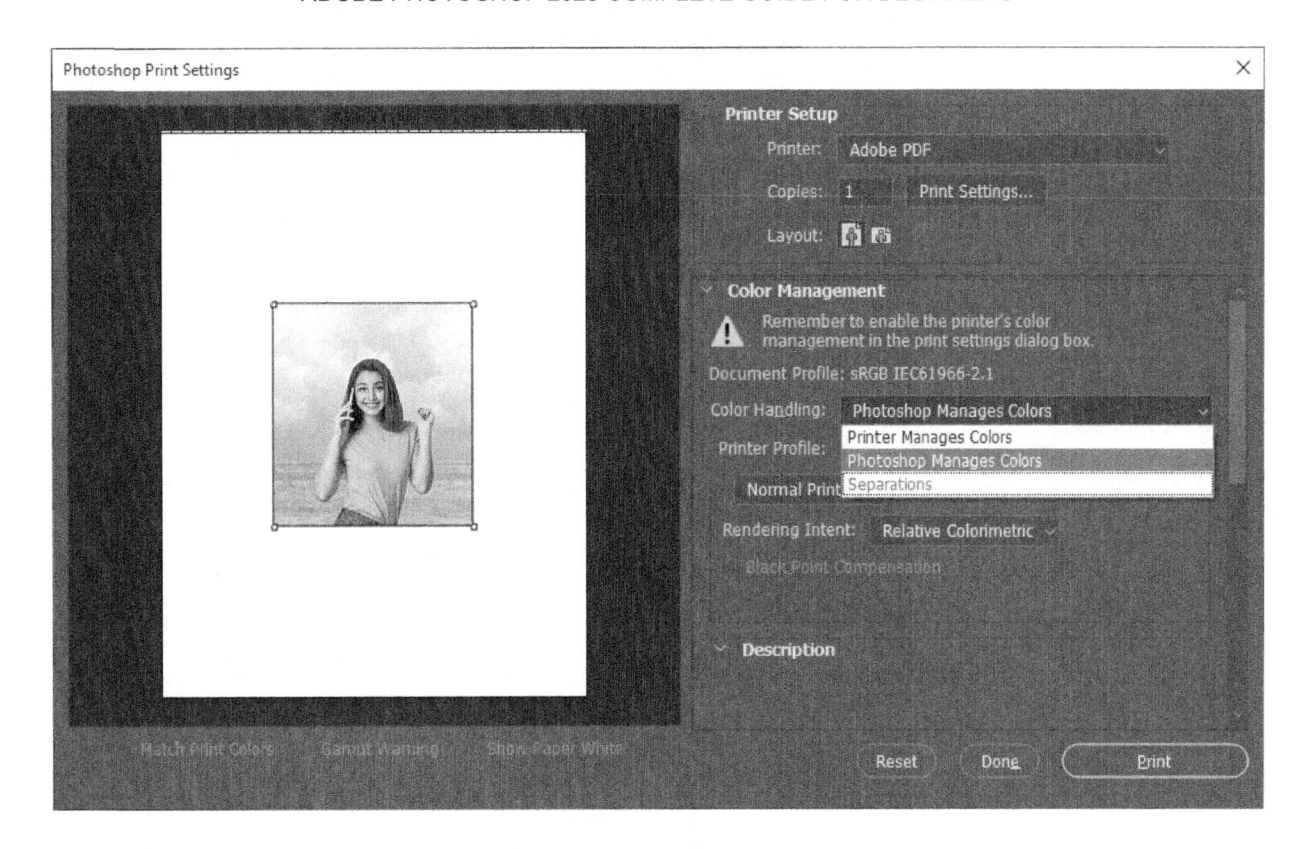

ADOBE PHOTOSHOP 2023 COMPLETE GUIDE FOR BEGINNERS

CHAPTER 15: EXPLORING NEURAL FILTERS

Understanding Neural Filters

Neural Filters is a feature in Photoshop that allows users to conduct intricate picture adjustments and upgrades with only one click by harnessing the power of artificial intelligence (AI). These filters conduct an analysis of the image with the aid of machine learning algorithms and then generate new visual content that is based on the original image. Because it is built on the Adobe Sensei AI platform, the Neural Filters feature can execute real-time analysis and alterations on the photographs that it processes. Users are now able to perform intricate and elaborate effects that were before difficult or impossible to do manually. This is made possible by a feature that is always learning and developing.

Here's how you can use Neural Filters in Photoshop:

• Launch Photoshop, select a picture to work with and go to the Filters menu.

• Make a selection in the Neural Filters drop-down menu to bring up the Neural Filters dialog box.

• The Neural Filters dialog box gives you a range of different filter settings that you may use in the picture. These contain a broad number of settings, some of which are Style Transfer, Colorize, and Super Resolution.

• After picking whatever filters option you desire to use, make any required modifications to the filter settings to get the effect you want.

• When you are done making modifications to the settings, pick the image to which you wish to apply the filter, and then click the Apply option.

A large array of effects, ranging from artistic transformations to technological breakthroughs, may be produced with the use of neural filters.

The following are samples of some of the most common neural filters:

Style Transfer: This filter provides you the option to duplicate the style of one image and apply it to another. For instance, you may offer a snapshot of the appearance of a well-known artwork by replicating the painting's style and so providing an original and creative impression.

Colorize: This filter provides you the option to add color to a monochrome image. The image is examined by the AI filter, which then applies color to the image depending on its context and the subject matter of the image.

Smart Portrait: With this filter, you may automatically improve the appearance of a person's face in a portrait. The filter enables modifications to be made to face expressions, may eradicate imperfections, and can balance out skin tones.

Super Resolution: This filter takes use of artificial intelligence to boost the image's resolution while keeping its quality intact. This is especially beneficial for images that have been decreased in size or otherwise manipulated.

Depth-Aware Haze Removal: This filter helps you to reduce haze from an image while keeping the three-dimensionality and depth of the scene. The filter utilizes AI to analyze the depth of the image and eliminates haze depending on the distance that exists between the elements in the picture.

In general, the Neural Filters panel in Photoshop is a highly useful tool for altering and transforming photographs. This tool can assist users save time and effort while also enabling them to build more complicated and nuanced effects. However, it is vital to keep in mind that Neural Filters might not always deliver the outcome that is expected. Therefore, it is vital to exper-iment with a number of unique alternatives and settings to get the ideal outcome that is attainable.

Exploring the Neural Filters workspace

The Neural Filters workspace in Photoshop is where users may apply and set multiple picture alterations and improvements enabled by artificial intelligence. Users may employ a range of filter choices in this workspace, which are aimed to automate tough editing operations and provide one-of-a-kind aesthetic effects.

When you visit the Neural Filters workspace for the first time in Photoshop, a dialog box will display a list of the various filter choices to pick from. These options are organized in certain categories, such as **"Face Cleanup,"** **"Style Transfer,"** and **"Super Resolution,"** amongst others. Each filter choice comes with its own specific set of controls and settings, which may be modified to achieve a range of distinct effects.

In Photoshop, the Neural Filters may be divided down into the following categories:

Featured: These are the final filters that were released. The results of these filters fulfill severe standards and are in conformity with all applicable legal, identity protection, and inclusion requirements. To begin utilizing a featured neural filter, navigate to **Filter > Neural Filters > All Filters > Featured** and pick an option from the drop-down box.

Beta: You can try these filters if you have the beta version. The procedures or models utilized for machine learning are presently undergoing further improvement. You are free to use and test these filters, but bear in mind that the results may not be what you think. To begin working with one of the highlighted neural filters, go to **Filter > Neural Filters > All Filters > Beta** and pick one from the available options there.

Wait List: This category comprises filters that are currently unavailable but may become so in the not-too-distant future. To understand more about what's to come, go to **Filter > Neural Filters > Wait List** and pick anybody from the list. You can then examine what's on the horizon.

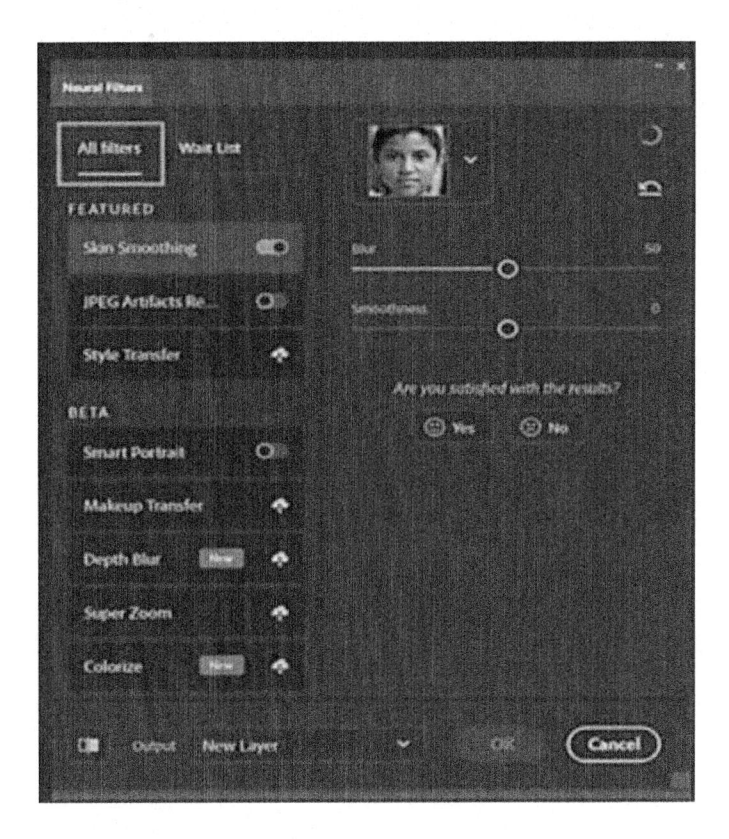

Output options

Your resultant modifications are stored as output in one of the following ways:

• Current layer - Destructively apply filters onto the current layer.

• New layer - Apply filters as a new layer

- New layer masked- Apply filters as a new layer with a mask of the resulting pixel output.

- Smart filter -Convert the current layer to a Smart Object and apply filters as an editable smart filter.

- New document -Output filters as a new Photoshop document.

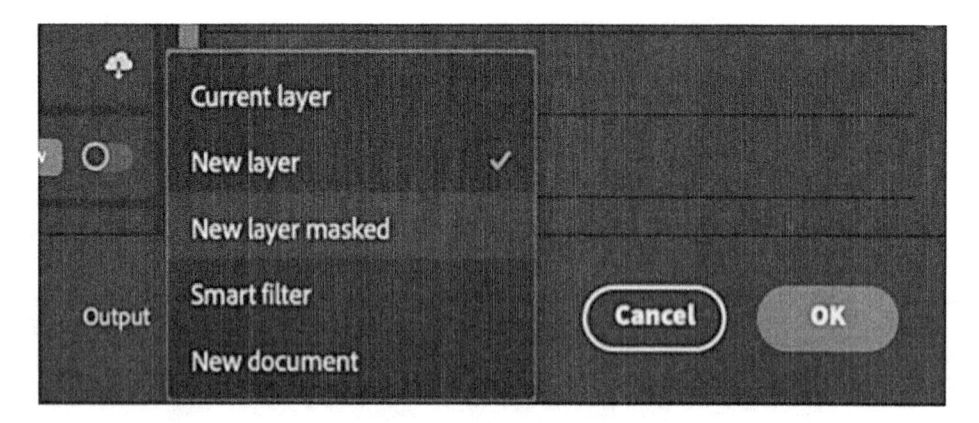

Additional Features

PREVIEW CHANGES

To flip between the before and after preview for each filter, click on the preview mode icon in the lower-left corner of the gallery.

RESET

To restore the impact of any filter to its initial values, click on the symbol at the upper right corner of the gallery.

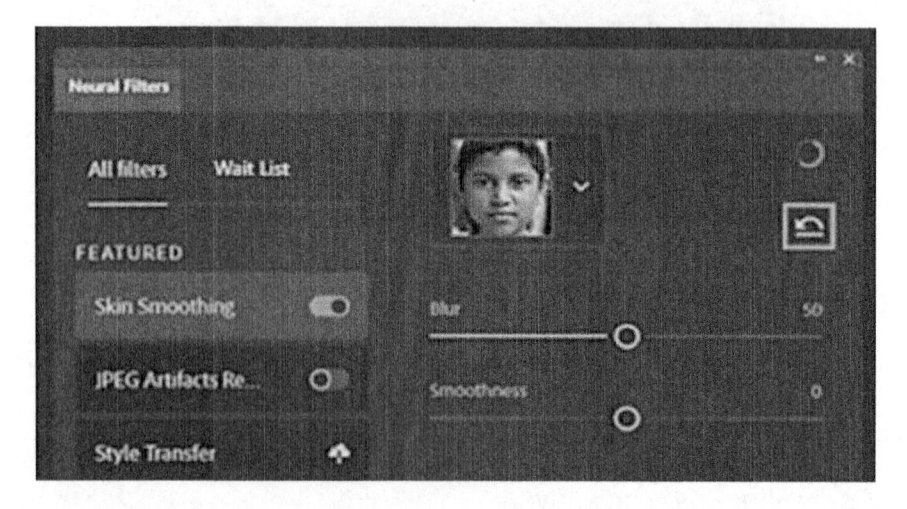

Restoring an ancient portrait picture

Scroll down until you reach the Restoration category in the list of filters, and then click the toggle switch that is positioned next to the Photo Restoration filter to activate and apply that filter. (If there are no available choices, but a Download button does appear instead, you should click the Download button as this implies that the filter has not yet been installed. The filter will automatically install itself when the download is done, and it will then be ready for you to use.) To examine the changes between the current version and the one you started with, utilize the Show Original button found at the very bottom of the workspace. If you click once, the alterations will be concealed, and the original will be visible; clicking again will show the changes again. If you don't see any improvement, try raising the magnification to 100 percent or more.

NOTE: Some Neural Filters might have a label that reads "Beta," which implies that they are functioning but are presently being worked on. You can use them, but bear in mind that when the final version is made public, the filters could produce different results, or some of the choices might be updated.

Make any required edits to the first two Photo Restoration selections, and then proceed to assess your work by going back to step 2:

• Scroll to the top of the image or zoom out as much as necessary till you can see it. Scratches and rips may be observed in that particular region of the photo print.

• Reduce the quantity of scratches to around 20 percent. There is a potential that a progress bar at the bottom of the image will hint that it will take some time. When it is done, the scratch is immediately removed, and you may check to see whether it was successful by tapping the Show Original option.

TIP: If you choose to make the value of a Neural Filter choice higher, you should be aware that this may have unforeseen and negative effects on some components of the picture. In most circumstances, it is advisable to preserve little imperfections, such as spots and wrinkles, and then fast clean them up using various retouching procedures. Using the Restoration Neural Filter allows you to make considerable modifications to this image. Select Smart Filter from the drop-down option labeled Output, and after that, click OK to leave the Neural Filters window. You should now close the document to save your modifications.

Adding color and depth blur

Using the Neural Filters in Photoshop to add color and depth blur to an image as a method of improving the visual impact of the shot is an amazing approach to accomplish. The color and depth blur filters may give a picture additional dimension and depth by emphasizing specified sections of the image with a selected color and blurring the backdrop.

This may be performed by emphasizing particular sections of the image.

1. Start by opening the picture: Launch Photoshop and load the image you desire to alter into the application. You may use this approach on any image to which you desire to apply color and depth blur.

2. Convert the picture into a smart object: To apply Neural Filters on the image, you will need to first transform the image into a smart object. Simply right-click on the picture layer then goes to the drop-down menu and choose the "Convert to Smart Object" option.

3. Navigate to the workspace for the Neural Filters: In Photoshop, you can reach the Neural Filters workspace by heading to the Filter menu and selecting Neural Filters from the drop-down menu.

4. Pick the Colorize filter: In this stage, you will pick the Colorize filter from the available options in the Neural Filters workspace. Utilizing this filter, you may selectively add color to the image.

5. alter the parameters: After you have picked the Colorize filter, alter the settings to add color to the image. The quantity of color that is added to the image may be changed, as well as the color that you like to add. You may also make use of the mask tool to pick the sections of the image to which you would want to add color.

6. Apply the Depth Blur filter: After you have completed adding color to the image, it is time to apply the Depth Blur filter so that the image will have more depth and dimensions. Choose the Depth Blur filter from the drop-down menu of choices that displays when you're working in the Neural Filters workspace.

7. Modify the parameters to add depth blur to the image. Once you have picked the Depth Blur filter, change the parameters to add depth blur to the picture. You may decide which sections of the image are fuzzy by changing both the amount of blur and the depth range of the effect.

8. view the changes: After applying the Colorize and Depth Blur filters, you can view the changes by clicking on the Before/After button in the Neural Filters workspace. This will bring up a window that displays the image before and after the filters have been applied. This offers you the chance to compare the edited image to the original image and make any appropriate alterations depending on the results.

9. Make any essential modifications to the settings: You may make any necessary adjustments to the parameters of the Colorize and Depth Blur filters to acquire the appearance you desire. You may finetune the sections where you wish to add color and blur by altering the quantity of color and blur, as well as the settings for the mask. This provides you with greater control.

10. Save the image: Once you are pleased with the edits that you have made, save the image using a format that has excellent quality, such as JPEG or TIFF. This will supply you with a digital duplicate of the edited image that you may maintain for a substantial length of time in the future.

About Output Options in Neural Filters

A Neural Filter may give numerous alternatives for applying filter results to the document, in the Output menu. The number of possibilities you see may be different than in the picture below, depending on which filter and filter settings are selected.

Your option influences the amount of editing flexibility you have afterwards.

The current Layer applies the result to the specified layer. This permanently modifies the original layer. The only way to back out of it is to undo it before you shut and save the document. We recommend utilizing one of the following choices instead since they keep the current layer intact.

New Layer transfers the result to a complete copy of the specified layer, keeping that original unmodified.

New Layer Masked transfers the result to a copy of the chosen layer with the altered regions showing via a layer mask. This helps guarantee that sections of the image that were not meant to be modified remain as they are on the original layer.

Smart Filter adds the result to a Smart Object produced from the specified layer. You may adjust the filter parameters later by double-clicking that layer's Neural Filters instance in the Layers panel.

New Document applies the result to a duplicate document containing the filter results on one layer.

The trade-off you intend to make between file size and flexibility might impact your selection. More editing versatility is afforded by extra layers and Smart Objects, however the file sizes they output are frequently greater. When you make several adjustments inside a filter, such as modifying individual faces in a group image using a different filter, all of those edits are mirrored in the final output. If you apply Smart Portrait and Style Transfer to the same layer, for instance, both of those effects will be applied to a single layer, which is referred to as a Smart Filter. It's pos-sible that the results that Neural Filters generate won't be immaculate straight immediately. By applying the outputs of Neural Filters as a distinct masked layer, you may freely mix them with the original layer to produce a more convincing end, while still saving several steps in contrast to more conventional ways that demand more work.

Creating a more convincing composite

When integrating multiple pictures in Photoshop, it is fairly unusual to stumble into tone and color discrepancies between the individual images. This might convey the sense that the com-posite is neither coherent nor convincing.

The good news is that there are a few different Neural Filters that can aid in addressing these challenges and providing a picture that is more consistent and cohesive.

1. Color Matching: You may use the "**Color Match**" filter to get the colors of two distinct images to appear the same. Using this filter, you may pick one image to use as a reference for the color tone you wish to obtain, and then apply that color tone to another image. This is especially beneficial when integrating several images that were acquired with various cameras or under diverse lighting settings.

2. Colorization: The "**Colorize**" filter enables you to add color to an image that was previously in black and white. When working with images from the past or ones that are black and white, this approach might be beneficial. You may obtain a look that is more consistent by adding color to the image. The color tone of the photograph will match the color tone of the other photos in the composite.

3. Texture Synthesis: The "**Texture Synthesis**" filter may be used to construct a new texture from an existing texture in the image. When merging photographs with varied degrees of detail or texture, this approach might be beneficial. You may achieve a more consistent appearance for the composite by synthesizing a new texture from an existing one. This will allow you to match the texture of the photographs that are included in the composite.

4. Depth Blur: The "**Depth Blur**" filter can be added to an image to give it a better feeling of the depth of field. When compiling images that were shot at varied distances or with a range of lenses, this is a really valuable method to have.

5. Lighting: The "Lighting" filter may be used to adjust the lighting of an image. Adding depth of field to a photograph helps you to achieve a more consistent appearance that matches the depth of field of the other photos that are included in the composite. When integrating images that were taken under a range of lighting circum-stances, this is a really handy method to have. You can create a more consistent appearance across the composite by changing the lighting of the image so that it corresponds to the lighting of the other photographs in the composite.

You may produce a composite image that has a more consistent tone and color by applying these Neural Filters to resolve differences in tone and color that exist across several photographs. Because excessive use of these filters might result in a composite picture that does not have a natural appearance, it is crucial to bear in mind that they should be utilized with care and finesse when being employed. The formulation of a well-balanced approach is crucial to the construction of a decent composite image.

Improving Photoshop using your usage data and images

Training features that are based on machine learning using examples of both good and terrible outcomes is a keyway that software developers employ to strengthen features based on machine learning. Any business that makes use of machine learning requires a technique to train the models that its software employs, preferably using examples that represent the interests of the product's end users. However, the majority of software developers do not have access to extraordinarily massive data sets that include genuine customer files, and even if they do store client files in the cloud, they typically do not have consent from customers to use their files to train software. Adobe included a Product Improvement pane in the Preferences dialog box in Photoshop so that it would be easy to make adjustments and enhancements to Photoshop. This is not necessarily confined to machine learning as the Photoshop Improvement Program wants to request permission to exploit your images and use statistics to aid in enhancing Photoshop features; yet this is the core focus of the program. The option that reads "Yes, I'd like to participate" is turned off by default; nevertheless, if you choose to take part in the survey, you may turn it on. Adobe researchers can acquire, utilize statistics, cloud documents, and other photographs that you edit using Photoshop when this function is active.

The decision of whether or not to take part in the Photoshop Improvement Program is in part a question of personal taste. If you feel that the method Photos hop manages the types of images changing that you complete may be enhanced with the help of your usage statistics, then you might wish to consider taking part in our research. However, you should be aware of the potential consequences of participating in the Photoshop Improvement Program if you work for a company or organization that deals with confidential documents, if you need to protect the privacy or proprietary data of your customers, or if you are legally bound by nondisclosure agreements. In any of these instances, you may be forced to keep specific information private.

Common challenges and limits when using Neural Filters in Photoshop

It is vital to be aware of some regular difficulties and constraints that may occur while employing the Neural Filters in Photoshop before commencing your investigation of these filters. Neural Filters are a strong tool that may be used to improve images; nonetheless, there are several scenarios in which utilizing them may not deliver the effects that are expected.

When dealing with Photoshop's Neural Filters, it is vital to be aware of the following constraints and issues that are among the most prominent.

Limited Control over outcomes: Neural Filters in Photoshop have various downsides, one of the most prominent of which is that it is difficult to exert complete control over the outcomes they generate. The output of a filter is ultimately selected by the neural network on which the filter is based, even though you may adjust the settings and parameters of the filter. Be-cause of this, it is conceivable that you may not always be able to attain the precise outcomes that you are seeking.

Compatibility Issues: Another problem of utilizing Neural Filters in Photoshop is that the filters may not be compatible with some of the accessible picture formats. Certain filters may work better with various sorts of images or under particular lighting settings. A filter that increases the look of skin texture, for instance, may not function as well on an image that has a lot of contrast or harsh shadows.

Limited Resolution: The resolution of the picture you are working with might be a limiting issue for the Neural Filters in Photoshop. It's probable that these filters won't operate as well with images that have a really high resolution as the neural networks, they deploy are pretty sophisticated and demand a lot of processing power. If you want the absolute best results from a Neural Filter, you might discover that you need to down sample your image in specific scenarios.

Limitations on Customization: Although the Neural Filters in Photoshop may have their settings and parameters modified to obtain a range of various effects, the filters themselves are ultimately meant to only produce one sort of outcome. Because of this, it is probable that you will not have as much control over the end outcome as you would if you were using another form of image-processing tool inside Photoshop. If you want more granular control over the look of your final work, you may want to investigate Photoshop's various different ways and tools.

Limited Consistency: Another problem of utilizing Neural Filters in Photoshop is that they may not always offer consistent effects across many photographs or various sections of the same image. This may be a difficulty especially when working with complicated photos. Because of this, utilizing Neural Filters in a manufacturing process where maintaining consistency is vital might be problematic. It is necessary to test your filters on a selection of different images and in a variety of lighting circumstances to guarantee that they are provid-ing the correct effects.

Despite these constraints, the Neural Filters in Photoshop may be a highly valuable tool for editing images and creating effects that are one of a kind. You may apply Neural Filters more successfully and receive the maximum results from your picture editing process if you are aware of these challenges and restrictions. Neural Filters allow you to edit your images in ways that were not imaginable previously, but with enough testing and creative thinking, you can attain these results.

Best practices when applying Neural Filters in Photoshop

It is vital to guarantee that you acquire the absolute best results feasible when utilizing the Neural Filters in Photoshop by following ideal practices whenever you do so.

When working with Neural Filters in Photoshop, it is crucial to keep the following recommendations and ideas in mind:

1. Use High-Quality Source Images:

The final output that a Neural Filter creates can be substantially impacted by the quality of the picture that acts as its source. Utilize high-quality images that are well-exposed and well-lit to improve the possibility that the results you acquire will be as positive as they can be. It is likely that the Neural Filter will not be able to provide a result that is convincing if the source picture is of poor quality, noisy, or fuzzy.

2. Experiment with Different Filters

Photoshop features a broad range of Neural Filters, each of which is aimed at producing a particular category of effect. It is vital to practice with a number of filters to focus on the one that offers the most desirable effects for the image you are working with. It is crucial not to be intimidated to experiment with alternative filter combinations or to adjust the settings of a filter to acquire the effect you desire.

3. Understand the Limits of Each Filter:

Each Neural Filter in Photoshop comes with its own set of needs and constraints. It is vital to have a thorough knowledge of what a filter can and cannot do before applying it to your image. When applied to specific kinds of images, certain filters may function better than others, while others may fail to achieve the intended effect under particular kinds of lighting. You can use each filter more efficiently and avoid spending time on filters that won't work for your image if you understand the restrictions of each filter and how they relate to your image.

4. Make Adjustments in Small Increments:

It is crucial to make modest alterations while adjusting the parameters of a Neural Filter, and it is also important to evaluate the results frequently. Because Neural Filters can occasionally yield results that are difficult to foresee, it is vital to avoid making major modifications all at once to prevent obtaining unanticipated consequences. You may acquire a better idea of how each parameter affects the outcome by making some very tiny tweaks and assessing the results after each change.

5. Apply Filters in Stages

Instead of applying certain Neural Filters all at once, it is occasionally more effective to apply them in phases instead. Before going on to the next filter, you will be able to examine its influence and make any required modifications to its settings owing to this function. Applying filters in phases makes it significantly simpler to undo or make adjustments to individual filters if this becomes required.

6. Save a Copy of Your Original Image:

It is advised that you make a saved duplicate of the original image before applying any Neural Filters to the image you are working with. If the Neural Filter gives surprising results, you will be able to return to the image before applying the filter. Keeping a duplicate of the original image and the processed version makes it much simpler to inspect both of them side by side and assess whether or not you are happy with the result.

7. Make Use of a Powerful Computer

Because Neural Filters are so computationally demanding, the application of these filters can be excruciatingly slow on machines that are either older or less capable. Utilize a powerful computer that has a huge amount of RAM and a swift CPU if you want to acquire the highest performance and keep away from bothersome slowdowns.

Exploring third-party Neural Filters for Photoshop

The user may access a range of third-party Neural Filters in addition to the built-in Neural Filters, which provide even more capabilities and opportunities for customization. The following is a list of some of the most prominent third-party Neural Filters that are compatible with Photoshop.

Topaz Labs AI Clear

Topaz Labs AI Clear is a powerful Neural Filter that makes use of artificial intelligence to improve the clarity of images by removing noise and bringing out previously hidden aspects. The image is examined by the filter, which is driven by machine learning algorithms, and selective noise reduction is applied to selected regions of the image as a consequence. Additionally, it can increase sharpness and detail without creating artifacts or adding undesirable distortion.

LuminarAI

Neural Filter is one of the AI-powered tools and features that are featured in the all-in-one photo editing software known as Luminar AI, which also incorporates a range of other AI-powered tools and features. The Luminar AI Neural Filter is capable of creating a number of effects, such as the enlargement of portraits, the deletion of objects, and the replacement of the sky. It analyzes photographs using powerful machine learning algorithms to enhance them and give the results to customers at a level equivalent to that of a professional.

DxOPureRAW

DxO PureRAW is a Neural Filter that can clean raw RAW picture data by eliminating artifacts such as noise and distortion. The photographs that are created as a consequence of the filter's analysis and processing are cleaner, sharper, and more accurate than those that would have been produced without the filter. It is especially beneficial for photographers who shoot in low light or high ISO settings as it may greatly boost image quality in these conditions. This makes it particularly advantageous for photographers who shoot in low light or high ISO conditions.

Skylum Aurora HDR

Skylum Aurora HDR is a Neural Filter that was built specifically for the benefit of high-dynamic-range (HDR) photography. The final image created by the filter contains a broader diversity of tones and hues than ordinary images do as a consequence of the deployment of machine learning algorithms to analyze and enhance many exposures of the same subject. Users may fine-tune the output to their liking due of the filter's comprehensive customization options, which are incorporated in the filter as well.

ONI Photo RAW

Neural Filter is one of the numerous AI-powered tools and features that are included in the sophisticated photo editing application known as ONI picture RAW, which also incorporates a range of other tools.

The filter may be used to accomplish several distinct effects, such as improving portraiture, changing the sky, and decreasing noise. It analyzes and processes photographs by employing strong machine learn-ing algorithms, which results in outputs equivalent to those generated by experts with significantly less labor.

AI Gigapixel

The AI Gigapixel Neural Filter was created to increase image quality in terms of both resolution and detail. This filter takes use of powerful machine learning algorithms to evaluate and enhance photos, which eventually results in shots that are more detailed and sharper.

It is highly beneficial for photographers who need to increase images without sacrificing quality, such as those who work in print or large-format photography. This may be achieved with the aid of this tool.

Tips and techniques Photoshop 2023

Select Colors from Anywhere

Let's start with one of the easiest Photoshop hacks. Stop screenshotting items only to take colors from them! Simply choose the Eyedropper tool, minimize Photoshop, click the dropper into your canvas, and then drag anywhere outside of Photoshop.

Install Custom Photoshop Brushes

Don't feel confined to utilize simply the brushes that come pre-installed in Photoshop. Try adding one of the many brushes the internet has to offer by heading into your bushes, hitting the Gear button, and choosing Import Brushes.

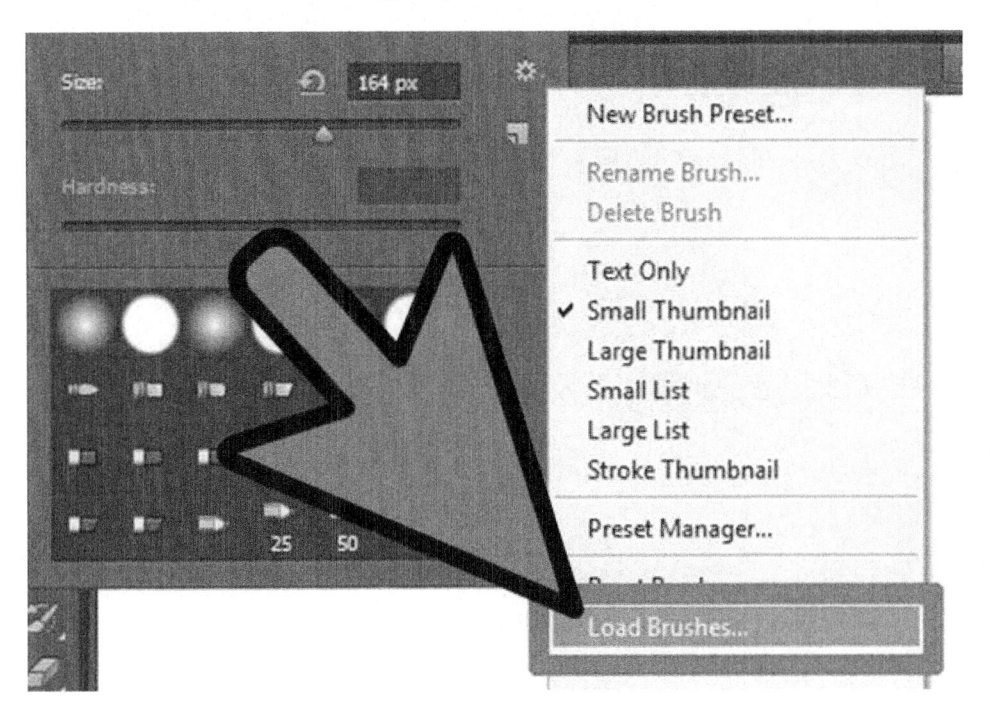

How to Create a Rain Texture

This free Photoshop trick will come in handy for you! If you want to add some drama to your photographs, capturing raindrops as they fall is a terrific method to do it; but nature does not always cooperate with your ideas. You can create your rain by making a new layer that is completely black, adding some Noise to it, then applying a Motion Blur using an angled brush, and then setting the layer to Screen. Simply by introducing some contrast, you can make it rain immediately.

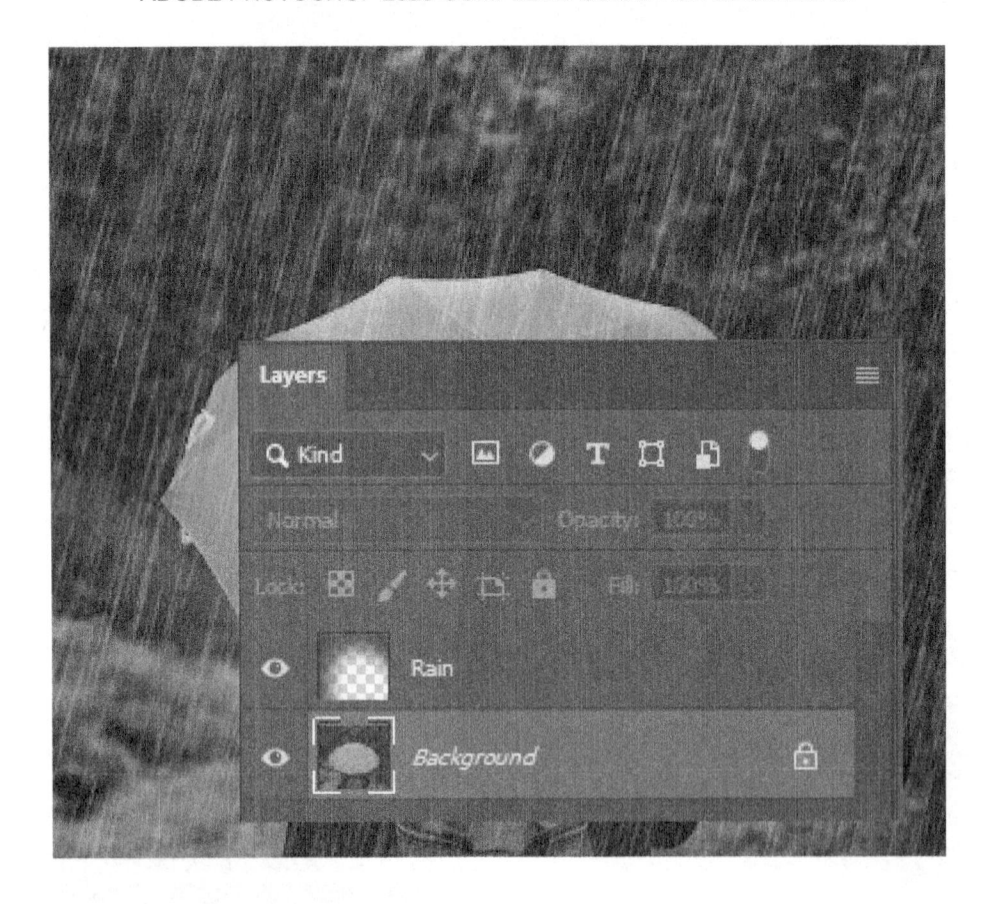

Create a Quick Light Bleed Effect

Create a new layer and paint white towards the top of your photo using a wide fluffy white brush to generate a small light bleed that will assist merge any image. This may be done by establishing a new layer. To put the finishing touches on it, lower the layer's level of transparency. It's worth your time to educate yourself with this amazing Photoshop tip!

How to Use Blend If

We're only started this Photos hop tips & techniques list! Here's another one: utilize Blend If to blend anything onto everything by double-clicking the layer you'd want to blend, going down to Blend If, and while holding Shift, experimenting with the sliders.

The uppermost layer will start merging into the ones below.

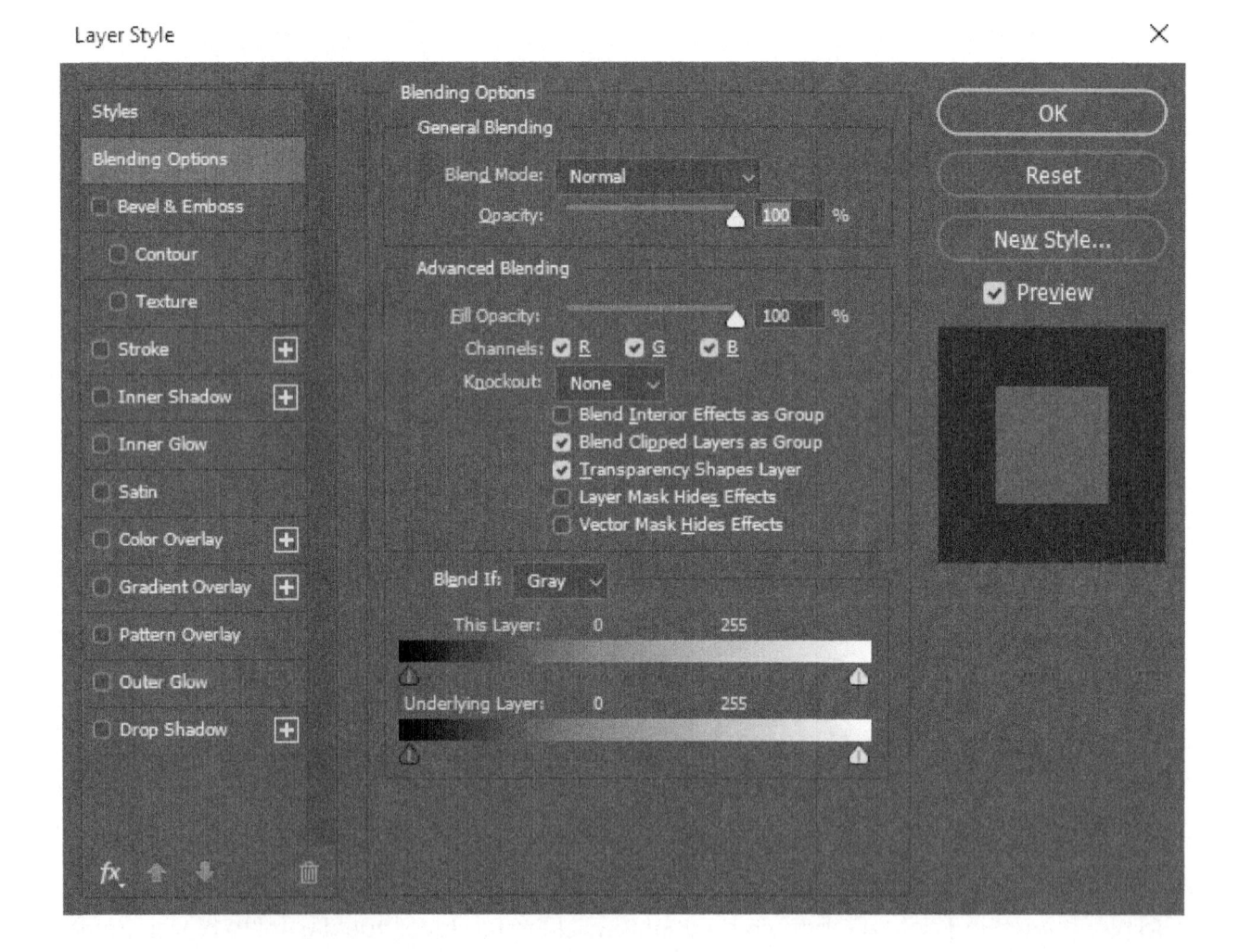

How to Copy Layer Styles Quickly

Do you have a layer style that you want to apply to multiple layers at the same time? The following is a Photoshop hint: Keep the Alt key held while you drag the FX symbol from the originating layer to the layers you want it to affect. There is no need to muck around with the settings as the layer styles will be applied instantly.

How to Create Multiple Stroke Effects on Text

Why does one line stroke when you may have two? Double-click the text layer to apply a Stroke layer effect. Press the Plus symbol to add another Stroke. Add as many as you'd like!

Make a Trendy Double Exposure Effect

Here's one of my favorite free Photoshop tips: Create a simple double exposure effect by taking one high-contrast black-and-white image, and then clipping a second image onto it. Set the sec-ond image to Screen. The actual charm is in the smart composition.

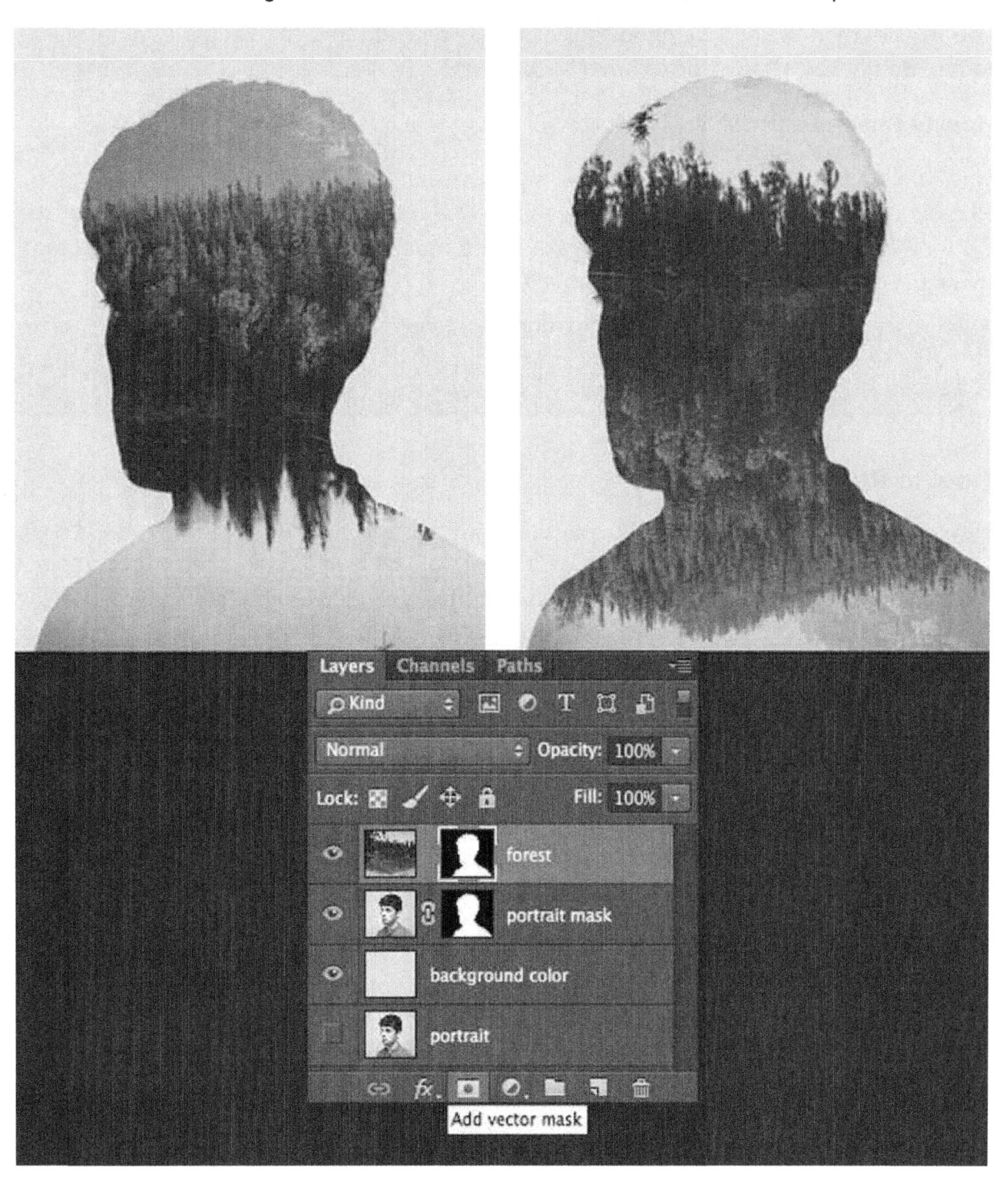

How to Merge Shapes

Looking for amazing Photoshop tricks? Create quick bespoke forms using the ones you've already produced by choosing your shape layers and then Right-Click > Merge forms. Barn! Now several forms have become one.

How to Change a Brush's Flow Rate

Have you attempted to combine your shadows but failed? Make use of this Adobe Photoshop tip: Choose the Brush, move your way up to the top tool bar, and lower the Flow of the Brush. Now, with each stroke of the brush, the color will gradually build up, making it great for shading and lighting effects.

How to Paint Makeup

Have you forgotten the importance of employing a makeup artist for your shoot? No worries! There is a variety of lore and wisdom about this issue. Make a new layer, adjust the blending mode to Soft Light, and then add the eyeshadow by hand! You will rapidly become an adept post-production makeup artist if you take advantage of the Soft Light and **Overlay** layer settings.

How to Make a Frequency Separation Photoshop Action

Do you ever find yourself interested in how photographers keep such perfect high-fashion skin? This phenomenon is known as frequency separation! Create two layers of your photo, one of which should have a Gaussian Blur filter applied, and the other should have a High Pass filter applied. Adjust the dial to Linear Light.

You can restore the color and skin tone by using the blurred layer and you can repair the texture by using the high pass layer.

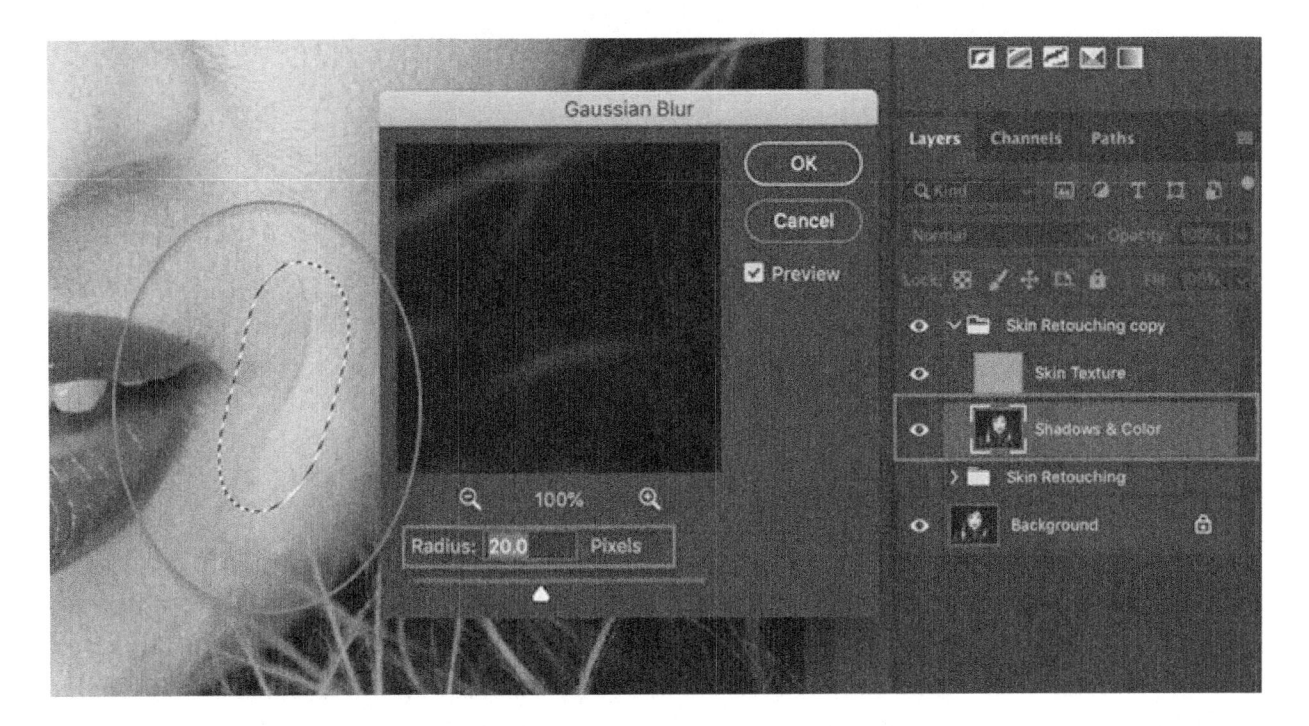

How to Create Chromatic Aberration

Do you long for the days of broken VHS tapes and glitchy computer screens from the 1990s? After duplicating your layer, double-clicking it, unchecking the R channel, and shifting it over by three to five pixels, you should now have a new layer. Finally, it's time to put on your 3D glasses!

Hide Layers Quickly

You want to concentrate on a particular layer, but the other layers are getting in the way. While holding down the Alt key, click the Eyeball icon that corresponds to the layer that you desire to isolate. When you click Alt once again, the other layers will automatically turn themselves back on.

Extra Tips

Keyboard Shortcuts

The workflow of your Photoshop work may be enhanced greatly by getting familiar with and making use of many keyboard shortcuts. Learning the most frequent keyboard shortcuts for critical tools and processes including selection tools, brush choices, and layer management can help you save a great amount of time. As an example, hitting "B" will pick the Brush tool, whereas using "Ctrl + J" would duplicate the layer that is presently active.

Customizing the Workspace

You have a great lot of choice over how the workspace in Photoshop is put up, including how the panels, tools, and menus are structured to meet your unique workflow. Make the most of this adaptability by choosing a configuration for your workstation that optimizes your production in the least period of time. You may build and keep several personalized workplaces, which can be used for a number of applications including photo editing, digital painting, and website construction.

Non-Destructive Editing with Adjustment Layers

Utilize adjustment layers so that you may preserve your flexibility and prevent making alterations that are irreversible to the original picture. Adjustment layers allow you the opportunity to make adjustments to a picture, such as modifying the brightness, contrast, levels, and color balance, without impacting the pixels that were there originally. You also may update or delete these adjustments at any point, which makes it simple to experiment with alternative ways and fine-tune your alterations.

Smart Objects for Scaling and Transformations

Utilizing Smart Objects is particularly useful if one is involved in raster-based picture editing. You will not suffer any reduction in picture quality if you execute non-destructive modifica-tions on an image after converting a layer into a Smart Object. These transformations include scaling, rotating, and warping. You also may apply filters and adjustments to Smart Objects in the form of Smart Filters, which can be modified and amended at a later time.

Content-Aware Fill

When it comes to eliminating undesirable sections from your images or filling in gaps, the Content-Aware Fill tool is a game-changer that you won't want to live without. It then produces a seamless replacement after completing an intelligence study on the surrounding pixels. To employ this function, first, create a selection around the region you want to get rid of, then go to the Edit menu and click Content-Aware Fill, and last, sit back and let Photoshop do its job.

Blend Modes

Blend modes give an endless number of creative alternatives when utilized for photo editing. Experimenting with the various blend modes available in Photoshop may help you produce one-of-kind effects and improve the mood of your images as a whole. Each blend mode interacts with the underlying layers in its own way, enabling you to achieve some extremely remarkable results. These mixed options include screen, multiply, overlay, and soft light, among others.

Brush Customization

The brush tool is a fundamental feature of Photos hop, and the degree to which you customize it may substantially enhance the number of creative possibilities accessible to you. By altering the brush's size, hardness, opacity, and flow, it is possible to produce brush strokes that are precise and controlled. In addition, experimenting with different brush presets and designing your own could aid you in producing traditional painting media effects or attaining specific texture effects.

Layer Masks for Seamless Edits

With the use of layer masks, it is possible to selectively expose or conceal sections of a layer without irrevocably erasing any pixels. You may modify the visibility of various portions of the layer by painting the layer mask in either black or white. The mixing of photos, the development of composites, and the application of modifications to select locales are all areas in which this ap-proach excels.

Automating Tasks using Actions

Utilizing the Actions tool in Photoshop could assist you save a considerable amount of time if you find yourself conducting actions that are comparable to earlier ones. With actions, you may record a sequence of steps and then utilize that recording to apply those steps to several photographs with just one click. Actions enable the ability to automate and simplify a broad range of editing actions, from very basic ones like resizing and applying filters to more intricate procedures.

Utilizing Photoshop Plugins

Explore a vast range of third-party plugins to enhance the capabilities of Photoshop and add new features. These plugins give you access to a greater array of editing tools, filters, and effects, which may assist improve your editing abilities and provide you with fresh new creative paths to explore. There is a plugin available to fulfill practically all of a creative person's requirements, ranging from those that replicate film effects to those that add beautiful brush strokes or advanced retouching capabilities. Investigate numerous dependable plugin vendors, and then select the plugins that best meet your editing tastes and needs after doing so.

Utilizing Photoshop's Content-Aware Tools

Photoshop includes many content-aware tools that might save you time and effort in different editing chores. The Content-Aware Move tool allows you to move items within a picture while automatically filling in the backdrop flawlessly. The Content-Aware Patch tool helps you eliminate undesired items by replacing them with surrounding textures or patterns. Experiment with these tools to simplify your editing routine.

Utilizing Photoshop's Selection Tools

You may isolate and change particular sections of a photo with the use of Photoshop's many selection tools, which are accessible in the application. The Quick Selection tool, the Magic Wand tool, and the Lasso tool are three of the selection tools that are used the most commonly. You'll be able to gain accurate selections and make targeted adjustments or edits to specified sections of a picture if you master these tools and combine them with modifier keys so you can accomplish both at the same time.

Utilizing Photoshop's Healing Tools

When it comes to editing images and getting rid of imperfections and other flaws, the Healing tools in Photoshop, such as the Spot Healing Brush, Healing Brush, and Clone Stamp tool, are crucial. These approaches may flawlessly combine pixels and offer results that look as if they were taken organically, which are essential whether you need to eradicate blemishes, wrinkles, or unwanted objects. Experiment with a range of healing instruments and make required modifications to their settings to obtain the outcome you desire.

Utilizing Photoshop's Layer Styles

The deployment of effects and upgrades to your layers may be achieved in a swift and time-saving method by applying layer styles. Layer styles may swiftly transform the look of your layers, offering them effects like drop shadows, inner glows, bevels, and gradients. Experiment with the different options and settings available in the Layer Styles tab to achieve one-of-a-kind and visually beautiful outcomes.

Utilizing Photoshop's 3D Tools

The 3D capabilities in Photoshop allow you to construct three-dimensional things and give your ideas greater depth, which opens up a world of creative possibilities. The 3D tools in Photoshop offer a solid foundation for your creative activities, whether you want to make 3D text, change 3D models, or add textures and lighting to your compositions. You can achieve all of these things with the 3D tools in Photoshop. Invest some time in becoming familiar with the principles of 3D modeling and rendering to open up a new arena of creative possibilities.

Frequently Asked Question

What are layers in Photoshop?

Layers are one of the main aspects of Photoshop. They make it possible to layer various components of an image or design on top of one another, which simplifies the process of editing and modifying particular elements of the composition without impacting the others. Each layer has the capacity to house a range of items, such as text, shapes, or photos, and may be altered in its own right.

How can I remove the background from a photograph in Photoshop?

To remove the backdrop from a picture in Photoshop, you may use numerous approaches, such as the Magic Wand tool, the Quick Selection tool, or the Pen tool. These tools allow you to pick the backdrop or topic you wish to remove and eliminate or isolate it using layer masks or the background eraser tool.

Can I use Photoshop for digital painting?

Yes, Photos hop is frequently used for digital painting and making artwork. It features numerous brushes, configurable brush settings, and painting tools that resemble classic art processes. Artists may create digital paintings from scratch or improve and change existing photos utilizing Photoshop's painting features.

Is Photoshop just available on Windows?

No, Adobe Photoshop is accessible for both Windows and macOS operating systems.

Adobe maintains cross-platform compatibility for their program, allowing customers to access Photoshop regard-less of their operating system.

Can Photoshop restore blurry or damaged photos?

Yes, Photoshop offers various tools and approaches to restore blurry or damaged photographs. You may use the Sharpen tool, Filters, or the Camera Shake Reduction function to increase the sharpness and clarity of photographs. Additionally, Photoshop contains tools for erasing scratches, dust, and other flaws from damaged images.

Can Photoshop be used for site design?

Yes, Photos hop is often used for web design. It lets designers develop website layouts, design user interfaces, and optimize pictures for web use. Photoshop's capabilities, such as layer styles, smart objects, and slices, simplify the development of online visuals and content.

What is the difference between Photoshop and Adobe Lightroom?

Photoshop and Lightroom are both pieces of image editing software that were produced by Adobe, although they were meant to handle unique jobs. Photoshop is a sophisticated editing application that may be used for a range of difficult image editing, retouching, and graphic design jobs. On the other hand, Lightroom is especially meant for photographers who work with RAW files and is directed towards the organizing, editing, and improvement of vast collections of photographs.

Can I use Photoshop on mobile devices?

Yes, Adobe has a mobile version of Photoshop called Adobe Photoshop Express, which is accessible for both iOS and Android smartphones. While it may not have the complete range of functionality as the desktop version, Photoshop Express allows you to conduct basic image editing activities on your mobile phone or tablet.

How can I build a panorama in Photoshop?

In Photoshop, the Photomerge feature may be used to assist the construction of a panoramic image. With the aid of this feature, a single panoramic picture may be made by integrating a number of pictures that overlap with one another. You need simply make a selection of the images you desire to combine, go to the "File" menu, click on "Automate," and then pick "Photomerge." The pictures will be aligned and blended together in Photoshop in order to build the panorama.

Can Photoshop be used for 3D modeling and rendering?

Yes, Adobe Photoshop has rudimentary 3D modeling and rendering capabilities. It lets you design, edit, and modify 3D models and add textures, materials, and lighting effects. While Photoshop's 3D features are not as extensive as specialist 3D software, it may be a handy tool for simple 3D jobs and incorporating 3D components into your designs.

How do I erase red-eye in Photoshop?

Red-eye is a typical problem that happens with flash photography, where the subject's eyes appear red in the acquired image. Photoshop has a Red Eye tool that can automatically identify and fix red-eye. Simply choose the tool, modify the size and intensity settings, then click on the red-eye regions in the shot. Photoshop will replace red with a more natural tint.

Can I generate animated GIFs with Photoshop?

Yes, Photoshop allows you to make animated GIFs by merging many photos or frames into a single file. You may use the Timeline tab to specify the duration and sequence of each frame, apply effects or transitions, and even add text or objects to create fascinating and interactive animations.

How can I resize or crop a picture in Photoshop?

Changing an image's proportions in Photoshop, as well as cropping it, is a pretty straightforward task. To modify the dimensions of the photo, go to the "Image" menu, then click "Image Size" from the drop-down menu that displays. You also have the option of employing the Crop tool, which allows you to choose and eliminate areas of the photo that aren't wanted. Photoshop provides options for pre-serving the aspect ratio of a picture, altering the resolution, and picking portions within an image to crop.

Is Photoshop adequate for professional photographers?

Yes, Photos hop is commonly used by professional photographers to improve, retouch, and alter their images. It features powerful editing capabilities, including adjustment layers, curves, and brushes, allowing photographers to fine-tune their photographs, fix exposure and color, remove distractions, and add creative effects. Additionally, Photoshop's interface with Adobe Lightroom enables a smooth workflow for photographers.

Can I produce and edit videos with Photoshop?

Yes, Photos hop has rudimentary video editing tools. You may import video files, cut and organize clips, apply transitions and effects, alter colors and tones, and export the finished film in multiple formats. While Photoshop's video editing tools are not as sophisticated as professional video editing software, it may be a handy tool for modest video editing jobs.

What is the difference between Photoshop CC and Photoshop Elements?

Photoshop CC (Creative Cloud) is the full-featured version of Photoshop that is offered through Adobe's subscription model. It enables access to all the newest features and upgrades, as well as interaction with other Adobe applications. Photoshop Elements, on the other hand, is a simpler version of Photoshop that targets casual users and amateurs. It includes minimal editing features and is offered as a one-time purchase.

Can Photoshop open and edit RAW files?

Yes, Photoshop can access and edit RAW files, which are uncompressed and raw picture files taken by digital cameras. Photoshop features enhanced tools and controls particularly built for RAW processing, allowing photographers to change exposure, white balance, sharpness, and other aspects with more flexibility and accuracy.

Is it possible to automate operations in Photoshop?

Yes, Photos hop has a tool called Actions, which allows you to record a sequence of processes and apply them to many photographs. This automation tool might be handy for repeated activities or bulk processing. Additionally, Photoshop enables scripting using JavaScript, enabling you to develop custom scripts and automate complicated procedures.

Can I interact with others in Photoshop?

Adobe has developed collaboration tools in Photoshop that enable many people to work on the same project concurrently. This capability, known as "Coediting," enables Realtime collaboration, where changes made by one user are instantaneously mirrored for others. It enhances teamwork and simplifies the creative process, particularly for design teams and distant collaborations.

Conclusion

Throughout this thorough book, we have studied the numerous features, tools, and methods available by Photoshop, empowering users to unleash their creativity and generate stun-ning visual material. With its enormous array of features, Photoshop has become an industry standard, adopted by professionals and hobbyists alike throughout the globe. We began by presenting the core ideas of Photoshop, offering a firm basis for those who are new to the software. We discussed crucial subjects such as the Photoshop workspace, including the toolbar, panels, and menus, allowing users to navigate through the software with ease.

Adobe Photoshop is a sophisticated and extensively used image editing program that offers a wide variety of tools and capabilities for modifying and enhancing digital photographs. It has become the industry standard for graphic designers, photographers, and digital artists because to its adaptability and wide features. Users are able to execute a broad number of tasks, including altering photographs, adjusting colors and tones, making digital artwork, integrating several images, and applying a variety of special effects. Users have a great level of control over their creative process due to the product's user-friendly interface, which is accompanied by a large collection of tools and settings. Users are allowed to make alterations to a photo in Photoshop's non-destructive editing mode, which is one of the program's most significant benefits. This option helps users to avoid making alterations to the source file that are irrevocable. Users have the ability to experiment with a number of creative possibilities owing to this functionality, which permits iterative editing and allows for experimentation.

Photoshop also allows a seamless connection with other Adobe Creative Cloud tools, such as Illustrator and InDesign. This link promotes a fluid workflow and encourages cooperation across diverse design specialties. It supports a huge variety of file formats, which enables it to be compatible with a wide number of devices and systems. In addition, Adobe continuously adds more capabilities to Photoshop and makes changes to the application, ensuring that users have access to the most recent breakthroughs in digital image processing. Because of these changes, which often involve user feedback and stay up with industry trends, Photoshop is a perpetually changing application.

However, it's worth remembering that Photoshop has a high learning curve, and mastering all of its functions may need time and practice. Additionally, its subscription-based price strategy may be a hindrance for certain customers who prefer one-time purchases or free alternatives. Generally, Adobe Photoshop is a vital tool for professionals in the creative business, delivering excellent image editing skills, adaptability, and a broad collection of functions to bring their artistic vision to reality.

ABOUT THE AUTHOR

Anishe Morrisa is a seasoned graphic designer, digital artist, and Adobe Certified Expert with over 15 years of experience in the field. His journey began with a simple point-and-shoot camera and a desire to capture the world in a unique light. Quickly realizing the power of post-production, he dove headlong into the world of Photoshop, turning simple photographs into compelling pieces of art. Over the years, he has worked with leading advertising agencies, design studios, and photographers, contributing his skills to various award-winning projects.

Anishe's expertise doesn't stop at basic retouching and color correction. He is proficient in high-end beauty retouching, compositing, 3D modeling within Photoshop, and even video editing. His advanced skill set includes mastering selections, layer styles, vector drawings, and color grading. It's not just about making things look good for **Anishe**; it's about understanding the technical intricacies that make a well-edited image stand out, including color spaces, resolution aspects, and intricate layering techniques. His in-depth knowledge on these topics is precisely what inspired him to write the "Adobe Photoshop 2023 Complete Guide for Beginners."

Having witnessed the evolution of Adobe Photoshop from its earlier versions to the latest Photoshop 2023, **Anishe** felt the need to create a comprehensive guide that covers both fundamental and advanced aspects. Understanding the software's increasing capabilities, especially with features like Neural Filters, excited him about the creative possibilities that could be unlocked, even by someone new to the platform. This enthusiasm is what you'll find weaved into every chapter of his book.

The guide is not just a collection of tutorials, but a curated journey. The initial chapters provide solid groundwork, ensuring that even complete beginners can follow along easily. As you turn the pages, the complexity of the projects gradually increases, introducing you to advanced tools and techniques, including cutting-edge features that make Adobe Photoshop 2023 a powerhouse for digital editing.

In addition to his professional career and writing, **Anishe** is a dedicated educator. He has conducted several workshops, both online and offline, aimed at simplifying complex design and editing concepts for students and professionals alike. He's a regular contributor to graphic design forums and photography blogs, where he shares tips, tricks, and tutorials on Adobe Photoshop. He believes that knowledge is best used when shared, a principle he applies by openly distributing a wealth of resources to budding artists and photographers.

What sets **Anishe** apart is his ability to explain complex subjects in a straightforward, easy-to-understand manner. He understands that Adobe Photoshop can be intimidating for beginners, but his teaching methodology, now reflected in this book, aims to demystify the software and make it accessible for people of all skill levels.

So, whether you're new to Photoshop or looking to refine your skills further, **Anishe Morrisa's "Adobe Photoshop 2023 Complete Guide for Beginners"** is the go-to resource you've been waiting for. It's not just a book; it's an invitation to explore the limitless world of digital art and photography.

Happy reading and creating!

Printed in Great Britain
by Amazon